W9-DAZ-162

Also by John Mosier

The Myth of the Great War

The Blitzkrieg Myth

CROSS OF IRON

CROSS OF
IRON

THE RISE AND FALL OF THE

GERMAN WAR MACHINE, 1918–1945

JOHN MOSIER

A HOLT PAPERBACK

JOHN MACRAE BOOKS / HENRY HOLT AND COMPANY · NEW YORK

Holt Paperbacks
Henry Holt and Company, LLC
Publishers since 1866
175 Fifth Avenue
New York, New York 10010
www.henryholt.com

A Holt Paperback® and ⑰® are registered trademarks
of Henry Holt and Company, LLC.

Copyright © 2006 by John Mosier
All rights reserved.

Distributed in Canada by H. B. Fenn and Company Ltd.

Library of Congress Cataloging-in-Publication Data

Mosier, John, 1944–
   Cross of iron : the rise and fall of the German war machine,
1918–1945 / John Mosier.—1st ed.
     p.   cm.
   Includes bibliographical references and index.
   ISBN-13: 978-0-8050-8321-7
   ISBN-10: 0-8050-8321-9
   1. Germany—Armed Forces—History—World War, 1914–1918.
2. Germany—Armed Forces—History—World War, 1939–1945.
3. Strategy—History—20th century.   I. Title.

D531.M63   2006
355'.033043'09041—dc22   2005052660

Henry Holt books are available for special promotions
and premiums. For details contact: Director, Special Markets.

Originally published in hardcover in 2006 by
John Macrae Books / Henry Holt and Company

First Holt Paperbacks Edition 2007

Designed by Victoria Hartman

Printed in the United States of America

2   4   6   8   10   9   7   5   3

Fought with Frederick in all his wars; chose disgrace when obedience was incompatible with honor.

—*Epitaph, tombstone of*
General Johann Friedrich Adolphe von der Marwitz

CONTENTS

Introduction: Truth and Error   1

1. The German Army in 1918: Secrets of Success   11

2. The Army Before Hitler: Hollow Victories,
   Shattered Illusions   25

3. Breaking Out of the Cave: Hitler and the Wehrmacht's
   Jewish Problem   45

4. Planes, Personalities, and Conflict in the Luftwaffe   68

5. Paper Tigers: Hitler's Tanks   90

6. Bloodless Victories, or Nearly So: Toward a Greater
   Germany, 1935–39   108

7. The Fall of the West, September 1939–June 1940   123

8. A Few Distractions on the Road to Armageddon   144

9. The Soviet Collapse   165

10. The Death Ride: Russia, December 1941–December 1944   182

11.　Failure and Philosophy: The End of the War　　　　204

12.　The Criminals　　　　228

13.　Conclusion: Myths, Realities, and Achievements　　　244

　　　Notes　　　　257

　　　Acknowledgments　　　　305

　　　Index　　　　307

CROSS OF IRON

INTRODUCTION:
TRUTH AND ERROR

The truth must be repeated over and over again; because error
is repeatedly preached among us, and not only by individuals,
but by the masses. In periodicals and cyclopedias, in schools
and universities—everywhere, in fact, error prevails, and is
quite easy in the feeling that it has a decided majority on its
side. Often, too, people teach truth and error together, and stick
to the latter.

Goethe[1]

During the First World War, the German army was astonishingly successful. British and French gains of territory were generally measured in meters, German gains in kilometers. As late as spring 1918, the Germans broke through the British and French lines on the Western Front, driving a series of wedges between the British and French forces and coming to within seventy kilometers of the heart of Paris. These achievements are all the more impressive because German losses were substantially fewer than those of the Allies.

In writing about the First World War, Winston Churchill observed that although the Allies did poorly on the battlefield, their propaganda was remarkably successful in covering up their losses of men and territory and in spinning every incident into a seamless account of triumph, an observation also made by British prime minister David Lloyd George in his memoirs.[2] For the first three years of the war, the Allies rationalized their lack of progress by claiming that German victories came at a heavy price: German casualties were much higher than Allied ones. As that assertion slowly eroded in the face of investigations made by the French government, the numbers shifted: casualties were roughly equal.

After the armistice, the last claim, aided considerably by a pacifist campaign against war, became an established fact: the war on the Western Front had been an inconclusive, bloody stalemate. The Allies were finally victorious in the fall of 1918, the legend went, because the British beat the Germans on the battlefield, while, back at home, Germany was driven to the brink of surrender by the success of the blockade. This, too, was a largely British triumph, and although London had allies, it was the British who beat the Germans and forced them to surrender.

Like all great legends, the one about the Great War gave comfort to the survivors, nurturing their illusions. It justified the behavior of the governments concerned, and, by demonizing the Germans, it insulated their postwar treatment against a small but growing chorus of critics. Morally, ethically, philosophically, Adolf Hitler seemed the proof that his nation's detractors had been right. The case was closed.

After June 1940, however, these legends abruptly came back to haunt Germany's foes. If the Allies had indeed been victorious in 1918, why had they been beaten so quickly in 1940? One legend thus demanded another, and in the aftermath there was no shortage of ingenious explanations of Hitler's takeover of western Europe. Nobody, then or now, seemed much concerned about the philosophical implications of the rationalizations. But each story, each explanation, no matter how artful or reasonable, came down to the same premise: it empowered Hitler and enfeebled his enemies.

The first step in understanding the rise and fall of the German military, then, is a difficult one. It requires us to discard the seductive myths of the First World War and replace them with a more complex reality in which the Germans are seen to be enormously successful on the battlefield. They were better in 1940 because they had been better in 1914.

Although this idea is hard for many historians to accept, the facts have always been there, the most significant one being the casualty exchange ratio. During the war, André Maginot and Abel Ferry analyzed the casualty figures and came to the conclusion that the Allies were not winning the war of attrition, that French and British soldiers were not dying in fewer numbers than their German adversaries; a decade later, Churchill studied the final reports of the combatants and came to a more drastic conclusion.[3] Recently, Niall Ferguson and I, working independently of each other, have established that the ratio of German soldiers killed to Allied soldiers killed approached 3:1 and was certainly 2:1.[4]

So the first question this book answers is this: Why were the Germans so successful?

Their triumphs were not a function of better equipment, novel concepts, brilliant senior commanders, or the feebleness of the enemy soldiery. When I began studying the German military and the world wars in 1969, I accepted the traditional paradigm and taught it to my students. Germany's achievement was a resounding tale of great captains like Erwin Rommel and Heinz Guderian, marvelous technological innovations (jet planes and guided missiles), and startling developments like the blitzkrieg. The Third Reich lost mostly because it was finally crushed on the battlefield by the Soviet Union, which not only bore the brunt of the fighting but was primarily responsible for the victory. There were two other factors as well: the combined Anglo-American air and land offensives, which stretched the Wehrmacht past the limits of endurance, and the fact that the leader of Germany was a madman whose decisions fatally crippled the machine.

Like the British legends of the Great War, very little in these standard accounts is true. The Wehrmacht's superiority in combat was not a function of better equipment. As chapters 4 and 5 make clear, German matériel was mostly inferior to that of its adversaries. Nor, as I explain in chapter 11, was the country ever able to produce enough supplies. Canada probably produced more trucks than Germany did.

Nor were the victory years of 1939–41 the result of some radically new concept of warfare. The blitzkrieg is such a wonderful notion that it is not likely to die, even though it hardly existed and certainly does not characterize the German army of 1939–40.[5] In the eighteenth century, scientists attempted to explain the process of combustion by arguing that flammable materials all contained a substance that made them burn. This substance, which was odorless, colorless, and otherwise not amenable to detection, was called phlogiston. Blitzkrieg is the phlogiston of modern military history.

But legends have provenance not just because they are remarkable stories. They also endure because they provide us with easy answers to basic questions. The great advantage of the old story of the German army was that it offered clear answers to two implicit questions of some importance. On the one hand, it explained why the Wehrmacht was so good: great leadership, impressive weaponry, startling new tactics.

In strictly military terms, the truth is both simpler and less satisfying. The superiority of the Wehrmacht on the battlefield derives almost exclusively from intangibles such as leadership, doctrine, and institutional memory.

Superior leadership is difficult to measure. As I explain in chapters 1 and 2, however, we can quantify three significant factors that have a distinct impact on leadership. Historically, German officers existed in greater numbers and were much better educated than their counterparts in other nations. The selection process after 1918 ensured a high level of competence in the officer corps that would direct the military in the next war. The weakness of this process was that it yielded a group of able tacticians but sacrificed the traditional diversity of the German officer corps. The new leaders were great captains but lousy generals, one reason why Hitler found them easy to manipulate.

The other reason for German success is that the military built on its achievements in the Great War. In chapters 1 and 2, I show how these superior doctrines emerged, why they were retained in the army's memory, and why they were universally ignored by Germany's once and future opponents. Briefly: the Allies started believing their mythical accounts of the Great War. Because they had beaten the Germans in battle, there was nothing they could learn from the losing side. In reality, not only had it been the other way around, but the Germans themselves believed that they had been victorious and had been cheated by the maneuverings at the war's end. That seems to me to be pretty much the case, even though it is still resolutely denied by most historians.

The mention of Hitler leads to a major theme in this book, one which differentiates it from some of the fine work that has been done on the war. The early victories of the Wehrmacht did not happen because of a purely military superiority. In large measure they came about because of Hitler's evil genius and the incompetence of the governments opposing him. The fact that Hitler was a supremely wicked man should not blind us to the fact that his judgments were generally shrewd, and nowhere more so than in foreign policy and military strategy. This observation contradicts the cherished beliefs of many biographers. But I believe that chapter 6 establishes a clear pattern of the moves that essentially led to the checkmating of the Allies even before the shooting started, in September 1939.[6]

Complementing this theme is another: an analysis of the claims made by the surviving generals, whose testimony has too often been taken at face value and never questioned. The dominant conclusion that emerged from the interrogations of Hitler's generals was that had he only listened to them, they might well have won the war. But even the most cursory scrutiny of their claims suggests that Hitler, although a supremely wicked man, was a better strategic thinker than any of his subordinates.[7]

Hitler was both more rational and far shrewder than is generally allowed. Many people, I think, will find this idea hard to swallow. Reflection, however, suggests that my portrait makes him considerably more evil than the conventional depictions of him. Madmen are generally thought to be less accountable for their actions than the sane.

As I said earlier, the chief benefit of legends and myths is that they provide us with convenient answers to apparently intractable problems. In the legendary war, Germany's downfall results mostly from Hitler's mad pride, which led him to attempt to conquer the world, notably the Soviet Union, and was matched only by his interference in the direction of the war.

This tale provides us with a great explanation of why, if the Wehrmacht was so good, Germany lost the war. But it is nothing more than a tale. As chapters 8, 9, and 10 demonstrate, there was nothing irrational about Hitler's decision to attack Stalin, nor did it lead inevitably to Germany's defeat. I used to believe that the war was won on the Eastern Front, and taught the concept to my students. I don't think the facts support the case. Once we strip away the veneer of pro-Sovietism that coats every account of Stalin and the Red Army, what stands revealed is a tottering edifice presided over by a man whose paranoid brutality was exceeded only by his military ineptitude.

Had the United States not entered the war at the end of 1941 and mounted a series of massive invasions of Europe (and North Africa) in 1943–44, there would not have been, in my view, any reason why the Third Reich would not have prevailed. Arguments to the contrary ignore the battlefield impact of what would have essentially been a 50 percent increase in German combat strength had the Wehrmacht not been forced to deploy troops all over western Europe to confront the American assaults.

In my account of the First World War, I remarked that the intervention of the United States was decisive in tilting the war to the Allies. This claim brought down a firestorm of criticism from British reviewers and their American fellow travelers. I should remark in passing that the more I look at the matter, the more cut-and-dried it seems: were I to write *The Myth of the Great War* again, I would make the argument much stronger.

Be that as it may, I do not see how anyone can assert that the Second World War was not basically won by the United States, with only minimal help from an exhausted and overstrained Britain. So Hitler's decision to declare war on the United States after Pearl Harbor is probably his one great military error. In Chapter 11 I explain why this was so, and why he made the decision. At bottom, it all came down to Hitler's philosophy of the world, his belief in the power of the great man over the soulless industrial state.

If there is one consistent thread that runs through accounts of the rise and fall of Hitler and the National Socialist state, it is that their only philosophy was a corrosive racism and hate mongering. It was a tenet that allowed Hitler to justify the murder of millions of innocent people. The failure of the Allies at Nuremberg to deal adequately with Hitler led to a situation in which many people who should have known better declared that all or most of the excesses and atrocities of the war were committed by Hitlerite fanatics.

The traditional German military observed the rules of war, the surviving generals claimed, and to a surprising extent they have been believed. But as I explain in the penultimate chapter of this book, the facts are otherwise. Although the senior officers in the army and the air force may not have realized the scale of mass murder Hitler ordered, it is impossible to argue that they were unaware of the crimes German soldiers under their command committed against their uniformed opponents. Although these seem insignificant when weighed against Hitler's fourteen million civilian murders, they constitute clear examples of unambiguous criminality. Each case contravenes the rules of war as understood and practiced by the German army for centuries. Those actions started long before the brutalities of the Eastern Front.

The crimes and the German conduct of the war are more closely related than most people suppose. The decisions Hitler made during his last months become explicable in the light of earlier mass murders; there was no chance that the global conflict could end without trials for war crimes. One reason the Germans fought on so stubbornly was that many of them had much to fear if they surrendered outright.

Hitler's insistence on murdering the Jews played a major role in the Third Reich's crusade. But here again, the situation is far more complicated than has traditionally been thought. As chapter 3 explains, the contingent of officers of Jewish origin was surprisingly large when Hitler came to power. The National Socialists immediately tried to purge the military of Jews. To the extent they succeeded, they weakened the armed forces. Despite the rhetoric and the killings, however, men of Jewish descent continued to serve in the military, right through the war and at high levels. That the Wehrmacht was not as racially pure as it is often depicted—one of the many bizarre paradoxes of the war—is not simply another weird fact about the National Socialists. Rather, the conflict between Hitler and the military on this issue, and the passive-aggressive behaviors it triggered, became the model for their future struggles.

In my view, these behaviors explain much of what was going on in the German high command, revealing why the survivors could claim disobedience and defiance even though they did nothing whatsoever about the crimes that were being committed after September 1939. As to the notion of Hitler as a meddling madman and his generals as unwilling sufferers: I would suggest not only that he was not but that the leadership of the Wehrmacht was every bit as culpable in his atrocities as the fanatics of the Sicherheitdienst and the Einsatzgruppen, to whom the majority of killings of the innocent are justly ascribed.

Although there was a war at sea as well as in the air, both lie outside the scope of this narrative.

The story of the Luftwaffe, for example, is basically that of a tactical air force, so it has been easy to fold it into this volume. Germany never intended to have much of a strategic air force; the British and the Americans had strategic bomber forces and used them. As the bomber barons and the airpower apostles have it, the air war was a separate war, and they go so far as to attribute the collapse of the Third Reich almost entirely to the bombing campaigns. In my view, this idea hardly stands scrutiny; in any event, the Germans never developed a parallel doctrine.

As to war at sea, the chief contributions of the Kriegsmarine in the Second World War were two. Before the fighting started, Germany's attempts to get around the restrictions of the Versailles Treaty gave rise to the idea that the basis of its supremacy in 1939 was two decades of systematic cheating on naval design. This notion, still widely believed, confuses intentions with results. In key areas nothing much was achieved, and although German naval design was first-rate, Germany entered the war with a minuscule surface fleet and a short-range, coastal defense submarine force. The surface fleet was fatally wounded in the Norwegian campaign, and even though the submarine war in the Atlantic captured the popular imagination, its effect on the outcome of the war was less than imagined. Admiral Erich Räder's brilliantly successful Norway campaign was the only decisive contribution made by the navy, and one with only limited results.

Thoughtful readers may disagree with my conclusions—as they may disagree with Winston Churchill's belief that all the leaders of the Third Reich should have been taken out and shot at the end of the war (I cheerfully plead guilty to this opinion as well). Germany was, by 1939, a country where wickedness was rapidly becoming a way of life; it was controlled by a man who was planning to murder millions of his fellow human beings and enslave uncounted millions more. And Hitler had plenty of willing helpers. None of these circumstances should blind us to Germany's military accomplishments. On the contrary, they should remind us that the wicked are often enormously successful.

THE GERMAN ARMY OF 1918:
SECRETS OF SUCCESS

Since the broad mass of the lower officers gives an army its character, the German Army of the World War could be called an army of armed students.

Konrad Heiden, *The Führer*[1]

Because of Germany's traditional prominence in science and engineering, the nation could provide its military with high-tech weaponry. Its well-educated officers quickly learned how to use these weapons (and when to demand new ones). The prestige of the military meant that educated young men found it attractive and wanted to be associated with it. Educated soldiers who understand how to use the sophisticated weapons they have been given are clearly going to be much more successful on the battlefield than their opponents.

But the key was the ability of the army to attract the educated and intelligent and put their talents to work. In 1900, Germany hardly had a monopoly on education and intelligence. What it did have was a society in which young men wanted to be officers.

The distinguished British travel writer William Harbutt Dawson summed up the situation perfectly: "The institution which, next to the throne, is the most popular in Germany, is the army. Its popularity runs through all classes of the population, and so does the popularity of what in England is wrongly called conscription."[2]

The reason why was simple. Before 1871, there was no Germany. The state had been created by the army. Although one could say this was true of most states, for the Germans the birth had occurred recently. In 1914, men were still alive who remembered 1871, who had defeated the enemy. Moreover, even before 1871, the military's record of success enhanced its prestige. The institutional tradition of the German military was victory, from the triumphs of Frederick the Great on. By 1900, they included decisive wins in wars with Denmark (1864), Austria (1866), and France (1870).

These victories did not come about by chance. The chief factor was the general staff system that had been evolving in the Prussian army since the start of the nineteenth century. By 1914, all armies had general staffs of some sort, but the German system differed from the others in fundamental ways. In other armies, staff officers were simply the eyes and ears and messengers of the commanding general. In the German army, they were empowered to give orders and even assume command. Staff officers of relatively junior rank continuously moved up and down the system, from central headquarters to units in the field.

When the Germans mounted the initial siege of the Liège fortresses in August 1914, a chance Belgian shell killed the senior field commanders. Command passed to the senior staff officer, Erich Ludendorff, a mere colonel, who then directed the successful attack. That the same officer who had planned the Liège offensive and then became its commander was later dispatched by Helmuth von Moltke to take over as chief of staff of the forces fighting the Russians gives an idea of the importance of staff positions.[3]

In this system, junior officers, who were relatively young, were entrusted with significant responsibilities. In 1916 the head of operations—Abteilung I, the most prominent general staff department—was only a major. The head of the second department, in charge of heavy weapons and munitions, was a lieutenant colonel, and the director of the Abteilung IIIb (military intelligence) was another major. Of the twelve men listed in the organizational chart as being directly below the supreme commanders, only three were generals. The other nine were either majors or lieutenant colonels.[4]

The employment of junior officers in positions of authority was widespread. The chief of staff for Army Group A was a major. The officer the high command brought in to reorganize the defensive positions on the Somme in 1916, and who assumed the position of chief of staff for the First Army, was Colonel Lossberg. The manual on defensive tactics that enabled the army to withstand repeated attacks with such success was written by Captain Geyer. When, at the end of 1914, the army decided to develop new assault tactics, it turned first to an engineering officer, Major Kaslow, who was then replaced by Captain Rohr.[5]

So one reason the military attracted talent was that it promised responsibility for relatively young men in a way unique among armies. France had bright young officers as well, but the French system, like the Russian and the British (and the American), gave them little to do.

The practical result was that Germany entered the war with many more officers than any other combatant. The French general Maxime Weygand estimated that, in 1913, Germany had 42,000 officers and 112,000 noncommissioned officers, while the French army had only 29,000 officers and 48,000 noncommissioned officers.[6] The imbalance is dramatic. Both countries had peacetime armies of about the same size, and planned to expand them enormously in the event of war. By today's standards, these armies consisted essentially of reservists; only between one-fifth and one-third of the soldiery would be made up of what we would call regulars, or active-duty troops. Clearly, the country with the biggest leadership cadre would have an enormous advantage in war, because it would have an impressive ratio of officers to soldiers. As the French figures indicate, Germany had a quantitative advantage. Whether or not German officers were better educated than their future opponents, the nation had created a substantially larger corps of leaders. In fact, the Weygand estimate seriously understates the case.

In France the prestige of the army was declining. Fewer young men wanted to be officers. In 1894, there were 2,079 candidates for Saint-Cyr, France's school for future officers. In 1906, there were 1,046 candidates. Six years later, the number had dwindled to 880.[7] Ironically, the Germans and Austrians had the opposite problem: they had more young men seeking to be officers than they had room for in their armies, or money to pay them.

In response, an important alternative means of military service was established. Provided he had the proper background and education, a young man could fulfill his military obligation by a year of voluntary service, ultimately emerging with a commission as a reserve officer. The catch was that the future reserve officer was eligible only if he had obtained his *Abitur*, or diploma, from an advanced secondary school, known as a Gymnasium in Germany and Austria-Hungary. Reserve officers thus represented an elite not only socially but educationally, and not simply within their countries. By 1913, there were 120,000 men with reserve commissions in Germany, or over three times as many reserve officers as regular officers. The German superiority over France was not four to three, as Weygand's figures suggest, but about six to one.[8]

Both classes of officers were highly educated. The excellence of the German school system before 1914 is notable; less remarked upon is the extent to which the numerous military academies emulated the rigors of the Gymnasium. They were first-rate schools, a fact admitted during the war even by the British: "Of the general education provided by the college, apart from its system, I have nothing but praise," wrote one disaffected Englishman who had gone through the system, going on to provide a brief description of a course of study in which "a love of literature and the drama, and of the fine arts generally, was fostered; and if any cadet showed a strong musical or artistic proclivity, he was encouraged and allowed to practice these pursuits." In addition, students were expected to know either French or English, as well as Latin, and although advanced mathematics was not obligatory, it was offered in the curriculum and students were encouraged to take it.[9]

The military schools provided a stepping stone for young men whose family finances would not allow them to attend a Gymnasium. The youthful Heinz Guderian, future creator of the German armored divisions, was one of them. His father wanted him to become an officer, but he was a man of "limited means," Guderian reveals in his autobiography,

explaining that for those two reasons he went to the cadet school at Karlsruhe.

> Our course of studies was based on the up-to-date civilian schools, the
> *Realgymnasium*, the main emphasis being on modern languages, math-
> ematics and history. This provided a good preparation for life, and the
> standards reached by the cadets were in no way inferior to those of simi-
> lar civilian institutions.[10]

Although both Britain and France had schools as good as any Gymnasium, they had no equivalent system for future officers. Nor did they feel
one was required.

There was one other crucial difference. In the United States, West
Point provided an excellent education for men of modest means. Ulysses
S. Grant and John J. Pershing went there not because they wanted to become professional officers but because it gave them an education they
could not otherwise have obtained. But there was only one West Point,
while in Germany and Austria-Hungary, there were a dozen.

Although officers passed into the ranks of the elite in civilian life, the
best career officers were expected to continue their education in military
affairs. The early experiences of Werner von Blomberg, later a field marshal and minister of defense during the early Hitler years, is typical. He
entered Gross-Lichterfelde, the most famous of the cadet schools, at the
age of sixteen, and was commissioned a *Leutnant* (what Americans
would call a second lieutenant) three years later. Despite having an army
officer for a father, von Blomberg was not rapidly promoted. He didn't
become an *Oberleutnant* (first lieutenant) until 1907. He then attended
the three-year course at the War College, was promoted to *Hauptmann*
(captain), and spent the next three years in the topographical section of
the general staff. Like von Blomberg, Guderian did advanced studies—
in his case, the War School at Metz in 1907–08.

The great advantage in the sheer numbers of educated officers explains why the Germans were better at training soldiers than anyone else
and why they were so adept at developing tactics that made full use of

the revolutionary technology with which the country supplied its army. Before 1914, British experts reckoned that the Germans could train soldiers in about one-third of the time that the British could. Once the war started, however, it was assumed that this advantage would quickly be overcome. As one respected British officer remarked ruefully: "When the war began we were all prepared for the Germans to be successful at first . . . but we argued that very soon we should become better than they. . . . The exact contrary has been the case." Or as the talented French general Emile Fayolle wrote gloomily in his secret diary: "The great superiority of the German army lies in its organization and methods of instruction."[11]

As Fayolle realized, the increasing complexity of the tools of modern warfare demanded a high level of education and an effective training system. Germany, as a technologically advanced nation, was able to give its soldiers sophisticated weaponry. The army's advantage in education, training, and leadership meant that it could use the new weapons effectively. A lead in technology does not automatically guarantee superiority, though, and in matters military, it is often exaggerated. But the German army in the First World War was a unique case: it had both the technology and the human resources to use properly on the battlefield.

The new weapons demanded a shift in the perception of warfare, both tactically and strategically, and in both cases the German army was far ahead of its opponents. The successful offensives and the casualty imbalance were not the result of Allied ineptitude or of chance. They were the logical outcome of fielding an army that, quite simply, outperformed those of its foes.

Of the two broad areas—tactics and strategy, on the one hand, technology on the other—the first was of greater importance, but the Germans had a substantial advantage in both, particularly in heavy artillery. In wars fought before 1914, most casualties—about nine out of every ten—were inflicted by rifles. In the First World War, the figures were reversed: about eight out of every ten casualties resulted from artillery fire. Although the French had invented the first modern artillery piece, the famous 75-millimeter field gun, it was the only long-recoil weapon they had in service in 1914. Artillery would prove crucial on the battlefield, but most French weapons were obsolete mechanical-recoil weapons that dated from the 1870s. Not only were they inaccurate, but they were also heavy. While the British had up-to-date guns, they were even heavier, and required days to assemble on site.

The Germans, for their part, systematically developed a family of mobile long-recoil weapons designed for indirect fire at high angles. German gunners could rain shells down onto infantry hiding behind walls and houses and in trenches. The Allies had only a handful of weapons capable of such precision, and those few were so heavy that they had to be transported in sections. Assembly took several days. By contrast, the German 21-centimeter howitzer could be towed behind a transporter and put into action immediately. The Austrian 30.5-centimeter howitzer used by the Germans on the Western Front could be transported by road and deployed within six hours—not surprising, considering that the inventor was Dr. Ferdinand Porsche.[12] The Allies had nothing comparable until late in the war.

The Germans not only entered the war with better weapons; they had more of them—an advantage of three or four to one in the number of long-recoil heavy artillery, road-transportable heavy weapons, and motorized gun transporters. They had mastered the production of gas shells for their guns—and were firing the shells onto the battlefield—while the British were still relying on the wind to disperse gases. It was the Germans who figured out how to synchronize the rate of fire of a machine gun with the revolutions of the propellers of their airplanes, so that pilots could fire directly ahead in their line of sight.

This superiority extended all the way down to the way the ordinary soldier was equipped, starting with the fact that his steel helmet (introduced in late 1915) was infinitely better than that of his opponents. Even a shell's near miss could generate a shock wave that would throw the soldier through the air, turning him into an unwilling missile in which his all too vulnerable head and neck were at risk. Flat helmets were of no use. But the German coal-scuttle helmet protected the back of the neck;

moreover, the flared edges transmitted the shock to the shoulders and thus the rest of the body, reducing traumatic head injuries.

German soldiers were the first to have reliable hand grenades (or hand grenades at all), their own transportable artillery (infantry mortars), flamethrowers, and armor-piercing ammunition for their machine guns.

The ability to manufacture sophisticated weapons was rooted in Germany's highly developed industries, while their skill in deploying the armaments in the field was an attribute of the educational achievement of the soldiery. And the realization that such equipment was needed was a function of an educated officer corps, men who approached warfare rationally, as a business or a scientific enterprise. But it was the combination of these factors that gave the German army its decisive edge in combat and resulted in tactical innovations that formed the basis for its success in both wars.

In the First World War, the Germans had three tactical challenges and one strategic issue to confront. The army identified the problems correctly, and had made reasonable progress toward solving them. Indeed, in my view, they *had* solved them. In the next war, German offensive doctrine would rely on these principles; only the hardware would change.

The three tactical questions were these: First, in an age where weaponry was making frontal attacks by massed infantry a recipe for suicide, how could local offensives succeed without massive casualties? Second, given the calamitous, unprecedented effect of heavy artillery on the battlefield, how could the defenders survive such bombardments and repel an opponent who was willing to let his infantry be massacred in order to seize territory? Third, in light of the increasing depth of the battlefield and the enormous armies involved, how could local offensive successes be translated into breakthroughs that would either force the enemy into a disastrous retreat or surround and capture its forces?[13]

The Germans had been worrying about the first problem since before World War I, and with particular urgency, since any offensive through Belgium into France would have to deal with the massive belt of fortifications both of these countries had built. It was this situation that provided the army with the motivation to develop heavy mortars as well as

road-transportable heavy guns. Organizationally, it stimulated the formation of combat engineer units, the Pioniere.[14] These soldiers, organized
in companies and doled out to infantry divisions, one or two per division,
were unique—combat infantry with engineering training. They were
also unique in having their own organic heavy weapons. At first these
consisted of 17.5- and 25-centimeter mortars, but as the war progressed,
other weapons were added, notably flamethrowers.

Once the Germans broke through the Belgian forts and penetrated
the French fortification line, the Pioniere were employed in both an offensive and a defensive role. German doctrine blended the two concepts
in the following way. On the attack, the officers preferred to seize a position and force the enemy to attack it frontally in an attempt to regain it.
On the defense, the Germans, after letting the enemy attack a frontal position that had been largely abandoned, would mount counterattacks
from positions behind that line, outside the immediate zone of attack.
Either way, the German practice involved a lot of engineering, but the
Pioniere units had been designed for offensive operations, and within
the first six months of the war, a mixed unit of combat engineers and
elite infantry had been assembled to develop small-unit assault tactics.

The infantry was drawn from the Jäger battalions.[15] Although often
thought of as light infantry, Jäger battalions had, by 1914, more machine
guns than regular infantry regiments, and during peacetime they were at
nearly full strength, while the regular infantry regiments operated with a
greatly reduced number of men. So these combined units, which would
eventually become known as *Sturmabteilungen*, or storm troops, were
initially drawn from the units where the concept of firepower generated
by mixed weapons had replaced the traditional idea of infantry units as
men firing only rifles.

By January 1915, the commander of the first *Sturmabteilungen* unit,
Captain Rohr, had his men in action in the Vosges Mountains. Instead
of the massed infantry assaults of the Allies, Rohr's men relied on their
artillery (the mortars of the Pioniere) to pulverize a small section of
trench, which they then attacked from the ends. Instead of rifles, they
relied heavily on hand grenades and machine guns manhandled into

position. Enemy strong points were bypassed rather than assaulted, to be dealt with by artillery fire called in by forward observers. As the war progressed, more weapons were added: flamethrowers in early 1915, and the portable 7.5-centimeter mortar by the end of 1916.

The German tactics were successful, and by February 1916 were in widespread use. The method of teaching the new techniques was simple. Units were formed, and the men in Rohr's unit began instructing them. As these units mastered the skills, they in turn taught others, spreading the tactics throughout the army. The Allies eventually noticed the existence of these units, but they failed to understand how they functioned. According to the British high command, the Germans had skimmed off the cream of their infantry and put them into special units, the famous storm troopers, thus fatally weakening the rest of their army.[16] On the contrary, their primary role was educational, and as the war continued, most German soldiers in active (as opposed to reserve) units became storm troopers. By 1918, the army was closing down the separate detachments, so that only about one-third of them were in operation at the end of the war.

The emphasis on combined arms extended beyond the creation of combat units with organic heavy firepower. Allied doctrine meted out heavy artillery at the army group level, where it was centrally controlled. The Germans, by contrast, parceled out their heavy artillery regiments to the combat units that needed them, thus giving divisional commanders authority over their use.

The Germans believed that offensive operations incurred fewer casualties than defensive ones. Since they were fighting on three fronts, however, they had to pick and choose their operations carefully. As a result, the army became expert at defensive warfare. A significant part of the German success on the defense came from superior engineering. They did not simply dig trenches. They constructed field fortifications in depth, so that their defensive positions consisted of three separate lines, with the rear ones anchored by formidable strongpoints made of stone, concrete, and earth.

When the Allies began their preparatory shelling, the German defenders withdrew into their shelters, which, when properly constructed, were basically impervious to even the heaviest shells. The Allies had to stop the bombardment once their infantry started the assault. The resulting massacre of the attacking infantry was based on a simple calculation: the defenders could emerge from their shelters and set up their machine guns faster than their opponents could cross no-man's-land. Sometimes the remnants of the Allied infantry were able to get into the first line of the German trenches, but at that point, the new offensive tactics would promptly drive them out.

One key reason for the German success on both offense and defense was that company, battalion, and regimental commanders had the authority both to withdraw from areas threatened with attack and to order counterattacks to contain any potential local breakthroughs. By contrast, their Allied counterparts were invariably forced to wait for orders from the divisional or even corps command. Given the primitive nature of communications during the war, these delays were fatal, because the German movements were always within the Allied decision cycle: by the time orders came back down the chain of command, it was too late.[17]

The Germans knew that success at the small-unit level on offense and defense would not win the war. The traditional idea was that the only way to defeat the enemy was to engage it in a massive battle, or series of battles, in which its forces would be destroyed. Once both sides had fixed defensive positions, however, this idea became problematic. But the British and the Italians persisted in it throughout the conflict. Joffre, the supreme French commander until late 1916, saw correctly that what was required was an offensive that would rupture the defensive lines on such a scale that the Germans would not be able to contain it, particularly if the rupture created a big enough hole. Although Joffre was replaced midway through the war, his notion lived on, and on the German side, Ludendorff had essentially the same opinion.

The problem with the idea was set forth by General Fayolle, who observed succinctly that it wasn't easy to pass an army through an army.[18] His remark reflects the inherent limitation of Allied tactics. If you were willing to lose one army in the initial mass attack, you might succeed.

But how would you then move the next army through the debris left by the first attacking force and across the cratered battlefield your artillery had produced?

Since the Allies never solved this problem, a generation of analysts were led to conclude that a large-scale breakthrough could not be staged on a broad front, because of the rudimentary communications between the units doing the attacking and the commanders behind them. German achievements to the contrary were either ignored or explained away by the inferiority of the Russian, Italian, and Romanian armies. But in March 1918, with breakthroughs of fifty and sixty kilometers on broad fronts, the Germans obviously had figured out a solution, and they promptly repeated the feat, in April, and then again in May.

The key lay in the application of the small-unit tactics developed early on. Instead of bombardments that went on for days and massed infantry attacks, the Germans favored short, intensive assaults that caught the defenders unawares. The initial assault used relatively small numbers of men who worked their way through the rubble. The solution to Fayolle's question, then, lay in his precise formulation: since it was basically impossible to pass an army through the remains of an army, don't deploy the first army at all, thus avoiding the logistical problems that the Allies were never able to solve. So at the level of the battle, the Germans had figured out how to mount successful breakthrough operations; the successes of the spring of 1918 were simply the latest examples.

But at the strategic level, the idea didn't work. In modern warfare the opposing sides were simply too big and too powerful. Each side could absorb a horrifying number of defeats and still keep fighting. The British solution was a war of attrition: we have more men than they have, so if losses are roughly equal, we will finally prevail. That was why the Allies kept insisting that German losses were either worse than theirs or the same, and why there was consternation in the French government in late 1916, when shrewd observers began to argue that such was not the case.

Leaving aside the willingness to slaughter one's citizenry, the idea seems logical, but it is seriously flawed. By early 1916, French troops moving up to the front were bleating like sheep in protest, and local commanders were delaying attacks in every way they could.[19] Moreover, the idea could succeed only if there was an equal exchange of casualties. It is hard enough for an army to get accurate information as to its own losses; having solid data about your enemy is even more difficult, and figuring out whether it still has soldiers left is more challenging still. During the First World War, the Allies failed totally in both areas. Their notion of German losses were fantasies, and their calculations of the available manpower pool were simply wrong. Although the whole idea exuded scientific precision, it was junk science: there was no way to determine the precise figures required in evaluating the chances that the strategy would work.

The second and most successful German presiding general, Erich von Falkenhayn, understood this dilemma and had argued for a much different strategy, which he outlined in a letter to Kaiser Wilhelm II in December 1915. You can't destroy the enemy's armies; they are too big and powerful. Nor do you need to. The real objective is not to win some great battle but to make France quit the war, to make "clear to the eyes of her people, that militarily they have nothing to hope for"; and to do this, there's no need to rely on "the uncertainty of a breakthrough." Not only was this "beyond our strength," but it "is not necessary. The objective can be satisfied with limited forces."[20]

The objective is to achieve a sort of systemic shock of your opponent. In July 1916, when the Germans stopped the Verdun offensive, the French positions on the ridge above Verdun consisted of isolated soldiers crouching in piles of rubble. That the victory was fatally incomplete resulted primarily from the lack of overall control of the various theaters by von Falkenhayn, with the commander of the Eastern Front, von Hindenburg (and his chief of staff, Ludendorff), doing everything possible to undercut him, to the extent of withholding troops as the twin battles of Verdun and the Somme came to a climax.

Von Falkenhayn was aiming at a blow that would shock France into quitting the war. The idea was profound. At lower levels the Germans had gotten around what was regarded as the great checkmate of modern firepower, had overcome their numerical inferiority, had learned how to smash through the enemy's defensive positions. Now, at the higher level, that of strategy, they had figured out how to bring wars to speedy conclusions without the problematic battle of annihilation.

So in the First World War, the German army was successful because it had managed to attract the country's best and brightest, men who were constantly astonishing their opponents (or at least those who fought and died on the battlefield) by their resourcefulness and ingenuity.[21] In the war that followed the army was successful because it did pretty much what it had already learned how to do. The men of Hitler's military, the commanders of the Wehrmacht, really contributed nothing new to warfare. On the tactical level, they were content to do what they (or their fathers) had done in the last war. On the strategic level, as we shall see, they mostly proved the old saw that terrific captains don't necessarily make great generals.

THE ARMY BEFORE HITLER:
HOLLOW VICTORIES, SHATTERED ILLUSIONS

> Still more important is the image, which all Germans firmly
> maintained, that in reality the Germans had won.
>
> Sebastian Haffner[1]

The reasons for the German success in the Second World War are not difficult to find, although many people will consider them difficult to accept. The first reason, I think, is unexceptionable: in May 1940 the Wehrmacht had the advantage of five weeks of experience in battle, and many more in logistics—the latter was the result of the occupations of Austria and Czechoslovakia, the former the result of surprisingly hard-fought battles in Poland.

The other reason is more complicated, more controversial, and less overtly military. There was a widespread and deeply held belief, articulated by Haffner, that the Germans had won the First World War militarily but had been tricked at Versailles; that they had not, in other words, been beaten into submission, exhausted by the blockade and the British army. The corollary was that what the Allies—particularly the French—really wanted was nothing less than the destruction of Germany.

It's not difficult to find evidence that Germany was not nearly so defeated as was claimed. "This country does not have the image of a vanquished nation," General Fayolle wrote on December 26, 1918.

"Everything breathes order, prosperity, wealth. Germany is not at all destroyed. If left alone, she'll start the war all over again in ten years, perhaps even before."[2]

Fayolle's remark is the departure point to an understanding of the rebirth of the army. The Germans built from success, not failure, and their feelings of being wronged gave them a focus, an edge. Among themselves, they argued that they had only asked for an armistice because of the Americans. There was no dispute about the decisiveness of the U.S. intervention among the present and future leaders of Germany.

One day in Munich, Adolf Hitler was talking to an early supporter, Ernst Hanfstängel, who challenged him on this subject. " 'Well now,' I said, 'you have just fought in the war. We very nearly won in 1917 when Russia collapsed. Why then, did we lose it?' 'Because the Americans came in,' [Hitler] said. 'If you recognize that, we are agreed and that is all you need to know.' "[3]

Hitler was simply repeating the more precise judgment of Paul von Hindenburg, who, from September 1916 on, had commanded all German troops in the field and, after 1925, served as president of the republic. Thanks to an enterprising American reporter, we know what von Hindenburg actually thought in November 1918. Here was his answer when asked "Who won the war?"

"I will reply with the same frankness," said Hindenburg, faintly amused by our diplomacy. "The American infantry in the Argonne won the war. . . . [W]ithout American troops against us, and despite a food blockade which was undermining the civilian population of Germany and curtailing the rations in the field, we could still have had a peace without victory. The war could have ended in a sort of stalemate. And even if we had not the better of the fighting in the end, as we had until July 18, we could have had an acceptable peace. . . . Even the attack of July 18, which Allied generals may consider the turning point, did not use up a very important part of the German army or smash all our positions. . . . But the balance was broken by the American troops. The Argonne battle was slow and difficult. It was bitter and used up division after division. We had to hold the Metz-Longuyon roads and railroad. . . . [F]rom a military point of view the Argonne battle as conceived and carried out by the American Command was the climax of the war and its deciding factor. . . . I repeat, without the American blow in the Argonne, we could have made a satisfactory peace at the end of a stalemate or at least held our last positions on our own frontier indefinitely—undefeated— the American attack won the war."[4]

This was hardly the view the British and the French wanted to hear, and in the years that followed they created one of the most dangerously delusional ideas of the century: that they had pounded an exhausted Germany into abject submission; its armies had been defeated in the field. But the Germans didn't feel beaten; they felt tricked and swindled, and their anger, fueled by their helplessness, was the ire of the righteous man who feels he's been beaten by a bunch of cheaters.

The Allies added insult to injury by insisting that Germany alone bear responsibility for the war. As the hostilities had continued, as the Allies suffered reverse after reverse, as the casualties mounted, the demonization of Germany and Austria-Hungary became ever more intense. What began as wartime propaganda emerged, soon enough, as the official Allied war aims, which then duly entered the historical record. There they became enshrined as the truth, part of a curious antihistorical vision in which the events of the First World War are seen through the prism of the Second.[5]

In the immediate aftermath of 1918, however, the kaiser's flight, and the willingness of the leaders of the new Socialist government to accept the burden of guilt, fueled an equivalent German fantasy stemming from the perceived contrast between the leader of the army, von Hindenburg, remaining at his post, and the emperor fleeing the country and abandoning his subjects. It was this concept that gave yet more psychological support to the notion that the government had stabbed the nation in the back, while the army had remained steadfast.

But the problem ran far deeper than the comforting British and French notion that the German ideas about who had won and lost were a delusion held only by a few, and became significant only when Hitler stirred them up. By January 1919, Germany was in the middle of a civil war, while at the same time it was threatened by external forces. The brutal fighting of those years would set the course of the Wehrmacht, giving it a taste of success and, perhaps more important, a thirst for blood.

After the kaiser abdicated and fled the country, Germany became a respectable democracy. It had always been more of one than its enemies pretended, and the man presiding over the government of what would be known as the Weimar Republic was Friedrich Ebert, the founder of the German Socialist Party. In the years before the war, it had become one of the country's major political organizations.

But Ebert's government fell squarely in Lenin's sights. Lenin had never put much stock in the idea of Bolshevik revolution in Russia, believing, instead, that the chances were better in Germany. Once in power, he preached a Bolshevik holy war: his followers would spread the gospel into the West, and all Europe would become Communist. That a great power like Germany should become a model Socialist state was too much to bear. So the Bolsheviks embarked on a course of bloody insurrections and uprisings, in the Baltic region, Hungary, and Germany itself. Lenin then compounded his misreading of history by unleashing a reign of terror that would continue, unchecked, for decades inside the newly formed Soviet state.

In Berlin, Ebert and his colleagues pondered the fate of their fellow Socialist Aleksandr Kerensky. When the Russian politician had assumed leadership of a provisional democratic Russian state in 1917, he extended to the Bolsheviks the courtesies of a genteel Western democracy, as though they were simply another political party. But Ebert saw that the Bolsheviks aimed to take over the state, that their preferred method was violence, and that their target was Germany—where Lenin wanted a Communist state, Britain and France wanted one stripped of power and territory. By January 1919, both seemed distinct possibilities. But Lenin and the Allied leaders had fallen victim to their own mythology: the Germans were neither defeated nor inclined to Communism. In November and December 1918, when German troops marched home, often as intact units, and carrying their weapons with them, their attitude was that they hadn't beaten the French and the British for four years only to find the country taken over by the Reds.

Although the Bolsheviks tried to proclaim that theirs was a spontaneous popular revolt against a despotic government, the only truly spontaneous reaction was from those millions of German soldiers. They organized themselves into combat units, subsequently known as the Freikorps, and started shooting back. So on January 6, 1919, as the Bolsheviks briefly seized Berlin, the government there simply incorporated all the Freikorps units into the army.

Ebert's tactic worked. By summer 1919, regular and Freikorps army units had restored order to Germany. They had overcome full-scale Communist revolts in Bavaria aimed at creating a Soviet-style government and seceding from Germany. The Polish offensive, aimed at incorporating all of Germany east of the Oder River into the recently formed Polish state, had been blocked, as had Bolshevik efforts to reclaim the Baltic provinces of Estonia, Latvia, and Lithuania.

Legally and organizationally the ad hoc units that spontaneously arose to combat the Bolsheviks after November 1918, the Freikorps, became part of the army of the new republic.[6] Their status was not a legalism. Virtually every army officer of any note was involved at some level with the Freikorps, whose combat forces were organized exactly like regular army units.

The situation in the Baltic makes this point clear. During the war, German troops occupied the bulk of the future countries of Estonia, Latvia, Lithuania, and Poland.[7] In November 1918, when Germany itself collapsed, there resulted a complex series of struggles: nationalists fighting for freedom, local Communists trying to determine the nature of the governments of the emerging states, troops from the Red Army hoping to regain the territory for the Bolsheviks, and stranded German troops seeking to defend the interests of local German minorities.

In December 1918, the high command of the new German republic appointed a military leader for the Baltic, Count Rüdiger von der Goltz, whose three divisions were charged with restoring order. In addition to the First Guards Reserve Division, he commanded two division-size Freikorps units: the Baltische Landwehr (which, as the name suggests, consisted of forces raised from the ethnic German population) and the Eiserne Division. The Eiserne Division had three infantry regiments, a cavalry regiment, four artillery companies, a tank unit, combat engineers, and even airplanes. The Baltische Landwehr Division was not equipped with armor, but it had considerably more artillery, and both divisions had all the normal supporting units. They were about as far from being bands of irregulars as one could get, right down to having some of the best officers of the old army—men who would go on to become leaders of the Wehrmacht.

Heinz Guderian, for example, was one of the staff officers of the Eiserne Division. Immediately after the armistice, he had been attached to the main office for Eastern Frontier Defense, located in Berlin.[8] In January 1919 he was with the Southern Frontier Defense Command, in Breslau; two months later he was assigned to the Northern Defense Command, at Bartenstein; and in April he moved to the Eiserne Division. By October he was commanding the Tenth Reichswehr Brigade, in Hannover.

In January 1920, Guderian became a company commander in his old unit, the Tenth Jäger, whose headquarters was at Goslar. The battalion was particularly active in the first half of 1920, putting down the uprisings (Guderian called them "disturbances") in Hildesheim, Dessau, Bitterfeld, and the Ruhr. Guderian's service record in the years immediately following the war tracks the major military actions perfectly, illustrating the extent to which the regular army, career officers, and the Freikorps melded together.

Guderian's was hardly an isolated case. There was no real difference between the army of the Weimar Republic and the Freikorps. General Werner von Fritsch, for instance, initially served as chief of staff for the Northern Frontier Defense Headquarters.[9] It is difficult to find a senior officer of the German army in the Second World War who was not involved at some level with the Freikorps. And in these bloody struggles, the future officers tasted real victory.

Regardless of their opponents, the Germans were successful on the field of battle. Although forced to withdraw from the Baltic states, by May 22, 1919, the Germans, together with Russian and Latvian forces, had conquered most of the area, including the port of Riga. The fall of Riga had an importance far beyond the Baltic. It marked the collapse of Lenin's dream of pan-European revolution. What is more, the Germans had learned that they could defend themselves: while fighting was going on inside Germany, they were confronting the Poles over Silesia, which the new state claimed as its own.

The struggles there were largely overlooked, since by early 1920 the Russo-Polish War was under way. Unlike the Balts, who were forced to depend heavily on German soldiers, the Poles had a large, surprisingly well-equipped military, aided by the French, who saw in an independent Poland the necessary counterweight to Germany and Russia. The resulting conflict put the gravestone on Lenin's ambitions. The war began on April 25, 1920, and by late July, Polish forces, supported by French armored units, routed the Red Army, took more than fifty thousand prisoners, and drove deep into Belorussia. Lenin's insistence on a campaign of terror had produced a Poland much larger and more powerful than the Allies had anticipated, wanted, or intended.

In Silesia, however, the Poles were less successful. German units ejected their forces from Silesia, only to see the region handed over to the Warsaw government anyway, by France and Britain. Thus at one stroke the Germans realized their military prowess, fueled their dislike for the Poles, and saw confirmation of their worst suspicions about their own government—and the Allies.

The Allies had already determined (in May 1919) that there would never be another German army of any significance. They dictated a minuscule force of 100,000 men and prescribed the equipment and the number of officers, thus reducing the military to the size of Belgium's. The Germans weren't even allowed to build frontier fortifications, despite their obviously defensive nature. In contrast, the Versailles Treaty encouraged the other nations to arm themselves to the teeth. The point isn't whether or not this was fair. The point is that the Germans perceived it as grossly unfair.

Moreover, despite their earlier pronouncements about trying German leaders as war criminals, what the Allies actually did was to demand monetary and territorial reparations. So those Germans who had been opposed to the kaiser, who were as pacifist and antimilitarist as could be desired—a substantial minority in 1914—were now backed into a tragic corner: they felt themselves to be innocent, and good patriots to boot. And yet the whole country was being punished.

People who feel that a rule is unfair are likely to cheat. Ignoring the terms of Versailles quickly became a cottage industry, giving rise to endless complaints about perfidious Germans and to the idea that much of their early success in the next war was a function of this cheating. Germany, so the legend ran, had flouted Versailles and armed itself to the teeth while the hapless Allies stood by, impotent and somnolent.

By now this legend is enshrined in the historical record as fact, but the evidence to support it is highly ambiguous. The military gained little from the clandestine research, and what was achieved was more than offset by the fact that the key businesses involved, interested mostly in financial solvency, started selling their wares to foreign countries.

The highly profitable Krupp enterprise is often cited as the primary example of how a collusive effort, involving German industrialists, rapacious Swedes, and weak-kneed Allies, enabled the company to shift its key patents out of Germany. By 1921, the firm had substantial control of the Swedish arms manufacturer Bofors, allowing former Krupp employees to manage the "development and production of the latest Krupp-designed artillery, antiaircraft guns, and light tanks."[10]

The most notable Bofors gun to be developed under this scheme was a 40-millimeter rapid-fire weapon designed at the request of the Swedish navy in the early 1920s. The device went into production in 1930 and quickly established itself as the preferred antiaircraft gun, primarily because of its reliability and extremely high rate of fire (more than 120 rounds per minute). By 1937, it had become the de facto standard antiaircraft weapon for anyone who had the money to purchase it.[11]

The problem is that the Bofors weapon had become the standard gun for the British army, not the German, and by 1941 it had become standard for the Royal Navy as well. Indeed, the principal consumers of Bofors guns were nations that used them in 1939 and 1940 to fight off the Germans: other Scandinavian countries, the Netherlands, Belgium, and even Poland. The Germans themselves relied on entirely different types of antiaircraft guns, all of them developed in the early 1930s—long after the advent of the Bofors company's most successful design. So much for the idea of clandestine rearmament.

In terms of organizing the minuscule army allowed by Versailles, the Germans did somewhat better. The proverbial "father of the German army," Hans von Seeckt, was the son of a Prussian general and hailed from an old Pomeranian family.[12] As one might expect from the graduate of a Gymnasium (this one in Strasbourg), he was an educated young man clearly bound for great things: commissioned in 1887 in an elite guards regiment, picked for the three-year course at the Kriegsakademie in 1893, and, four years later, selected to be a member of the general staff.

In 1914 he was chief of staff for the Third Army Corps as it moved through Belgium. Von Seeckt established himself as the embodiment of a senior staff officer: not only did he direct the planning of operations, but in October 1914 and again in January 1915, he staged counterattacks that resulted in serious losses for the French. As a result, in March 1915 he was named chief of staff of the Eleventh Army, and spent the remainder of the war in the east.

The commander of the Eleventh Army was General August von Mackensen, and the von Seeckt–von Mackensen team produced some significant victories, beginning with the Galician offensive (usually known as the Battle of Gorlice), in which German troops advanced about 120 kilometers in two weeks, forcing the Russians to withdraw all the way to the San River. Gorlice was the first of several major successes. In October 1915 the Eleventh Army, operating with Austrian and Bulgarian forces, overran Serbia, driving the remnants of the Serbian army out of the Balkans entirely. Von Seeckt, who was instrumental in stopping the rout caused by Russian general Alexei Brusilov's great 1916 offensive, went on to become chief of staff for a joint Austro-German army under Archduke Joseph.

Von Seeckt's career had not been contaminated either by failure or by contact with Erich Ludendorff, regarded inside the officer corps as a shameless self-promoter with a tendency to panic. But the worst problem was that Ludendorff, like von Moltke and von Falkenhayn, had failed to deliver the military victory that the German officer corps felt should have been achieved.

Nor did it hurt von Seeckt's reputation that he was a well-educated aristocrat with a general for a father, an exemplary private life, and a legendary field marshal as his patron.[13] So it's not surprising that in the successive reshufflings of the army command after November 1918, von Seeckt was at the center of things. In January 1919, he became the leader of the hastily created Northern Frontier Command, and was thus the army officer nominally in charge of the operations in the Baltic and in Poland. In April 1919 he was sent to Versailles as part of the vain German attempt to ameliorate the emerging Allied diktat, was named head of the commission charged with studying the shape of the postwar army, and then, after the failure of the Kapp putsch in March 1920, appointed chief of staff, remaining in total control of the army until 1926.[14]

Technically there was no such thing as a general staff, as it had been abolished at Versailles because of its alleged contribution to Germany's militarism, but under von Seeckt the Truppernamt, or training organization staff, was simply the general staff with a different name. Similarly, von Seeckt undercut the 100,000-man limitation on the army by filling it up with noncommissioned officers. By the end of his tenure, the Reichsheer had only 36,500 ordinary soldiers—the other 63,500 were all noncommissioned officers, easily enough to form the cadres for an army of one million men.[15]

Von Seeckt's appointment can also be seen as the resolution of a conflict that had marked the army's officer corps for decades: east or west? Otto von Bismarck's foreign policy had been predicated on close relations with Russia, thus ensuring that Germany would never have to fight a war on multiple fronts. Bismarck's successors, despite their self-proclaimed skills, mangled that policy, and the French had, with a certain dexterity, stepped in and secured an alliance with Russia.[16]

For the staff officers and senior commanders of the 1890s, this unwelcome turn of affairs meant that in the event of a European war, they would have to face the unpleasant likelihood of fighting on two or even three fronts. So the question reduced itself simply enough: If you had to fight a war against both France and Russia, whom would you try to defeat first? Alfred von Schlieffen, the alleged military genius of the German army, had opted for taking on France first. Although the German army's actual offensive plans (drafted by Ludendorff when he was von Moltke's director of planning) transformed the old general's vision in every respect, in one key way it remained the same: in the event of a war with both powers, the Germans would initially attack France, and stay on the defensive in the east.

In the fiercely independent world of the German general staff, however, this idea was never completely accepted, and by 1914 there were two factions: the easterners and the westerners. Military officers are almost always divided into factions. In the French army before 1914, these divisions were so extreme that a name was coined, or appropriated, for them: *chapels*, a term redolent of religious intensity and monasticism, suggesting deeply held beliefs rather than simple disputes over tactics or technology.

The easterners were one such *chapel*: officers who followed the lead of Helmuth von Moltke the Elder (1800–1891), who had argued that, in the face of the most likely war scenario (Germany versus France and Russia), Germany should stay on the defensive in the west and strike to the east. Ludendorff and von Moltke the Younger had attempted to square this circle: the army would strike hard in the west, destroy the French, and immediately go on the offensive in the east. As events developed in August and September 1914, the movement from west to east was first seen as France's salvation and then as a sign of how Germany had botched things.

But the real problem was that the easterners had promptly gone over to the offensive on their own, defeating the core of the Russian army and then demanding more troops to follow up on their early successes. So it was certainly possible to make the case that the westerners had been wrong from the start: wrong to insist on an offensive in the west, and wrong to continue to pour resources into the fighting there. After all, the Germans had defeated Russia, forcing the Bolsheviks to come to the table and sign a peace treaty, proof that the strategy was possible, proof that the westerners had been both wrong and inept.

As a result of von Seeckt's control over the military, this approach became the new orthodoxy. But his main impact on the army was in personnel, as he decided, himself, who would be in the four-thousand-man officer corps. Given that in the early 1920s Germany probably had at least fifty thousand veteran officers, the selection was a formidable task, and there's no doubt that in this respect, as well as in training and doctrine, von Seeckt shaped what would eventually become the Wehrmacht. The army already possessed a coherent doctrine derived from its experiences—suitably critiqued—in the previous war, and von Seeckt added little to this store of knowledge. It is primarily in the deployment of human resources that he made his mark.

Taking a relatively nonpartisan posture placed von Seeckt squarely in the central *chapel* of the traditional Prussian officer corps, whose members were studiously apolitical, who saw themselves as belonging to a technical profession exclusively concerned with the art (or science) of war. They despised von Falkenhayn, Germany's talented war minister and commander in chief (from September 1914 through August 1916), because he was too political, and for the same reason, they had no use for Ludendorff, who had spent most of his time on the Eastern Front involved in the administration of German-occupied territories, while men like von Seeckt had directed the war.

Von Seeckt's selection of officers profoundly tilted the nature of the corps. Over the short life span of the Second Reich (1872–1918), a variety of forces had combined to create an officer corps that was surprisingly middle class and diverse. By 1914, the corps had a much lower percentage of aristocratic surnames than the French or the British, and even this comparison overstates the representation of the nobility, since Germany was full of families whose titled surnames were belied by their social status. In fact, the rise to prominence of men like Max Hoffman (often touted by British analysts as being the military genius of the Eastern Front) and Erich Ludendorff offers us an accurate glimpse into an astonishing underlying reality: socially, the officer corps of the army of the Hohenzollerns was indeed an inclusive affair.[17]

To von Seeckt, however, this was precisely the problem. There were too many potential Ludendorffs. Or worse: the uprisings of 1918–19 had seen more than a few officers on the side of the Reds. So von Seeckt relied on criteria that seem in retrospect to be more social than military. In light of the capability of the officer corps in winning battles, it would have been difficult to make bad choices. Only an incompetent could have botched the process, and von Seeckt, educated, intelligent, with proven military savvy, certainly did not. Although he was sacked in 1926, he left a lasting mark on the army.[18]

A disturbing undercurrent emerged from von Seeckt's personnel selections. As he carefully made his choices, the tone of the new officer corps became profoundly professional and quasi-aristocratic, composed predominantly of men from the eastern regions, especially Prussians. This is not to say that the officer corps contained only men entitled to use the aristocratic "von." On the contrary, of the roughly fifty officers who are generally considered to be the senior leadership of the German army of the Second World War, only eighteen, or slightly over one-third, fit that description.[19]

But in developed societies such as Germany and Britain, the families constituting what might be referred to as the ruling classes are defined by complex social criteria that often resist understanding. There was no single benchmark that could be used in the selection process. But von Seeckt seems to have had a set of standards intended to ensure a socially homogenous and reliable officer cadre, and when geography, family background, and service records are factored in, it is clear how he made his decisions.

Of the other two-thirds of the senior leadership, those men whose surnames did not indicate an aristocratic background, most came either from a military family or were connected with the east; probably close to half of the total officer cadre fit this criteria. Consider, for example, Hermann Balck. Although, surprisingly, not well known, Balck may be fairly considered the prime mover in Germany's drive toward a mechanized army.

In 1938 he would become the head of the inspectorate for mobile troops. In May 1940, Balck's First Motorized Infantry Regiment stormed across the Meuse at Sedan.

There is no doubting Balck's personal courage, his leadership (as a Jäger officer in the First World War, he won an Iron Cross), or his military competence. And at first blush, the fact that he was chosen by von Seeckt to be part of the four-thousand-man officer corps suggests that the head of the new German army had a nose for talent. But a closer inspection of Balck's record may reveal entirely different reasons: his father had been a general in the army of Kaiser Wilhelm II, his family hailed from Danzig Langfuhr, in East Prussia, and most of his military service had been on the Eastern Front.

To take a more famous case, consider Heinz Guderian. Like Balck, his family came from the east. He was born in Kulm, a small town near the Vistula, in East Prussia. His family were farmers and army officers; his father was on active duty until 1908. Guderian's prewar service had been in an elite unit, the Tenth Jäger, and during the war he had served on the staff of another kind of elite unit, the Fifth Cavalry—membership in cavalry units in European (and the British) armies drew their officers from those families judged to be socially prestigious.

The resulting officer corps was hardly the sort of group to represent a government that was by definition Socialist, but it is incorrect to assume that the army was therefore going to agitate against the government. On the contrary, the officers of the Reichsheer, by and large, prided themselves on being apolitical technicians. Von Seeckt's officer corps was certainly conservative, but no more so than the professorate, and much less political. In the context of the polarized citizenry of the Weimar Republic, its simple conservatism placed the army leadership more or less in the middle. When Hitler came to power, the officer corps was the least disposed to National Socialism of all the key groups in Germany.

The fatal flaw, or besetting sin, of von Seeckt's leadership cadre was neither its lack of political orientation nor its conservatism: armies, being inherently hierarchical, are instinctively conservative. The immediate problem was naïveté, a worldview that had long existed in the German and Austrian officer corps, many of whose members subscribed to a way of life that had more in common with the monastic than with the secular. They lived apart, and the uniforms they wore on almost all occasions differentiated them from the population at large. Junior officers had to remain bachelors, and the statutory celibacy further separated them from their countrymen. They were required to subscribe to a code of honor, and to defend it by offering up their lives through the duel.

But democratization of the army during the years before 1914 had provided the officer corps with a leavening of practicality and cynicism. Max Hoffman spent most of his early years in the army drunk. Before the war, Erich Ludendorff had taken enough time out from directing the army's planned offensive operations to engage in a scandalous romance. And at the highest levels, the necessity of dealing with the court and the kaiser demanded a certain realism about the affairs of the world—courtiers of all nations not being noted for either their unworldiness or their naïveté.

But the strain had always been present. It is quite marked in the literary treatments of the army before the war. Arthur Schnitzler's fictional Lieutenant Gustl, for example, is naive to the point of being neurotic, a tendency he shares with the protagonists of other great German-language novels treating the officer class; Hermann Broch's von Aschenbach (*The Romantic*) and Joseph Roth's Carl Joseph von Trotta (*The Radetsky March*) are the most outstanding examples. In the dinner party that takes place early on in Theodor Storm's famous novel of Berlin, *L'Adultera*, the wealthy and shrewd van der Straaten belligerently lectures his brother-in-law about the contemporary political scene, in a way that suggests the good major's complete innocence when it comes to politics, even though he is a member of the general staff.

One could multiply these fictional examples at length. The young men of the turn of the century and after who constituted the potential officer pool were in many ways sheltered, privileged, and unworldly. The realities of combat hardly remedied the situation, and may have in fact exacerbated it. Unfortunately, von Seeckt's criteria loaded the officer corps with men who were innocent, and ignorant, of the ways of the world.

Von Seeckt would live for ten years after his dismissal, but his power over the army was gone.

Werner von Blomberg, appointed by von Hindenburg as Reichs-wehrminister in 1933, is a good example. An easterner from a military family (he was born in Pomerania and his father was a lieutenant colonel), he was a natural choice for the Reichsheer, and by 1925 was a colonel in charge of army training. After von Seeckt was fired by the Socialist government, von Blomberg assumed command of the army. The sequence is, in miniature, the perfect emblem of why Weimar failed: the left drove a relatively apolitical man out of the key military job and managed to replace him with a series of nonentities and fawning Hitlerites.[20]

Although he was an able officer, von Blomberg's remarks reveal a man confused by the world. At one point he confessed that he had almost become a Bolshevik, and then he distinguished himself by his enthusiasm for Hitler, whom he believed was the greatest man who ever lived. But the best example came in 1937, when the fifty-nine-year-old general fell head over heels in love with a twenty-four-year-old secretary, whose past hardly qualified her to be Frau General von Blomberg, as soon became sadly obvious.

There's certainly nothing unusual about a middle-aged man becoming involved with a much younger woman. The real marker of the good general's character is that he proposed to her. Hitler, who had a surprisingly keen nose for public decorum (as well as an understanding of women), was suitably furious, and von Blomberg was promptly sacked. The incident is generally viewed as some nefarious Nazi plot to strengthen control over the military, but given von Blomberg's pliability and his worship of Hitler, it's difficult to see why anyone would have bothered scheming to have him replaced.

Indeed, von Blomberg did not just passively aid Hitler's agenda for the military; he actively abetted it. It was von Blomberg who authorized the addition to the uniform of the eagle and swastika patch, the *Wehrmachtsadler*, thus linking the military explicitly to Hitler's party and to

Hitler himself. As defense minister he signed a decree ordering that uniformed personnel honor the boycotts of Jewish merchants being organized by party cadres. He was not a National Socialist or Hitlerite, simply a naive man with a weak character.

But except for a few outspoken individuals such as Ludwig Beck, the officer corps von Seeckt put together was, like the future Frau von Blomberg, easy to persuade, a susceptibility that to the more worldly is frequently (if not invariably) taken as a sign of innocence. There were plenty of veteran officers, former leaders of the Freikorps, who were cynical and sophisticated and shared the same traditions that produced the von Falkenhayns and the Ludendorffs. Von Seeckt ensured that, instead, the officer corps would be filled with their opposites.

How else to explain, for example, that, in 1943, Rommel suggested to an astonished Hitler that German foreign policy could be made immeasurably easier if it weren't for the rumors about the treatment of the Jews and that the solution might be to make a Jew one of the party administrators, a Jewish gauleiter? In 1943? Here's a man who knew absolutely nothing about what was going on in his own country, and, as Hitler himself observed after Rommel's departure, who had failed to grasp what Hitler's Germany was all about.[21]

More to the point in discussing matters military, the naïveté was not restricted to politics and the bedroom. After 1918, plenty of internal criticism was directed at the army from officers. To a certain extent, the criticism was a good thing. What is curious, however, is that the negative appraisals were concerned almost exclusively with tactical problems. For instance, the only reason the Germans lost the Great War was that they had failed to come up with a decent light machine gun and lagged in tank production. The mostly technological nature of the issues resonated with the leading theorists outside of Germany, men like John Frederick Charles Fuller and Giulio Douhet, who saw warfare in mechanistic, abstract terms.

This emphasis on the technological—or tactical—was not offset by any grand strategic thinking. The lack of interest in the larger picture started with von Seeckt, whose sole excursion from the tactical occurred when he bruited the idea of an all-volunteer army, as distinct from the traditional army base of the Kaiserreich.

What was the purpose of the army? To von Seeckt, whose appreciation came from the war with Russia, it was to engage the enemy in a battle of annihilation and destroy its army. Nowhere was there any recognition that this aim was no longer possible, or that it would necessarily win a war.

This was a departure. In dramatically different ways, the leaders of the old German army had sought to develop means of conflict resolution—which is to say, they had possessed a sense of grand strategy, subordinating actual combat to the end in view. Von Falkenhayn, for instance, had seen right to the heart of the problem: Germany (and by extension other nations) lacked the overwhelming force required to defeat an enemy on the field of battle. Armies with millions of men were simply too large to be defeated—or surrounded and forced to surrender. What was required was to destroy the enemy's will to fight, indoctrinating its citizenry with the message that their cause was hopeless.

The von Hindenburg–Ludendorff approach had been more classically Frederickian, albeit it on a grand scale. Take out each one of the Allies, until the survivors realize they can't win. The emphasis was not so much on the destruction of the enemy's army as on ending his interest in continuing the fight, and thus the doctrine merged into von Falkenhayn's idea. Neither Romania nor Italy was destroyed, but its morale had collapsed, along with its ability to pursue the war except in desultory fashion.

Ludendorff and the easterners failed to comprehend where von Falkenhayn had been headed. After the containment of General Alexei Brusilov's June 1916 offensive and the abortive Romanian invasion of Hungary—January 1917 at the latest—the war in the east was over. The great spring 1918 offensives in France should have been executed in the spring of 1917, and could well have been. Instead, the Germans continued to grind away at the Russians (and then diverted resources to smashing the Italians). Why? Because Ludendorff and von Hindenburg had not grasped that in the new warfare, all you had to do was destroy the enemy's will to fight, something that required neither great battles nor formal treaties of peace.

It is also true that Ludendorff got sidetracked, or seduced, by the historic Germanic vision of *Drang nach Osten*, an expansion to the east, but this too was an integral part of the vision of the easterners. At bottom, their preference for an offensive against Russia (as opposed to one directed at France) reflected ideas that were as much nationalist (or chauvinist) as military or political.

The fact that neither strategy was ultimately successful in the way that had been planned does not mean that the ideas were stupid or inherently unsound. Indeed, the German military leaders of 1914–18 were, in this respect, surprisingly sophisticated: they realized that wars could not be won by the traditional practice of pursuing battles of annihilation, that wars could be won without ever destroying the enemy's army or fighting a decisive battle.

Great captains do not automatically make great generals. Great generals do not necessarily become great commanders in chief. Dwight Eisenhower had never had any substantive field command, and John Pershing's had been restricted to counterinsurgency warfare in Mexico and the Philippines.

The difference was that both Pershing and Eisenhower (like the Duke of Wellington in an earlier age) pretty much had to fight with whatever officer corps their country had given them. But von Seeckt was cherry-picking his officer corps, ensuring that only men that met his standards went into the army, and these were the men who would become the leaders (and the trainers of the leaders) for the next war.

On the political or personnel side, what von Seeckt ended up with was a remarkably naive group of technicians, and hence the ease with which Hitler dazzled, coddled, and manipulated them. The dominance of men from the eastern *chapel* also ensured that they would be receptive to Hitler's reversion to *Drang nach Osten*—the idea that Germany's future lay in the east, toward Poland, Ukraine, and the Baltic. That tilt had already been sanctified, in the minds of most Germans, by the bloody combat in Upper Silesia and the Baltic, by the sacrifice of Memel and the historically German-dominated territories around Posen.

So the result was to produce an officer corps that consisted of brilliant technicians and tacticians, of great captains, if you will, very few of whom had the aptitude or the inclination to become great generals. The key word here is "great." Operationally, the Wehrmacht would prove itself an excellent army, and no wonder: it was run by men with high levels of technical expertise.[22]

Hitler would dominate them not merely because they were the sort of men who were easily dominated but because he was the only one in the room who had any real concept of grand strategy. Hitler had been only a lowly corporal in World War I, but he understood strategic thinking, and he had an uncanny instinct for strategic moves, just as he had an uncanny instinct for the wicked. As the war continued, he became—like all truly evil men—increasingly convinced of his genius, distrustful of his generals, and inclined to micromanage the war, with results like the German near-paralysis on June 6, 1944. But he was the only one who understood strategy at the grand level.[23] The others were simply excellent tacticians and technicians.

BREAKING OUT OF THE CAVE:
HITLER AND THE
WEHRMACHT'S JEWISH PROBLEM

If someone had come to me in 1914 and said that one country
would attempt to exterminate the Jews, I would have said then
"no one can be surprised at the depths to which the French
can sink."

George Mosse[1]

Lenin's main achievement in Germany and the Baltic was to foment a
bloody revolt that considerably strengthened the most extreme opponents of the Bolsheviks. As the eminent French historian François Furet
observed, "The Soviet terror was one of the fundamental reasons for the
popularity of fascism and nazism."[2] A denial of the Red terror thus leads
to a total misunderstanding of the rebirth of the German military, whose
struggles against the Bolsheviks (and the Poles) in the years after the First
World War gave it both a sense of confidence and a taste for blood.[3]

As the National Socialists began their ascent to power, a similar denial would distort the nature of Hitler's political success. The result is a
cartoon image of Germany in 1933 that prevents us from understanding
both the hopes and the fears of the officer corps, as well as the inevitable
conflict between its members and Hitler.

In his campaign for votes, Hitler had capitalized on memories of the crushing of the Bolsheviks in 1919–20, linking the party with the struggle in highly effective symbolic ways. The use of the swastika dates from the immediate postwar violence: the emblem, crudely daubed on helmets and armored vehicles in 1919–20, suggested an association with and a continuation of the anti-Communist military deployments of the civil war. The same is true of the party's appropriation of the term *Sturmabteilung* (storm troopers), usually abbreviated by the National Socialists as SA: the term deliberately recalled the nation's military successes in the Great War and subsequent civil war, as did the term Schützstaffel, or SS, and, indeed, the death's-head badges used as their insignia.[4]

It started out with only a handful of supporters, but by the 1932 elections, Hitler's party received nearly one out of every three votes cast in Bavaria, and close to four out of ten in other key states. By July of that year, the National Socialists had won well over a third of the votes and had managed to fill 230 seats in the Reichstag. For Anglo-Americans, accustomed to a two-party system in which there is generally a majority, as distinct from a plurality, these figures seem to support the idea that Hitler did not have a real power base, and that most of the German people repudiated him.

But in a multiparty system with complex rules for determining electoral representation, a party that captures one-third of the seats often becomes the dominant group, either because the other parties are hopelessly fragmented and sprawled across the political spectrum, or because it is able to secure a coalition of like-minded politicians. Although Americans may question whether this is the best way to manage things, it is how most major European states determine which party forms the government even today. Since, as a result of the 1932 elections, the National Socialists were the single largest party in the Weimar Republic, Hitler would, in the normal course of events, have become the leader of the government.

And in fact this is what happened, albeit circuitously. In January 1933, Hitler was duly named chancellor (prime minister). He promptly called for another round of elections; when they were held, on March 5, 1933, the National Socialists received an astonishing 43.9 percent of the popular vote. With their coalition partners they had a majority of the popular vote (just over 50 percent) and 288 of the 647 seats in the Reichstag. In the Weimar Republic's complicated electoral system, these figures amounted to a landslide.[5]

For many writers, this observation is so horrifying that they can hardly bring themselves to admit it, much less record it, but the figures are nonetheless accurate, and any understanding of what happened next must begin with an acceptance of this reality. Hitler did not seize power. He was elected, he was popular, and initially he governed by relying on the same extensive powers his predecessors had wielded. Dictators are most often seen as men who seize power through force, after either a revolution or a military coup. But Hitler rose to power legally, through votes. He was propelled into office by a population that was both polarized and exhausted, one that had lost faith in the idea of democratic capitalism and was still traumatized by the Bolshevik terror.

Hitler was also a genuine revolutionary. He aimed to transform German society, and he gained power by persuading people to vote for him in astonishing numbers. As the photographic evidence makes abundantly clear, he was a genuinely popular leader, and, despite much of what has been said, or assumed, he was a shrewd politician, a canny foreign minister, and no mean military strategist.[6]

Support for Hitler and the National Socialists was particularly strong in the universities, which were Nazified (to use the rather inelegant expression) well before he became chancellor. It is suggestive, I think, that it was there that the most open and brutal acts began. That they started almost immediately after the March elections demonstrates how entrenched the party already was in this important area of society.

These men and women believed—to use a metaphor of Martin Heidegger's, appropriated from Plato—that they were breaking out of the cave, out of the darkness and despair of Weimar and what Hitler liked to call its Marxist government. In Baden, for example, the new rector of Freiburg University was forced to resign in April 1933, after having held office for only a few weeks. His successor, Heidegger, was elected unanimously by the faculty—minus its Jewish members, who had already (in April 1933) been purged as part of what the National Socialists called the *Gleichschaltung*.

Although not a member of the party at that time, Heidegger was more than sympathetic to its aims and enjoyed considerable backing in the party-dominated student association. In May 1933, Heidegger, who had joined the party on May Day, was duly inaugurated rector. The "Horst-Wessel Lied," the party's anthem, was printed on the back of the program and the ceremony concluded with everyone singing it—including the fourth verse, in which all present were supposed to render what was the functional equivalent of the party salute.

I have chosen Martin Heidegger as an example because of his enthusiastic endorsement of Hitler and his party, the overwhelming vote for his rectorship by men who knew very well what their backing meant, and the mutual support that existed between the new rector and the student associations. But the choice is deliberate in another way: Heidegger was one of the most important philosophers of the twentieth century. His eager pronouncements about Hitler illuminate a key principle of National Socialism that is of enormous significance in understanding the conflict that soon developed between Hitler and the officer corps. No one saw the basic premise of National Socialism more clearly, and he put it plainly enough in an address to Freiburg students at the start of the 1933 winter term:

> Let not your being be ruled by doctrine or "Ideas." The *Führer* himself and he alone *is* the German reality, present and future, and its law. Study to know: from now on all things demand decision, and all action responsibility.[7]

Considered narrowly, "doctrine" presumably means theology, and "Ideas" refers to what Heidegger saw as the slavish adherence of German philosophers to Plato. The passage applies to political systems as well, and Heidegger was consciously rejecting both democracy and Marxism-Leninism, a self-described philosophical system that also rejected Plato in no uncertain terms.

Perhaps the concluding "Heil Hitler" at his inauguration was simply pro forma and demanded of anyone in his position, but no one held a gun to Heidegger's head and made him become rector. Nor is there any indication that he was troubled by the purging of the Jewish faculty (including his former patron, the distinguished philosopher Edmund Husserl) as part of the *Gleichschaltung*, by the student-dominated book burnings, or by the formation of paramilitary student groups—all of which took place while he was rector.

The point here, however, is not to indict Heidegger. I leave that to the philosophers—although it seems to me that they have thus far done a remarkably sketchy job of it. Rather, it is to show just how firmly established the National Socialists were in key areas, how quickly Hitler's ideas were put into action, and how powerful his support was. We often assume that the National Socialists were a party composed of thugs, hoodlums, and nonentities and that Hitler seized power by force, stole the government, tricking the population at large. The votes cast remind us that the latter is not true; the name Heidegger gives the lie to the former.

Heidegger's pronouncement was not simply idle theory. Hitler began his reign by openly reserving the important decisions to himself—as well as the right to determine what constituted an important decision. By promoting a social system in which competing groups and individuals, each of whom had to appeal to him for a final decision (which was often not final at all), Hitler made certain that he was truly the ruler of the country. And this principle was to a certain extent—most notably with Hermann Göring—recapitulated throughout the leadership.

But there was more to it than that. The restoration to greatness that Hitler had campaigned on depended on raising the standard of living, which, rightly or wrongly, most Germans felt had deteriorated to the point of intolerability under the Socialist government of the Weimar Republic. We often speak of the national defense dilemma posed to a nation by invoking the phrase "guns or butter." Hitler aimed to provide both and, much conventional wisdom notwithstanding, he was quite successful at it.

After 1933, regardless of the objective indicators of economic prosperity, the subjective indicators were positive, as were many of the traditional ones: "Hitler's National Socialist Germany demonstrated that it was possible to achieve a high standard of living under a rigid dictatorship."[8] So much so that it is fair to say, as some Germans have conceded, that had Hitler died in 1938, he would have been regarded—at least in Germany— as the man who restored his country to its place in the sun.[9]

In short, Hitler behaved like a man who feels he has been given a mandate by the nation at large and who plans to use that mandate to implement the policies that got him elected in the first place. Retrospectively, the most notorious of those programs was his aim to rid German society of the Jews. Although his project was begun immediately and with great success, nowhere more so than in the universities, not all of the country's institutions were so enthusiastic. The most resistant was Germany's most respected and powerful institution: the military.

In 1933 the officer corps was the least Nazified of any group in Germany. Paradoxically, while the Jewish professorate was purged within weeks of the March elections (and the persecution of the German Jews in other areas of society began as well), in the military the purges took longer, were met with a surprising amount of disapproval, and were much less successful.

Those characterizations have to be carefully qualified. The military was hardly unified, in many cases its motives were suspect, and its resistance was a far cry from that of July 1944 (when a small group of officers narrowly missed assassinating Hitler). Moreover, there's not much doubt in my mind that had Hitler been victorious, he would have had every person of Jewish descent murdered. But, although these are important reservations, they should not blind us to the fact that what actually happened in the Third Reich was confusing, complicated, and of great significance to an understanding of the relationship between Hitler and the military and—since the military represented Germans at large in a way that, say, the universities did not—of importance to an understanding of what in retrospect is often seen as a sort of descent into national madness.

I suspect that the main problem that most readers have with the paragraphs directly above is far simpler: for half a century or more the conventional wisdom has been that there were no Jews in the German army, not even in the army of the Hohenzollerns, and certainly not in Hitler's military. In fact, the absence of Jews in Kaiser Wilhelm's military is often taken as yet another instance of how backward, repressive, and even feudal Wilhelmine Germany was.

The contention is false in almost every way. In 1866 there were 26 Jewish officers in the Prussian army; by 1870, there were 120. One of these men, Walther Mossner, rose to the rank of general and was ennobled by Kaiser Wilhelm II.[10] It is true that the numbers were small to begin with, and that in peacetime they were even smaller: in 1906, for example, there were only 16 Jewish officers in the Prussian army. But the Jewish population of the German empire created in 1871 was small. The usual estimate is about half a million out of a total population (in 1913) of 67 million, or about three-quarters of 1 percent. We should hardly expect to find all that many Jewish officers in Kaiser Wilhelm's army, for the simple reason that there weren't all that many Jews in Germany.

Given the sweeping generalizations that have been made about the subject, though, the figures are revealing: small is not the same as none. Moreover, in the Austro-Hungarian army at the same time, there were 2,180 Jewish officers—a significant percentage of the officer corps. So the claim that there were no Jewish officers in the German army is untrue.

As we have seen, in Germany and Austria-Hungary, the reserve officer phenomenon was widespread. By 1914 there was a sizable pool of officers with reserve commissions in both empires. In both armies, Jews were allowed to hold reserve commissions.[11] When reserve officers are counted in, the picture changes dramatically. In the decades before 1914, about 300 Jewish reserve officers served in the Prussian army and more than 50 in the Bavarian. During the First World War, 3,200 Jewish officers served in the German army, and about 100,000 enlisted men; 12,000 of them were casualties. Precise Austrian figures are not available, but we have enough data to say with confidence that the numbers there were probably three times as great.[12]

When Hitler came to power in 1933, the National Socialists discovered that there were a surprising number of Jews in the Reichswehr. How many? The National Socialists had difficulties in computing solid figures for the Jews in the general population, much less in any one part of it. A special department was formed, charged with ferreting out what Hitler regarded as the Jewish menace. One of the experts there, Achim Gercke, wrote in 1935 that it would take a thousand researchers three decades to come up with a precise estimate of the numbers. The National Socialists quickly became aware that the situation was substantially more complex than they had assumed it to be.

The numbers that exist are wildly incomplete (and will probably never be fully known), but research has identified at least twenty-seven generals and admirals, one field marshal, and forty colonels of Jewish descent serving under Hitler. The figures are not trivial: they are too widespread for us to dismiss as the result of some sort of confusion in identification.

The problem the National Socialists had uncovered was simple enough to explain, incredibly difficult to resolve. Hitler began with a simple distinction: Jews constituted a race whose members were, by definition, reasonably easy to identify. He was well aware that Jews and gentiles had sex with each other and intermarried, so there would be people of mixed racial descent. In fact, the National Socialists had a name for these people: *Mischlinge*, which literally means "mixed."

In traditional Jewish law, the children born of such marriages, particularly when the mother is Jewish—or when the family practices traditional Judaism—were considered to be Jewish. And when pushed to extremes, traditional Judaism believed, or claimed to believe, that, in practice, the offspring of marriages between Jews and gentiles were Jewish, and couldn't be altered by a simple religious confession (to use the German word) that one could change at will.

Small numbers of Jews in German society remained easily identifiable by their dress and their physical appearance: in contemporary terms we would call these Orthodox Jews, who practiced the religion of their ancestors. But in the prosperous, developed regions, these Jews were in the minority. Not only had an increasing number of non-Orthodox Jews intermarried; others had abandoned religious practice, still others had converted, and some had done all three.

The vast majority of the people affected either did not regard themselves as Jews or were not aware that they had Jewish ancestors. To a great extent, the same thing held true at the more educated levels of German society with respect to gentiles as well. In other words, to Hitler's biological definition was opposed a cultural definition. Most Germans—like people around the world—categorized people by using a combination of both. But over the course of time, as more Jews and gentiles intermarried, the biological indicators became harder to rely on. The general term for this process, sociologically speaking, is *assimilation*. The word refers to a complex and difficult-to-identify process, but the idea is clear enough. In Germany and Austria-Hungary, the Jews had assimilated to a remarkable degree. They were, in many respects, more German than the Germans; they thought of themselves as such and were generally accepted, simply because it was becoming increasingly difficult to tell who was Jewish and who was not.

The statistical data suggest the magnitude of what was going on. Of every three marriages in which one of the partners was identified as a Jew, one of the marriages was to a gentile. This pattern was stable, and it had been in place for decades. The children of these marriages, and the grandchildren of those marriages, the *mischlinge*, were numerous. The National Socialists weren't sure of the numbers, but they quickly became aware of the immense difficulty in singling out Jews: in 1935, when universal conscription was reintroduced, researchers estimated that there were close to 100,000, and maybe as many as 150,000—or even 200,000—eligible males of Jewish descent in the Third Reich.

There are two areas in which the information is exact. On the one hand, discussions inside the government reveal that the National Socialists readily grasped the size and complexity of the problem; on the other, we have precise identifications of individuals of Jewish descent who served in the armed forces after 1933, either because they were discharged when their Jewish descent became known or because we have subsequently been able to document their Jewish heritage.

But the multiple categories of religious adherence are beside the point. Before 1933, outside of Jewish traditions, there was no real answer to the question, Who is a Jew? Consider Edmund Husserl, one of the more important philosophers of the twentieth century. He was born in 1859, in Moravia, in the Austro-Hungarian empire, of Jewish parents, Adolf Abraham Husserl and Julie Selinger Husserl. Husserl studied at Leipzig and then Vienna, where he received his doctorate in 1883. The following year his father died, and within a few years' time, Husserl converted to Christianity, married Malvine Steinschneider, and had two sons, Gerhard Adolf and Wolfgang. Both sons received reserve commissions and were at the front in 1914. Wolfgang was wounded and then ultimately killed in 1916. Gerhard survived the war as a highly decorated officer.

Theirs was hardly an isolated case. Helmuth Wilberg was commissioned in 1912, and by 1915, as a captain, he commanded the Fourth Army's Feldflieger Abteilung 11. After the war, he became one of Hans von Seeckt's aviation experts, rose to the rank of general, and served in the Luftwaffe until he was killed in an airplane crash in 1942. Curiously, despite the official idea that the Luftwaffe would become the most National Socialist of the branches of the military, the man who was essentially its operational leader after 1933, Erhard Milch, was, like Wilberg, a Jew.[13]

Once it was discovered how pervasive the problem was, the National Socialists came up with a process as bizarre as it was formal, in which an individual with non-Aryan ancestors could be declared racially pure. Despite their increasingly strident racial rhetoric, the National Socialists created a bureaucratic system that allowed men of Jewish descent to be Aryanized.

Some of this was simply by fiat. Göring had documents produced establishing that Milch's parents were not his biological parents. That is to say, his biological father was not the man who was married to his mother but some impeccably Germanic male who had been sexually involved with her.[14] There's a certain weird logic here. As Hitler's creatures soon realized, any data attempting to identify Jewish officers (or enlisted men) were predicated on something vague and unknowable: who was actually Jewish and who was not. It is unknowable because there is no way of telling which definition the individuals in question used, if they were aware of the ethnic components of their heredity, or if they thought of it as being in any way important.

This happened because, over the course of the nineteenth century, the Jewish population in the German lands had essentially migrated from one definition of Judaism to another, and the shift was significantly aided by a comparable movement among German Protestants. *Migration* is preferable to the term *assimilation*: as the Jews of Western Europe found to their dismay after Hitler came to power (if not before), they had never truly been assimilated into the gentile populations of Franco-Germanic Europe; and in fact their neighbors—particularly in France—were more than willing to identify them and see them taken away to be murdered. Even so, the Jews had completed a remarkably successful migration, from regarding themselves according to scriptural depictions of Jewishness to accepting a more elastic, abstract definition of their religion.

A parallel migration was taking place among Protestants. Just as Jewishness became less based on public worship and on a concept of a distinct people, so did the Christianity observed by the affluent, educated segment of the population. If we substitute for the Jewish sense of "people" the Christian idea of "denomination," or sect, the migration is indeed similar.

The great German novelist Theodor Storm neatly sums up the Protestant shift when he describes the religious beliefs of one of his characters. Franz is an attorney, an enlightened man who "belonged to that growing community of people who saw Christianity not as a supernatural sign but rather the natural result of man's spiritual development. He therefore refrained from attending church."[15] His young wife is a pious Roman Catholic, but it is his hope (which in the course of the story becomes realized) that she follow his migratory path, putting behind her the rituals and public observances of faith while retaining its ethics and spirituality.

Such men saw themselves as morally and ethically Christian, but they did not necessarily base their religious beliefs either on Scripture or on the body of Christian doctrine, nor did they consider it necessary to share in a liturgy of public worship. The position held by Franz in Storm's story was not only tenable but typical.

A similar tendency could be seen throughout European Jewry: Jewishness became increasingly a function of tradition and ethical precepts rather than of ethnicity or of ritual. Ethically and spiritually, there is little difference between the attenuated Christianity evinced by Storm's character and the attenuated Judaism of many German Jews of the era. I don't wish to push this comparison too far, only to make the observation that socially and legally, the distinction between Jews and gentiles was increasingly blurred. Technically, of course, the parallel is dubious: few Jews, regardless of how ethical and abstract their convictions had become, would be comfortable reciting the Nicene Creed, the key statement of Christian belief. But at some point in the nineteenth century, men and women began to evince a certain inconsistency when it came to their religious beliefs. They considered themselves "good" Christians (or Jews) without feeling that they had to subscribe to the literal sense of their religious identity, or even believe in it.[16]

The best evidence of this—evidence that would have major repercussions after 1933—is the increase in interfaith marriages, particularly between Jews and gentiles. According to Jewish law, the offspring of such marriages would be regarded as Jewish if the mother was Jewish. But the real question is, how did the children—and the parents—regard themselves? Complicating the issue further is the matter of conversion. The Jew who regarded himself as holding beliefs equivalent to those of Storm's attorney, seeing religious belief as a set of ethical and spiritual precepts, would not necessarily feel inhibitions about converting; or, more precisely, would experience roughly the same inhibitions as a Baptist who became a Presbyterian or an Anglican.[17] Or maybe not. Since we lack a time machine to go back and interview him, his feelings are unknowable, and we can only make inferences based on observed behavior.

We know conclusively the extent to which Husserl thought of himself as German, but we do not know the extent to which—before Hitler—he thought of himself as Jewish, or how he defined the term.

By attempting a logical, racial definition of the relative Jewishness of the population, the National Socialists had opened a Pandora's box. The newly renamed Wehrmacht had a sizable Jewish component, men who had one or more Jewish grandparents. In proportion to the general population of Germany, the half a million or so Jews were a small percentage, but this was not the case in the military. In one sense, however, there was a parallel: just as some of the country's most distinguished professionals, academics, and intellectuals were Jews, so were some of the military's most competent officers.

But there was a key difference, and one that sets the military apart from the universities and the population at large. The Wehrmacht was not nearly as enthusiastic about the purging of their ranks as the professorate.

The primary reason had little to do with enlightened tolerance. Rather, the traditions of the German army had included a system of evaluations based on competence, not on class, ethnic background, or social status. By later standards it was a very imperfect system, but by comparison with the armed forces of Britain, France, and Russia, it was enormously effective— and one obvious result was the Wehrmacht's battlefield performance.

So the military's response to the aggressively pursued racism of National Socialism, together with Hitler's personal involvement at every level in this internal conflict, ensured—guaranteed—that an atmosphere of mutual distrust would develop. In fact, the response of the military to this particular goal of National Socialism—the eradication of Jews from German life—may be profitably seen as the model for whatever resistance to Hitler there was.

I say this because the pattern that developed early on was psychologically complex. There was little if any overt defiance or disobedience, much less any serious attempts to eliminate Hitler. In this sense, the traditional hard-line consensus of analysts that the military was, by and large, an enthusiastic supporter of Hitler is true: he had no significant opposition until late in the war, when the officer corps realized that the nation was well on the road to defeat.

The problem is that this view rests on a flawed model of human behavior: you are either conspiring to overthrow or you are actively in support. But the most common form of resistance is not defiance or rebellion; rather, it is manifested by what we now call passive-aggressive behavior.[18] Not coincidentally, the phrase has military origins. Although today the phenomenon is thought of exclusively as a mental disorder, the term was coined by American army psychiatrists in 1945 on the basis of their work with soldiers. They saw a fairly widespread pattern of passive resistance to orders, coupled with complaints, privately expressed hostility (grumbling), and reluctant compliance (but only when the soldiers had no choice).

While generally seen as a maladaptive pattern, passive-aggressive behavior, in a military (or educational) context, is in fact a rational response when individuals are deprived of their autonomy—that is, in an authoritarian system shaping all their overt actions. It allows the individual to maintain a feeling of independence without the risk of open confrontations, to shirk responsibility for the failure of his or her actions, and to create a series of seductive behavioral rationalizations.[19]

One of the most interesting results of such behavior is that it often produces a kind of inversion, in which the reasonable person (or the person in authority) is maneuvered into displays of anger or arbitrary acts, after being continually frustrated by instances of passive aggression. As anyone who has exercised even the mildest authority will attest, passive-aggressive behavior is a difficult form of resistance to counter; I suspect that many of the stories of Hitler's tirades are in fact representations of the understandable (if extreme) response of someone in a position of authority who is constantly being thwarted. Similarly, the insistence on unquestioned obedience can be seen as a normal reaction on the part of a leader faced with manifestations of such behavior.[20]

I believe that the phenomenon of passive aggression explains the deep ambivalence displayed by the officer corps. Few of them were committed National Socialists; indeed, the more they were faced with government demands, the more they resisted them. But at the same time, they had bought into Hitler's premise and accepted his goals to the extent that they understood them. Freeing Germany from its shackles—breaking out of the cave into which they believed the country had been imprisoned— restoring it to its rightful place in the sun, eliminating the social disorder that plagued the Weimar Republic, and reclaiming the lost territories were the aims they shared with Hitler, and indeed with most Germans.

The divergence began with Hitler's insistence on the key point of his philosophy, one that Heidegger had understood very quickly, the *Führerprinzip*. Heidegger's attempts to impose that concept on the (by definition) feudal, anarchic modern university were laughable and often ludicrous. It was one reason why his tenure as rector of Freiburg was short and unhappy. But however ham-handed his dictates were, he was, after all, Martin Heidegger, and therefore possessed of insights denied to ordinary men and women. His articulation of the basic principle was, I think, right on target: Hitler aimed to seize control of the state in a way that no German or Austrian had previously attempted. His power would be absolute.

Given the traditions of the German army, there was bound to be a clash—not over goals but over power. The armed forces reserved to themselves the prerogative of deciding who was a Jew, not because they had any philo-Semitism but because they realized that the strength of the military rested on its autonomy in personnel selection. The officer corps in both Germany and Austria-Hungary formed its own society. It lived by the rules it had promulgated during the course of the last century.

At the top—the level of the supreme command—the military deferred to the government, traditionally personified by the monarch. So when Hitler, infuriated by Werner von Blomberg's infatuation with a much younger female secretary of dubious morals, sacked him, he was operating in accordance with a theory the officer corps understood. The principle that the overall commander served at the discretion of the state was clear enough. Likewise, Otto Gessler's sacking of General von Seeckt in 1926 had not caused a mutiny in the Reichsheer.

But as Hitler's precepts spread throughout German society, as the principle of the *Gleichschaltung* began to be applied, the military realized that one of its most cherished and inviolate principles was on the chopping block—the right to pick its members and reward them (or not) according to its own criteria. Nor was this simply an expression of military privilege. The officers had seen firsthand what happened when government intervened in personnel selection. In France, when the Republicans tried to consolidate their power before 1914, they had selected as minister of war General André, who instituted a veritable purge of officers not thought to be sufficiently Republican: Catholics, Monarchists, and Freemasons. The result was to staff the army with men who were politically reliable; unfortunately, they were also militarily incompetent.

As in any poorly run organization, a few able people managed to slip through—one reason that the French didn't lose the war in the first few months of fighting. But the cost was frightful, and proof that the German system was correct. But now Hitler, or anyway his followers, were proposing to change the rules, by insisting that the military, like society at large, purge itself of its Jews. Moreover, National Socialism sought to alter the system in another, equally fundamental way: the question of who was or was not Jewish would now be formally decided, and the only acceptable definition would be based on kinship.

Both in theory and in practice, the government edict caused the military serious problems. Hitler's intention was to identify all military personnel of Jewish descent and discharge them from the service. Given the numbers involved, the difficulties of identification, and in many cases the passive resistance of their fellow soldiers, the process quickly bogged down. Some men were identified and discharged. But others managed to evade the purge, and after the fighting started, they were aided by the fact that armies in wartime tend to have contempt for the regulations put forth by those not in harm's way. And because German soldiers were scattered throughout Europe, there was a simple logistics challenge— trying to keep up with the whereabouts of men even when they had been identified and declared to be of Jewish descent.

At the same time, a complication arose that Hitler had clearly not considered. Since the distribution of the sexes in large populations tends to be equal, there was, for every man of Jewish descent eligible to serve in the Wehrmacht, a woman of Jewish descent of the same age. And, contrary to its fond hopes, National Socialism was not able to stop the pattern of intermarriage between gentiles and Jews.

For that matter, it could not prevent German males stationed outside Germany from marrying local women. We have no real idea just how many German soldiers became sexually involved with young French women, but we do have a pretty good estimate of how many children resulted—about 200,000, a number that gives us some idea of how widespread the situation was and how many German soldiers either wanted to marry young women of Jewish descent or have relationships with them.[21] Hitler most emphatically did not want German soldiers consorting with French women, but the numbers suggest that his directive on the subject was simply ignored, despite the penalties, and there are a surprising number of cases in which his proscription against marriage with Jews was also disregarded.

Compounding this complicated and confusing situation was Hitler himself, whose behavior was paradoxical, to say the least. At the same time that he was moving toward the outright murder of all Jews in German-controlled territories, he was granting waivers for Jewish Wehrmacht personnel who had served with distinction in combat.[22] But then, Göring had already done the same thing in the case of Milch. Although no exact figures can be compiled, it appears that the Luftwaffe—supposedly the most National Socialist of the branches of the armed forces—was the one with the most influential, high-ranking officers of Jewish descent: Milch, Wilberg, and Milch's main assistant, Karl-August von Gablenz.[23]

The number of individuals covered by the various stratagems is unknowable, but the available data provide some indications. There may have been as many as 16,000 officers who, although of Jewish descent, were exempted from discharge and served in the Wehrmacht, and the number of applications for exemptions appears to be in the tens of thousands, with roughly (very roughly) about one-fifth of them granted.[24] That being the case, it is no particular surprise, I suppose, that we have records showing that men of Jewish descent were serving in the SS, often at precisely the same time as their friends and extended family members were being carted off and murdered.

In retrospect, it is obvious that Hitler's view of Greater Germany was one in which the Jews had been eliminated, most of them by murder, with the few remaining traces disappearing in a few generations. And by summer 1941, this goal was becoming increasingly clear, particularly to armed forces personnel. Paradoxically, of course, we can comprehend the impact on Jewish members of the Wehrmacht—as well as on their comrades, in at least some cases—of Hitler's vision. The more threatening the consequences, the more serious the attempts to hide, to conceal one's identity. Or, as we have seen, to escape from it by being declared an Aryan.

The soldier who did either one oftentimes had an even more powerful motive than self-preservation—the security of a wife, children, an immediate family. So there's no mystery why such men would not only continue to serve but serve with distinction, nor why their comrades might enable their survival.

The real question is how to account for their motivation before Hitler's true aim—murder—became so clear. We have too many recorded instances of men who were devastated by being discharged from the military, men who accepted what was going on, men who, at one level or another, remained supportive of National Socialism. How could this be the case?

The answer, I think, lies in two elements, which, although distinct in theory, largely converged in practice: the power of the cultural definition to which everyone, to some extent, subscribed, and the inconsistency of Hitler and his minions.

We've already seen examples of the inconsistency, in which Jewishness was trumped by state decree. But if the German Jews and their Austrian counterparts thought of themselves as German in specific ways, they also had a clear picture of Jewishness. It was not cultural or ethical; it was geographical and racial: the Jews were those people who lived in the eastern ranges of the two empires (and in Russian Poland and Ukraine). They formed pious communities scrupulously practicing the religion of their ancestors. They lived apart, as easily identifiable by their dress and their language as the western Jews of the German lands were not.

Operationally, that description was what was meant by the word *Jew*, and this point of view included the Westernized assimilated Jews as well. When men of Jewish descent serving in the Wehrmacht encountered the segregated rural Jews in Poland, they experienced a sense of disgust. That reaction is, I think, a fair characterization of the response of western Jewry. So when Hitler and the National Socialists used the word *Jew*, many German Jews simply assumed that these were the people he was mentioning—and to a startling degree, they nodded in approval.

There's nothing surprising in this view, which parallels the distaste that many urbanized Anglo-American Protestants have for those Protestant sects characterized, inaccurately, as fundamentalist. Such comparisons make people uneasy, but they serve as a reminder that there was nothing unusual in the attitudes of the western Jews toward their eastern counterparts. Regardless of the degree to which they perceived themselves as being genuinely accepted (or assimilated) into German life, the western Jews were free from the sporadic terror visited on the Jewish communities of the east. There were no pogroms in the two German empires.

As a result, German Jews could not imagine themselves being abused and expelled from Germany. Again and again the cry would be raised that they were as German as the Germans. Thus we find the distinguished philosopher Edmund Husserl insisting that he was as much a German as anyone else, and that his dismissal from Freiburg University because he was a Jew was the "supreme affront" of his life: "I fancy I was not the meanest among the Germans (of the old style and the old school), and that my house was a place of true national sentiment, as evinced by *all* my children, who volunteered for service in the field or (in Eli's case) in a military hospital during the war."[25]

The western Jews who lived in the German lands saw themselves as Germans (or Austrians) first and foremost. They generally thought of their Jewishness in pretty much the same way that many Christians thought of themselves as Lutherans or Calvinists or Roman Catholics, and when they heard denunciations of Jews, they interpreted the tirades as being aimed at foreign people from the east with whom they had little or nothing in common. This rejection is, in hindsight, delusional, but it explains the curious reaction of Germany's Jews to National Socialism.

Moreover, Hitler cleverly pandered to this illusion. Consider this extract from his first speech, in April 1922. The denunciation of the Jews has a curious beginning:

> The million workmen who were in Berlin in 1914 have remained what they were—they are workmen still, only thinner, worse clad, poor; but the 100,000 Jews from the East who entered Germany in the early years of the war—they arrived in poverty and they are now "made men" riding in their motor-cars.[26]

This linkage allowed the German Jews to assume that Hitler was exclusively concerned with the *Ostjuden*, not them, and his concern was one they themselves, by and large, shared. Over the next decade, more than one Jewish-German nationalist would make an open appeal for the removal, from German society, of traditional, racial Jews. In hindsight it is easy to criticize both their utterances and their ignorance. But the fact of the matter is that Hitler manipulated them just as effectively as he would later manipulate the Wehrmacht's officer corps: both groups were surprised when the movement began to expel anyone of Jewish descent from government service and from the professions.

For that matter, regardless of their sentiments toward the Jews, the population at large interpreted Hitler's pronouncements in pretty much the same way as a good many German Jews did. When Hitler promised them power and prosperity, he certainly did not say that these achievements would come about through the expropriation of the wealth of one segment of society and then through the conquest of their neighbors. It is all very well to ask, in shock and horror, how they could have been so naive, but doing so is a serious mistake. They weren't blind, they were lied to, and it is the measure of Hitler's evil genius that he was able to deceive not only the Germans and many German Jews but much of the rest of the world as well.

In the speech quoted above—which set the pattern for most of his subsequent political speeches—Hitler made another important link that contributed to the deception. First, the "Jews" were really the people "from the East," and not good Germans at all. Second, these "Jews" were Communists, and the leaders of the Bolsheviks were almost entirely Jewish. A few paragraphs later in this speech, Hitler observed that

> while now in Soviet Russia the millions are ruined and are dying, Chcicherin—and with him a staff of over 200 Soviet Jews—travels by express train through Europe. . . . The 400 Soviet Commissars of Jewish nationality—they do not suffer—the thousands upon thousands of Sub-Commissars—they do not suffer.

By now it is customary, indeed obligatory, to regard Hitler's speeches as nothing but falsehoods aimed at fomenting mischief and stirring up hate, but Hitler was like any skilled fabricator: he interwove the true with the false, using the former to convince his hearers of the latter.

There was a significant Jewish component in the leadership of the Bolsheviks, particularly in the regions with which most Germans were familiar, such as Hungary, the Baltic, and Munich (in the abortive effort to found a Soviet republic in that city). When Bela Kuhn attempted to institute a Hungarian Soviet republic, virtually all his political leaders (the commissars) were Jews, as was Kuhn himself. In other words, Hitler was not lying, and for a long time he usually linked the word *Jew* with the term *Bolshevik*. Because the German and Austrian Jews tended to be prosperous, established members of society, as well as deeply patriotic Germans and Austrians, they viewed Bolshevism with the same animus as did most others.

In the repressed and repressive Jewish communities of the Romanov empire, Bolshevik ideas fell on open ears. There had always been an interest in messianism, and by 1900 this interest had more or less secularized. Even the Jews in the west were not immune from its appeal.

But the secular messianism in the West was benign. Zionism, as first enunciated by the Viennese Theodor Herzl, was a peaceful response to the rational perception that assimilation had real limits and that the tolerance and stability that European Jews enjoyed was not a reliable constant but a shifting dynamic. The principles of Zionism also reflected the growing tendency to see human beings as members of ethnic groups, and inside the Hapsburg empire, with its heterogeneous population, this tendency was at its most visible.[27]

The logical response to concerns about anti-Semitism was to emigrate, and during the First World War, the British had been persuaded to let Jews return to their traditional lands in the Middle East, largely in response to the Zionist goal of creating a Jewish state. Zionism was a peaceful, practical, and realistic solution to the situation as it was perceived by members of the Jewish intelligentsia in 1900. And emigration to a land where a state could be established whose citizens could live free from fear of persecution certainly resonated with Anglo-Americans and European Protestants, both of whom had engaged in extensive emigration for precisely those reasons—that is to say, because of their religious beliefs and the concomitant persecutions they had endured.

Bolshevism as it had emerged before 1917 fit into this pattern of secular messianism. The Bolsheviks too wanted to create a society, one based on freedom from want, in which there would be real equality and an end to the exploitation of the workers for the selfish needs of a few. Thus it's easy to see why Jews were attracted to Bolshevism in disproportionate numbers. They lived in a society widely regarded by Westerners as being repressive and intolerant.

In the West there had always been two alternative responses to repression and intolerance. One had been to relocate, what we might call, after its most famous exponents in Anglo-America, the Puritan response. The other had been to attempt to transform the state itself, the model employed in the French Revolution. The responses of European Jews fit neatly enough into the two categories: Jewish Zionists wanted to emigrate; Jewish Bolsheviks wanted to overthrow the state and create a new one.

The problem was that the latter program, which depended heavily on violence, had, historically, two outcomes. The first, which the Bolsheviks explicitly endorsed, was the French (and then the Soviet) revolutions of 1789 and 1917, successful attempts to change a government through armed rebellion. The second was failure; as happened in both cases, a reign of terror that commenced almost immediately. It was the tragedy of European Jewry to become identified so closely with the failed Bolshevik revolutions of 1918–20 outside of Russia, as well as the repressive and brutal regime that was emerging in Russia itself.

Although the linkage—between the Jewish intellectuals of the East and the Bolsheviks—has often been denied, it occurred, and it gave those seeking to foment hatred of the Jews a plausible excuse. Although there are certainly speeches in which Hitler decoupled the terms *Jewish* and *Communist* (or *Bolshevik* or *Marxist*), they were, by and large, made to the growing number of party cadres. In the more public speeches, he preserved the phrase with great consistency.[28]

But regardless of whether he was believed or not, Hitler's clear intention—to get rid of the Jews—created an irreparable fissure in the military and established a model that ultimately led not only to the destruction of Germany but, perhaps more important, to the destruction of the honor of the military itself. The key word here is the verb: it *led* to that fate. It was not the sole cause of the collapse. But it was very much the critical first step.

PLANES, PERSONALITIES, AND
CONFLICT IN THE LUFTWAFFE

Hitler will never ask me how big our bombers are, but only how
many we have.

Hermann Göring[1]

As Hitler began his ascent, his most important henchman and colleague was a decorated aviator of the First World War, Hermann Göring.
It was Göring who was made head of the Prussian State Police and who
began the process of turning it into a branch of the National Socialist
party. It was Göring who was named Hitler's successor and who took
charge of the economy. Given his background in the air force, it was
only natural that he would be made head of what was shortly to be called
the Luftwaffe.

But Göring had entirely too much on his plate to be an effective military chief. So the development of the air force was, in effect, handed
over to a cabal of senior airmen who were left to fight it out among themselves as to the type of air force Germany would have—and to fight it out
with the other services and the civilian economy for a share of the resources. As a result, the same sort of confused, contradictory state of affairs held in rearmament as in the treatment of the Jews in the military,
the outcome of the increasingly passive-aggressive behaviors manifested
by the military leadership.

In the long run, Göring's emulation of Hitler's divide-and-compete management style was disastrous for the air force. But the ruin was not immediately apparent, because the fledgling air arm he inherited was the result of years of planning, throughout the 1920s, in which German specialists absorbed the lessons learned during the First World War about the uses and limitations of airpower.

In that war, the Germans had been at the forefront of developing long-range bombers. Over the course of the war, the first strategic bombing campaign against London killed 1,413 people and wounded 3,407, most of them civilians.[2] When the Germans looked at the data, however, they decided that their strategic bombing campaign was not much of a success.[3] Consequently, in German doctrine after 1918, the air force was firmly subordinated to the army: "The Air Force, as an independent arm, is not called upon to conduct an independent war apart from the Army and the Navy"—which is to say, it was supposed to function tactically, not strategically: its objective would be to support the aims selected by the ground forces.[4]

The German raids had made a lasting and painful impression on the British and the French, and in the decades after the war, the air forces of the two nations moved in a different direction—the one posited by the Italian theorist Giulio Douhet, who advised countries to put their faith in a strategic bombing force. Although the British had an impressive fighter component, the orientation of the Royal Air Force was strategic, not tactical. Moreover, because both the British and the French air branches preserved the ancient rivalries between the navy and the army, they would fight their own war in their own way. So the German rearmament effort was a serious departure: as the Luftwaffe emerged, it would be a tactical air force, organized around ground-combat-support missions. Its chief opponents would, on the contrary, see airpower as a strategic force, devoted to the destruction of the enemy's resources and the protection of their own airspace from enemy bombers.

The difference was not perceived in the 1930s, because the military aircraft in service were remarkably similar, regardless of their intended function. Both the British and the French developed an interceptor force designed to stop the strategic bombers that would attack their cities. But such planes—fast, well armed, and maneuverable—were also required in the German scheme, which demanded control of the airspace above the battlefield, so the ground-support planes could operate without annihilation. In practice, the British Hurricane and Spitfire were pretty much like the Messerschmitt fighter, the Me-109, that was the mainstay of the Luftwaffe during the Second World War.

Despite the insistence of the airpower enthusiasts on strategic bombers—planes that could reach the enemy's major cities and factories and drop heavy loads of explosives on them—no such aircraft was available during the prewar era. The specifications for the American four-engined B-17 bomber were set only in 1934: the first flight didn't take place until July 1935, and a few planes began to enter service in early 1937. British development lagged substantially behind: the specifications for the Lancaster weren't set until 1936, and the aircraft didn't enter service until 1941.

Before then, the bombers in service were essentially tactical aircraft, because of their short range and limited payload. Although newspapers, politicians, and experts terrorized France and Britain with assertions that airpower could obliterate their metropolitan areas in a few hours, the only major city the RAF's Bomber Command had the ability to attack intensively was Paris, and the French were in even worse shape.[5]

There was a final way in which the distinction between tactical and strategic, between medium (or light) and heavy bombers, was fatally blurred. A city close to a battle zone was thought to be simply another enemy headquarters and supply depot and could become a legitimate tactical target, the destruction of inhabitants and structures considered to be collateral damage.

To the people being bombed, the distinction between tactical and strategic, like the one between deliberate and accidental, was pointless, and the Spanish civil war obliterated the differences for everyone except a few airpower experts. This explains the apparent paradox: the Luftwaffe was designed to be a tactical arm subordinate to the army and at the same time was perceived as a strategic weapon capable of destroying major population areas and killing millions of innocent civilians.

Nonetheless, German planners aimed at a purely tactical force that would support ground operations, and even though the Luftwaffe was touted as the most National Socialist of the three services, few changes were made to what had already been decided long before Hitler's ascent.

Seeing airpower as subordinate to objectives set by the ground forces, the Germans considered it to consist primarily of tactical bombers and reconnaissance planes. Because neither craft would have much chance of surviving on the battlefield by themselves, the Luftwaffe would need control of the air. This view was in marked contrast to that of the British and the French, who assumed that bombers could operate with impunity over enemy airspace, and gave little thought to the idea of securing hostile skies. According to the Allied perspective, no country would be able to protect all its airspace; the bombers could always find some safe route to the target, and catch the enemy by surprise.

Despite the data available from the First World War, the British and French air forces persisted in the belief that antiaircraft defenses were useless—the main reason why the bomber would always get through. Going hand in hand with this conceit was one no less fatuous. It was simply assumed that if a bomber flew over a factory and dropped a tonnage of explosives sufficient to obliterate it, this was what would happen. Because the mission could be precisely calculated, the question of whether the target was actually hit was off the table.

This is where the tactical versus strategic issue came seriously into play. German ground commanders demanded the same precision from the air that they were accustomed to receiving from artillery fire. The requirement was difficult to meet. At 13,000 feet, only 2 percent of the bombs dropped during level-flight bombing runs would fall inside a circle with a diameter of 200 meters.[6] Lower altitudes would result in a corresponding increase in accuracy, but a circle 200 meters in diameter is an awfully big area, and 2 percent an awfully small number, so *accuracy* is a wildly misleading term.

Although it was possible to improve this figure by releasing the bombs at lower altitudes, the math makes the problem clear: cut the altitude in half and the accuracy could conceivably be quadrupled, up to an impressive 8 percent. Not much of a gain, not much chance of hitting a target—and the chances of the plane being destroyed on its bombing run were probably about 50 percent, based on the disastrous Allied experiences in May 1940.[7]

The plan that offered the most promise was that of the dive-bomber. The pilot would simply fix the target in his sights and plunge directly toward it. At the last minute, he'd release the bomb and pull up, but the bomb would continue on the path the plane had been on. Compared with level-flight bombing, the accuracy was phenomenal: a pilot could put one out of every four bombs inside a fifty-meter circle.

By the late 1920s, airframe design had progressed to the point that planes could be built that would withstand the enormous stresses inherent in diving into a target and then abruptly pulling up at the point of bomb release. The navies of the major powers were intrigued, and both the French and the Americans developed dive-bombers for use by their naval aviation units. But the Reichsheer was the only army with any interest in the principle, and by 1929 the Germans had plans for an actual dive-bomber. Made by Henschel, it was known as the Hs-123. A serviceable biplane, it was rapidly replaced by the He-50, which in turn (by 1937) was replaced by the Ju-87.

This last plane became so notorious (it is generally referred to as the Stuka, a shortening of the German word for dive-bomber) that the concept is associated with the German air force of the Hitler era. But the decision to employ the dive-bomber in a serious role had been made long before 1933.

The decision was still controversial, however. Inside the air force (both before and after Hitler's ascent) there were serious questions raised. Dive-bombers could operate successfully only if two conditions were met. First, the side deploying the craft must have command of the air and keep enemy fighters out of the skies over the target area. From their experiences in the First World War, the Germans knew this was a difficult proposition.

The other condition that had to prevail was an absence of effective antiaircraft support for the side being attacked. Of course, this was also true for level-flight bombers, which were, if anything, more vulnerable, but with the dive-bomber there was no particular need for accuracy: all the ground forces had to do was create a curtain of fire over the target; the bomber would have to dive right into it to deliver its payload.

A good many air experts were skeptical that both conditions could be met, and Wolfram von Richthofen, chief of the air force's technical services bureau, was basically opposed to the idea. But in 1936, von Richthofen was replaced by one of Göring's favorites, a fighter ace from the previous war, Ernst Udet. Udet, who was as ignorant of airpower theory as a goat, had been impressed by the naval planes he had seen on his trips to the United States and was convinced that the dive-bomber was the weapon of the future.

The von Richthofen–Udet dive-bomber case is the perfect example of how Hitler's leadership principle worked. Since Hitler himself made all the important decisions, access to him was all important, and this scheme was repeated on down—the same thing held true for Göring himself. What gave access was not one's official position, but character or reputation, which in turn impacted on the leaders. Udet was the surviving German ace with the highest number of confirmed kills (sixty-two) and had received the coveted Pour le Mérite. That gave him instant access, and was why Göring had lured him out of retirement, gave him a commission in the Luftwaffe, and then made him inspector of fighters and dive-bombers in 1936.

Because of Udet's access—and his belief in the dive-bomber—the issue was never really debated. In effect, von Richthofen, who despite his famous name had not joined the air force until late in 1918, never got to argue his case, so Udet carried the day. In June 1936, Göring replaced von Richthofen as head of the technical bureau. From then on, the dive-bomber was a foregone conclusion.

At one level, Udet was correct. He and Hitler sensed the Allied deficiencies. Although in theory the assumption that there would be no serious challenge for command of the air and no effective ground-to-air defenses was highly dubious, it was, in practice, exactly the case. Udet's estimate, however he derived it, was right, and von Richthofen's was wrong. So the dive-bomber case established a pattern in which the amateur was more nearly correct than the professional.

In the long run, Udet was mostly wrong, but even that judgment has to be qualified. The initial Ju-87 took flight in 1937, and it served the Germans well for the first years of the war. By 1942, antiaircraft defenses made its dive-bombing missions suicidal, but the plane then became an effective ground-attack aircraft. Thanks to its sturdy design—a necessity for a dive-bomber—modified Ju-87s, equipped with 20-millimeter guns mounted beneath each wing, were extensively used on the Eastern Front against armor and light-skinned vehicles from 1942 on, while a subsequent modification, using 37-millimeter high-velocity guns, was capable of destroying Soviet T-34 tanks.[8] Over five thousand were produced, partly because the air force was unable to develop a successor; still, the number suggests the soundness of the design.

But the Udet example is important in another way as well. Having refused to pay much attention to the professionals and having been right once, Udet kept pushing his own ideas, even when they were idiotic. And who could tell him otherwise? Hitler and Göring knew less about the technical side of aircraft design and airpower than Udet did.

So the ultimate result was a catastrophic design failure for German bombers, because Udet insisted that they all had to be capable of dive-bombing, regardless of their intended purpose. And as head of the technical services department, Udet was in a position to determine the types of aircraft to be produced. The air ministry, after looking into the matter, had decided that there was no point in sending a bomber out with fewer than eight 250-kilogram bombs; the heavier payload of two metric tons was necessary to compensate for the inherent inaccuracy of level-flight bombing.

None of the bombers then in service could carry this load over a reasonable operating range and still have any chances of survival.[9] Consequently, a new bomber was necessary, and two American-born designers working for Junkers promptly came up with a plane, the Ju-88. A prototype was flown at the end of 1936—certainly a record for development time, as the specification had been laid down only in early 1935.[10]

The Ju-88, produced in greater numbers than all other German bombers combined, was in its original design exactly what the air force needed: a fast, medium-range bomber with a heavy payload. But Udet decided that the plane had to be capable of dive-bombing, so the plane doubled in weight. Not surprisingly, it turned out to be inferior in every respect to the planes it was supposed to replace. Although subsequent design modifications made it an efficient aircraft in a variety of roles, the air force, thanks to Udet's obsession with the dive-bomber, was stuck with its obsolete bombers for most of the war.

This was the Hitler problem (or *Führerprinzip*) in a nutshell: the same intuitive flash that gave the Wehrmacht its initial successes was the reason for its ultimate defeat. If Udet and the dive-bomber is the textbook example of this, the failure to develop a true strategic bomber illustrates the other troubling aspect, the importance of one or two key individuals who, on a lower level, embodied the *Führerprinzip*.

Heidegger had shrewdly put his finger on the underlying premise of National Socialism: an emphasis on leadership over tradition, law, and reason. Udet's rise to power exemplified this. He gave the Luftwaffe a deadly weapon none of its opponents had. He also impeded the development of planes the air force desperately needed in the future, but the problem was not entirely Udet's fault. Had not fate intervened, the Luftwaffe would have entered the war with a serious long-range bomber force.

Although German doctrine was firmly tactical, the new chief of staff of the air force had transferred to it from the army and so had missed that part of the decision-making process. Walter Wever was no ordinary officer. Von Seeckt felt that he was the best subordinate he had, despite the fact that Wever was one of the relatively few dedicated National Socialists in the senior ranks.

Not only was Wever a dedicated National Socialist; he had even read *Mein Kampf*, a fact that may well have made him unique in the Wehrmacht leadership. What is more, he had pondered its military implications. They were clear enough, and, in terms of airpower, they were strategic, not tactical. Hitler was, like General von Mackensen, von Hindenburg, and even Ludendorff, an easterner. He had no real interest in settling scores with France, reclaiming Alsace, making Belgium a German satellite, and engaging in a ruinous naval competition with Britain. Where Hitler did see expansion and, presumably, conquest was toward the east.

When Wever looked at the map, the implications were obvious: the only way Germany could destroy the Soviet Union was to destroy its industrial centers, to carry the war to the Soviet heartland in precisely the way that airpower theorists like Douhet had envisioned in the 1920s. So Germany needed a strategic bomber force, planes capable of striking over distances of two thousand kilometers.

The British and the Americans had come to the same conclusion, although their reasons were primarily defensive, not aggressive. The United States needed a long-range bomber, one that could fly across much of the Pacific and the Atlantic, deliver a reasonable payload, and then return safely. The RAF needed a bomber that could get to Munich and back, somewhat less of a technical requirement, because the distance is only about nine hundred kilometers. But the idea of a true long-range bomber was appealing, since the British empire was spread around the globe. Moreover, given the sums involved, the ability to maintain a strategic strike force that would lay waste to an enemy's cities should it attack seemed doubly attractive: it was a cheap and effective deterrent.

By the mid-1930s, then, both the United States and Britain were trying to develop true long-range bombers. But Wever was actually first off the mark. In 1934, he asked both Dornier and Junkers to produce four-engine prototypes. The two firms were still thinking in terms of medium-range bombers. The prototype Do-19, which first flew in October 1936, had roughly the same power-to-weight ratio as the initial B-17 (which had made its first flight fourteen months earlier), but its range was a disappointing sixteen hundred kilometers, albeit it with a reasonably impressive three metric tons of bombs. While the Junkers prototype, the Ju-89, had more powerful engines, it was considerably heavier, so the performance was about equal.

The point is not that the competing German planes were disasters. They had about the same flight characteristics as the British Wellington, and could have easily dropped heavy payloads on the United Kingdom in the 1940 bombing campaign. This was one important reason to develop strategic bombers: the shorter the distance the bomber must travel, the heavier the load it could carry. But neither plane was in the same league as the U.S. B-17, and so, in spring 1936, Wever ordered a new specification—for a bomber capable of flying 5,000 kilometers with a 500 kilogram load, at a speed of 500 kilometers an hour. For the time, early 1936, the specifications were remarkable. Wever was years ahead of the Allies in strategic bomber development.

Both by personality and position (chief of staff), Wever was a key player in the emerging air force. Considered properly, his demand for a true strategic bomber was unassailable; moreover, he had *Mein Kampf* on his side. He also had the sort of personality capable of juggling the various egos involved. This was important, because the decision makers in the air force, men like Udet and Göring and Milch, were basically fighter pilots, constitutionally incapable of getting enthusiastic over strategic bombers. In the increasingly personalistic world of the Third Reich, the fact that Wever was pushing for strategic bombers meant they would get built.

Unfortunately for the Luftwaffe—and fortunately for the Allies—it also meant that if Wever was out of the picture, they wouldn't get built, and at that point fate intervened. The good general had entered the air force without knowing how to fly, but, conscientious officer that he was, he soon learned. But if one were to list Wever's many skills, piloting an aircraft would not be among them. On June 3, 1936, Wever took off from an airport near Dresden, in a plane he had never flown before (an He-50), without bothering to do a preflight check.

As anyone who has been in the cockpit of a plane (however small) can attest, this is monumental stupidity. And for good reason, as Wever promptly illustrated: a preflight check would have revealed that the ailerons were still locked. The He-50 rose off the ground, then stalled, dived into the ground, and exploded.

And that was the end not only of one of the Luftwaffe's most competent leaders; it was the end of the strategic bomber program. Göring promptly appointed Albert Kesselring chief of staff, largely because Kesselring and Udet hated each other (and they both hated Milch). This was Hitler's basic management principle with a vengeance. Göring thus divided the management of the Luftwaffe into three parts, which meant that only he could break deadlocks, and he kept the ambitious and unscrupulous Erhard Milch from replacing him.

Milch had worked for Junkers after the First World War, rose to become head of Lufthansa, and was lured by Göring into the air force, where, after 1933, he became head of the air ministry. After 1940, Milch became de facto head of the air force, but in 1937, he had little say in what sort of planes were being built, the key players being Udet and Kesselring, the new chief of staff, who had spent the last war as a gunner, not a pilot. But he was as opposed to the idea of the strategic bomber as Udet was. So after two planes were built, the program was canceled, in April 1937.

But the cancellation affected only the Dornier and Junkers projects. The assigment for a true long-range bomber had been given to Heinkel, and development continued throughout 1937. There was a rationale for abandoning the Junkers and Dornier planes: the Heinkel project was technically the most advanced and in theory held the most promise. Both Junkers and Dornier had four-engine bombers already in the air. The drawback was the lack of power, but this was a common problem, one the Allies faced as well, and there is little doubt that BMW and Daimler-Benz (whose engines powered the two prototypes) could have solved it.

But here again a basic pattern of the Hitler era emerged, with resources being pulled from a project that was already built to a project that was still on the drawing board. The proposed Heinkel plane was the sort of bizarre engineering project that was the Achilles' heel of much German design. Heinkel proposed a plane with four engines but only two propellers. The engines would be twinned in two single nacelles, each pair driving a four-bladed propeller.

That the design was not going to work very well became quickly apparent: the first five prototypes didn't survive their tests in 1940. But by now the need for a heavy bomber was too obvious to be ignored, so the plane went into preproduction. Of the first fifteen aircraft, eight crashed during tests, killing seventeen men. Some of the trouble could be traced to Udet's dive-bomber fetish, sill unchecked. But the basic flaw was in the design itself. Neither Heinkel nor Arado (which ended up producing many of the planes that went into service) could get the design sorted out. Most He-177 losses were due to equipment failures rather than to enemy fire.

There is one final element of importance in the strategic bomber disaster. Like the other features, it also set the pattern. Despite his politics, Wever was highly regarded, and so it was logical to trace the failure of the program to his premature death. Postwar, however, Kesselring argued that the decision was eminently defensible: Germany simply lacked the resources to build both heavy bombers and the tactical planes it needed to support its ground troops in offensive operations. Since there were not enough resources to do everything, this argument sounds sensible enough, and has duly made its way into most, if not all, studies of the Luftwaffe, where it is accepted as fact.

But the idea is completely contradicted by the continuation of the He-177 strategic bomber program, which gobbled up all sorts of the allegedly precious resources. A good bit of this was owing to technical ineptitude and managerial incompetence, but as the Dornier and Junkers programs had already resulted in airworthy bombers, it is difficult to escape the conclusion that it would have consumed less resources to produce either of these planes than to pursue the chimerical vision of the He-177.

The Kesselring rationalization is false in another way. On paper, the Do-19 was at least as capable an aircraft as the He-111 medium bomber: it had the same cruising speed and could carry a much heavier load over greater distances. But the Do-19 (like the Junkers prototype) had the potential to become a strategic bomber, and the He-111 did not. Had either the Dornier or the Junkers bombers gone into production, they would have been more or less contemporaneous with the He-111, which was still being evaluated by the air force at the end of 1936. If there really had been a serious scarcity of resources this was the sort of thinking that should have been jettisoned.

But then the whole question of the scarcity of resources is basically a red herring. Except for the French, none of the Western democracies had much to spare for national defense. Germany was hardly any different from Great Britain or the United States in this regard. The real issue was not scarcity, it was allocation. Hitler had promised Räder an enormous surface fleet, and by 1936, work was already beginning on Plan Z. The real reason was simple: Räder had lobbied Hitler aggressively and persistently, while at the Air Ministry, the chief activity was fighting over who would be in charge of what.

That this was so is made clear enough by one of the more embarrassing incidents of the time. Either no one was paying any attention to bomb production, or it wasn't clear whose turf was involved, but it turned out that while the Luftwaffe was building up fleets of planes and terrorizing a gullible world in the process, they had forgotten to produce any bombs. If a war broke out, they would be reduced to dropping buckets of dynamite or large rocks. An exasperated Hitler, when told of this, made the not entirely idiotic suggestion that they simply fill up expended industrial cylinders with high explosive and use them as a stopgap measure. The experts were properly horrified, but it's difficult not to be sympathetic to Hitler's response.

One of the clinical hallmarks of passive-aggressive behavior is to come up with excuses that exculpate the individuals involved from any responsibility for what happens. The "we couldn't build a bomber because we didn't have the resources" claim fits this tactic perfectly. Most such excuses have some foundation in fact, of course—one reason they're often accepted at face value. Germany did have limited resources, and the senior air force personnel were probably more aware of the scarcity than the naval high command, simply because they were more closely integrated into party affairs, as a result of Göring's determination to make the Luftwaffe the most National Socialist branch of the military. But basically the alibi was an instance of the passive-aggressive in action.

Since so many senior officers in Hitler's air force were aging fighter pilots, it is hardly surprising that the Luftwaffe quickly capitalized on the technical excellence of the German airplane manufacturers and touted fast, modern fighter planes. More than any single plane, the Messerschmitt 109 epitomized the German air force. An excellent design, it soldiered on throughout the war, and therein lay the problem.

The Me-109 dated from a specification for a fast fighter plane laid down in 1935, at which point the standard German fighter was the He-51, an aging biplane. There was a competition of sorts, with the firms of Messerschmitt (the 109), Heinkel (the 112), Arado (the 80), and Focke-Wulf (the 159) competing. Willy Messerschmitt's design had one incontestable advantage: it was the only one of the four prototypes with a German engine. The other three used imported British engines (the Rolls-Royce Kestrel). The Focke-Wulf machine was—as would prove true in future designs—overweight and underpowered. The Arado had a fixed undercarriage, so the choice came down to Heinkel or Messerschmitt.

Now the case can be made that the Me-109 was the better plane to put into production, and not simply because it had a German-built engine. But as Willy Messerschmitt had much better connections with the National Socialists than did Ernst Heinkel, the final decision was tilted as much toward politics as anything else—not so much because of the defensible choice to make the Me-109 the standard fighter but because of the decision to keep Heinkel as far away from fighter plane development as possible. For the next five years, Heinkel kept coming up with terrifically fast and maneuverable fighter planes, only to be ignored. The result was a calamity for the air force, because although the Me-109 was a terrific plane for 1935, by 1940 it was already showing its age. The air force badly needed a replacement fighter to enable it to maintain air superiority in the face of the British Spitfires (a more recent design), the latest examples of the Soviet Chato series, and the slew of fast, potent American fighters that would eventually be deployed in Europe.

Neither Messerschmitt nor Focke-Wulf could create a design that was any better than the aging 109 for all-around performance. On the contrary, the new replacement fighters were, in key areas, inferior to the latest modifications of the 109, and so the craft had to be kept in service. Aside from the 109, Messerschmitt's planes were all basically failures. Its twin-engine long-range fighter-bombers were massacred by the RAF's faster single-engine planes, and none of its single-engine designs offered any advantages over the 109. This is not to imply that he wasn't a brilliant designer—the jet aircraft his firm designed and built was a spectacular piece of engineering. But when it really counted in 1940, Messerschmitt simply couldn't develop the right airplane.

Nor could Focke-Wulf, whose new Fw-189 fighter was in too many key areas inferior to the aging Messerschmitt, particularly in operating altitude. As Allied bombers flew higher and higher—and gradually began to have long-range fighter escorts—the ceiling of the 189 essentially made it useless for anything except ground attack.

What makes the situation all the more curious is that both firms were allowed to put their inferior designs into production, while Heinkel, which had a first-rate fighter plane, the He-100, already flying, was told to shut up and keep on turning out bombers. The reason, as Heinkel's historians gloomily admit, was party politics, which trumped objective evaluations. In fact, when Heinkel, along with Fritz Todt, Ferdinand Porsche, and of course Messerschmitt, was nominated for the National Socialist National prize in 1938, he was included only because of last-minute intervention by Hitler himself. Since Heinkel's fighter planes had consistently broken every speed record around, he could hardly be ignored—but the party faithful certainly tried. And even then, the air force basically refused to admit that his fighter planes existed, despite the obvious growing need for a new plane.[11]

This account simplifies a complex situation. All the other major aircraft manufacturers at one point or another during this period managed to produce planes that were duly pressed into service and then found to be totally overmatched. The RAF's Boulton Paul Defiant fighter, for example, was so outclassed by the Me-109 in May 1940 that the planes had to be withdrawn from action; the standard fighter planes for the American and French air forces of 1940 were quickly found to be outclassed by the planes of their German (and in short order, Japanese) adversaries.[12]

Moreover, evaluating which design was best proved to be, particularly in the days before computer modeling, a tricky business. Only extensive flight testing could provide evidence and even then the results were sometimes ambiguous. The American B-17 was certainly a successful design, but its early development was plagued by crashes, and, like almost every plane built anywhere, extensive modifications were required to enable it to survive in combat. One reason was that in 1939–41, only one air force had experience in anything resembling the conditions of the Second World War—the Luftwaffe, because of its experiences in the Spanish civil war (1936–39).

But that only brings us back to the initial point. The Germans should have known how tricky the design issues were, and how combat forced dramatic changes on machinery. It's difficult to escape the conclusion that basically, as with the strategic bomber failure (and the dive-bomber success story), everything came down, finally, to personalities and favoritism. As a result, the Luftwaffe was a Potemkin village affair: its prewar reputation was based mostly on clever propaganda in which prototypes were disguised as production models and senior officers lied about the quality and quantity of the aircraft in service. Once the war started, it had neither the planes nor the personnel to offer the level of support that German doctrine required. Consequently, ground commanders increasingly found themselves deprived of what they needed, and had to improvise as best they could.

Given the almost total Allied command of the air, it would seem the ground commanders were helpless. That they were not is a function of the other aspect of German tactical air doctrine. The Allied airmen, believing that antiaircraft defenses were useless, passed this function on to their army colleagues. The Germans, who had never accepted the idea that the bomber could always get through, not only developed antiaircraft weaponry on a systematic basis, they handed the whole area over to the Luftwaffe.

This was another departure from what everyone else was doing. Anti-aircraft defenses in everyone else's army were left to the ground forces to devise. When the war began, France and Britain were as well equipped as (or better equipped than) Germany in every area save antiaircraft systems, and the disparity would have fatal consequences. The two sides were, generally, asymmetrical. In May 1940 the French had about 3,800 antiaircraft guns strewn around the country, the majority of them antiques; the Germans deployed over 9,000, most of them embedded in the combat units.[13]

The Allies had no real way to fend off the German bombing and strafing, but the Germans were easily able to fend off Allied attempts to do the same thing. Somewhat by accident—or owing to Göring's desire to create an all-encompassing fiefdom—the newly created Luftwaffe would emerge as the perfect example of military integration. In addition to control over aircraft, it would control not only all the antiaircraft systems but also the airborne units.

The Luftwaffe had another serious advantage, the participation of German planes and personnel in the Spanish civil war. This participation, far from being some long-range scheme to test the new air force, happened largely by accident. When the uprising against the Spanish republic began in July 1936, the leaders of the coup were confronted with a difficult situation. The Spanish armed forces were essentially split between the rebels and the government, with the air force and the navy mostly declaring for the latter. The core of the army was a reasonably combat-effective force known as the Army of Africa, whose leader was Spain's youngest general, Francisco Franco. But as the name of the entity suggests, this force was in Africa (Spanish Morocco), so the immediate problem the rebels faced was how to get it to Spain in the face of a hostile naval force.

Both sides in the war immediately appealed for foreign aid. The government of the republic took the step first, going to France, where the Popular Front was then in power, and asking for massive military assistance. Representatives of the rebels went to both Italy and Germany, seeking help, mainly bombers and conventional weapons. The men sent to Germany managed to see Hitler himself at Bayreuth, where he was attending a Wagner opera. Shrewdly, he saw to the heart of the problem: if the rebels could get their combat-hardened African troops to the mainland, the coup would succeed. The quickest way to accomplish this was through an airlift. The only German plane available, the Junkers 52, originally designed as a bomber, was gradually being phased into a transport role. The planes could first be used for the airlift and then as bombers, and would be supported by a German expeditionary force. The mixed force of tanks, antitank units, and aircraft that Hitler ordered dispatched was handled in Berlin by the Luftwaffe's Helmuth Wilberg. Known as the Condor Legion, the force became notorious.

Although everyone claims that the civil war in Spain was a sort of test bed for the war that followed, the generalization is surprisingly difficult to nail down. The reason is simple enough: the war went on for about three years, and right up until the end of it the two sides were surprisingly well-matched, as both sides had access to the latest military technology as well as foreign experts.

Consequently, the lessons one learned from the conflict were largely a function of one's vantage point. In retrospect it is easy to see why this was the case. As one of Spain's more competent commanders remarked during the conflict:

> The trouble with this war is that almost nobody tells the truth of what he sees and knows, while many responsible people are actually incapable of rendering an account of what they have seen.[14]

Truer words were never penned. For the ground-warfare experts, the civil war simply confirmed whatever prejudices they had going in.

In the skies the situation was quite different. Thus the Germans learned that trying to destroy a bridge from the air took many more bombs than the experts had thought. They also found out how inferior their airplanes were. Although the Ju-52 transport and the He-51 fighter initially performed well, once the Soviets began shipping their planes to Spain (and letting them be flown by Soviet pilots), the Italo-German air force promptly lost mastery of the air. The situation improved greatly once the Germans responded with the Me-109 fighter and the He-111 bomber, but the proxy Nationalist air force had mastery of the air only at the end of the war, largely because of the withdrawal of the Soviet personnel.

There were certainly times and places in which the Italo-German air units dominated the skies, but the air war was largely an indecisive seesaw—and this too was an ominous portent for the Luftwaffe, since the planes deployed in Spain in 1937 would be basically the same planes used throughout the Second World War.[15]

But the Republicans had never done much to develop their ground-to-air defenses, so when the Nationalists had temporary air superiority, they could bomb and strafe with impunity. In this one area, the two sides were not evenly matched: the Germans had brought their antiaircraft units with them, and the recently deployed 8.8-centimeter gun established its value as an effective weapon.

This asymmetry led to the widespread notion that the Nationalists, thanks to their German and Italian air contingent, had command of the skies while the forces of the republic were reduced to fighting with bolt-action rifles. On the contrary: their air force had slightly more planes than the Nationalists, and the Russian aircraft deployed were at least as good as anything the Germans and the Italians had.[16]

Be that as it may, the destruction of the historic Basque town of Guernica, on April 26, 1937, gave the world the idea that the Germans were not only wicked but supremely powerful. The apocalyptic proclamations of the airpower enthusiasts thus converged, in the West, with Stalin's vociferous anti-Fascist campaign. The former had by now convinced a great many people that bombers could obliterate cities in short order; the latter portrayed the Nationalists and their allies as a gang of thugs capable of any atrocity. In Guernica both groups had the proof their zeal demanded.

Like most overblown myths, this one backfired on all concerned. Guernica was about fifteen kilometers behind the front lines. Whether it was a legitimate target or not, it was a tactical, not a strategic, one. It was also a modest target, since the town had a population of fewer than ten thousand people. Nor did the Basques have any air defenses.

So the claim that Guernica demonstrated the overwhelming power of the bomber was a generalization unsupported by the facts, as the relatively low casualties make plain. Moreover, the German bomber crews may have destroyed the town by accident. The key word here is *destroyed*. They clearly intended to bomb the village, but there was apparently no premeditated plan to obliterate it.

This is by no means to exonerate the personnel involved. There had already been examples of the machine-gunning of civilians and the destruction of small villages from the air. On March 31, 1937, for instance, German bombers had attacked the rail and road junctions at Durango. Like Guernica, Durango was a small town, important only for the junctions. Aerial attacks killed nearly 250 people, apparently all civilians, including a significant number of priests and nuns.[17]

Although, as we have seen, level-flight bombing was highly inaccurate, the Ju-52 was a slow plane with a good deal of lift: it could fly at extremely low speeds without stalling, and because the citizens of Durango were unarmed, there was no need to worry about antiaircraft fire. It is hard not to believe that the air crews were shooting at everything in sight, without regard for whether the target was a military one or not: a railroad line is difficult to mistake for a church, and yet the bombers hit at least two houses of worship.

The challenge in this case—and in others as well—is to decide if the attacks were part of a deliberate policy. Whether they were deliberate or not, the distinction became blurred, perhaps beyond repair. If the air force of the republic was less culpable, it was because the Nationalists had better antiaircraft defenses—and were in general better organized. Both sides established an appalling record of war crimes.

Of course if Guernica was, as a good many people have claimed (and with evidence that can't be swept off the table), a tragic error, it was a mistake that was bound to happen, given the concept of airpower that held sway in the 1930s. The problem was that the major air forces refused to admit that the level-flight bomber was an extremely inaccurate weapon, and the airpower theorists expressed no reservations about killing civilians.

On the contrary, both public figures and the press seemed to take a certain diabolical relish in describing the carnage. Even the usually more sober (and politically conservative) *Life* magazine weighed in: "On March 16, 17, and 18 the greatest test of General Douhet's theories ever given fell on the Spanish city of Barcelona," one essay began.[18]

And now the grisly claims came back to haunt all those concerned, from the politicians who had delivered the grim pronouncements, to the experts who had explained how it would come to pass—because Guernica the myth soon overpowered any rational or objective consideration of the situation. Not surprisingly, the citizens of the Western democracies were not enthusiastic about their governments' pursuing courses of action that, if they resulted in war, would—as those same governments cheerfully told them—mean they'd all be dead and buried under the debris of their own rooftops. So the net result of the airpower discussions was to sharpen the resolve of the pacifists and give them renewed traction in public policy debates.

Logically so: for innocent people on the ground, the only thing that mattered was that their homes, their neighborhoods, their friends and relatives, could well be slaughtered for no apparent military reason. Moreover, the National Socialists were more than happy to scare the daylights out of the rest of the world. Claiming, unofficially, that it was all a mistake only made the matter worse. That implied that if the air force really intended to destroy a town, it could do enormously more damage and murder still more people.

And once the war began, events were easily rearranged to fit the Guernica pattern—albeit on a much greater scale. It is an easy step from Guernica to the abrupt surrender of the Netherlands after the bombing of Rotterdam (whose destruction was also wildly exaggerated, mostly in an attempt to show how wicked the Germans were), and yet another easy step to the idea that the Luftwaffe, developed almost entirely as a tactical air force, could bring Britain to its knees. Nor was it much of a step to go further, as the Allies soon did, and believe that their strategic bombers could destroy Germany just as Douhet had said would happen.[19]

Thus somewhere between one-half and three-quarters of a million innocent men, women, and children were murdered during the course of the war in Europe by air attacks, most of them killed as a result of basic misunderstandings. So Guernica was not simply a crime, it was the opening act of a catastrophe. That the overwhelming majority of the people murdered were German is ironic. A few technical developments aside, the German air force personnel in Spain missed the most important lesson to be drawn. He who dances to the devil's tune must pay the devil his due.

PAPER TIGERS: HITLER'S TANKS

In war only the simple can succeed. I visited the staff of the
Cavalry Corps. What I saw there was not simple.

Paul von Hindenburg, commenting on the 1932 maneuvers[1]

German armor development was, if possible, even more of a muddle
than aircraft design. The Luftwaffe at least entered the war with excellent, if aging, aircraft. Tank commanders began with underpowered,
overweight vehicles that were completely unsuitable for combat, even
though the Reichsheer had been secretly developing and testing armored vehicles at the Kama site in the Soviet Union since 1929.[2]

Hitler's accession marked the end of the Russo-German cooperative
efforts in testing and training. The Red Army promptly pulled out and
the Germans went home, taking their test vehicles with them. Heinz
Guderian, the great German armored expert, sums it up well:

> Although tank construction in the 'twenties was marked by great techni-
> cal improvements over the tanks built during the First World War, it was
> still inadequate to fill the tactical requirements of the tanks to be em-
> ployed in the new role which we had envisaged for them. It was not pos-
> sible simply to order the mass production of the experimental models
> then available. The construction of new models was essential.[3]

Basically, then, German armored development didn't begin until 1933,
when the army set a specification for a five-ton tank equipped with two

machine guns in a rotating turret. Although this specification was for a tank that was lower and lighter, and had a substantially greater range and higher ground speed than the French Renault FT17, it was the same concept with the same weaknesses, even though the Renault tank had been designed nearly seventeen years earlier.

The mass-produced FT17, with its rotating turret, was the forerunner of all modern tanks. It was underpowered and lightly armored, but in 1917 no engine had the power to propel a tank properly on the battle-field, so weight had to be kept to the minimum.

Initially the various tank specifications were antithetical, but Renault was on the right track: most subsequent tanks used the same revolving-turret principle as the FT17.[4] By the time the German Mark 1 tank was being produced, a reasonable international consensus had developed about what constituted a light tank. By this standard, the Mark 1 was a wretched machine. With its 13-millimeter armor and twin machine guns, it actually had less armor and less firepower than the old FT17.[5]

It looked like a tank, and it had a rotating turret, but in reality it was a tankette, or what the French and the British called a machine-gun car-rier, albeit a machine-gun carrier that desperately needed to be put on a diet. These small combat vehicles, lightly armored and weighing about two tons, could be used in reconnaissance or to tow guns.[6] They were all based on a British Carden-Lloyd design of the late 1920s, heavily modi-fied and then produced locally. Thus the Czechs had the Tancik Vz33, the French had the Renault VE, and the Italians had the Fiat Ansaldo CV3, which was exported to other countries, notably Austria. By con-trast, the Czech LTM, with its turret-mounted 37-millimeter gun and 25-millimeter armor, is a good example of contemporary light-tank design. Its 120-horsepower engine allowed it to reach speeds of up to 40 kilome-ters an hour; it had a range of nearly 200 kilometers and excellent cross-country performance.

Basically, the Mark 1 represents a dead end in tank design. In his memoirs—the single most important eyewitness account we have of German armored development—Heinz Guderian makes clear that he was aware of the many deficiencies of the Mark 1. His argument is that production was justified because it gave the army a stopgap tank to use while the real tanks the army needed were developed and put into service. This sounds logical enough. If German tankers were to learn how to deploy these vehicles, they had to have equipment to drive around that vaguely resembled a tank, and thus the Mark 1.[7]

But Guderian is like Kesselring. Much of what he says is highly disingenuous. The Mark 1, a contemporary of the Czech LTM, went into production in 1935, and the planned replacement tanks went into production less than a year later. But the Germans kept on producing the Mark 1 anyway. On September 1, 1939, there were 1,445 Mark 1 vehicles deployed. The Polish campaign revealed—not surprisingly—that the Mark 1 was unsuitable for combat. Nonetheless, the army still deployed 523 of them in May 1940. Astoundingly, 843 were in service at the end of 1941.

One year after production of the Mark 1 began, the army issued a specification for a second vehicle, to weigh about seven tons and be armed with a 2.0-centimeter gun. The Mark 2 repeated most of the mistakes of the Mark 1: its 15-millimeter armor was hardly an improvement, its operating range had deteriorated, and its weight had gone up dramatically—at over nine tons, it weighed nearly as much as the Czech LTM. Compared with everyone else's tanks, it was a joke. The 2.0-centimeter gun was the puniest in service in any tank, its armor negligible. In the Spanish civil war, its performance in the field against Russian and British tanks was pathetic.

It is difficult to avoid the conclusion that the Mark 1 and the Mark 2 represented German engineering at its sorriest, but by August 1939, the army had 930 of them in service, and by May 1940, the total had grown to 1,092.[8] Two years later, well into the Russian campaign, there were still 860 Mark 2 vehicles in service.

In his memoirs, Guderian claims that in the proposed armored divisions, two types of tank would be required. The first would be a light tank "with an armor piercing gun and two machine guns. . . . The light tanks would equip the three light companies of the tank battalions."[9] The projected light tank (as opposed to the vehicles the Germans were busily turning out like tin cans) was designed to be the basic vehicle of the armored divisions still in the planning stage. Essentially, the Mark 3 was a large version of the Mark 2, and it replicated most of the flaws of the earlier models. Designed as a light tank, it qualified only in the sense that it was lightly armored and seriously undergunned—which guaranteed its inferiority in any tank-versus-tank battle.

The Mark 1 was simply a small combat vehicle that weighed more than twice as much as any other light combat vehicle. The Mark 3 was a light tank that weighed nearly twice as much as everyone else's light tank. But then the Mark 3 vehicles that went into production in 1938 weighed about the same—and had essentially the same bulk and profile—as the support tank Guderian mentions, the Mark 4. In later modifications, only an expert can tell the two vehicles apart.

The Mark 1 excepted, all three designs had some advanced features, as one would expect from a German-engineered project. From the start, the Germans had gone for welded armor, which was inherently superior to the other two processes then in use, riveting and casting. After the FT17, the French, who were well ahead when it came to tank design, solved the problem by casting. Although casting was an expensive method that produced a heavy vehicle, it made French tanks basically invulnerable to enemy fire, as the Germans would find out, to their dismay, in May 1940.

Welding was clearly the best of the three techniques. The individual pieces could be shaped, and the welds connecting them, far from being the weak points (as was the case with riveting), would be stronger than the pieces joined. Electric welding had revolutionized the shipbuilding industry in the 1920s, and the Germans were smart to apply the technique to tank construction. But so were the Russians; and the Americans, too, had realized the inherent problems of riveted armor and had begun to shift over to what might be called a composite construction, in which certain components (the nosepiece of the hull) could be bolted on to a welded chassis.

Moreover, despite the obvious technical inferiority of riveted armor for tanks, the Germans were not concerned enough about the defects to prevent them from deploying hundreds of the two Czech light tanks once they had occupied Czechoslovakia and had access to its unexpectedly large tank park. Both Czech designs soldiered on until well into the Russian campaign: in January 1942 there were 197 of the earlier Czech LTM-35 tanks (known in the German army as the 35t) still in service, and 1,144 of the more modern TNHP-S vehicles (the 38t).

The other intelligent feature in German design was the emphasis on a two-man turret for the two larger tanks; the commander now had someone to load the gun while he directed the driver, since in these early models only the commander had a decent field of vision. But the Czech tanks were similarly outfitted — putting two men in the turret was hardly a patented idea.

The German tendency to overengineer their designs had a fortuitous effect: as the army belatedly realized how wretched its tanks were and desperately began to upgrade them, it found that the basic structure (hull, suspension, and turret) could easily accommodate more powerful engines, transmissions, weaponry, and even armor.[10]

If their tanks were this wretched, where did German armor get its reputation? During the first part of the war, the Allies never got a good look at a German tank, a fact that accounts for much of the misinformation surrounding the German tank force. By version J, which went into production in late 1943, the Mark 3 tank had become a formidable battlefield opponent for the Allies. Its high-velocity, 5.0-centimeter gun was almost as potent as the standard gun on the Sherman, and its upgraded armor made it hard to disable. Later versions of the Mark 4 could easily outgun any Allied tank. So there was a tendency to assume that vehicles like the Mark 3J and the Mark 4F were more or less the same vehicles that German armored divisions had deployed in 1939–40. No wonder they had rolled over their opposition!

But in reality these versions were all borne of the Russian front, and the Germans went to war in 1939 with surprisingly few of the admittedly feebly gunned and weakly armored originals. To be precise, in May 1940 the army possessed 3,695 tracked vehicles based on Mark 1–4 designs, of which 3,228 were actual tanks. And of that total, the two vehicles intended to be the basis of the armored force amounted to only 21 percent, or one out of every five vehicles, while the two Czech designs constituted another 12 percent. In that month, of the roughly 2,000 tanks the Germans deployed in the west, 1,478 were Mark 1 and Mark 2 tanks; thus two out of every three German tanks available for action were the Mark 1 and the Mark 2 tankettes, inferior, in every respect, to all British, French, and Belgian tanks.

In his memoirs, Guderian claims that this situation was a result of the resistance of the army's high command, who were opposed to his ideas, and everyone accepts this as being the case. But this claim is hard to square with the production statistics. Once the designs for the Mark 1 and the Mark 2 were approved, the army certainly had enormous numbers of them built. Clearly there was a willingness to build and deploy tanks.

The more logical explanation—and the one most experts have accepted—is that the army had decided to emphasize mobility over all other considerations. If one conceptualizes the tank as a vehicle designed to break through the enemy's infantry positions, moving rapidly through his lines and striking at the relatively vulnerable rear, then the Mark 1 was a decent enough weapon. It was fast and maneuverable, had a respectable cross-country range, and its twin machine guns (much less the 2-centimeter gun of the Mark 2) would certainly wreak havoc once the opponent's main positions had been either broken through or outflanked. This was exactly what Fuller was proposing in his theory of armored warfare: the tank was a breakthrough vehicle.

From that point of view, the German army didn't need thousands of heavier, more powerful vehicles: a few hundred would destroy any fixed enemy strongpoints (the 7.5-centimeter gun of the Mark 4 would do just fine), while the Mark 3 could deal with the few enemy tanks that might be encountered.

The Germans weren't the only people to fall into this trap. So did the Americans: speed and mobility were increasingly emphasized at the expense of armor and firepower when it came to tank design; the culmination was the otherwise inexplicable refusal of the army to give the

Sherman a decent gun. There was no need for one; tanks were break-through weapons, the argument ran, and had no need to be able to fight other tanks.[11]

But the principle was flawed. It assumed that the enemy had neither tanks nor antitank weapons (or the latter only at the front). But what if your opponent had tanks and also subscribed to the theory? While your tanks were rampaging through your foe's rear, his tanks would be rampaging through yours. Why hadn't anyone noticed this obvious drawback with the theory?

There are two answers. The first may be traced to men like Fuller, who completely distorted the armored combats of the First World War and then, like Douhet, postulated armored warfare as though the tank, like the bomber, was unstoppable. This simply denied reality. On the battlefield, the slow-moving, lightly armored tanks of 1917–18 quickly revealed themselves to be highly susceptible to antitank weaponry. At speeds of little more than a brisk walk (eight or nine kilometers per hour), they could be disabled by field guns and even mortars, while their armor could be pierced by the armor-piercing ammunition issued to machine-gunners or by the heavier armor-piercing round of the T-Gewehr antitank rifle. Most French tanker casualties came from bullets, not shells.

Moreover, on close examination, Fuller's great set-piece armored victory (or near victory) in Cambrai, France, was simply propaganda. The British tank force drove through the German positions, just as Fuller believed would be (had been) the case. But within forty-eight hours, most of those tanks were out of service for mechanical reasons, and within a few days, a successful German counterattack had overrun the British first-line positions. Cambrai was a victory only if one blew the whistle early and overlooked what happened after the initial breakthrough.

And this was against an enemy who had neither tanks nor proper anti-tank weaponry, whose infantry were forced to improvise defenses on the spot. What would be the fate of another Cambrai, this time against an enemy with tanks, antitank weaponry, and infantry trained to expect such an onslaught? Put that way, the prospects were grim. It was much more convenient to assume that your tank force would face no real opposition and that your enemy lacked all these things: that, in other words, the offensive weapons of 1930 would encounter the defenses of 1916 or 1918.

What is remarkable in these accounts is the extent to which self-serving statements were taken at face value and duly passed into military history as fact, as with Albert Kesselring's defense of the failure to produce a strategic bomber. Heinz Guderian is taken—correctly in my view—as the key player in armored development, so it's interesting to examine his remarks about what was going on. There are several problems with his account. In the first place, if they were supposed to be the main tanks, why did the army produce them in such leisurely fashion? By May 1940, three years after the start of production, there were only 381 Mark 3 vehicles in service—and this tank was supposed to equip three out of every four tank battalions. And there were nearly that many of the Mark 4 tanks (290) in service, so there was something wrong with the ratio from the start.

Guderian's defense boils down to production costs and development time. The first two vehicles were produced because they were cheaper and the designs were ready to go into production. But the dates don't corroborate the claim. The specifications for the Mark 1 were set in 1933, for the Mark 2 and the Mark 4 in 1934, and the Mark 3 in 1935—all within twenty-four months.

Working prototypes for the four tanks only complicate the issue. The Mark 2 and the Mark 3 were being tested at the same time (1936), while prototypes of the Mark 4 were being evaluated in 1935. The Mark 2 and the Mark 4 went into series production in 1936, and the Mark 3 followed the next year. A rational production scheme, then, would have quickly dropped both of the smaller tankettes to concentrate on what had been envisioned all along as the two main tanks for the armored forces.

Moreover, the cost argument can easily be refuted: a Mark 3 cost less than three times what a Mark 2 cost to produce, and the army would have been much better off if it had entered the war against France with another 350 Mark 3 vehicles instead of the 1,077 Mark 1 tankettes it actually deployed.

Production went on for the same reason the air force kept on produc-ing its light and medium bombers: to Hitler, as Göring observed, the only thing that mattered was quantity. So the army let the situation con-tinue, even though they knew they were producing a totally inadequate vehicle. Essentially what the army had managed to do by 1939 was to produce two variants of two tanks. The only real difference between the Mark 3 and the Mark 4 was the gun—and this was actually the result an internal bureaucratic fight. The tankers (according to Guderian, any-way) wanted the Mark 3 to be equipped with a 5.0-centimeter gun, while the army insisted that the existing 3.7-centimeter gun, the standard anti-tank weapon, would do just fine.

This tank would, in theory, be the main battle vehicle of the armored divisions, while its companion, the Mark 4, would be the tank Guderian envisioned for support operations: "The medium tanks would enable the medium company of the battalion to perform its dual role of, first, sup-porting the light tanks in action, and, secondly, of shooting at targets out of the range of the light tanks' smaller calibre guns."[12] The theory is sound enough; the problem lay in the guns themselves.

The 7.5-centimeter gun initially mounted on the Mark 4 was an ex-tremely low-velocity weapon. Although artillery pieces are always desig-nated by the aperture of the barrel (in this case, 7.5 centimeters), other important factors determine the destructive power of the shell. Chief among these (to simplify drastically) is the speed attained by the shell as it exits the barrel and the mass of the shell itself. In the 1930s the mass of the shell (its weight) was largely a function of the diameter of the barrel, and explains why guns are ranked by barrel aperture.

But this is misleading. Longer barrels give the rapidly expanding gases a larger containment area, forcing them to expand in only one direction—along the length of the barrel. As the length of the barrel in-creases, so does the muzzle velocity. Basically, ignoring other factors, the relative destructive power of a shell can be calculated once the muzzle ve-locity and the weight of the shell are known. That is why the Germans (like everyone else) could take the 7.5-centimeter gun, increase the length of the barrel, and produce a substantially more destructive weapon. The late-model version of the original L24 gun that equipped the Mark 4, for example, was six times as powerful.

The tankers wanted to equip the Mark 3 with a 5.0-centimeter weapon whose expended-energy destructive force would be half again as powerful as the bigger gun in the Mark 4. And since, for guns firing at relatively flat trajectories, power is a good indicator of range as well, Guderian's comments are simply untrue: the Mark 3 would have been more lethal than the Mark 4.

However, the actual gun fitted to the Mark 3 was the same gun the army was using as its antitank gun, a truly feeble weapon, with about a third of the hitting power of its French and Russian equivalents. What this means, recalling that German tanks were underarmored to begin with, is this: French and Russian tanks (and British tanks equipped with their two-pounder guns) could destroy any German tank, while their heavier armor would prevent the same thing from happening to them. Moreover, since the British and the French (and the Belgians and the Poles and the Czechs) were all using antitank weapons of equal or greater potency, German tankers were going to have difficulties in carrying out the armored thrusts envisioned.

The German tank commander General Kühne, a veteran of 1940, described the situation ruefully: "The only German gun that is effective against the French tanks is the 7.5 centimeter gun of our Mark 4 firing an armor-piercing shell. . . . The shell of our 3.7 centimeter tank and antitank guns is ineffective against French tanks at the normal range of combat. . . . The 3.7 centimeter shell does not perform its mission and is not suitable for modern tank warfare. . . . The high explosive 7.5 centimeter shell has no effect on the heavy French tanks at distances of 600 to 800 meters. The 2.0 centimeter shell will not penetrate any French tank and had only a moral effect."[13]

How to explain this well-nigh-total inadequacy? In the period between the wars, hardly anyone had serious combat experience involving armor, so although the Germans were operating blind, so to speak, they were not much more handicapped than the French or the British or the Americans. That being the case, it's hard to escape the conclusion that the culprit was Guderian himself. In 1928, when Guderian took over responsibility for the development of mechanization and armor, he had never actually seen a modern tank; his military background had been primarily as a signals officer, and by his own admission the only tank he had seen (until the first new German designs appeared) was the 1918 German vehicle still being used in Sweden.

Although several analysts have discussed the superiority of German intelligence in comparison to the Allies', on this most basic detail, either German intelligence failed or, more likely, Guderian and the other German tankers simply ignored what they were being told. How could the existence of nearly invulnerable French tanks be a secret? Leaving aside the fact that nothing in the French military establishment was ever a secret for long, there's the point that the main heavy tank—the one that gave Kühne's hapless gunners such fits—was already in service by the time Guderian took over armored development, in 1928. None of the other French designs were particularly new; all of them had been in the field before their German counterparts.

The failure is not intelligence (in either sense), it's curiosity. Lack of curiosity is a good sign of näiveté, testimony to the end result of the selection process begun by von Seeckt, which resulted in an officer corps that was narrowly focused and quite naive—the narrow focus that characterized British "experts" in 1914 who insisted that the super-heavy guns the Germans and Austrians were deploying in Belgium couldn't possibly exist.

The rapidity of the victories of 1940–41 on the surface seemed to indicate that Hitler and his growing band of disciples had guessed correctly. Thus was luck confused with success, and patterns that would ultimately lead to failure rewarded, with Germany's tank experts claiming that their triumphs were the result of deliberate preferences for speed and mobility.

Guderian had excuses as to why things fell out as they did, but it is difficult to take them seriously. After 1934, when the army high command began to realize that Hitler, by and large, thought they were disloyal (compared to the air force and the naval commands), Guderian promptly went to Hitler and protested, just as Räder would later threaten to resign when Hitler refused to fire his naval adjutant for marrying a woman of uncertain morals. Nor did either officer suffer as a result of his actions. Hitler, at least in those days, was willing to tolerate a surprising amount of dissent and resistance. No, the excuses are classic instances of the passive-aggressive behavior that had been triggered by the party's interference in military personnel matters. By the time Guderian and Räder looked back, each of them had accumulated a decade's worth of experience in explaining why it wasn't his fault.   .

One final glaring weakness needs to be explained. Although Fuller and his disciples had argued that all that was needed on the future battlefield were vast hordes of tanks, the French, who as usual were first off the mark in experimenting with divisional organizations, saw right off that the situation on the modern battlefield would definitely require infantry.

Initially, the model used relied on the old horse-and-foot distinctions. Some divisions would consist of tanks, and some of infantry. But given the revolution in motor transport, it would make sense to put the infantry in motor vehicles and abandon horses and feet entirely. Actually, the French had gotten a great deal of experience with mechanization beginning in August 1914, and by October they were moving whole infantry brigades by truck.

But nobody knew what the correct mix of vehicles and units was. Did you simply take an infantry division and put it in trucks? The problem was that you would need a very special type of truck to keep up with a tracked vehicle, no matter what its cross-country speed was, since the trucks of that era were designed for roads.

By 1918, all infantry divisions had cavalry and artillery attached to them. Should all the horses be replaced? And if so, with what? Wouldn't it make more sense to have a division with both tanks and infantry? That way, they could work together under a single command. And if that was the case, then the infantry would have to keep pace with the tanks, and so would the artillery and antitank guns.

To find answers, the major armies began to experiment with various combinations. There were mechanized divisions, light divisions, and several types of armored divisions. In addition, tanks (usually heavy ones) operated in independent battalions or brigades, controlled above the level of corps or division, just as heavy artillery had been handled at the start of the First World War. And since no army could afford to move all its equipment and personnel by truck, some men still traveled on foot and led (or rode) horses.

Guderian wanted all aspects of an armored division to be motorized, and he wanted specialization, so that some units, called motorized divisions, would be totally dependent on vehicles, while the men in others would walk (and use horses). Logically speaking, all the tanks would be concentrated in tank divisions, and since the German word for *armor* is *Panzer*, those units are called Panzer divisions, just as German tanks are, somewhat inaccurately, referred to as Panzers as well.

At first, the idea was that Panzer divisions would consist of hundreds of tanks (about four hundred), but ineptitude in production, coupled with Hitler's demands for numerous armored divisions, meant that by May 1940, the average tank strength for the ten armored divisions was only 268, with only three of them having a tank strength of over 300.

Actual wartime experience quickly established that the goal of armored divisions of three hundred tanks and no infantry was a poor choice, because as tanks became bigger and had more firepower, they needed more room to maneuver. So the Germans basically went for the model the French had been experimenting with. In the beginning, this deployment consisted of one tank brigade, one motorized infantry brigade, and a motorized artillery regiment, together with a battalion of motorcyclists and a motorized reconnaissance battalion. Initially, the armored component of the division would have totaled over four hundred tanks, and the U.S. Army duly put out the figure in 1941—by which time the tank component of most German armored divisions was well under half that, and closer to one-quarter. In fact, in the evolution of the armored division in Germany through the war, there was a steady reduction in the number of tanks and an increase in infantry with stepped-up firepower and all-terrain mobility. Interestingly, the French had been heading in just this direction before 1940 — and most major armies followed suit after the war.

But even before the war began, the Germans had run into a significant problem: they lacked the sheer numbers of motor vehicles — and the right kind of motor vehicles — necessary to mechanize their forces. We're familiar with pictures of German half-tracks, bristling with infantry; they epitomize the notion of mobility. But that vehicle, the Schützenpanzerwagen 250, didn't enter service until 1942, even though the army had issued specifications for six different models of half-track vehicles, rating them by load, ten years earlier.

But the army's intention was that half-tracks would be prime movers, not personnel carriers. The smallest of these vehicles, rated at one ton, was intended to tow an antitank gun, or one of the two howitzers that by then had replaced the traditional 7.7-centimeter field gun used by infantry divisions in the last war.[14] The vehicle's payload was too limited and its cross-country performance poor. Nevertheless, by 1942 the army had more than eleven thousand of them in service, even though increasingly — now that the 3.7-centimeter antitank gun was being eliminated — the three-ton half-track was mostly used for towed artillery and antitank (and larger antiaircraft) guns like the 7.5-centimeter antitank gun and the 8.8-centimeter dual-purpose weapon. The five-ton half-track was designed to mount a 7.5-centimeter gun, so as to provide mobile firepower for the cavalry units, while the eight-, twelve-, and eighteen-ton vehicles were all intended as prime movers for the army's heavy artillery (guns of 10 centimeters or larger). But as usual, production was a problem: the army had only four thousand of the three-ton vehicle in service by 1942. So the needs of the armored divisions for decent personnel carriers were in competition with the general necessity of supplying the artillery with prime movers and the cavalry with firepower, with no attention given to vehicles for personnel until later in the war.

Originally, motorized infantry units were transported mostly by truck; in fact, little thought was given to the motorization of the infantry. Although the British were hardly in the forefront of modernization, they had, at the start of the war, eight thousand tracked personnel carriers (these vehicles were suitable for towing light weapons as well). The French were more lavishly equipped; even the Belgians had made better provision for transporting infantry than the Germans.

In May 1940 the German army was the least mechanized of all the major combatants, and the situation never improved. Despite the German emphasis on speed—and the criticism of enemy tanks for being too slow—as late as summer 1941, most of the troops in the motorized regiments were truck bound: once they came close to their objective, they had to get out and walk, as the vehicles carrying them were incapable of moving off-road.[15] Most German soldiers walked into combat up until the end, and, right through the war, a surprising number of guns were still being pulled by horses.

The one exception to the lack of mobility, at least early in the war, was the large number of armored cars produced. The army deployed about 1,100 in 1940, mostly for reconnaissance. Since each armored division was supposed to have twenty armored cars, this was the one area in which the army was able to equip the divisions as intended.

The initial models had poor cross-country performance, and this failing wasn't remedied until well into the war, when a combination of better transmissions and more powerful engines gave the armored cars true all-terrain performance (something French armored cars had possessed from the beginning). Ironically, the improvements came at just about the time the army had decided to abandon wheeled vehicles as much as possible, because of the deplorable roads and weather in east and central Europe.

Were one to judge from the tables of organization of the new divisions, the logical conclusion would be that they were set up not around tanks or armored cars but around motorcycles. An exaggeration, of course, but two of the three infantry battalions in the two infantry regiments consisted of one motorcycle company and two infantry companies, while the third had three infantry companies. The infantry brigade, in addition to its two infantry regiments, had a motorcycle battalion of two companies, and the reconnaissance battalion had one as well. Indeed, the most common motorized vehicle for an armored division was the motor-cycle, a fact that hardly boded well for either the offensive striking power of the division or its ability to move cross-country. Even had the high command embraced the new theories of armored warfare, the army lacked the resources to carry them out.

The Germans certainly had the chance to learn all of these things in the Spanish civil war. Curiously, Guderian never mentions this, and al-most all the claims on the German side emanate from General von Thoma, who had been involved from the very early days, when he com-manded the Kama training facility, in Russia. In 1936, after Hitler au-thorized the beginning of German aid to the Nationalists, von Thoma was sent to Spain to command the German tank detachment there and to train Spanish tank crews.

Almost everything we know about these events comes from Basil Lid-dell Hart's interviews with von Thoma. Unfortunately, Liddell Hart tended to accept von Thoma's remarks at face value. Thus, for example, the general's comment that there "were never more than 600" ground troops in Spain at one time is taken as fact.[16] So there is some question about von Thoma as a reliable witness, an important point, as it is to him, via Liddell Hart, that we owe the idea that Spain was regarded by the Germans as a sort of practice with live ammunition for the army, and that this is so has duly been enshrined in military folklore.[17] Other than that, all we have of any substance is a brief sentence taken from Göring during his trial, in which he says that he had urged Hitler to aid General Franco, in order to allow various technical aspects of the air force to be tested. But this testimony is wobbly.[18]

But what did the Germans actually learn? Or, to put the question an-other way, what did they fail to learn? On this score, von Thoma was rather coy, admitting that the Russian tanks the Germans encountered

were of a heavier type than ours, which were armed only with ma-chine-guns, and I offered a reward of 500 pesetas for every one that was

captured. . . . By 1938 I had four tank battalions under my command—
each of three companies, with fifteen tanks in a company. Four of the
companies were equipped with Russian tanks.[19]

The Russian tank von Thoma is referring to was the T-26. It was indeed
bigger and heavier than the two small German tanks: it weighed just under ten tons. It had marginally thicker armor, was a little slower, and had
a significantly greater operating range. But the most important feature
was that it mounted a potent 45-millimeter gun. The German and Italian tankettes were helpless: on October 29, 1936, one T-26 destroyed
eleven Italian tanks, and the pattern of massacre would be repeated
again and again, with the Italians, who had deployed many more tanks
than the Germans, thus suffering many more losses—not that the Germans didn't suffer heavily as well.[20]

The T-26 was a vastly superior tank, but it was badly employed in
Spain. When the tankers were Russian (as was always the case at first),
there was a total lack of coordination with the infantry. Thus, although
initially the tanks were used in what was thought to be the proper
massed-formation style, there was no infantry follow-up to hold the
ground secured by the armored breakthrough and to mop up isolated
strongpoints that the tanks had bypassed. That was the case in the October attack. In later attacks, when more and more vehicles were (apparently) crewed by non-Russians, there was a tendency simply to
mishandle the tank units, as was the case in the doomed efforts to save
Bilbao from being overrun by the Nationalists in June 1937.

Republican ineptitude on the ground may well have been the chief
cause of difficulty in interpreting the lessons of the war. Stalin had given
the Republicans better tanks, but they couldn't use them correctly, and
their troubles may well have given the Germans a misleading sense of superiority despite the wretchedness of their equipment. But whatever von
Thoma learned, he didn't reveal it to Liddell Hart, and from Spain he
went on to command a tank regiment in Austria, and was thus shunted
away from the center of activity. So the one lesson the Germans should

have taken to heart from personal experience—the potency of Soviet armor—they missed entirely.

How entirely? In the words of Germany's greatest tank expert:

> We believed that at the beginning of the new war we could reckon on our tanks being technically better than all known Russian types; we thought that this would more or less cancel out the Russians' vast numerical superiority. . . . But one curious incident made me at least slightly dubious concerning the relative superiority of our armored equipment. In the spring of 1941 Hitler had specifically ordered that a Russian military commission be shown over our tank schools and factories; in this order they insisted that nothing be concealed from them. The Russian officers in question firmly refused to believe that the Panzer IV was in fact our heaviest tank. They said repeatedly that we must be hiding our newest models from them, and complained we were not carrying out Hitler's order. . . . It was at the end of July 1941 that the T34 appeared at our front and the riddle of the new Russian model was solved.[21]

In fact, the only real conclusion to be drawn from the ground war in Spain was that none of the major powers learned very much. As with the air war, everyone saw whatever it was he wanted to see.

BLOODLESS VICTORIES, OR NEARLY SO:
TOWARD A GREATER GERMANY, 1935–39

———————————

To blame individuals is to forget that politicians are the expres-
sions of public moods which are the masses' collective dreams.

Hugh Thomas[1]

Although badly equipped and deeply politicized, the Wehrmacht had
an institutional memory that enabled it to build slowly and steadily on
what it had learned in 1914–18. Such recollections translated into effective training and doctrine were important, but the real force behind the
drive to initial victory in 1939–40 was the series of spectacular foreign
policy successes Hitler engineered. Each of Hitler's moves had a practical benefit for the military, although this is generally unremarked. In
large measure, by 1939, Great Britain and France found themselves
checkmated even before the fighting started.

The return of the Saarland to Germany as a result of an open election
was the first of these triumphs, and one with enormous military implications. It had little to do with Hitler, although he certainly took the credit
for it. The Saarland is an irregular quadrilateral tilted to the west, abut-
ting Luxembourg and stretching for about two hundred kilometers
east toward the Rhine. Like Alsace, its Germanic cultural and political
identity dated back to the first part of the tenth century. But during the

early revolutionary wars after 1789, the French grabbed as much of the Saar region as they could, and the southernmost portion became French.

At Versailles the French argued that the whole area should become a separate territory, administered under a League of Nations mandate, the fiction being that the inhabitants would decide their fate at some time in the future. These mandates, however piously intended, were little more than thinly disguised territorial appropriations, but under British and American pressure, the French agreed that at the end of 1934, the inhabitants would vote, presumably to remain free of Prussian oppression. Fifteen years of French control had indeed made a great impression on the natives. On January 13, 1935, nine out of every ten voters elected to become part of Germany.

The National Socialists rode this cause to victory, although they had had little responsibility for it. But the election had significant repercussions for any future military conflict between France and Germany. The French had blithely assumed that the Saarlanders would vote to become a French puppet state; consequently, when the military began construction of the Maginot Line in 1929, nothing was planned for the old border between the two areas.

The fortifications were finished and the money spent before the plebiscite. When the dust from the ballot boxes had settled, the French army had an 150-kilometer gap in the middle of its fortified border (the breach was roughly from east of Metz to west of Bitche). The fortification plan had been based on the assumption that the entire border from the Rhine to the western frontier with Luxembourg would be so heavily fortified as to be impenetrable. If the Germans attacked, France would thus have time to mobilize its army. But as a result of the plebiscite, this ingeniously fortified line knocked the carefully planned idea into a cocked hat.

The Saarland plebiscite was problematic for Britain as well. In 1932–33, Hitler had persuaded people to vote for him—and they did. The plebiscite gave him even more legitimacy, by suggesting that the German people were overwhelmingly behind him. Thus emboldened,

Hitler now made his move, tweaking the noses of the impotent French. In 1919, the French had tried to annex the right, or German, bank of the Rhine, incorporating all the German lands opposite Alsace. Militarily the logic was impeccable: the Rhine was a major obstacle. If the French had troops across the river at the start of hostilities, they could carry the war directly into Germany. But this strategy was too much for even the most Francophile of the Anglo-Americans at Versailles, and the idea was basically hooted off the table.

The compromise had been to forbid the Germans to maintain any troops in the Rhineland or to build any defensive fortifications there. As Hitler never tired of pointing out in his speeches—correctly—this was an unprecedented intrusion in national affairs. But he moved cautiously. A year after the Saarland plebiscite, he ordered troops into the Rhineland, ostentatiously remilitarizing it. Although the action was symbolic, the military implications were not. The Rhine was too broad and too deep to be forded; the only way across was by bridge. A few German troops could easily blow up the bridges, preventing any French advance.

Taken in conjunction with the Saarland plebiscite, France's carefully constructed defense posture was ruined. Technically speaking, Hitler's decision, on March 7, 1936, to remilitarize the Rhineland was a violation of the Versailles Treaty, and much fuss would subsequently be made of this illegal act. In hindsight, the lack of any serious French and British response seems incredible, because it gave rise to charges of appeasement, weakness, and apathy.

But the British had already dumped a good part of the Versailles pact when they concluded the Anglo-German naval agreement the year before. Hitler had earlier broken the treaty when, on March 16, 1935, he announced the reintroduction of conscription and demanded an armed forces that went far beyond anything allowed by Versailles. Germany's remilitarization was thus a fact.

At the same time, the British and the French were faced with substantial international challenges that illustrated the impotence of the League of Nations: Benito Mussolini's Ethiopian adventure, the Japanese incursion into Manchuria, the war between Paraguay and Bolivia, and the deepening crisis in Spain.[2] All were more important threats to world peace than Hitler was.

And by 1936, public opinion in France and Britain had shifted decisively. People were simply unwilling to support military action against Germany, particularly when it involved the enforcement of a treaty (Versailles) that was more and more seen as grossly unfair. The situation was not, then, a failure of Anglo-French will; it was a rational political calculation, mostly made by the British, since in the decade ending in June 1940, France had endured no fewer than twenty-two prime ministers—a new government every five months. In March 1936, during the remilitarization crisis, for example, the French prime minister, Albert Sarraut, had been in office for barely a month. By the beginning of June, there was a new occupant, Léon Blum.

Stanley Baldwin, the British prime minister, was as experienced and stable as his French counterparts were insecure and temporary. Unfortunately, when it came to foreign affairs, probably his most significant achievement was to tell the House of Commons that "the bomber will always get through . . . the only defense is in offense, which means that you have to kill more women and children more quickly than the enemy if you want to save yourselves."[3] Baldwin, who read the *Times* like everyone else, was thus only repeating the conventional wisdom, but such words were not likely to inspire his listeners to dig in their heels and brandish their weapons over something as abstract as the militarization of the Rhineland or the introduction of conscription.

Hitler now had momentum, but the next decisive step came about largely by accident. The Saarland plebiscite had gone the wrong way for the Allies, but the vote had been decisive. The worst possibility was an election in which the votes are so evenly divided that there is no consensus. A year later, the world was indeed presented with just such a worst-case scenario, a country split precisely down the middle: Spain in the election of February 16, 1936.[4] The narrowly elected government then behaved in a way totally divorced from reality. Instead of building bridges, its leaders blew them up.[5]

That there would therefore be a revolt, whether in the form of a coup or an outright rebellion, was thus a foregone conclusion. What differentiated the revolt that broke out in July 1936—a revolt initially intended as a coup d'état—was that the leaders of both sides immediately went global, sending emissaries out to all and sundry seeking help, and that help was immediately given to both sides.

The Republicans appealed to the French prime minister. Blum, elected in France by a Popular Front similar to the one in Spain, promised aid, and Pierre Cot, the minister for air, began arranging transfers of aircraft.[6] Britain pressured Paris to remain neutral, but French aircraft continued to reach the republic, along with volunteers and funds, all carefully orchestrated by Stalin so as to feign neutrality. By contrast, Hitler's and Mussolini's open support of the rebels gave rise to the notion that the Spanish people were fighting on alone against the combined might of Germany and Italy, when, as we have seen, the Red Army was in Spain up to its ears.

But the most important point about the war in Spain is that while it was going on, Hitler made his final moves in Central Europe, thus presenting the Allies with a foreign policy overload as they tried to figure out how to cope with multiple crises. Having used the Spanish situation to boost Germany's military prowess, Hitler now took advantage of Allied helplessness to make a series of territorial acquisitions, each with a powerful military implication.

First came the move into Austria. Like the Spanish, the Austrians were deeply divided. The idea of becoming a part of Germany may not have represented the aspirations of the entire population, but the concept had considerable appeal. So in March 1938, Hitler, having settled affairs with Mussolini—who had wanted Austria to become an Italian protectorate—ordered the army to occupy the country.

As had been the case with the decision to intervene in Spain, Hitler made up his mind and issued his orders. The Reichswehr had at one point developed a plan for such an invasion, called Case Otto, based on the supposition that there might be a Hapsburg restoration in Vienna, a horror that all good Socialist states would feel compelled to prevent. The plan was dusted off and hastily applied. Guderian records that he was told late in the afternoon of March 10, given command of the motorized troops involved, and provided with his orders that evening; he communicated them to his commanders shortly before midnight. They assembled at Passau (just up the river from Linz) the next night, and were told to move into Austria at eight o'clock on the morning of March 12.

Guderian and his commanders had to plan on short notice how to cross great distances. From the Second Armored Division's base in Würzburg, it was a good four hundred kilometers to Passau, and almost three hundred more to Vienna. There was no lead time, no discussion, no preparation, no planning. Of course, Austria was hardly going to attempt to defend itself. On the contrary, German troops were greeted enthusiastically (an inconvenient fact for many historians); the only military problem faced was logistical.

But for a mechanized unit, the logistics were formidable. Armies, Napoléon had observed, traveled on their stomachs. Modern armies, he would have added, travel on their fuel supplies. This was a truth the hastily mobilized mechanized troops promptly discovered, along with the recognition that German motorized equipment was not the most reliable in the world. Although the advancing army did not, as Churchill later opined, litter its trail with abandoned vehicles like Hansel and Gretel's trail of bread crumbs, it did make the army realize the crucial importance of logistical support for armored and mechanized columns.[7]

Guderian lists half a dozen areas in which the army learned from the challenges it had encountered; paramount among them was the importance of fuel, as well as of maintenance services. What he glosses over was the extent to which the motorized units were using inherently unreliable machines. Unlike the French, the Germans had never subjected their vehicles to long-term endurance and reliability tests of the sort that would reveal the inherent mechanical weaknesses in the equipment. Nor, even though they realized the problem, did the army pay adequate attention to the problem and try to solve it. Mechanical weaknesses and unreliability would dog the armored divisions all through the war.

But the advance into Austria gave the Germans a unique advantage: the experience of having to improvise a rapid advance into a foreign country. That the foreigners were far from hostile made little difference when it came to such matters as supplying fuel, bypassing stalled vehicles blocking narrow roads, and finding one's way through unfamiliar territory. Insofar as there would be a military key to the German successes of 1939–41, it is to be found in Case Otto, because it was there that the armored and mechanized divisions learned that logistical support in operations involving advances of hundreds of kilometers was essential. This was the one area of mechanization where the Germans had an advantage even before the war began—they had worked out the basic problems of moving motorized columns long distances over European roads.

Strategically, the *Anschluss* was a mixed bag. On the one hand, it gave Hitler an enormous internal boost. Many Austrians, perhaps the majority, had wanted to be part of the Reich for nearly two decades; they had been unsuccessful; now, with one quick stroke, Hitler had accomplished the link. There were tangible results as well. The Austrian army was small but well trained and professional, the inheritor of a tradition of excellence in combat that is generally overlooked. Now Germany had access to Italy, Hungary, and Yugoslavia; the latter two nations promptly began to reconsider their foreign policies. Czechoslovakia was a nominally Slavic isthmus, with Germans on three sides, thus presenting it with an intractable defense problem. And since the German action was unchallenged, it encouraged Poland and Hungary to reconsider their territorial aims against the newly formed country.

On the other hand, the *Anschluss* was the beginning of the swing of the pendulum of public opinion in the Western democracies. Most people weren't familiar with the complicated interactions in Central Europe. What they saw instead was that Hitler had simply gobbled up a country, particularly since there was a great deal of play in the media regarding the sentiments of the Austrian population. The remilitarization of the Rhineland was abstract; the takeover of Austria was concrete. It was the beginning of a profound shift, particularly in Great Britain, where, for the first time, people (other than Winston Churchill) began asking themselves when and how Hitler would be stopped.

In the popular mind at the time—and for most people subsequently—

the next step, dismemberment of Czechoslovakia, was both the symbol of the spinelessness of the Western democracies and the high-water mark of Hitler's territorial machinations. "Munich," a word that became synonymous with its twin, "appeasement," entered the vocabulary as a pejorative. So did the name Neville Chamberlain, the British prime minister who negotiated the deal with Hitler.

Chamberlain has much to answer for. At the treasury, he had strangled the British military for years, long before he became prime minister. His behavior after August 1939 was shameless. On this one point, however, he is not nearly so guilty as is made out, because the situation with regard to Czechoslovakia was even more complicated than Spain.

In 1867 the Hapsburg empire had been divided, for administrative purposes, into halves. Many of the empire's Slavs found themselves in the Hungarian portion, and there was a sizable group under Hungarian rule whose linguistic affinities were closely aligned with the Czechs': the Slovakians. It was the genius of Tomáš Garrigue Masaryk, the founder of the short-lived Czechoslovakia, to see that when one added the predominantly Slovakian regions to the lands of the Czechs, the result would be a territory large enough to be a successful country. He also realized that the Slovakian immigrants living in the United States were the key to building support for his idea. So Masaryk negotiated a compact with the American Slovaks, the Pittsburgh Agreement. The document called for a state, Czecho-Slovakia, organized on the Swiss model. Each group would have autonomy in law, education, language, culture, and governance, just like the three main ethnic groups of Switzerland.

At Versailles, armed with this agreement, Masaryk's most important disciple, Eduard Beneš, convinced the Allies to acquiesce to the formation of the state. Moreover, he was successful in getting a strategically important area to the east, misleadingly called Ruthenia (to disguise the fact that it was basically a part of western Ukraine), attached to the Czech and Slovak lands as a League of Nations mandate.

Intellectually, the relations between the Czechs and the Slovaks were complex. There were cultural affinities that Masaryk supposed would provide a sound basis for a country. Unfortunately, when the Slovak leaders showed up in Paris to argue for more autonomy, the Czechs had them arrested and deported back to Slovakia, now occupied by troops of the newly created Czecho-Slovak army. They were promptly arrested and put in jail.

Whatever the merits of the Czech case, this incident started the nation off on a sour note, and for the next twenty years, relations between the Czechs and the Slovaks steadily deteriorated, to the point that it was no longer a matter of right or wrong but of perception. By 1938, Czecho-Slovakia was a failed marriage, the differences between the parties were irreconcilable, and the Slovaks wanted out. So did the ethnic Germans, the Sudeteners. Like the Slovaks, their grievances dated from Versailles, when their delegation was shunned.

The Allies had never cared what the ethnic Germans of Central Europe wanted. But now this long-ignored group found a new and forceful ally: Hitler and the National Socialists. The Sudeteners increasingly felt that they were suffering the same treatment as the Slovaks, only more so, and began agitating against the Czech government in Prague.

The series of crises that ensued has always been pinned on Hitler, but doing so is as inaccurate as putting all the blame for the war on Chamberlain. The problem was inherent, and it had begun to fester long before Hitler came along. It followed from Masaryk's misleading idealism, Beneš's misrepresentations at Versailles, and, most important, the failure of the Czechs to convince the Germans, the Slovaks, and the Ruthenians that they respected their autonomy. The situation was surprisingly like the one in Spain: a central government, confronted with a variety of complaints from separatist groups, acted as though the challenges were all the work of a few malcontents.

A commission had been appointed to look into the Sudeteners' grievances, and its chair, Lord Runciman, came to the obvious conclusion that by this point the only solution was partition. All this played into Hitler's hands, but Runciman was neither a puppet nor a naïf. Masaryk's experiment, however nobly intended, had failed. An anonymous editorial writer in *Life* magazine hit the nail on the head: the Czech "rulers have maintained the forms of democracy only by violating some of its spirit."[8]

So in 1938, Hitler met with Chamberlain, Edouard Daladier, and Mussolini at Munich, and they simply peeled off the Sudetener territories from the Czecho-Slovakian Republic and awarded them to Germany. Given the confused sequence of events that followed, Munich has been seen as the archetypal symbol of the failure of the democracies to stop Hitler. France, which had an alliance with the republic, should have come to its aid. The Czech army, it is said, was tough, its fortifications impressive; the autumn of 1938 would have been the time to stop Hitler once and for all. The German military at this time was much weaker than it was later, and the Third Reich would have promptly collapsed.

Save for the fact that the German military was certainly weak, however, this line of reasoning is nonsense. The problem the Allies had set out to solve at Munich was not Hitler but, rather, a repeat of the Spanish civil war. In that conflict, the military had fragmented, as is generally the case in a true civil war. In Czecho-Slovakia the situation would have been worse: the army, although top-heavy with Czech officers, was drawn from the population at large, which meant that approximately half the men in uniform would not have fought against the Germans. The Slovaks, the second largest minority in the republic, had already made clear that they would not lift a finger to protect the autonomy of a state they despised. Nor would the Sudeten Germans have fought for the republic.

At the same time, in the event of such a conflict, both the Hungarians and the Poles would have moved in on the eastern portion of the country. The Poles, who still wanted the Duchy of Teschen, made no bones about the feeling that their national security was best served by a common border with Hungary, a euphemistic way of saying that Ruthenia had to disappear.[9] The Hungarians felt, with a good deal of justification, that Versailles had dispossessed hundreds of thousands of Hungarians, who were now stranded in Masaryk's state. Both countries would have entered the war — provided they thought they could win.

Moreover, the Allies would have faced the same problem in coming to the republic's aid that they later faced in Poland, only more so: How could they assist a nation surrounded on three sides by its adversary? There was no way to transport troops there, nor did Britain possess the strategic bomber force with which to batter the German cities into submission—assuming, of course, that British public opinion would have tolerated a series of Guernica-style bombings.

Much has been made, subsequently, of the Czech system of fortifications, but again, it was more appearance than reality. These forts, modern, impressive, but seriously incomplete, ran along a key stretch of the border between northern Bohemia and Saxony. Had they been fully manned and equipped, they would have been a formidable obstacle—to an invasion from the north. But the German-speaking areas were mostly to the west and the south, along the borders with Bavaria and Austria. The fortifications were irrelevant to the situation of September 1938, even had the Czech army been a unified force.[10]

Initially, both Daladier and Chamberlain were mobbed on their return home by a populace gratified that there would be no war. The German mechanized columns that appeared in western Bohemia and trundled through Karlsbad (Karlovy Vary) were greeted by equally enthusiastic crowds of Sudeteners. And now events—and Hitler—conspired to give the pendulum a hearty push. Ironically, having engaged in all sorts of shameless manipulations of the world at large, Hitler was going to be nailed for a situation over which he had surprisingly little control: the collapse of the state Masaryk had conjured up at Versailles.

Most people believe that, having devoured the Sudetenland and thus rendered the Czech Republic defenseless, Hitler decided to grab the rest of it. Both claims are wrong. The state that had originally been envisioned in 1918 did not include the Sudetenland or the fortifications in the areas where the bulk of the German population lived. Militarily speaking, the country was no less capable of defense after the first partition than it had been beforehand. In terms of morale, however, the story was different. What Munich signaled was that Central Europe was essentially going to be left to the German sphere of influence, and the nations there reacted accordingly—the Czechs no less than their neighbors.

The Poles still wanted the Duchy of Teschen and the end of Czech-mandated Ruthenia, the Slovaks wanted their own country, and the Hungarians wanted the frontiers between their country and the Czechs (and the Slovaks) redrawn, as well as Ruthenia. Since most of this territory was in what the Slovaks planned as their new country, Hungary's loudly expressed intentions were troubling. Nor were the Czechs willing to let the Slovaks or the Ruthenians steal away into the night unimpeded.

On October 1, 1938, German armored columns crossed the border into the emasculated Czech Republic, occupying the Sudetenland. Three days later, the Hungarians proposed to Hitler the annexation of Slovakia and Ruthenia. On October 8, the Ruthenians (Ukrainians living in the Czech Republic) presented Prague with a list of members for what would be an autonomous regional government. The Slovaks had already met two days earlier and had come up with a parallel proposal. On November 22, the Czecho-Slovak Republic officially became a confederation of Czechs, Slovaks, and Ruthenians, each group to have considerable local autonomy in its local areas.

But by then the Slovaks were beginning to panic. Negotiations with Hungary had broken down, and on November 2, representatives from Germany and Italy met in Vienna and readjusted the boundary between Czecho-Slovakia and Hungary; the latter thus got back the roughly 600,000 ethnic Hungarians who had been stuck inside the Czech Republic at Versailles.[11] Teschen was restored to Poland, and Germany acquired a small piece as well. The Slovaks, who had been hapless bystanders with no say in the foreign policy of the republic, saw that at this rate, they would end up again under Hungarian domination.

While some Slovaks sought real independence, as far as the Czechs could make out, the Slovak idea of autonomy was, for all practical purposes, de facto independence. Thus in February 1939, as the Spanish civil war slowly came to a bloody end, the Czechs drew up a plan to occupy Slovakia. The plan was so secret that neither the Czech prime minister nor his minister of defense knew about it; it nonetheless existed. On March 10, a version of the plan was put into effect, and Prague attempted to name a new Slovak government. On the thirteenth, the Slovak leaders went to Berlin, because Hitler had agreed the day before to guarantee the new state's independence (as it were). Without Slovakia, there was obviously no more Czecho-Slovak Republic, so events happened quickly: by March 15, German armored cars were in the streets of Prague. On that same day, the Ruthenians declared their independence, only to see Hungarian troops invading the country, with the tacit approval of Warsaw.

Although it soon became established in the West that Hitler had orchestrated all these events, the motivating tensions predated Hitler's rise to power by decades. Considered from the point of view of diplomatic history after 1918, Hitler's decision was harmless. The Slovaks had always (post–1918) wanted their own country, they were as entitled to one as anyone else, and Germany had every right to guarantee its existence and to insist that Hungary and Slovakia settle their differences peacefully. Hitler would insist on the same thing with Hungary and Romania, embellishing his credentials as a man who had unified Germany peacefully and had reversed the injustices of the Versailles and Trianon treaties without a shot being fired.

From the point of view of the Germans, the Poles, the Slovakians, most Hungarians—and some Ruthenians—this was a perfectly logical development, and one probably viewed favorably (in private at least) by a good many foreign ministries in the West as well. For the French and the British public at large, however, the dismemberment of the Czecho-Slovakian Republic was the last straw. Again the complexities of Central European ethnicity were, for most people, not merely abstractions; they were daunting abstractions of the sort that only the professional diplomats of the previous century understood. The disappearance of an entire country, though, was concrete enough. It was rendered all the more so by the defiant "come and get us" speeches that Hitler had been making through the fall of 1938.

For the officers of the Wehrmacht, the events of 1938 were astonishing and persuasive. Whatever feeble ideas had been circulating inside the German military about a coup were aborted, because national opinion was now firmly set on the opposite trajectory. Hitler had not only restored the country to its former greatness; he was well on his way to extending its borders past the limits of 1871 or 1914, and all without a shot being fired.

It was this last consideration that dissuaded the senior officers from whatever notions they had been entertaining. Their opposition to Hitler, never very marked, had been based primarily on the fear that his actions would precipitate another war, a conflict that, given the attitudes and strengths of France and the Soviet Union, would be a calamity for their country. But bloodless victories are difficult to counter, particularly when accompanied by delirious crowds lining the roads. The matter was as true in Bohemia as it had been in Austria—that it existed at all suggests the complexity of the situation.

Hitler, wickedly shrewd, judged both the mood of the times and the tenor of his foreign opposition perfectly. And his cleverness, no less remarkable for being profoundly evil, in turn allows us to understand his increasing hold over the military leadership—at precisely the moment when the British and the French people began to dig in their heels and demand he be stopped.

They were also more perceptive than their leaders. Germany had no sooner absorbed the last of the Czechs than Hitler took two significant steps. About one of them—perhaps the more important—relatively little is known. But at some point the Germans and the Russians began serious talks that resulted in the infamous pact of August 23, 1939, in which they agreed not to attack each other and to divide northern and eastern Europe into two zones of influence. We don't know the exact date when the decision was made, but on April 17, 1939, to everyone's surprise, the Soviet ambassador to Germany made a speech in which he observed that differences in ideology certainly shouldn't prevent the two countries from getting along with each other.

Stalin's creatures had been instrumental in shaping and intensifying the prevailing climate of anti-Fascist opinion in the West among the

Communist parties, and had used the war in Spain to whip the world
into a frenzy. So the ambassador's remarks, an astonishing about-face,
were dismissed as an utterance of no consequence whatsoever. If noticed
at all, they were seized upon as a indication that Stalin was not in complete control of the party and the state. In reality, the speech was the fore-
cast of a sea change in the relations between the two great tyrants.[12]

The actual agreement, which caused consternation when it became
public, was subsequently subjected to a series of torturous deconstruc-
tions by scholars who were simply unwilling to admit that the two great
tyrants had been feeling each other out for months and months—since
the spring of 1939 in fact.[13] But they had been, and they came to an
agreement easily enough, thus dooming Poland before a shot had been
fired.

The other step we know about definitively: on April 3, 1939, Hitler directed the military high command to prepare for an invasion of Poland.
The era of bloodless victories was over. The Second World War was
about to begin.

THE FALL OF THE WEST, SEPTEMBER 1939–JUNE 1940

He who cannot stand misfortune does not deserve good fortune.

Frederick the Great[1]

On March 24, 1939, the Allies announced a formal guarantee of Poland's territorial integrity. A week later, Hitler was directing the general staff to plan an offensive against Poland. Hitler had finally gone too far: the Poles would fight, the British and the French would fight, the war the Germans feared was now at hand. An interesting legend, but the problem with the idea is that by July 1940, France had been defeated, had sued for peace, and had become a German satellite. The British army, chased back to its island, left most of its weaponry behind. The Germans were in control of Belgium, Denmark, the Netherlands, and Norway. Poland had once again ceased to exist. The war that broke out on September 1, 1939, was a conflict that Hitler won.

Although after September 1939 the conventional wisdom—aided considerably by German propaganda—was that Poland had been squashed like a tin can, its military was tough, aggressive, and fairly well equipped. It had decisively beaten the Red Army in 1921, but in 1939, geography was against the nation. Most of the old Czech-Polish frontier was now the border with Slovakia, a German ally, so the Poles had to face the possibility of an attack on three sides: from the west out of Germany proper, from the north out of East Prussia, and from the south out of the Czech protectorate and Slovakia.

Key industrial areas were right inside the frontier, as were major cities, and the only outlet to the west was the Polish Corridor, a salient running through German territory, roughly eighty kilometers wide, connecting the country to the Baltic ports of Danzig and Gdynia. The corridor was indefensible, Danzig heavily Germanic (and technically a statelet under the aegis of the League of Nations). Without an outlet to the sea, the Poles would be dependent on neighboring countries: an openly hostile Lithuania and the Soviet Union to the north and east, an unstable Romania to the southeast. To defend Poland was a national defense nightmare.

The Polish high command knew this. Their idea, Plan Z, drawn up in 1938, was modified in light of the collapse of Czechoslovakia: it called for a defense of the frontiers, relying heavily on the natural barriers posed by its main rivers. So the Poles divided the military into three army groups (Łodz, Pomorze, and Kraków) and several smaller independent commands (the Narew Group; the Carpathian, Modlin, and Poznan armies). They had little choice. The only strategic alternative was to abandon all the territory to the north of the Bug River and west of the Vistula; in other words, simply to give up the most prosperous and developed half of the country.

Clearly this was an impossibility. Moreover, the abandonment of a large section of the country without a fight would do away with one of Poland's few defensive strengths: Poland is a large country whose terrain is divided into clear sections by its major rivers. A fighting retreat slowly south and east, destroying the bridges across the rivers, would have a powerful effect on the speed of any advance. This was an important consideration, because the Poles believed that if they could stall the German assault for two to three weeks, Allied pressure would bring an end to offensive operations in Poland.

But Poland had no good options for a defensive strategy, other than a fighting withdrawal to the eastern part of the country. Perhaps for that reason alone, the Poles—and the Allies—put an enormous amount of faith in the idea that if Hitler actually started a war, his government would collapse almost immediately. On the other hand, a determined army of nearly two million men was not going to be overcome without substantial combat, and the Poles had recovered from a massive invasion before, having defeated the Soviets on the outskirts of Warsaw.

The Germans had their own troubles, potentially crippling ones. If France and Britain were to be believed, an offensive against Poland would become August 1914 in reverse: smaller forces would have to hold off the French in the west while the bulk of the army conducted offensive operations in the east. But in Poland the road and rail system was sketchy. It would be more difficult for the Germans to move divisions from Kraków to Karlsruhe, Germany, than from Metz, France, to Frankfurt an der Oder. Germany would not be able to mount an offensive with anything approaching the overwhelming force that prudence required. Although they had quantitative and qualitative superiority in tanks, planes, and mechanized forces, the Germans could hardly manage a war on two fronts.

Hitler, who had already considered this problem, came up with a solution. He had carefully laid the groundwork for his maneuvers in the east, intervening directly in peacetime military operations. As a result, the Allies were checkmated almost as soon as they moved the first pawn. Hitler left the planning of the offensive to the army high command, and concentrated on two important areas. The first, the alliance with the Soviet Union, doomed Poland to an attack from the rear as soon as Stalin thought it was prudent. He was no more interested in having the Poles around than was Hitler.

To understand the military significance of Hitler's second move, we have to go back to 1920. Immediately after the stabilization of the eastern frontier with Poland, the high command of the Reichsheer, worried about further Polish aggression and forced to operate with a small standing army, tried to fortify the frontier. But the Allies were adamant that Germany not be permitted even defensive positions, so any attempt at military construction was blocked.

After 1933, however, Hitler approved the appointment of a new head of engineers, Colonel Förster, whose grandiose plans envisioned a Maginot-style defense on the Polish frontier. The relationship between

Förster's projected fortifications and the French ones was much the same as the relationship between German tanks and French and Soviet tanks: overengineered and undergunned. In early 1938, Hitler inspected what had been built, and realized—correctly—that the engineers had gone off on a tangent. The centerpiece of each major French fort was a series of invulnerable turrets and casemates, each with clusters of rapid-firing guns and mortars that could interdict any enemy action taking place within a circle of from five to ten kilometers. The French forts were like battleships: everything centered on delivering high explosives to the enemy. Förster was building battleships, too, but he had forgotten to equip them with their batteries of heavy guns. All he had were enormous underground infantry shelters.

Hitler scornfully rejected the plans, arguing that all the engineers were doing was moving men underground where they would be besieged or exterminated. He then made two decisions, one technical, the other of great strategic interest. In July 1938 he personally wrote out the precise specifications for the types of fortifications that should be erected, opting for smaller (and infinitely cheaper) blockhouses that would form a defense in depth, each structure housing a combination of automatic and antitank weapons. In essence, it was the same type of system that the French had begun building to supplement the Maginot Line after 1934.[2]

There was nothing unique or even unusual about the specifications—although the fact that Hitler was drafting them himself is a good indicator of the essential rudderlessness of German military projects in the Third Reich. The striking thing was the change in strategic direction: Hitler aborted the eastern projects and demanded that the engineers turn their attentions to the west.

As the campaign against the Czechs intensified in the late summer of 1938, so did the pace of construction. When Hitler began his increasingly strident public denunciations of the Czechs, they were accompanied by statements about the fortifications in the west, thus in effect daring the Allies to attack him. Although the peak period was fall 1938, the work continued afterward, and by mid-1939, the Germans had a dense system in place.

Lacking expertise in turret and gun design (and stubbornly determined to go their own way), the German engineers carried out Hitler's strategic plan by supplementing the weakly armed fortifications with a combination of mines and tank obstacles—belts of stubby concrete pylons first used (apparently) by Czech engineers in northern Bohemia. The idea was to control the path of the attacking armor, forcing the tanks into channels that were actually minefields. This, in turn, would separate out the infantry from the armor, ensuring that any attack quickly degenerated into the suicidal onslaughts of the previous war, where the Allied infantry had been hurled against machine guns firing out of protected concrete shelters.

Thus Hitler's preparations for a campaign against Poland had begun nearly sixteen months before the directive of April 1939, since the Allied response to an offensive against Poland would, by definition, be the same as one aiming to stop an invasion of Czechoslovakia: a military offensive into Germany itself. If that attack stalled out on the new defensive fortifications on the country's western frontier, then the bulk of the army would have a free hand to conduct offensive operations in the east. Provided the Germans could overpower Poland quickly enough, that country's allies would be confronted with a fait accompli and no satisfactory way of responding.

Although a shrewd move, Hitler's fortification plan ignored the impact of what Britain regarded as the twin pillars of its national defense: strategic bombing that would destroy the enemy's means of production and take the war to the population at large, and a naval blockade that would starve the enemy of food and war matériel.

Clearly, however, a blockade would not work. By 1938, Germany had become the dominant player in the Balkans and thus benefited from a steady stream of agricultural and industrial goods from Hungary and Romania. It had also established reliable supplies of minerals and metals from Spain and Scandinavia. Given Italy's support of Germany—and the size of the Italian fleet—the British would have a difficult time controlling shipping in the Mediterranean. And the Scandinavian countries, all neutral, could ship materials to Germany without having to risk the high seas.

At the same time, the Germans, uniquely, had put a great deal of effort into their air defense system. Given the range of British bombers, the adherence to the idea that bombers were capable of offensive actions on their own, and a wildly optimistic belief in the accuracy of level-flight bombing, it hardly took a genius to conclude that the strategic bombing campaign would be a dud—at least at first.

Unless the reconstituted German military proved to be a failure in the field, Poland would have to fight alone, without any real help from Britain. The offensive capabilities of the French were a different matter entirely, but Gamelin, the French army commander, had informed the Poles they'd have to hold for at least two weeks, and it was reasonable to assume that it would be closer to a month before the French superiority in tanks, mechanized units, and artillery would be able to break through the western fortifications. In that case it would be a close-run affair, because to overrun Poland might well take more than a month. Germany needed a quick victory, and Hitler had everything in place to make sure that one occurred.

The one questionable link in the chain was the army itself. To the reader accustomed to tales of slashing armored advances deep into Poland, the actual disposition of German forces comes as something of a surprise. The initial plan set forth five separate axes of attacks, and divided Poland into unequal halves, the demarcation zone being roughly a line running from Warsaw to Cottbus (a city about midway between Berlin and Dresden).

In the northern half, Army Group North consisted of the Third and Fourth Armies. The Fourth Army would attack the Polish Corridor, and the Third Army, operating out of East Prussia, would attack all across a nearly 200-kilometer section of the northern Polish frontier, headed for Warsaw, some 250 kilometers to the south. Despite its importance, the Third Army consisted of only eight infantry divisions, a cavalry brigade, and a tank brigade. But then the Fourth Army, which had only four infantry divisions, two motorized divisions, and an armored division, was responsible for the whole northern section of the border.

Army Group South, the stronger of the two commands, would attack all across the roughly six hundred kilometers of frontier. The Eighth Army, composed of five infantry divisions, would march out of Breslau toward Todz. The Tenth Army, the strongest of all the groups, with six infantry and seven motorized divisions, would head in the direction of Czestochowa (Tachenstoschau), while the Fourteenth Army, consisting of five infantry and three motorized divisions, would attack toward Kraków.

The aim was to attack on three separate fronts simultaneously. No distinction was made between armored divisions and motorized divisions: the assignment of objectives had little or nothing to do with the degree of mechanization or armor in the units.[3] So the German strategy was entirely conventional and entirely predictable.

The Germans attacked on Friday, September 1, 1939. Although driven back on all fronts, the Poles fought desperately. Strategically, they had an unexpectedly decisive ally. Despite claiming he needed a two-week lead, Gamelin, the French commander, had thrown together an offensive into the Saarland by the following Wednesday.[4] Nor was the RAF slow to begin strategic bombing operations.

But neither Allied offensive had much success, nor could it have had, given the German preparations, and by Tuesday, September 12, the French high command was beginning to have second thoughts. German static defenses were difficult to break through, and the news from Poland was bad. Already on September 8, German newspapers were claiming that their troops were on the outskirts of Warsaw. Ironically, the next day the Poles mounted a determined counterattack, and heavy fighting went on until the twenty-first. But by then the Poles had lost. Stalin had belatedly sent his forces into action. On September 17, the Soviet Union attacked and the Polish government fled to Romania; on the twenty-eighth, Warsaw surrendered.

The Germans had quickly achieved control of Polish airspace, mostly because the Poles had made a decision to move their aircraft out of range of initial air strikes, thus preserving their air force for future use. They succeeded, but this proved a serious mistake, and one that was a good example of the failure of airpower doctrines. Before the war, the Allies had pressured the Poles into not making any belligerent moves that might give Hitler an excuse to attack (not that he needed one). So on that fatal weekend of September 2–3, the Poles were still mobilizing and hence extremely vulnerable to tactical airpower.

The correct solution to this problem was to put everything up in the air that could fly, to prevent the Luftwaffe from gaining supremacy—and from massacring the ground troops before they could form up into their units and be deployed. In military terms, this was the only real Polish mistake. In the ground fighting, those Polish troops that had been able to form up and deploy as units gave a good account of themselves, and the survivors were still holding out as best they could into the first week of October, although by then the campaign was clearly over.

Despite subsequent claims about the impact of armored units, German tactics were conventional.[5] The only novel tactic was the deployment of the air force, but little was happening on the battlefield that hadn't been seen in Spain three years earlier. Nor did the new mixture of armored, mechanized, and light divisions prove particularly successful. The third group was promptly scrapped, and the armored commanders gloomily dealt both with their serious losses (about a fifth of the tank force) and with the realization that most of their tanks (the Mark 1 and Mark 2) were unsuitable for modern warfare.[6] Like men waking up after a prolonged debauch, though, the German commanders pondered a far worse situation than the failure of the tank industry: they were now at war with France and Britain.

Hitler's propagandists immediately claimed swift victory, and the French and the British were only too glad to help them out: the idea that Poland had fallen in a few days (a week or so at most) directed attention away from their failure to bring any meaningful aid to their ally. From the boasts issuing from Berlin it was only a short step to the assertion that the arrogant, reckless Poles had only themselves to blame; such a charge was quickly made, and duly repeated by subsequent historians. The one war that the Allies were capable of winning was the war of excuses.[7]

Unlike his generals, Hitler was unfazed; indeed, he was brimming with confidence. Even before the last Polish garrison had capitulated, Hitler was insisting that France be attacked. Field Marshal Walther von Brauchitsch received a directive from Hitler to that effect early in October. In this (as usual) lengthy document, Hitler insisted, "The attack is to be launched, if conditions are at all possible, this autumn."[8]

Von Brauchitsch was so flushed with success after Poland that he promptly went to Hitler and said the idea was impossible; according to General Siewert, his adjutant, "when he found he could not convince the Führer, he began to think of resigning."[9] Instead, he and the other senior generals dug in their heels, and there followed a series of confrontations, with Hitler "ordering" an attack on France no less than eleven times between November 1939 and April 1940. Each time, the order was canceled, and the only action German troops saw before May 10, 1940, was in Norway.

There was method in Hitler's apparent madness: despite their losses in equipment and the need to replenish stocks of ammunition and fuel, the Germans, in October 1939, would have caught the Allies still mobilizing for war. Most of the British Expeditionary Force was in the process of setting up shop on the Continent, and French war production was just hitting high gear. The Allies were substantially stronger in May 1940 than in September 1939, whereas the Germans were hardly better equipped than they had been earlier. That the result was an Allied disaster should not blind us to the fact that there were other possibilities.

The internal wrangling worked to Germany's benefit. The recurrent threats of an offensive tied down the French, and as time passed, the infighting allowed for a reconsideration of the feeble and predictable offensive plan that the general staff in Berlin had produced. But the big advantage for the Germans came directly from the Allies themselves; it was handed to Hitler by Stalin, whose unprovoked aggression against Finland, at the end of November 1939, fueled a growing obsession with Scandinavia in London.

The passage of time was helpful to the Germans in two other ways. It fueled the not-yet-extinguished hopes in London and Paris that some sort of peace could be negotiated, and it permitted the various Communist parties to reorient themselves in conformance with Stalin's directives: Hitler was no longer the enemy but a friend—the days of the anti-Fascist front were over.[10] Because of the strength and discipline of the French Communist Party, the defense industry would be seriously crippled, as indeed it was.

Once Hitler had a plan of operations for the offensive in the west in front of him, he was justifiably critical. The best the planners could offer was, essentially, to reproduce the offensive that von Moltke and Ludendorff had come up with before 1914: a great sweep through Belgium moving to the south, only this time the Netherlands would be included as well. It was difficult to imagine that the French wouldn't be prepared for the assault, and although this time the Germans would be able to use their entire army, they would have more to contend with on the part of their enemies: a large Belgian army, the growing British Expeditionary Force, and a small but determined Dutch military.

But fate intervened, in the form of Stalin's aggression against Finland, an attack that galvanized the West and convinced the high command in London that the best chances for victory lay in a long war during which their superiority in strategic bombers and surface vessels would allow the Allies to strangle Germany economically. Aware that, as noted earlier, a blockade would have little effect on food supplies, because of the German hold on Central Europe and the Soviet alliance, the British, mostly at Churchill's urging, considered the idea of cutting off Germany's iron-ore imports—the one serious area of vulnerability that would have an immediate impact on the nation's ability to manufacture arms. The Russo-Finish War thus provided a perfect excuse for Allied intervention.

The less said about this bizarre conceit the better; the point is that Scandinavia began to occupy the attentions of the Allied governments to the exclusion of France. At the same time, Gamelin was receiving continuous reports of an impending attack, since Hitler kept issuing directives to that effect. By January 1940, the Allies were operating schizophrenically:

planning an invasion of Scandinavia with one hand and standing on the defensive in France with the other. The result was a curious mixture of fatigue and diversion, all of it to the advantage of the Germans.

While the army leadership wrangled over changing the basic plan for the offensive, Räder pondered the grand strategy of this new and unexpected war. Like a great many other people (Neville Chamberlain, for instance), the good admiral had taken Hitler at his word and assumed there would be no war for many years—and certainly not with Britain. Like nearly everyone else, then, he was astounded when the war actually started. When recovered, he set out to examine what the navy could do with its limited resources.

Räder began to consider Norway. If the Germans seized that country, all sorts of advantages would accrue. They could stopper the upper end of the North Sea, protect the flow of raw materials into Germany, interdict Allied supply routes, and threaten the main base of the Royal Navy at Scapa Flow, in northern Scotland. If Hitler really intended to strike east and fight the Soviet Union, Norway would be invaluable: from bases there, the Germans could shut down one of the main supply routes into Russia.

This was thinking on the grand strategic level, and Räder was basically alone in his point of view; he was, in other words, the only senior German commander, Hitler excepted, who was thinking strategically. And Hitler, who was, at the same time, becoming interested in Erich von Manstein's ideas about the ground offensive in the west, not only agreed with Räder; he put the navy in charge of the whole operation, even though it would involve a substantial allocation of Luftwaffe strength.

Either by chance, German efficiency, or Allied bumbling, Räder's Norwegian operation beat the Allies to the punch. Their expeditionary force was already at sea, headed for an invasion of neutral Norway, when the Germans landed there. Embarrassingly, despite the Royal Navy's regarding the North Sea as its private pond, the whole German naval force had managed to get by them. There was a price to pay: Räder lost a sizable portion of his already heavily outmatched surface fleet, and the airborne troops tied up in Norway fighting the British around Narvik were not available for the May offensive, thus forcing the Germans to improvise (very badly) for the airborne component that was needed in Luxembourg.

Although run by the navy, the German operation in Norway was a startling lesson in the power of the Luftwaffe. German planes repeatedly attacked British ships, sinking one destroyer and preventing additional landings, while the roughly five hundred transport planes landed about thirty thousand men, together with thousands of tons of supplies, negating what should have been the substantial Allied advantage, its overwhelming naval superiority.[11]

The Allies lost on every level. Despite control of the sea, coalition troops (British, French, Polish, and Norwegian) were unable to wrest Norway from the outnumbered and undersupplied German airborne and mountain troops—an ominous portent for any future ground combat. Some of their best troops and officers—personnel the Allies desperately needed in France—were still stranded in Norway on May 10, 1940: the French alpine division, a brigade of the Legion, the Scots Guards, the Sherwood Foresters, the Yorks and the Lancs, the Leicesters—and far too much equipment, which was already in short supply.[12]

Although the Royal Navy was justified in claiming victories at sea over the Germans, it lost what was essentially an entire carrier battle group. That, too, was a grim omen for the future of the war at sea. What was perhaps worst of all, however, was that, thanks to Räder, the British and French governments were fixated on Norway to an extent that today seems incredible.[13] So was public opinion. When the Germans struck west, the only people paying attention were the Dutch. It is a truism in war that it is difficult to recover from faulty initial dispositions. For the Allies, this would prove, fatally, to be the case.

The first German offensive plan involved the same massive sweep through Belgium that von Moltke and Ludendorff had hit on before 1914, mostly because of geography. But by 1939, the Germans estimated they would have to fight their way through Belgium—one reason they were so unenthusiastic about the campaign.

Erich von Manstein had been thinking about this problem. His idea was simple enough: it was doubtful the Allies would remain on the defensive. Instead, they would move into Belgium in force, coming to the aid of the main Belgian defensive line whose fortifications dominated the Meuse River valley. So von Manstein proposed a grand flanking movement that was the opposite of the one being considered—it would come out of the left side of the German line rather than the right, move to the northwest rather than to the west and southwest. The advancing Germans would thus trap the Allied armies inside Belgium, cutting them off from their bases.

Since flanking movements had always been the preferred German offensive method, there was nothing particularly innovative about the idea, and its aims were classical: envelop the enemy and then annihilate it in a great battle (or force it to surrender). The novelty of the concept lay in the fact that it was a major gamble of the same sort that had characterized Räder's Norway campaign. The admiral had reckoned that he could not only move the invasion force to Oslo—and hold it—before the Allies could arrive but that his task force could elude the Royal Navy. He was right, but it had still been a gamble.

What von Manstein was proposing was even more of a risk: he was betting that the Germans could traverse the rough terrain on their left and get behind the Allied armies pouring into Belgium before those forces could either reach the Meuse or turn around and extricate themselves from the trap. Both operations had a fatal flaw. The British navy was slow to react and easy to fool, but once the battle was joined, it was a formidable opponent, and particularly when it outnumbered the adversary. Räder's officers would find this out the hard way. In the Narvik fjord, the British slugged it out with his destroyers and annihilated them on April 10–13, 1940.

The equivalent flaw in von Manstein's plan was his assumptions that the Germans could execute this massive left-flank advance in the face of the powerful French forces along the frontier. There weren't that many roads leading into France, and the area was split up with rivers. And if the French air force started bombing the roads and bridges, few tanks would be left by the time the most vulnerable part of the frontier was reached. The question was not—as was claimed at the time—whether mechanized columns could be run through the rough terrain of the Ardennes Forest, which straddles the frontiers of the three countries. The question was whether the Allies would allow this to happen. Simple prudence— assuming that your enemy is competent—suggested they wouldn't.

But Hitler was enthusiastic. The idea of a sudden bold stroke appealed to his instincts, and was, moreover, consistent with what Heidegger had seen (correctly) as his philosophy. The great man lived in the moment; his existence was realized by his immersion in it. He could seize the moment and astound both friend and foe with his boldness. Nietzsche had spoken of those people, contemptuously, as *die Herde*, the herd, which by January 1940 pretty much describes how Hitler felt about the army's senior commanders. They were suppressing the real talent, men like von Manstein. The only one with any spark to him was Räder (and Luftwaffe officers like Kurt Student, who were pushing for the airborne invasion of the Netherlands).

So with a stroke of his pen, Hitler empowered three wild gambles: Norway, the von Manstein plan, and the twin aerial assaults on the Netherlands and the Belgian forts. Chronologically, this is an oversimplification: these operations were proposed and authorized at different times, but basically the events merged in the first quarter of 1940—much to the chagrin of the high command, whose generals doubted that any of these plans would work.

Although much was subsequently made of what was claimed to be a brilliant shift in German plans dictated by von Manstein and Hitler, the actual deployments were similar to the initial dispositions, and the internal wrangling meant that German commanders had no real objectives when—and if—they broke through into France.[14] Heinz Guderian records that when, in March 1940, he briefed Hitler on how, in five days, he planned to move through Luxembourg and Belgium and cross the Meuse River at Sedan, Hitler asked him what he intended to do then, after he had established a bridgehead across the Meuse. "He was the first person who had thought to ask this vital question," Guderian records.[15]

This was an ominous portent for future campaigns: flashes of brilliance marred by a failure to enunciate objectives clearly and precisely, accompanied by a good deal of foot-dragging and nay-saying.

For no particular reason, the attack of May 10, 1940, caught everyone except the Dutch by surprise. In London, the new prime minister, Winston Churchill, woke up to find that war had broken out in earnest— and on what was essentially his first day on the job. An unpleasant reality, and for the Allies, things went downhill from there.

In light of the numerous accounts of these fateful weeks, including my own, I will content myself with singling out some of the more significant events that shaped the course of the fighting, both in France and afterward. One part of the great gamble was the airborne invasion of the Netherlands, in which a combination of parachute drops and assault landings would secure vital sections of the country and hold them until the ground forces could arrive. As the Netherlands was, to a great extent, separated from the other theaters of action in the west, events unfolded there separately. And since the nation surrendered after five days of bitter fighting, certain developments are often passed over.

Chief among them is that although the airborne assault succeeded, it did so at considerable cost to the Germans. Dutch landing fields were littered with Ju-52 transport planes, and the Luftwaffe lost a large proportion of its carrying capacity in those few days: of the 430 transports deployed, 280 were destroyed.[16] But then the Dutch air force, unlike its counterparts, had launched everything it had into the sky in a desperate bid to halt the offensive. Its tiny (123 aircraft) force was annihilated (88 planes lost), but by the time the fighting was over, the Germans had lost over one-third of the 900-plus planes deployed for the operation.

That the government of the Netherlands quit the war when it did is proof of the efficacy of prewar propaganda, in which it was opined that cities would be destroyed from the air. The fate of Warsaw seemed to confirm what an unholy combination of propagandists, pacifists, and airpower theorists had claimed was the case in Spain. In reality, Warsaw was bombed and shelled because its inhabitants refused to surrender; it was a legitimate military target. Moreover, much of the damage was done not by bombs but by shelling.

The fate of Rotterdam was less ambiguous. Through what seems to be, in retrospect, a horrible accident involving communications between the Dutch and the Germans (and German ground observers and pilots), the city was heavily bombed.[17] By later standards, the number of dead (under one thousand) was minimal. But the government, shaken to its core, promptly quit the war, an event that empowered the strategic-bomber enthusiasts, who now had proof of the effectiveness of their weapon. It's no exaggeration to say that Rotterdam thus set in motion the great bombing raids that epitomized the Second World War.

The government's decision to quit, however commendable its humanitarianism, was militarily foolish; the Dutch army felt it was holding its own, and Dutch soldiers were more than willing to continue the fight, an observation that I think reveals the true cause of the Allied defeat. It had little to do with what the armies were doing and everything to do with the overly hasty willingness of the governments involved to surrender after the first disaster.

As the Wehrmacht struck the Netherlands, it also launched a startling operation against the great Belgian fortress of Eben Emael. At one level, the assault was a repeat of August 1914. Because of the steep hills on both sides of the Meuse River as it makes its way south into France from Belgium, the German forces had to be able to cross the river at the one place where the terrain was relatively flat, north of the Belgian city of Liège, close by the Dutch border. To prevent the Germans from succeeding, the Belgians had ringed Liège with forts long before the First World War. Fire from their guns would block attempts to cross the river to the north of the city. Henri-Alexis Brialmont, the great Belgian military engineer, had seen that one additional fort was necessary, but the work involved was so formidable and the cost so great that the government didn't carry out the project. In 1914, this mistaken penury, which was of a piece with the Belgians' refusal to spend enough money to maintain a decent army, cost them their country.

After the First World War, however, wiser heads prevailed; the missing fort was duly constructed, thus giving the Germans an even greater challenge, because Eben Emael had been tunneled into an enormous outcropping overlooking the river. It was so large as to be a sort of Belgian Gibraltar, and its batteries made any German crossing of the river impossible.

By now (post-Poland) Hitler had begun to take a keen interest in what the Wehrmacht was planning. Like von Moltke the Younger, he realized that a successful invasion depended on what the older general had called a coup de main against the Liège forts. The resulting plan was probably the most brilliant operation of the war: combat engineers would land on the fort by glider. Armed with hollow-charge explosives, they would disable the numerous turrets and gun emplacements, thus enabling the ground forces to stream across the river. Parachute descents involved planes, and the drops resulted in men being scattered all over the landscape. Moreover, German paratroopers dropped without any weapons, and had to retrieve them from canisters when they landed. By contrast, men in gliders landed together, had their weapons, and could carry equipment with them—in this case, the hollow-charge packs.[18]

In the French fort system, each fort could give covering fire to its neighbors, so that if troops were landed on top of the structure itself, they would be decimated by artillery fire.[19] The Germans were aided in their assault by the size and isolation of Eben Emael, and, as well, by the fact that the Belgians had not given any thought to the possibility of an infantry assault, mainly because Eben Emael is basically a sizable plateau, and only one side has a sloping approach: the other three sides are close to vertical. So a glider assault was practicable (whereas with the French forts it wasn't, since their engineers had littered the terrain with wire and vertically mounted rails).

The assault involved fewer than one hundred men, was a brilliant success, and opened the door into Belgium and thence into France. It was also unrepeatable: glider troops were uniquely vulnerable as they descended, and the gliders landed without harm only because the Belgians didn't realize what was happening until it was too late. A few rolls of wire, a few hundred rails stuck vertically into the ground, half a dozen machine guns, and the landing would have been a slaughter.

But the operation went well, and the Germans were now able to mount a two-pronged thrust: north of Liège on both sides of the river, and to the south, through Luxembourg. Clearly the success of these sweeps depended on not being attacked from the air, and the Luftwaffe had gone into operation from the first moment of the assault, smothering the Belgian, British, and French airfields. The Belgian air force was particularly hard hit, but then its airfields were the closest targets.

Although Allied planes were in the air from May 10, their efforts were mostly futile. The French and the British air forces relied exclusively on level-flight bombing at low altitudes, a tactic that ignored both the impact of antiaircraft fire and the inherent inaccuracy of the bombing technique. It worked reasonably well against large targets like airfields but was a miserable failure against bridges and highways. And strafing attacks simply didn't work against infantry with antiaircraft guns. In short order, it became obvious that neither air force could operate for long with the level of losses sustained in those first few days.

Basically the air commanders were saying that their forces in the sky were more valuable than either the armies or the national territory—a variant of what had doomed the Poles in September. The arguments are complicated: had the fighting in France continued for long, the idea might well have worked. But at this comparatively early stage, five days into the fighting, a factor emerged that had devastating repercussions.

In the early morning of May 15, Paul Reynaud, the French prime minister, telephoned Churchill to say that his country had been defeated and that all was lost. No greater instance of panic among politicians exists. At that moment the three Allied armies were still intact, and one of them, the British, had done little fighting. French armored forces had won a tactical victory in Belgium and been involved in a real slugging match as their heavy tanks tried to stop the German forces now crossing the Meuse at Sedan.[20]

It was certainly true that the breakthrough was bad news, but it was hardly a defeat. On the contrary, the French had been fighting hard, and their commanders on the ground were confident—particularly those who remembered the horror of August 1914, when French armies, beaten everywhere in the field, were streaming back toward Paris. Nor did Hitler believe he was on the verge of a great victory. In fact, he was planning to move his headquarters farther west, to a specially constructed command complex in the Belgian village of Brûly-de-Pesche (north of Rocroi).[21] On May 17 he was at the headquarters for Army Group A at Bastogne, nervous about what he—and the staff—believed would be a massive French counterattack directed against the German left flank. He was determined to be directly behind what everyone assumed would be the German lines in southwestern Belgium, as the next phase of the war began.

But Reynaud's panic attack collapsed the Allied war effort. The British promptly began to retreat, alarmed that if the French front collapsed, their forces would be cut off from the Channel bases of departure. At this moment, as far as the top levels of the various governments were concerned, it was every bureaucrat, politician, and ancient general for himself. So while French field commanders fought on desperately, the British were ordered to retreat back to Dunkirk. And retreat they did, without bothering to inform the Belgians about what they were doing. Thus with one hysterical phone call, Reynaud had set in motion a domino effect: the British retreat, sensible enough if all was lost, opened a hole in the line, cut off the Belgian army from the Allies, and resulted in its eventual capitulation. Although I'm always suspicious of historical events that are attributed to the actions of one man, it is difficult to escape the conclusion that with his hysterical phone call, and given the situation on May 15, 1940, Reynaud lost France and ensured that Hitler's gambles would pay off.

It is a commonplace that the Germans won in 1940 because they were superior at every level, but this notion is simply not true. They stretched themselves thin, gambled hugely, and won because their adversary panicked. Generally, French and Belgian troops fought their adversary to a draw, and most of the engagements were resolved by an Allied retreat in obedience to orders, and not, as had been the case in

1914, because they were beaten in the field. The scope of the German victory was not without a cost: 27,074 men killed in action, and another 18,384 missing—most of whom were in all probability killed but their remains were never found. By the end of the fighting, the French had at least 92,000 men killed in action.

Like the Dutch, the Belgians fought hard.[22] The casualty figures tell the story: the Dutch had 2,157 men killed in action, the Belgians 7,500, and the British 3,457 (most of the losses were incurred during the fighting around the ports). The overall ratio of Allied to German dead was about two to one—slightly worse than it had been throughout the last war.[23]

Allegedly the French had no concept of how to use tanks, but in the first great tank battles of the war, at Hannut and around the Gembloux Gap in Belgium, French tanks scored what the Germans themselves thought was a tactical victory over two German armored divisions. That the armor of the misnamed French Corps de Cavalerie more than held its own against the Panzers of the German Seventeenth Army Corps, and that the French Third Armored Division and Fifth Motorized Infantry Division then fought the Germans to a bloody draw on the heights of the Meuse suggests that the notion animating many accounts of 1940 is fundamentally awry.[24] So does the fierce Anglo-French defense of the evacuation ports, and the failure of the Luftwaffe to penetrate that defense.[25]

Even after the evacuation of the British and the capitulation of the Belgians, the French army fought on tenaciously. German casualties in June were significantly higher than in May. The battle was intense enough that Michael Pössinger, a major in the Gerbirgsjäger, won the coveted Knight's Cross for his actions at Juvigny on June 6, 1940. He was credited with destroying seven French tanks.[26]

Examples like this suggest that the conflict was not nearly as one-sided as is often claimed. Had the Allied troops been allowed to stand and fight, had they possessed a leadership with the determination of Joffre, Gallieni, and Kitchener, the first phase of the war in the west would have ended far differently. Instead, the governments fell back on the one thing at which they excelled—blaming others for their own failings. The

British publicly blamed the Belgians, and privately blamed the French. The French returned the favor. The civilians in both governments devoted a great deal of energy to blaming their armies. There was plenty of ill will to go around.

When they stopped blaming one another, the one thing these mediocrities could agree on was that the Germans had won because they were better equipped and used a radically new form of warfare that had caught the Allies by surprise. Ironically, it was the one claim that was untrue. Hitler's gambles had paid off handsomely, not because his army was better but because his opponents panicked at the first serious setback.

But for the Wehrmacht, success spoke for itself: the heady triumph in the west recalled the halcyon days of 1870, of von Moltke the Elder and Frederick the Great. The Germans had always known that they were the best. Now they had the victories to prove it. They also had combat experience against some well-armed, well-led, and highly motivated opponents. Regardless of its numerous deficiencies in matériel and leadership, the army would be tough to defeat.

A FEW DISTRACTIONS
ON THE ROAD TO ARMAGEDDON

It was unfortunate that as its responsibilities grew, the status of
the General Staff should steadily decline.

Walter Goerlitz[1]

General Wever, one of the few senior officers who was both a dedicated
National Socialist and a reader of *Mein Kampf*, had taken away from that
book the unexceptionable conclusion that Hitler's intentions, his priorities, were to the east. I don't think there's any doubt that this was true:
Hitler was talking to the senior commanders about a Russian offensive as
early as July 1940. However, as the only sensible time to begin a Russian
campaign was at the start of summer—the middle of May—when an invading force could count on somewhere between two and a half and
three months of decent weather, the talks were simply general conversations. The actual order to start planning didn't come until mid-
December, by which time the beleaguered military planners had come
up with the blueprints for no fewer than five separate operations.

On July 16, 1940, Hitler gave the order to start work on a plan for the
invasion of Britain in September. Two weeks later, he directed the air
force and the navy to intensify efforts against the British, which suggests
that the invasion would take place in early September (the stepped-up
offensive started on August 8). The logic is easy to follow. Britain was the

last remaining adversary: after a month of aerial attacks, the country should, in theory, be devastated. Given that the Royal Navy had been totally unable to prevent the seaborne invasion of Norway—and was now considerably weaker than it was then—the idea of a cross-Channel invasion was as possible as it was predictable.

But the notion of a successful bombing campaign was problematic. Unlike the Lufwaffe, the RAF had entered the war with a sizable strategic bomber force. By June 1940, the RAF had lost over six hundred bombers and achieved nothing of any significance.[2] Losses in the early raids had been so high that Bomber Command switched to nighttime missions—ensuring that bombs would be strewn randomly around the countryside, since attacks in the dark were even less accurate than those conducted during the day.

The situation was a repeat of what had happened in the First World War, when both Allied and German strategic-bombing missions had promptly careened toward disaster.[3] But the airpower enthusiasts simply ignored the historical record, assuming that technological advances would make bombers unstoppable. As the RAF was discovering, however, the developments in aircraft technology had been more than matched by innovations in air defenses.

So the idea that the Germans could do with a force of short-range tactical bombers what the British had been unable to do with their much more powerful bombing force is simply the triumph of wishful thinking. But Göring was convinced that the Luftwaffe could destroy Great Britain from the air, and Hitler let him try. By July 17, 1940, the Germans had 2,600 aircraft positioned in French, Belgian, and Dutch coastal airports, and another 190 operating out of Norway. The attacks began on August 13.[4]

The Germans promptly encountered the same problems the RAF had. Unescorted bombers had no chance of survival over enemy airspace if the enemy had a decent air-defense system, and the only way to even the odds was to attach a fighter escort to fend off the foe's response. But in 1940 the fighter component of most air forces consisted of short-range fighter planes like the Lufwaffe's Messerschmitt 109. German efforts to produce a long-range fighter had failed. The Me-110, which in theory could provide long-range support, was no match for the British interceptors. So the RAF could simply move its planes farther north, where German losses would be prohibitive when the bombers attacked, since they would have no fighter support.

The German air force command was surprisingly adept at shifting its strategy as the challenges mounted, and the aerial offensive switched to cities, and then to cities being bombed at night. This inevitable regression did no real damage to the targets, left the RAF intact, and caused consternation among German air force personnel, who saw in the changes only indecision.

For the inhabitants of England, the Battle of Britain quickly assumed mythical proportions, but in retrospect there was no chance whatsoever that the German offensive would be successful. The campaign lasted for about two months, beginning in August 1940. By the end of October, the Luftwaffe had lost seventeen hundred aircraft and accomplished very little except the deaths of thousands of civilians. Although the RAF had lost nearly a thousand of its planes, British military production was hardly affected at all, and the morale of the population, despite a decade of being pestered by experts warning that civilization would be destroyed from the air, was, if anything, higher than before. Or, rather more accurately, the British were now considerably more united in their determination to beat the Germans.

Perhaps more to the point, by November 1941 the Luftwaffe was a considerably less potent force than it had been a year—or two years—earlier. The losses in planes could be compensated for, but, under Göring, training of aircrews had lagged significantly. A high percentage of aircrew deaths over Britain had been of experienced men, and the most important measure of actual combat strength, the number of trained and experienced pilots, dropped dramatically during 1940. By November, trained crews were at only three-quarters of the June 1940 strength.[5]

The air force had already been overextended in September 1939. Two years later, the situation had substantially worsened. In addition to the losses of trained personnel, German industry had not managed to produce any airworthy craft. The Me-109 was still the only true high-performance fighter and, like all the other planes in service, was now either obsolete or approaching that condition.

More perceptive than his creatures in the air force, Hitler abandoned the aerial offensive by early September. Abruptly, the focus shifted to the other end of Europe, with directives for plans coming (and going) with dizzying frequency. In September, Hitler began discussing an operation to seize Gibraltar, and thus stopper the Mediterranean. About a month later, on October 12, 1940, the invasion of Britain, code-named Sea Lion, was suspended. One month after that (literally) came the order to produce a plan for seizing Gibraltar. That order coincided with one directing the army to prepare an offensive against the Suez Canal in conjunction with the Italians. A week earlier (on November 4), Hitler had been talking about an invasion of Greece, and the directive was sent down on December 13.

A few days later, on December 18, Hitler directed that planning begin for an offensive against the Soviet Union. Since the plan envisioned an assault commencing on May 15, 1941, and the Greek operation, code-named Marita, was supposed to start on April 6, it seems at first glance that Hitler had simply gone mad with power and assumed he could conquer the world. Indeed, a current leading biographer of the dictator opines that the idea of attacking the Soviet Union is in itself sufficient grounds to question Hitler's sanity.[6]

This is a conclusion that can be reached only by suppressing—or ignoring—an enormous amount of evidence. Taken alone and considered on merit, Hitler's reasoning for a Soviet offensive beginning in mid-May was logical and well thought out. Starting at the end of June was risky, mounting successive operations even riskier. But Hitler was not some wild-eyed risk taker. His triumphs so far were not the result of luck but of careful planning and an uncanny ability to divine the responses of his enemies and adapt to the changing situation. His problem in the summer and fall of 1940, however, was not the behavior of his opponents but of his allies, who managed to scupper his main strategic plan quite thoroughly. And the main culprit was his staunch supporter and fellow dictator Benito Mussolini.

Their alliance in Spain had drawn Hitler and Mussolini together, just as the Italian strongman's support for Germany's Austrian and Czech adventures had given Hitler a sense of profound gratitude for his Italian colleague. Mussolini was, of course, more than willing to profit from their close association. Directly after the collapse of the Prague government in 1939, he had sent the hapless Albanian king, Zog, an ultimatum; on April 7, Italian forces occupied the country. On the twelfth, the Albanian parliament (such as it was) voted to fold the nation into Italy. Mussolini was well on his way to turning the Mediterranean into an Italian lake, while his adventures in Libya and Ethiopia had not only given him a colonial empire but had put the main British route to India and the east in peril (as well as the French connection to Algeria). But September 1939 found him reverting to the traditional hesitancy of Italy when it came to an armed conflict within Europe. Rome, like Madrid, sat on the fence and watched, waiting to see who the winner would be.

By the end of May 1940, Mussolini thought he knew. Italy promptly entered the war, and once again the hapless Italian army was thrown into alpine combat. The French had a profound distrust of Italy, and in the 1920s they had fortified the Franco-Italian border. Although its existence is largely obscured today, the southern extension of the Maginot Line was, if anything, more potent than the more familiar northern sector. Militarily, the Italian offensive achieved absolutely nothing. Diplomatically—or rather territorially—it was a success: the Italians got back the portion of southeastern France that Paris had acquired a century and a half earlier.

The Italian high command had seen its share of setbacks in Spain. In this offensive it had proceeded with caution, knowing that the population would not stand for a repeat of the disasters of the Great War, in which Italy had nearly as many men killed as Britain. But Mussolini was ambitious, and his greed drew Hitler into unexpected and unwanted conflicts in the Balkans and Africa.

Mussolini had badly overreached himself. Flushed with Hitler's success, he declared war on Britain and ordered his African troops to take the offensive. Theoretically, numbers alone should have carried the day. There were fourteen divisions in North Africa (more than 170,000 men) and an even larger army in Ethiopia—280,000 troops, although only 80,000 were Italian. To oppose this, Britain had fewer than 50,000 men, although this figure included one armored division in Egypt.

Both African campaigns began well. On July 4, 1940, the Italians invaded the Sudan, and by August 3, British Somaliland had surrendered. In the middle of September, the Italian Tenth Army, attacking out of Libya, penetrated into Egypt proper. But Marshal Rodolfo Graziani, the Italian commander, was cautious. He had been in North Africa long enough to learn that war in the desert was based on mobility and was entirely dependent on good logistics. Both of the Italian armies in Africa were stationed at the end of a tenuous land and sea route, both desperately needed supplies and equipment, and Italy was simply unable to meet their needs. In the desert, sheer numbers counted for little unless you could furnish them with food, vehicles, and other necessities.

Contrariwise, the further the Italians advanced, the better the supply situation for the defending British. So Graziani stopped at an obscure Egyptian town called Sidi Barrani and waited for his supply situation to improve. Mussolini was furious. He wanted Graziani to go all the way to Alexandria, an impossible feat. But Mussolini can hardly be accused of being reasonable. In September he had decimated the air force by sending two hundred planes to participate in the aerial offensive against Britain.

Then, not content with the events in North Africa, he decided to extend Italy's reach into the Balkans. On October 28, 1940, the Italian army, moving out of its Albanian base, invaded Greece. Subsequently the Italian army was treated derisively by both its enemies and its allies, but this is to miss the point. The Italians had the resources to fight one war, but not two or three, particularly on different continents.

Although its planes were, like Germany's, rapidly becoming obsolete, Italy had entered the war with a world-class air force. Some of it was spread out in the two African theaters and put to good use. A British offensive in November to regain Somaliland foundered in the face of

Italian air superiority. Italy also had a first-rate navy; yet as the war progressed, its losses—mainly of destroyers and lighter vessels—mounted in the face of desperate British attacks. In 1940, however, the navy dominated the Adriatic Sea, a fact that, in theory, was bad news for the Greeks. But for reasons that still mystify all concerned, Mussolini refused to authorize either the navy or the air force to participate in the Greek invasion. Possibly he thought that Hitler still intended an amphibious assault across the Channel, in which case the fleet and the air force might have a crucial role.[7]

Despite the African commitment, the Italians still had sizable forces at home, since they had been fighting the French only a few months earlier. What was required in the Balkans, of course, was an overwhelming show of strength, and particularly of a mechanized force that could strike quickly and break through the Greek defenses before winter set in. The Italian army had three armored divisions, but the largest and most powerful—together with most of the army's tanks—was in North Africa; so were most of the relatively scarce mechanized units.

Had the Italians been able to put all their resources into the Greek offensive, they probably would have prevailed. By the standards of 1940–41, the army had decent equipment, while the Greek army consisted, more or less, of men with rifles. But spread out as it was, with its forces not only diluted but to a great extent in the wrong place, the Italian army soon stalled in its various offensives. The Greeks attacked on their own, and in December the bottom dropped out of the Italian adventures on both continents.

In Egypt the British counteroffensive took Sidi Barrani and pressed on, in an illustration of what would seemingly become a fundamental rule of desert warfare: when a town is lost, the only alternative is to move back to the next one, no matter how many kilometers to the rear it is. The Libyan port of Tobruk fell, and by early February 1941, the Italian province of Cyrenaica had passed into British hands, together with more than 100,000 prisoners. What had begun as a great victory was now turning into a great defeat.

Mussolini was desperate. Unlike Hitler, who as chancellor was head of state, he was technically only the prime minister. Italy still had a king, and the *Fascisti* were thus simply another political party—they depended on the support of the population, and in the face of military defeats and heavy losses, that backing was threatened. This is not to say that Mussolini could have been dismissed or voted out of office—although eventually (in 1943) the king did dismiss him—only that he was considerably more vulnerable than Hitler was, almost by definition. But his reputation, and the reputation of the Italian military, had peaked in 1938, thanks to the Italian involvement in the Spanish war and the conquest of Ethiopia. Mussolini had no choice but to turn to Hitler for help.

Now this is, I think, the most curious thing about Hitler. He had a surprising weakness for those whom he considered in some way his loyal supporters—one could almost go so far as to say friends.[8] Mussolini's support, his acquiescence, had been the crucial element enabling the Austrian takeover—and an emotional Hitler had sworn he would never forget. Nor did he, despite the way Mussolini had weaseled out on the war until France was on the verge of surrender and the British had fled the Continent.

Strategically, logically, or in terms of national self-interest, there was no reason for Hitler to help the Italian dictator. Hitler's experiences with Franco had set the precedent. Whatever his regime owed to Hitler and Mussolini, Franco had declined to join their war in any formal sense, thus confirming the old diplomatic adage that nations have enemies but no friends.[9] Germany had no particular interest in Africa, and the Balkan countries were already in the German sphere of influence: Romania and Bulgaria were allies; Yugoslavia was pro-Axis; and until Mussolini had stirred them up, the only thing the Greeks desired was to stay out of the conflict.

More to the point, there was a pressing reason for the Germans not to get involved in the Italian adventures. By February 1941, the date for the Russian offensive had already been fixed: May 1941. Neither Hitler nor his commanders could afford to be distracted. Nor could Hitler simply wave a magic wand and change Mussolini's fortunes. Anything Hitler did to aid Mussolini would require troops and equipment that might still be tied up when the summer began in Russia. There was, in other words, every reason not to bail out Mussolini, and no real reason to support him.

But Hitler decided to help. His decision was a momentous one, and had fatal consequences—insofar as these things can ever be known. Hitherto Hitler's decisions had been shrewdly calculated. There was nothing irrational about them. They were shrewd and successful: France was defeated, Britain nearly so. Now, improbably, Hitler erred, largely if not exclusively because of his feelings for his fellow dictator.

Largely but not exclusively: there certainly could have been an element of calculation. Rather than more futile attacks on Fortress England, why not strike at the source of its power and prestige—its colonial empire? Since the British were in the process of aiding Greece (troops had not yet arrived but were in the offing), there was no better place to humiliate them a third time, to make it clear to the rest of the world that the empire was on the downward slope, that it could neither help its allies nor maintain its colonial possessions.

If this was part of Hitler's calculation, the thinking was not entirely off the mark. The British were desperate to reverse their losing streaks and equally determined that Greece should not become an Italian possession. They were stubbornly pursuing the war in Africa; in the first quarter of 1941, after weeks of hard fighting in both theaters, they managed to regain control of the territories in northeast Africa and had pushed the Italians far back into Libya.

However, it was now London's turn to watch as the bottom dropped out. On February 12, 1941, a German expeditionary force, accompanied by the other two Italian armored divisions, landed in North Africa. Hitler had sent his most famous general, Erwin Rommel, to command the force, which became famous as the Afrika Korps. Rommel had been a first-rate infantry commander in World War I. He had commanded the army detachment assigned to protect Hitler in 1939, and had then asked for and received command of an armored division in 1940.

Brave, clever, resourceful, and politically naive, he was the model of a military commander in the Third Reich. A Swabian from a comfortably bourgeois background with an exemplary personal life, Rommel had soon been turned into a great captain by the National Socialists, magnifying his exploits in France considerably. The Rommel myth was largely deserved. Although his experience had been entirely in the infantry, Rommel understood well the possibilities of armor, and in May 1940 he had proved himself a real tank commander. Even though the German contingent was small (fewer than ten thousand men), Mussolini could hardly complain, since he was getting Hitler's top general.

Rommel promptly smashed the British forces and started the march eastward, only to encounter the same difficulties that had bedeviled Graziani and the British commander in the Middle East, Archibald Wavell: how to maintain an effective combat force with such tenuous lines of supply. Rommel's early successes, coupled with the presence of German troops, created a profound depression in the British commanders, who, to a certain extent, became psychologically terrorized by his reputation. In reality, the secret weapon Rommel brought to Africa consisted of the two excellent Italian divisions, the mechanized and the armored core of the Italian army. And the British now had a serious handicap. British and Commonwealth units had been stripped from Africa to fight in Greece: by March 1941, around fifty thousand men, including an armored brigade.

The British were doing well in the other African theater, where Indian troops were instrumental in the reconquest, but those successes could hardly compensate for the setbacks in Libya. And just as the British were staggering back from that assault, Hitler launched a massive attack in the Balkans.

The planning for the invasion of Greece, code-named Marita, had been in the works since November 1941, as the Germans gloomily anticipated the collapse of Mussolini's Balkan adventure. The high command juggled the various factors involved: the amount of time required to put the operation together, the need to start Barbarossa (the code name for the German invasion of the Soviet Union) in mid-May, and the weather. It would take seventy-eight days to prepare, and the Germans wanted the greatest possible amount of time to elapse between the two operations. If preparations began immediately (in December), operations could begin in early March. Assuming the affair was concluded in a few weeks, the units would have only six weeks to be refitted and moved to their new positions. The time line was barely realistic.

Given the weather and the geography, early March was judged unfeasible. Because early April was the first practicable start date, the forces earmarked for Marita would not be available for Barbarossa. As the force ultimately assigned to Hitler's Balkan adventure grew to nearly thirty divisions, the allocation was clearly going to have an impact on the scheduled Soviet offensive.[10] Over one-third of these divisions were the relatively scarce armored and mechanized units—precisely those most needed for a Russian attack.

There was another serious problem. Germany has no common border with Greece. The only way German forces could reach the nation (by land) was to use Bulgaria as a springboard. But Bulgaria has no common frontier with Germany. So in order for the Germans to strike at Greece, they would have to move their forces through Slovakia, Hungary, Romania, and then into Bulgaria.

Then another wrinkle developed. Hitler had been negotiating with the Yugoslavian leaders, trying to get them into the corral along with Bulgaria, Hungary, and Romania. The Yugoslavians were interested, but not if their participation involved giving transit rights to the Wehrmacht to run over the Greeks. The affair was one of those on-again, off-again diplomatic operations so beloved of foreign ministries, and in February and early March, Hitler met with officials in Belgrade. Both Hitler and the British thought that progress was being made, but then everything collapsed. On March 26 there was a coup in the Yugoslavian capital, and a Serbian-dominated government was installed. Although the new government immediately tried to reassure the Germans, Hitler threw in the towel and told his commanders to add an outline for the invasion of Yugoslavia to their list.

Because the start date for Marita was April 6, 1941, army planners didn't have much time to figure out how to dismember yet another country, so there was a mad scramble to synchronize the two attacks. In fact, the Yugoslavian campaign was organized on such short notice that it never got one of the code names the German military was so fond of. Instead, it was known simply as Operation 25, after the number of the planning directive Hitler sent to the staff.

Logistically, Operation 25 was an amazing feat; militarily, it was less impressive than it might seem. With the military coup, the country was on the verge of a civil war. The Croatian and the Slovenes, figuring that they would be better off with the Italians than with their fellow Serbs, weren't much interested in fighting Axis troops. So when the invasion started, the civil war began as well. The Croatians (and some of the other traditional minorities) in the Yugoslavian army either surrendered or started fighting the Serbians. By April 11, five days after the attack, the Croatians had formed their own state and were demanding the release of all Croatians from military service.

In one key way the Yugoslavian situation simplified Marita. German forces could move through Yugoslavia now, and since the two operations began at the same time, that is indeed what happened. The Germans had another advantage as well. In 1940 the Greeks had moved most of their army to the west as they fought off the Italian offensive coming out of Albania. Although aware of the German threat, the Greek high command decided not to alter the disposition of its forces, leaving them to counter the Italians, planning (or hoping) that the British forces would suffice to check the German advance in northeastern Greece.

Despite desperate Allied resistance, the Germans moved quickly through Greece, and with minimal casualties: about 1,200 men killed in a military campaign that lasted for only a few weeks. By contrast, the army had suffered about the same number of deaths in December 1940—when there was no campaign going on.

British casualties were also light (about 2,000 men killed in action), but the losses in equipment were substantial: thousands of tanks and motor vehicles and more than two hundred planes, at a time when the troops in North Africa needed every tank and truck they could get their hands on.[11] The real disaster was to Britain's reputation: it had sent 58,000 men to Greece at least partially to put an end to the myth of Dunkirk, to demonstrate that Britain could protect its allies. The way things turned out was precisely the opposite. Whatever the strategic value of Greece—which was dubious for either side—the damage to British prestige was substantial. To most independent observers, it looked as though the Wehrmacht was unstoppable. And now came the crowning achievement: the airborne invasion of Crete.

Retrospectively, the Germans had no more need to attack Crete than the British to defend it. The operation was eloquent proof that poorly thought out geomilitary ideas had begun to dictate military operations, just as they had for the Allies with Norway. But the usual retrospective justification—that a British airbase in Crete would have allowed the RAF to bomb the Romanian oil fields, while a German base there would have threatened the Suez Canal—represents fairly the level of strategic thinking on both sides.

Theoretically, there was some truth to the proposition. The Romanian oil fields around Ploesti were, at 1,045 kilometers from Crete (or central Greece), a distance that was only about 10 percent greater than the distance to Berlin from southern England.[12] But in spring 1941, the RAF was having a tough time—despite all the support the home country could afford—inflicting any damage on Berlin, or even on closer German targets. The idea that a bombing campaign could be mounted from a primitive island like Crete was wishful thinking at its most optimistic. Not only would the British have had to build major airbases, but the navy would have had to keep them supplied—not a very likely possibility in what was basically an Italian lake.

Nor was there any chance that the Germans could use Crete to further an attack on Egypt. Nearly 900 kilometers separated the RAF bases in Egypt from southern Greece: the British had been forced to fly their aircraft there and use Greek bases, as the distances were too great for tactical aircraft to make round-trips. At 600 kilometers, Crete was closer, but the distance was still too great for existing German aircraft. By comparison with the Mediterranean, the distance from the French coast to London was trivial. If Egypt fell, it would be because the British lost the war on the ground—aided by German planes based in North Africa itself.

But geopolitical grandiosity was now the order of the day on both sides. The plan for Crete, called Mercury, was devised by Kurt Student, commander of the Eleventh Air Corps, which in turn was part of the Fourth Air Force, the main German air component in the Balkan campaigns. Student and Hitler had worked together before, on the plan for the airborne offensive against Belgium and the Netherlands. At the moment, he was one of Hitler's favorites; one reason was that the airborne troops were considered— correctly in most cases—to be exemplary National Socialists. The idea of a daring swoop onto Crete typified the kind of success Hitler was basing his regime on. And, of course, Göring liked the notion of an airborne invasion of Crete simply to demonstrate the power of the air force, whose prestige had clearly fallen after the Battle of Britain.

The whole affair is perhaps the best example of Hitler's strengths and weaknesses as a military leader. He saw clearly enough that the members of the general staff were hopelessly unimaginative. They had failed to understand the importance of Norway in the new kind of warfare that Hitler realized had begun. Their initial plans for Case Yellow had been archaic. And, as we shall see in the next chapter, their first ideas about Barbarossa were equally anemic. Frustrated, Hitler was prepared to bypass them, and to listen to men outside the hierarchy who had good ideas. So far so good, one might say.

Moreover, Hitler's basic instincts on these matters were generally better than anyone else's, and that was true here as well: Student's plan had been for the offensive to come entirely by air; Hitler insisted there would have to be a seaborne component. In this he was either very shrewd or very lucky. One important factor that would seriously complicate the British defense on Crete was to figure out how to position their forces to handle two entirely different German assaults.[13]

Then there was the downside to these arrangements. The army staff, with surprising realism, was opposed: the earliest date for the operation was May 20, 1941, barely a month before the start date for Barbarossa, and one didn't need a great general to foresee the consequences of tying up two or three divisions of crack troops—and half the Luftwaffe's transport strength—on the eve of such a large-scale offensive.

The problem was that the German high command's preferred plan, although strategically probably better than Student's, was unrealistic: an invasion of Malta. Practically speaking, Malta made more sense than Crete. The island lay squarely across the Italian (and now German) supply routes to Berlin's forces in North Africa, only 160 kilometers from southern Sicily and about 600 from Taranto, in southern Italy. Seizure of Crete might at some future date have a vague influence on the war; seizure of Malta would allow the Germans and the Italians to move men and matériel to North Africa unimpeded. Since that campaign had already begun, clearly Malta made more sense.

But Malta is simply one big fort sitting in the Mediterranean. The main island (there are three islands—technically Malta is an archipelago) is not a lot bigger than Washington, D.C. There were few if any decent places to put down airborne troops, and the island was bristling with antiaircraft defenses. It was also an important naval base for the British, and as the Germans had no ships in the Mediterranean, any attack on Malta would require a major fleet action by the Italian navy.

By April 1941 the British navy, which had bloodied its Italian counterparts continuously, had more capital ships in the Mediterranean than Rome did. There was no way the Italian navy would enter such a fight—nor would any other competent naval staff. German airpower could probably compensate, but that recourse would involve a major relocation. It was one thing to move the German Fourth Air Force from Greece to Romania, from which it could support Barbarossa, quite another to transport the forces from Greece to southern Italy and Sicily. To offer Malta as an alternative was basically to provide no alternative at all.

So on April 20, 1941, Hitler chose Crete. Although Göring assumed direct command of the operation, Loehr, commander of the Fourth Air Force, was the overall commander and Student, in charge of the Eleventh Air Corps, now called an airborne corps, was the man on the spot making the decisions. Student had an impressive force: over five hundred planes and one hundred gliders would transport the reinforced Seventh Airborne Division, backed up by the Fifth Mountain Division and a regiment from the Sixth Mountain Division, 25,000 troops in all. Air cover would be provided by the Eighth Air Corps, under Wolfram von Richthofen, 650 fighters and bombers plus reconnaissance aircraft.

The mountain troops would mostly land by sea, and the Germans had put together a ragtag force of captured Greek boats that they planned to organize into two convoys sailing under the protection of the Italian navy. The plan was simple enough, and mimicked the airborne offensive in Belgium and the Netherlands: 15,000 men would descend from the air, the first wave landing on the existing airfields so that subsequent arrivals could arrive by plane. Meanwhile, the seaborne force would set sail, and transport the heavy weapons and supplies, together with the mountain troops, who would then mop up the resistance. Because it took a month to organize the details, the attack didn't begin until May 20, 1941, one month before the final start date for Barbarossa.

The actual course of the struggle has been dealt with extensively, and only a few points are of serious interest.[14] Just about everything that could go wrong went wrong. German intelligence was a failure at every level. The Luftwaffe believed there were only 5,000 (possibly as many as 10,000) troops on the island, when in reality there were 32,000 British and maybe as many as 15,000 Greek soldiers there. Student assumed that his first assault wave had been successful simply because almost all the transport planes returned safely to base. He knew nothing of what was transpiring on the ground, where the two senior commanders had been killed and the paratroopers were being dropped mostly in the wrong places and massacred as they tried to retrieve their weapons containers.[15] Despite German mastery of the air, a British convoy carrying supplies to Crete blundered into the first enemy convoy as it rounded Cape Spatha, on the night of May 20, and sank virtually the entire convoy.

What saved the day for the Germans was a series of fatal blunders on the other side. Bernard Freyberg, a New Zealander, was in command of the island. Freyberg, who had distinguished himself in the First World War, became the youngest British general of his generation. He was brave, honorable, and utterly conventional. Under his command, the defenders were divided into self-contained battle groups, each charged with protecting a likely landing spot. The idea was good: Crete was mountainous and had few roads, so there was no possibility of shuttling reinforcements from one area to the next.

Then came the bad part. Freyberg's military experience was in the ponderous style of warfare the British had followed in the previous conflict. The fighting was slow and, perhaps more to the point, it was all offense. Now he was charged with conducting a defensive operation, one in which speed of response was all-important. This is a good example of the main Allied problem—the slowness with which crucial battlefield lessons were transmitted. In theory, the British should have learned from the Dutch example in May 1940: the only way to counter an airborne offensive was to throw everything available at it from the first moment. It was like smothering a fire: the best time is when you see the first flames, not when they start shooting out the windows.

This bit of wisdom had not yet penetrated, either to Freyberg or to the soldiers from Australia and New Zealand who made up the bulk of the defenders. Basically they dug in and waited for the Germans to come get them. And despite all sorts of setbacks, they promptly did; on May 28, Freyberg was evacuating the island.

From the British point of view, Crete was an unmitigated disaster. Freyberg left behind more than 12,000 imperial troops and nearly all of the Greek troops. In light of the German command of the air, it was surprising that the British managed to get anyone off, much less 17,000 men. But the cost was high: the navy lost three cruisers, six destroyers, and 1,823 men.[16] British naval forces in the area were mauled: three battleships, seven cruisers, four destroyers seriously damaged; the navy's sole aircraft carrier in the Mediterranean, the *Formidable*, was out of action for months. As a result, even after its serious defeats, the Italian navy was superior to the British Mediterranean fleet, so the navy had lost any hope of controlling the Aegean. The incident was distressing proof of the vulnerability of surface ships to air attacks.[17]

Crete was a major disaster for the Germans as well, although perhaps not in the way it is sometimes portrayed. Fewer than 15,000 of the Ger-

man troops who went into action were airborne, and, given the grim nature of the accounts of their struggles, the death toll is fairly low: 1,653
paratroopers killed in action out of a total for the campaign of 3,352
deaths, with casualties of all sorts coming to about 7,000.[18]

Student, who admitted he had miscalculated, later testified, somewhat melodramatically, that Crete was the graveyard of the German airborne. It would be more accurate to say that Crete was the most
spectacular in a series of miscalculations as to the effectiveness of sending troops directly onto the battlefield by air. In many respects, the aerial
assault on the Netherlands was an even worse disaster, and Hitler's idea
of using paratroopers to seize the main bridge into southern Greece had
backfired as well. In the jubilant days of May and June 1940, the heavy
toll of men and aircraft in the Dutch offensive had been overlooked, but
now the trend was seen, and Hitler—sensibly enough—was unwilling to
continue to mount operations with such a high death rate. Moreover, the
Luftwaffe's transport arm had taken another heavy hit: at maximum
strength the air force had only about one thousand transport planes, and,
one way or another, about two hundred of them had been lost over
Crete. The Germans concluded that large-scale airborne operations
didn't work as advertised.

Crete may well be the most written-about campaign—relative to its
scale and importance—of any part of the war. But two features deserve to
be mentioned, as their significance goes far beyond what happened on
the island. Hitler was furious with Student, whose reputation and influence abruptly deflated—an interesting reminder of the extent to which
the dictator had preserved one aspect of the traditional German military
system, in which the bar for success was set much higher than in other
armies.

In the Allied armed forces, generals soldiered on even after the most
abject failures or a clear demonstration of serious incapacity. But Crete
changed that practice dramatically for the British as well. "I am far from
reassured about the tactical conduct of the defense by General Freyberg," a furious Winston Churchill wrote on June 13, 1940, and Freyberg

never again held an independent command. Unlike previous British wartime leaders, Churchill was going to be ruthless about failure and would keep on replacing generals until he found one who could win.[19]

For Hitler, the abrupt change in the traditional British way of absorbing failure and spinning it into success was bad news indeed. After Crete, the spinning stopped. The British had been in control of the seas around Crete; they had put some of their best troops on the island; and they had enjoyed the inestimable advantage of knowing what was coming, thanks to their success in breaking the German codes. With all this, they still lost. Although, at one level, blaming Freyberg was patently unfair, at another level it was a long overdue recognition that the British problem was leadership, pure and simple. Crete may fairly be said to mark the end of the snobbish and condescending complacency about inept generalship that had, by this point, nearly been the end of Great Britain.

It's easy to see why the Germans missed this—it would be months before the results would become clear, and the string of British disasters was hardly over. But Crete marked something else that Berlin should have seen as worrisome. The bulk of the British infantry consisted of Australians and New Zealanders, together with bits and pieces of elite British regiments (the Leicesters, the First Welsh, the Black Watch, the Yorks and Lancasters). They proved themselves remarkably tough opponents.

I think it can fairly be said that the fighting on Crete was actually the first serious extended ground infantry combat of the war, and it suggested that the historic superiority of the German infantry in combat against its traditional opponents was no longer a given. In most situations German units had historically inflicted many more casualties than they received, regardless of their numerical inferiority. Casualty-exchange ratio is a rough but still significant indicator of superiority in combat.[20] There are, of course, all sorts of excuses for the German side, and many Anglo-American writers would deny the idea, but on Crete, at the bare minimum, the Commonwealth troops gave as good as they got. The bitter fighting should have served as a wakeup call to the Wehrmacht. The day when German generals could assume that their men would simply walk over their enemies, regardless of the situation, was coming to an end.

But all this was in the future. With the humiliating evacuation of Greece, followed by the surprise loss of Crete, British fortunes were at an all-time low. Despite Britain's historic emphasis on airpower, the RAF had been unable to halt the German aerial offensive, and the navy had been unable to prevent the loss of an island lying in the middle of a sea that the British had complacently regarded as an English lake. By June 1941, the German military machine seemed unstoppable.

Although Hitler's involvement had been triggered as much by his feelings for Mussolini—and an awareness of the need to keep the Italian leader in power—as by any sort of strategic calculation, Berlin's new conquests would make it extremely difficult for the Allies to bomb the Romanian oil fields that increasingly had become German pumping stations. With Romanian oil and French and Swedish iron ore, the German military machine was not going to be stopped for lack of resources.

It would be years before the Anglo-American strategic bomber force would have any significant impact on the German war effort, and with all due respect to the courageous aircrews of the Royal Air Force, much of that damage was inflicted by the Americans, whose entrance into the war in the spring of 1941 hardly seemed much of a possibility. In other words, the threat to Germany's raw materials was at best a potential threat that would take time to materialize. And if Hitler's plans continued to be greeted by success, Germany would have Soviet oil and grain, and hardly be dependent on a supposedly vulnerable Romania at all.

In the greater scheme of things, though, it's tempting to say Hitler gained Greece and lost Russia. Here's why. Although casualties in the former were negligible, equipment losses were not. The Germans had deployed nearly half of their armored divisions and a third of their mechanized divisions. Neither category had anything like the vehicle strength required, and after two weeks of mobile warfare, more than one-third of the wheeled vehicles were out of action because of mechanical failures. Mobile warfare in rough terrain was particularly hard on tires and treads,

two items in short supply. Among the many failures of German tank design was a woefully insufficient tread life. The relatively short distances
the tanks had to travel in Poland and France masked this deficiency. But
the dash through Greece made it all too obvious.

After three weeks of such movement, a German tank needed a complete overhaul, and the time between the end of Marita and the onset of
Barbarossa simply didn't allow for the level of maintenance the tanks demanded. For that matter, it hardly allowed for the divisions to get to their
new start line. As it was, one of the armored divisions was still stuck in
Bulgaria when the attack began in late June.

Although overall casualties were light, airborne casualties were a serious problem. In every campaign thus far, the Wehrmacht had made use
of airborne troops through some combination of parachute, glider, and
transport-plane delivery. But the losses in Crete meant that Barbarossa
would have to proceed without an airborne component—in precisely
the situation where it would have had the greatest impact.

Of all these setbacks, the loss of time was the most significant. In
northern Russia there was only a limited period of good weather between
the cessation of the spring thaw and the onset of fall rains, basically a 110-
day window that began about the middle of May. Despite a quarter of a
century of Communism, Russian roads were still generally unpaved, and
a great many of them lacked even the most rudimentary of weather-
proofing, a covering of crushed rock. The logic of meteorology was compelling. A war of rapid movement was over once the rains came, which
meant, in this conflict, the middle of September at the latest. By delaying
Barbarossa until the end of June, the Germans lost a crucial third of their
window. Nor should it be forgotten that in the essentially impossible aerial attack on Britain, Hitler and Göring had decimated the Luftwaffe.

No one of these problems in and of itself was sufficient to derail Barbarossa. Add them together and the Wehrmacht was going into a major
campaign with way too many handicaps. And as we shall see, there was
worse news to come.

THE SOVIET COLLAPSE

The Bolshevists will have the finest army in the world in a very short time, with the finest mechanical equipment.

D. H. Lawrence[1]

There is a widespread idea that, by 1941, the Soviet Union was so powerful militarily that only a fool or a madman would consider engaging it in battle.[2] On the contrary, Hitler thought he could beat the Russians because, in the First World War, Germany and Austria had defeated them so decisively that the Bolsheviks had to sign a humiliating peace treaty at Brest-Litovsk (on March 3, 1918), in which they ceded Ukraine, Poland, the Caucasus, and their Baltic provinces. The government had collapsed in February 1917, a year earlier, and the army was unable to mount serious operations after the summer of 1916.[3] The Germans continued the war in the east not out of military necessity but mainly because easterners—men like Ludendorff and von Hindenburg—wanted to expand eastward and exploit Ukrainian agriculture to counter the effects of the Allied blockade.

Moreover, the German victory against Russia had been achieved despite fighting on the Western Front, northeastern Italy, and the Romanian invasion of Hungary. But Hitler, who had no enemies left on the Continent, could draw on the troops of all the former Hapsburg lands, together with Finland, Italy, Romania, and Spain, as well as the foreign units of the expanding Waffen-SS.[4]

So the idea that Germany would not only win, but win quickly, was consistent with the historical record. And in 1941 the Germans did much better than they had in the First World War. The czar's forces still had control of Riga, the strategically important Latvian city on the Baltic, as late as September 1915. In the Second World War, Riga fell within a week (on June 29, 1941), while the town of Pinsk, anchor of the czarist army's defenses in late 1915, was occupied by the Germans on July 4, 1941.

Nor is there much to the claims about the power of the Red Army and the strength of the Soviet state. The Soviet Union was the most closed society imaginable. Its propagandists and admirers could say anything they wanted without fear of contradiction. Foreigners saw little outside of Moscow, and what little they saw was carefully controlled. Any appreciation of Soviet military strength in 1940–41 was guesswork—and remained so for the next forty years.[5] In reality, the czar's armies had been better prepared for war than Stalin's.[6] For one thing, the czar hadn't murdered nearly all his generals. Stalin had, replacing them with incompetents whose only virtue was sheeplike obedience.

As the Germans had discovered in Spain, the Red Army had some impressive military equipment: its mass-produced tanks and guns were better than anything the Wehrmacht possessed; its aircraft were at least as good. Western observers at the annual Moscow parades—the only time anyone actually saw the Red Army—were duly impressed. But the Soviet military establishment was a Potemkin village. Its thousands of tanks did not mean that it had effective armored divisions, nor did its thousands of planes signify that it had a tactical air force. Essentially it was an enormous warehouse, not a modern army. Its doctrines would prove calamitously unsuitable for modern warfare, its officers worse than amateurs, its command and control systems nonexistent, its logistics hopeless, its leaders appallingly incompetent.[7]

In the traditional accounts, much is made of the fact that the German high command knew so little about its adversary, but there's less here than meets the eye. What the Germans did have was history, the history of the Red Army on the battlefield in two separate wars against smaller countries that were, by contrast, poorly armed.

In the Russo-Polish War of 1920–21, the Red Army initially over-whelmed the Poles, advancing almost to Warsaw, but in July 1920 it was defeated so decisively that Poland stabilized its eastern frontier beyond the limits decreed at Versailles. Humiliated, the Bolsheviks agreed to a truce in September 1920 and signed a treaty confirming the new frontier (the Treaty of Riga) the following March. During this war the Red Army's casualties were roughly four times those of the Poles. In November 1939, the Soviet Union invaded Finland, a neutral country with a minuscule army and hardly any modern equipment. In three months of vicious fighting, the Russians lost at least a quarter of a million men, and Nikita Khrushchev, who was certainly in a position to know, thought the figure closer to a million.[8]

Supposedly this abysmal performance spurred serious reforms. But these changes, initiated at the top, had little impact on the military at large: they were more window dressing than substantial reform.[9] Hitler's decision to attack Stalin may have been wicked, and it may have been wrong, but it was not irrational.[10]

What was staggering about Hitler's idea was the scale. The operation he envisioned was unprecedented in modern warfare, encompassing a vast quadrilateral based on the cities of Berlin, Leningrad, Stalingrad, and Sevastopol. The top three sides were about 1,300 kilometers each, and the bottom section (Sevastopol to Stalingrad), slightly under 1,000. For much of the war, the front was roughly 1,500 kilometers long, about twice the length of the entire Western Front in the First World War. From Berlin to Stalingrad, as the crow flies, is 2,228 kilometers.

On a map, a straight line drawn from Leningrad to Stalingrad would pass just to the west of Moscow; the line would approximate the limits of the main German advance. Take the same map, draw a straight line from Berlin to Bucharest, and the two lines would be almost parallel—an approximation of the limits of the Red Army's advance to the west.

Except in the far southeast, where the Caucasus Mountains begin, the terrain the two sides would fight over is relatively flat, cut by large rivers, and north and west of Ukraine, mostly forest and swamp. In fact, the central feature of geography in European Russia is the Priapit (or

Pripyat) Marshes, the vast area of roughly 100,000 square kilometers that starts northwest of Kiev (the capital and chief city of Ukraine) and runs northward toward Minsk (the capital of what is now Belarus). The marshes lie between the Bug and the Dnepr rivers, and are bisected by the Priapit River before it makes an abrupt turn to the southeast and flows into the Dnepr above Kiev.

No one had ever been enthusiastic about campaigning in this enormous bog, and in the First World War it had formed a natural barrier, with armies fighting to the north and south of it. So any invasion force heading for Moscow out of western Europe would be forced to advance to the north of the marshes, moving in a straight line along the Warsaw-Moscow axis. The major cities along that route would be Vilnius (Lithuania), Minsk, and then Smolensk. The invasion route to Leningrad was likewise a straight line drawn from Königsberg, the capital of East Prussia, through Riga, the capital of Latvia, with the Lithuanian city of Kaunas a little to the south and the Estonian capital, Tallinn, to the north, and thence on to Leningrad. So there wouldn't be much surprise as to where the invaders were headed and how they were planning to get there.

In the fall of 1940, Hitler's planners returned with the obvious: a great thrust generally in the direction of Moscow, which would force the Red Army to stand and fight. Seize the capital and the war would come to a quick end. But there were major problems inherent in the army's idea. It ignored the redeployment of Soviet forces that had been taking place all summer and fall. Prior to August 1939, Soviet fortifications had been located along the frontier with that country. But after the invasion of Poland (and then the Baltic states in 1940), the Red Army was relocated far ahead of its prepared defenses.

There was, of course, no comparison between the older Soviet defensive line and the Czech or Maginot positions, but Hitler knew that highly effective defenses could be put together without the need to build elaborate French-style fortifications. For that matter, no one knew exactly what the system actually comprised.[11] On the tactical level, the Germans had some idea of the Red Army's methods and its equipment—but that was now several years old, and presumably great changes had occurred since then, and certainly since the Finnish disaster.

The net result of Stalin's territorial grabs was to give the Red Army a defensive position of great depth; therefore, heading directly for Moscow would be problematic. Moreover, the Germans were getting some information via Romania and Bulgaria to the effect that the Red Army was massing opposite their frontiers. In this sense, Stalin, who in spring 1940 abruptly confiscated from Romania the land between the Prut and the Dniester rivers, had tipped his hand.[12]

Neither Hitler nor Ion Antonescu, the dictator of Romania, had any illusions about the ability of the Romanian army to stand up against a Soviet offensive. But the initial German plan ignored the fact that an enormous Soviet force was committed to the southwestern front, opposite Romania and Bulgaria. In the event of a German offensive toward Moscow, the Russians could drive straight for the Romanian oil fields and Germany's armored and mechanized forces, as well as its planes, would quickly be out of gas. So the initial German plan, Otto, was like the fabled von Schlieffen plan, which von Moltke the Younger had sensibly pitched into the trash. It defied geography and ignored the size of the German army. Similarly, Otto assumed that the Germans could get to Moscow long before the Russians could get to Ploesti or Budapest.[13]

But these problems only illustrated how out of it the general staff was. They were still fixated on physically destroying the enemy, when the real issue was to shut down his means to wage war and seizing his resources. As the British and French had already realized, modern conflict was as much about controlling strategic resources as it was about winning battles. Although Norway was a fiasco, Churchill had the basic idea. The Third Reich needed oil, iron ore, and food supplies. A Soviet thrust through Romania would be a disaster, as indeed it was when it finally happened, in the summer of 1944. Conversely, seize Ukraine, the breadbasket of the Soviet Union, and the oil fields lying to the east of it, and the Russians would find themselves in the same position.

Resource protection and acquisition, therefore, dictated a strike to the southeast, and that was what Hitler insisted on. In this sense he was right, and the army was wrong. On the other hand—and in such cases there is always a contrary argument—Hitler's ideas committed the Germans to warfare on an extraordinary scale. Ukraine was bigger than Spain—and just as far away from Berlin. Voronezh, the historic center of Russian agriculture ("Black Earth" Russia, as it is still known), was as far from Kiev as Kiev was from Warsaw.

Distance was not the only problem. Although Ukraine is good tank country, the region has a series of rivers that make fine defensive positions or obstacles: the Dnestr, the Bug, the Dnepr, the Donets, the Don, and, finally, the Volga. The southern reaches of the last river mark the end of cultivatable soil as well as of European Russia: Voronezh, up the Don about 900 kilometers northwest of Stalingrad, was the key fortress for Russian attempts to keep out the Mongols. When the Germans got to Voronezh and Stalingrad, they had conquered the most productive part of the Soviet Union.

The basic problem was that the agricultural and mineral resources were at one end of European Russia (the southeast) and the industrial and political resources were at the other end, clustered around Leningrad. So Hitler decided that the offensive would move in two directions simultaneously. Whichever one Stalin tried to reinforce, the other would be fatally weakened.

In the long term, the Soviet Union, with its enormous manpower pool, could replace dead soldiers. But without its industry, it couldn't equip them, and without its agricultural base, it couldn't feed them. It was hardly able to feed them in peacetime, given the appalling state of Soviet agriculture and the disastrous failures of collectivization.[14] Move fast enough, and Stalin would lose the means to wage war, whether he lost his armies or not.

Underneath the bewildering array of plans, minutes, and directives, the internal conflict was simple: the general staff still saw warfare as a series of technical exercises aimed at destroying the enemy on the field of battle. Hitler viewed warfare as a means to an end, the seizure of the enemy's resources. But the plan actually executed in June 1941 was the same broad-front offensive that had marked Fall Weiss in September 1939 and Fall Gelb in May 1940. The only change was that the Germans now had enough experience to believe that they could move quickly through European Russia and seize the key objectives before the Russians could react.

If there was a flaw in this plan, it lay in the contradiction between Hitler's strategic thinking and the conventional ideas of his leading generals, a contradiction that had serious repercussions. On the planning side, it meant that the army commanders were given vague objectives.[15] On the operational side, it meant that there would be an inherent conflict between the more aggressive field commanders, who would see their instructions as providing them with license to fight their own war, and the army chain of command. Hitler was already suspicious of the army command, a state of affairs that encouraged direct communications with the field commanders. The net effect, noticeable almost immediately, was to reduce the army's high command to impotence and passive aggression, and indeed the manifestations of those attitudes, the smugly pessimistic "I told him what would happen but he didn't listen" syndrome, can be seen as early as July 1941.[16]

In its previous offensives, the Wehrmacht had achieved tactical surprise. Even though the countries being attacked knew they were threatened and that an attack was imminent, they were still caught off guard by the precise date, were uncertain as to exactly where the blow would fall, and were faced with tactics and technologies they hadn't equipped themselves to contain.

Given that the Third Reich leaked like a sieve when it came to military matters, that it was hardly possible to assemble an army of two million men in secrecy, and that the British, thanks to their code breaking, knew what was going on and passed the information to Stalin, the extent to which the Soviet Union was caught off guard by the German attack has always been a puzzle.

For a long time, even a discussion of June 22, 1941, by historians was off-limits in the Soviet Union, and it is, I think, impossible not to feel a certain instinctive agreement with Khrushchev's condemnation of Stalin in his famous speech of February 25, 1956. Stalin had established himself as the omniscient dictator who had created an enormous, invincible military. It was Stalin, and Stalin alone, who insisted that the attack was a surprise, when in reality he had been deluged with warnings from all sides.

But let us give Stalin, like the devil, his proper due. Retrospectives on intelligence generally overlook the fact that the correct information is embedded in packets of worthless and contradictory data. And so it was here. The very depth of the Soviet penetration of the West worked against accuracy: throughout most of the spring of 1941, the British believed that Hitler would not attack the Soviet Union until after the Germans had disposed of Britain. As the most recent Russian analyst with access to some of the archival materials puts it: "What the British and the Russians shared on the eve of the German-Soviet war was a conviction that a German ultimatum and possibly an agreement [with Britain] would precede hostilities."[17]

And from 1939 on, the German high command turned out plans for offensive operations like chickens laying eggs. They were all precise, they were all in response to Hitler's directives, and most of them were never executed, while those that were carried out occurred only after substantial delays. The fact that Hitler ordered the Wehrmacht to attack France in October 1939, for instance, could certainly be taken as an indication of his intentions, but the actual attack came only seven months later and was preceded by another ambitious operation, Norway.

There was (probably) no doubt in Stalin's mind that Hitler aimed to attack him at some point, just as there is reasonable evidence to suggest that Stalin planned to invade Germany. The question was when, and here the information is much more confused and contradictory than is often suggested. Moreover, given the diversion of the German military into Greece in the spring of 1941, together with the hastily planned Yugoslavian invasion and the Cretan airborne offensive, Stalin may be forgiven for thinking that Barbarossa would probably be postponed—like all the other operations thus far—and that the reallocation of resources for the attack on Crete was proof positive, since June 22 was simply too late to begin an offensive.

So Stalin didn't necessarily doubt the intelligence; rather, there was a good chance that it was out of date: in December 1940, Hitler seemed to be planning to strike the Soviet Union in May 1941. But was this still the case by April or May? All the decoding machines, all the spies, all the fellow travelers and moles in the world couldn't reveal what was inside Hitler's head. But there was a pattern—of offensives delayed or canceled—and in the absence of telepathy, the conclusion that Barbarossa would be postponed was sensible enough.

Nobody knows what was going on in Stalin's mind, either, but like a good many people in positions of power, he probably believed his own propaganda (as Hitler believed *his*). So the naive, sycophantic impressions generated by the feeble and the nervous outside Russia backfired badly. Stalin, receiving information from all sides as to the power of his military, may well have thought it to be true and assumed that any attack could be absorbed without great difficulty.[18]

Then there is the other, more imponderable, factor: Stalin's intentions. There is evidence to suggest that the idea of his own offensive against Germany was not far from Stalin's mind. Thus, once the critical window of May 1941 slipped by, he assumed, quite reasonably, that by the time the next opportunity for an attack came (May 1942), his offensive would be under way. The generations of analysts for whom the peaceful intentions of the Soviet Union are a given have always hooted this idea down, but it is consistent with the historical pattern of Lenin's state, Stalin's foreign adventures, and much of the evidence.[19]

Regardless of his intentions, there's one fact that helps explain the initial disaster, and that is the disposition of the forces. Whether for an offensive or a defense in depth, Red Army units were well in front of the prepared defensive positions, particularly in Belorussia and Ukraine. But whichever it was, moving the Soviet divisions so far forward was a major factor in the astronomical losses.

It's difficult to say, in retrospect, where the bulk of the Red Army was deployed, for the simple reason that the strength of its components was so erratic. On paper, an infantry division should have had a strength of nearly 15,000 men, which would make it the equivalent of a regular European division. But the average was far below that: the majority of the infantry divisions close to the front had 8,000 men, and those located farther back were even smaller. The situation was, if anything, worse for the mechanized units. The Fourteenth Mechanized Corps had only 520 light tanks, instead of an official muster of over one thousand medium and heavy vehicles, while its infantry would have to depend on requisitioned trucks for its transport.[20]

As deficient as the Germans were when it came to tanks and mechanization, they were not that badly off. Initially, one German armored division probably had more firepower than a Red Army mechanized corps, and there's no real comparison between what the Germans called an "army" and its nominal Red Army counterpart. Although the Soviet military had modern weapons, there's no indication that anyone understood how to use them.

For that matter, although, on paper, the Red Army possessed an enormous store of weapons, its ability to keep them in working condition is problematic. In June 1941, Stalin's army was essentially like that of Yugoslavia or Greece. The real question was how much of the old Russian army's reputation for toughness had survived the terror. A good question: in the years before the war, Stalin had nearly fifty thousand officers arrested, and a third of them were murdered; included in that number were almost all the senior officers, including the Red Army's most highly regarded combat commander, Mikhail Tukhachevsky.[21]

That the initial German assault fell on the hapless Red Army like a car crushing a tin can is hardly open to dispute. Stalin had a nervous breakdown, retreated to his dacha outside Moscow, and didn't reappear until July 3—eleven days after the start of the invasion—when he made a brief radio speech, notable mostly for the wobbliness of his voice. Still, even cloaked in the usual generalities, Stalin's admissions of territorial defeats were terrifying to anyone conditioned to believe in the supremacy of the Red Army: Lithuania, Latvia, parts of Ukraine, and Belorussia, this last being an ingenuous way of conceding the loss of most of Russian Poland.

By this time, of course, the crucial battles of the summer were over. The original defensive position shielding Leningrad and Moscow, a fortified line roughly on the axis Pskov-Ostrov, was gone, and the Russians were improvising defenses outside Leningrad. By the time Stalin got around to making his speech, the headquarters of the Northwestern Front, located at Pskov, had already lost contact with its units; most of them were already annihilated. Pskov itself fell on July 9. The Germans were already far into the Baltic: Riga fell on June 29.

The armies of the Western Front had already suffered the same fate, substantial forces being cut off by the advancing Germans, who had penetrated past Bialystock and Minsk by the end of June. Minsk fell on July 1, and the Germans claimed they had taken nearly 300,000 prisoners of war and captured 2,500 tanks.[22]

The Red Army claimed to be hanging on to Belorussia and the Baltic, but the damage had been done. Tallinn, the historic capital of Estonia, sitting opposite Helsinki, had been evacuated on August 28. Smolensk, the last major city before Moscow, had fallen on July 16, and Velikie Luki, the only town of any importance between Smolensk and Tallinn, on the twentieth.

Given the size and underdevelopment of Russia, control of the major cities, or even small towns of any substance, was important, considerably more so than in western Europe. It was only the urban areas that offered any of the services and amenities required for the logistical support of modern warfare. Control of them meant possession of shelter, railroad hubs, and stores of foodstuffs, as well as military supplies. This had always been the case, but the Stalinist obsession with industrialization and urbanization had accelerated the trend. The high command's initial impulse—that he who had Leningrad and Moscow had the source of Soviet power—may not have been true on the grand strategic level, but on a lower, more basic level, it was absolutely the case. The fact that, in czarist times, administrative districts such as Minsk and Smolensk were named after their major (and generally only) city makes the point well enough.

In these first months, the invading German forces swept over Belorussia and the Baltic states like a wave rolling up onto a beach. Its coverage was far from uniform: the debris of whole Soviet army groups were cut off. Some of these units were cut off owing to the rapidity of the advance and the lack of basic communications. But in many cases their fate came about because their commanders, blindly following the fantasies of Stalin's senior commanders, attacked straight into the path of the advancing Germans.

These attacks, all appearances to the contrary, were part of a deliberate Soviet strategy. Their initial effect was simply to run up the casualty figures still higher. Indeed, to a certain extent these attacks were so ineffective that the Germans failed to notice the pattern, assuming that their opponents were floundering around on the battlefield. But from the first, the Soviet high command had been obsessed with conducting offensive operations and blind to the losses such operations would incur, almost by definition, given the chaos and low level of expertise.

Either by design or by accident, however, the Soviet high command had hit on the weakness of the Wehrmacht. It was an army designed for offensive operations, and had been so long before Hitler came on the scene. Its doctrines regarded the best defense as a rapid offense, counting on superior mobility to enable the rapid redeployment of troops to enable such attacks—and to exploit them when they succeeded.

During the First World War, some Allied generals, notably Joffre, had a glimmering as to the antidote: make your own offensive big enough (or synchronize it effectively with others) and this superiority would disappear, forcing your enemy into the kind of slugfest that the German army hated and feared. The Allied problem, however, was that the manpower losses this incurred—given their tactical limitations— made the cost prohibitive.

But for the Bolsheviks, human lives meant nothing. Having let six million people starve to death in Ukraine simply to reach an obscure theoretical objective—the "collectivization" of agriculture—Stalin certainly wasn't going to let the deaths of five or six million more on the battlefield bother him when the stakes were both higher and more apparent.[23] Initially, the Russian attacks only ran up the death toll. But by November they were beginning to have an effect.

At first the Germans seemed unstoppable. By the end of July, the remains of three Soviet army groups were marooned to the southwest of Minsk, well inside Belorussia; four more were stranded southwest of Smolensk, and another seven in Ukraine. How to deal with these substantial forces now deep in the rear became an increasing worry for the German high command, intensifying the internal conflict developing in Berlin.

Given how close the Germans were in August to Leningrad and Moscow, it was tempting to throw all the available resources into a push for one (or both) of those cities. In other words, the army high command was still thinking in the framework of the original plan. But Hitler, who could see that resistance was stiffening the nearer the Germans got to the two cities, insisted that the major drive should be to the south. The Germans had broken through the established fortified position stretching roughly between Przemysl and Rawa-Russka within forty-eight hours, and Lwow had fallen by June 30.

The two major cities of Ukraine, Kiev and Odessa, would hold out for weeks longer: Kiev didn't fall until September 17, and Odessa survived for a month after that. But the advance had pushed far past Odessa by the end of July, and it was evident that Kiev was clearly going to fall soon. How far could the Germans go? In Hitler's view, all the way to Rostov, at the mouth of the Don River, and thence into the oil-rich areas of southeastern Russia.

Opposing all this was the textbook view of warfare. The Germans were not at all happy to discover that the Red Army had not yet run out of men and matériel. The losses were certainly astounding: in the first ninety days of fighting, the Soviet Union had two million men killed or missing, out of an initial effective strength of slightly more than three million men. If the wounded were counted in, the Red Army lost over four-fifths of its personnel in ninety days of combat.

But back in Berlin, men like General Halder, studying the intelligence reports, were grimly aware that this had hardly made a dent in the size of the army. For every unit the Germans destroyed, a new one sprang up in its place. Some of this was simply a sleight of hand: existing units in the rear were renumbered. But since the Germans never really knew how many units there were in the first place; from their point of view all of them were new.

Thus on paper, a new army appeared to be materializing behind the one that had been destroyed. The German appreciation was correct. In the spring of 1942, having suffered losses of nearly three million killed and missing, the Russian army was significantly larger than it had been at the start of the war: four million men as opposed to a little over three million.

So the conservatives—or the pessimists—in Berlin counseled a slowing of the tempo of offensive operations. The thing to do was to consolidate. The enthusiasm and energy of the armored commanders was all very well, but by now they were running out of tanks. Logistics and mechanical breakdowns were taking a toll on the advance, a toll that was probably even greater than combat losses. Then there was the problem of the tens of thousands of Soviet troops trapped behind the German advance. Prudence dictated consolidation, the mopping up of the bypassed units, and a concentration on creating a line of supply.

Confronted with these problems, Hitler waffled. Like Stalin, he was, increasingly, not just watching his generals but directing their moves. At first he agreed to slow things down, then changed his mind. Finally, on August 21, Hitler issued a directive: his forces should seize the rich areas along the Donets River, the Crimea, and the region around Leningrad. The advance on Moscow could wait, supposedly, but by mid-September, with the fall of Kiev, the Moscow offensive was abruptly reconsidered, and the German Second Armored Group, which had thus far been operating south of Smolensk, was directed to move north, while the enfeebled mechanized columns of the First Armored Group drove still deeper into Ukraine.

On October 16, Odessa, under siege by the Romanian Fourth Army, fell. On October 30, the Russians finally abandoned Kharkov, which German troops had entered on the twenty-fourth. The fall of Kharkov, together with Belgorod and Kursk, just to the north, gave the Germans a virtual stranglehold on the coal-rich Donets basin as well as the major part of Ukraine's agriculture.[24] At the same time, a renewed German offensive strike between Briansk and Rzhev overran Tula at the southern end and Kalinin to the north, creating a bulge on both sides of Moscow and trapping an additional six army groups.

The October offensive, coupled with the fall of Odessa and the encirclement of Leningrad, caused panic in Moscow, where, on October 16, there was widespread looting and a massive exodus from the city.[25] For the Russians, it was the darkest moment in the war; it was no accident that Aleksandr Solzhenitsyn picked the late fall of 1941 for the pathetic tale of Russian suffering in his short novel *Incident at the Kretchetovka Station.*

But Stalin stayed put. In August he had signed a decree specifying that soldiers who surrendered were to be regarded as traitors, their families imprisoned or sent into exile. Soldiers who made it through the fluid battle lines back to their own side were, in one of those horrifying Bolshevik euphemisms, termed "stragglers." They were herded into rail cars and sent to forced labor camps, where they were worked to death. The lucky ones were repatriated into the army and put in penal battalions, where they would spend the rest of their short lives clearing minefields by hand and being used as cannon fodder in the incessant Red Army attacks.

Despite the appalling losses, Stalin insisted not only on maintaining the tempo of Russian attacks but on increasing them, approving evermore-grandiose schemes. In the south, the German advance continued: the Germans actually seized Rostov and held it briefly but were too weak to withstand the inevitable counterattack. In the north, by the end of November, with the weather worsening, the Germans were frantically trying to keep their shrinking mechanized forces running; Stalin and his generals embarked on even more ambitious offensive plans. By the end of that month, the great German offensive of 1941 was over. Further operations would have to wait until the spring.

Insofar as the Germans had aimed to seize control of the south and capture both Moscow and Leningrad, their first stroke had failed. But the failure was relative. Hitler's initial instinct, which had led him to demand the conquest of Ukraine and then the Caucasus, had certainly not been wrong. On the contrary, the Germans now had control of the vast majority of Russia's agricultural and mineral (notably coal) resources. Leningrad, the industrial center of the country, was surrounded and under siege. The Red Army had lost nearly three million men, killed or missing, close to 25,000 tracked vehicles, over 60,000 pieces of artillery, and about 18,000 aircraft.[26] Although much industry had been forcibly relocated to relative security in central Russia, along with tens of thousands of people, the Soviet Union had lost half of its industrial capacity and most of its agricultural base.

The scale of human loss was so great that it seems almost to have a hardening effect on military analysts, as though the loss of three million Russians was simply an insignificant detail. There were, after all, millions more in the pipeline. This is of course to look at the loss from Stalin's perspective. After he had murdered, one way or another, fifteen or twenty million people even before the start of the war, a few million more were hardly of any concern to him.

Practically speaking, however, the magnitude of the Soviet loss in those first six months would have catastrophic implications for the rest of the war. When combat begins, every army makes mistakes. The Germans had entered Poland with large white crosses painted on their vehicles. They did not repeat that mistake in May 1940. Experience in combat is a harsh teacher, but the survivors, if left to themselves, learn valuable lessons. Those lessons are particularly valuable if the men involved continue to engage in more or less the same kind of operations as before, and this was certainly the case in the opening phases of Barbarossa, with its emphasis on speed, mobility, and hitting power. Their equipment was still mediocre—and still in short supply—but the Wehrmacht had learned a great deal. Already, by May 1940 its soldiers were killing at least four or five men for every soldier of their own—a phenomenal casualty-exchange rate. The exchange rate in the Balkans—excluding Crete—had been, if anything, even more to the advantage of the Germans: the British alone took nearly twelve thousand casualties out of their expeditionary force of slightly more than fifty thousand men.[27]

In the last half of 1941, the Germans had about 280,000 soldiers killed, almost all of them on the Eastern Front, which when measured against the Red Army's nearly three million dead or missing, gives us a ratio of nearly eleven to one. This suggests a serious imbalance of efficiency in combat, and I'll return to this figure on other occasions. Clearly there was a learning curve on the Russian side, as the ratio for the entire war in the east is only about six to one—an improvement, but not much of one. Those three million dead Russians in 1941 suggest the reason. There weren't enough survivors of the initial combat to pass on their experiences to the recruits who were filling the gaps in 1942. Consequently, the Red Army would lose another three million men in 1942, which only made the problem worse. The Bolshevik disregard for human life thus had a practical (as opposed to ethical) cost.[28]

But to conclude on a less ghastly note. By December 1, 1941, the Germans were right on top of the two major cities, had occupied all the territory up to Moscow and Leningrad, had seized almost all of Ukraine, and dominated both the Baltic and the Black seas. The basic question, then, was this: If the Red Army could not dislodge the German stranglehold by the spring, how far would the next German offensive go? That it would roll over all that remained of any importance was not far-fetched at all.

THE DEATH RIDE: RUSSIA,
DECEMBER 1941–DECEMBER 1944

The history of the war thus emerged as a bizarre cocktail of
facts, falsifications, and, above all, omissions.
                                                    Gabriel Gorodetsky[1]

At the end of November 1941, the Wehrmacht, although it had failed to
win the same sort of total victory over Stalin it had managed in earlier
campaigns, controlled an enormous portion of Russia's natural resources
and had destroyed much of its military. But the Germans in Russia were,
on a grander scale, in much the same situation as the Italians had been
in North Africa: significant early victories against the enemy that then
evaporated owing to a massive failure of logistics.

The basic structural problem was not that the high command hadn't
planned for the Russian winter. It was that the production of war materials
after September 1939 had continued at the same leisurely pace as before.
The failure to provide soldiers with decent winter gear was a symptom of
the deeper failure. The early victories had not only masked the problem,
they had compounded them, as the Germans continued to flesh out their
military with the stores of captured equipment from May 1940.

The situation was exacerbated by the delay in starting the operation.
Despite the mud and the rain in the fall of 1941, the Germans were still
mounting offensive maneuvers with success, as the listing of the cities

overrun after October 1 makes clear (see Chapter 9). Had the invasion begun in May instead of June, the tempo of advances extended a month, the damage done to the Soviet Union would have been irreparable. Such things are by their nature speculative, but it is difficult to escape the idea that Hitler's Balkan excursions cost him dearly on the Eastern Front, particularly when coupled with the air force losses in the British campaign and in Crete.

Insofar as there was any secret to the Wehrmacht's success in the early campaigns, it was in the integration of tactical airpower with ground operations. Although the Luftwaffe had simply destroyed the Soviet air force in the opening days of the war, thus enabling the command of the airspace over the battlefield that was a prerequisite for support of ground operations by bombers, the massive bomber force required had been too mauled by the RAF to have the same impact as it had in May 1940.

A more serious deficiency was the loss of transport capability. In each campaign thus far, air transport had played a major role. Despite being obsolete, the venerable Ju-52 transport planes had managed to funnel men and equipment into Norway, had been the backbone of the airborne invasion of the Netherlands, and had been almost totally responsible for the transport of the airborne troops to Crete. Despite its failings, the plane had a great virtue: like many transports designed at the end of the 1920s, it could land anywhere, so it was ideal for operations in eastern Europe and the Soviet Union. But there were never enough of them produced at any one time, and the losses of aircraft in the early offensives were never made up, thus depriving the Germans of the air transport capacity they sorely needed in the east.[2]

The real German failure, then, was not the failure to underestimate Soviet military strength. It was the failure of the National Socialist state to keep its military supplied with the quality and quantity of weaponry required if it was to conduct successful operations. The Ju-52 experience was typical. After six months of fighting, the German divisions in the east were still relying on obsolete equipment—and even that was in short supply.

Once the fighting began, however, there was a serious intelligence failure. The Soviet high command had thought about how to repel a German invasion long before the shooting started. Their idea was that the only way to blunt such an attack was with intensive attacks of their own. So once the German offensive began Moscow repeatedly ordered Soviet attacks, in conformance with the doctrines that had been set on high.

Until December, these ideas bore no relationship to the actual realities of the Red Army in 1941, and Russian losses were so catastrophic that the German high command failed to see that they were not isolated local attacks but were being carried out as part of a unified if insane plan of operations. While generals like Franz Halder were writing excuses back in Berlin, Soviet commanders in Moscow were patching together even more grandiose offensives. So December 1, 1941, marks the real turning point of the war on the Eastern Front, because from then on the war simply became a series of great hammer blows, in which both sides attempted enormous encircling offensives aimed at completely destroying the enemy's forces.

Given the appalling slaughter, conventional military wisdom—competence, one might say—dictated that the Red Army emulate the German example, and use the winter months to refit and reorganize. In November the German commanders had all pleaded for a halt, and even Hitler had recognized the advantage of a stop and had reconciled himself to the idea that the Germans would not have Moscow and Leningrad by Christmas.

Basically, the Germans were in bad shape, with only about one-third of their vehicles still running, and then only with difficulty (in the approaches to Moscow), as December was turning out to be unusually cold. The weather, along with the rapid advance, had a particularly adverse effect on air support. The Luftwaffe's short-range tactical aircraft were admirably suited to operating from hastily improvised airstrips. The difficulty was to care for them on the ground during those periods when the temperatures stayed close to zero degrees Fahrenheit. The Russian solution was to use heated hangars. Without them, the Germans were struggling, unsuccessfully, to keep their aircraft operational. So Stalin's decision to authorize a serious counteroffensive was reasonable.

However, it overlooked the fact that, as bad off as the Germans were, the Red Army was probably still worse: enumerating the divisions still available masks the inherent problem. In responding to the German onslaught, the Soviets had begun reorganizing their forces. But this reorganization was in reality simply a shrinkage: the reorganized infantry divisions, for example, had only three-quarters of the manpower, onethird of the vehicles, and less than half the guns of their June 1941 strength. Instead of forming divisions to replace the ones that had been annihilated, the Russians created tank and infantry brigades of fewer than five thousand men, while armored divisions were reduced to about two hundred tanks—and then reduced still further. By March 1942, what the Red Army now called an armored or mechanized corps was basically the equivalent of an understrength German division, and had fewer than one hundred medium tanks. The only new divisions created were— ironically, in light of the nature of the fighting—the eighty-odd cavalry divisions, hardly more than brigade-strength units.[3]

But Stalin was adamant. By the end of November, a dangerous bulge had developed on either side of Moscow, after the seizure of Kalinin (to the north) and Tula (to the south) as well as the disasters at Viazma in October. A similar envelopment had occurred below Leningrad. So the danger was that the Germans might once again beat their opponents to the draw and surround both cities.

Consequently, despite the appalling weather, on December 5, 1941, the first coordinated Soviet offensive began. These attacks were successful, in that they drove the Germans back from their potentially encircling positions, but a good deal of the success was due to the standard German doctrine, dating from the First World War, that encouraged commanders to cede territory instead of mounting costly defenses of captured ground. By January the Russians had retaken Tula and Kalinin and pushed Army Group Center back toward Rzhev and all the way to Velikie Luki. In fact, this area had become a dangerously vulnerable salient.

But the entire front had been pushed back, all the way from Leningrad to just south of Belgorod. Hitler was furious, and by the end of

December 1941, several of the key generals on the Eastern Front had been relieved: von Rundstedt (Army Group South), von Bock (Center), and even Guderian (Second Armored Army). The shock waves went right to the top: on December 19, Hitler took von Brauchitsch's resignation as army chief of staff and assumed personal control of the army.

Hitler's demand was that the army stand fast and not give up any territory. Both then and afterward, the senior army commanders were opposed, and saw Hitler's order of January 1942, ordering units to hold ground regardless, as an irrational act that eventually led to the destruction of their forces. Possibly so, but the German problem in January 1942 was inherent in the peculiar nature of the front itself. If the Germans ceded control of key cities, they would have to retreat a long way back—to the next town or city of any size.

Russia was not like France or Italy or Germany. In western Europe, when your forces retreated over the hill, they could take up new positions in another ancient and equally durable town and begin the defense all over again. In Russia, outside of the major cities (many of them, like Velikie Luki, little more than small towns), the geography worked the other way around. In the final years of the war, German commanders would experience this firsthand—it was easy to retreat, hard to find a new defensive position, harder still to coordinate the troops into a defensive line. Hitler was basically right.

The initial German indecision, however, in which retreat and resistance were jumbled together, encouraged Stalin to expand his plans. Instead of the tactically necessary attempts to keep the two major cities from being encircled, he ordered (on January 7, 1942) an offensive along the entire front. The Red Army lacked the men, the equipment, and the tactical leadership to succeed. When, in March, the offensives stalled completely, Stalin's main accomplishment was to weaken his forces even further: one way or the other, half the men in the Red Army were casualties; and the ratio of Russian to German dead and missing remained more than four to one.[4]

Stalin still had an enormous manpower pool. But it was shrinking. Moreover, in the winter offensives, he had committed—and lost—some of his best officers and his best troops (for example, the airborne units destroyed in the futile attempts to expand the bulge south of Moscow). Aid from the United States and Britain was beginning to arrive, together with tanks and planes from the relocated factories. Ultimately the lavish flow of American trucks, railroad stock, and armored vehicles would more than compensate for what was lost—and for what the state factories were unable to produce. But in April 1942, the Russians were largely on their own, and could ill afford the losses they had sustained in futile attempts to destroy the Germans.

On February 8, Fritz Todt, the head of the German armaments industry, had been killed in a plane crash. Hitler promptly appointed as his successor Albert Speer, who had been serving as Hitler's architect. Under Speer's administration, German armaments production increased dramatically, particularly given the proliferation of complex designs and Hitler's meddling. The Third Reich would eventually run out of gas, but it would never run out of tanks and planes.

The German military establishment had been curiously complacent about Soviet arms, with Guderian ingenuously expressing surprise when the first T-34 tank was encountered. So the winter campaigns had been an unpleasant surprise. Red Army tank commanders had no idea how to use their armored vehicles, but both the ground and air forces were discovered to have some excellent equipment.

Given its lethargic production and retrograde design initiatives, the German tank establishment was going to have a difficult time catching up, but the Germans proved themselves adept at improvising quick fixes. High-velocity 7.5-centimeter guns began to appear on the Mark 4 (still the only decent tank in service), enabling it to take on the T-34 with something approaching parity. The production of antitank guns was still pathetic, so the standard Soviet 76.2-millimeter gun, available in enormous quantities, was modified, and proved to be a potent weapon.

The real innovation, however, was one the tank establishment, and Guderian in particular, fought tooth and nail. For a true tank enthusiast, a rotating turret (with the main gun mounted in it) was the only solution in tank design. But for many tasks, there was no need for a rotating turret. Tracked vehicles mounting artillery pieces, for example, could operate quite effectively. For that matter, so could antitank guns: if armies were deploying thousands of towed weapons for that purpose, it was hard to fault the logic of putting the weapon on tracks and making it self-contained.

The debate was not just theoretical: the turret was the most complex and expensive part of the tank. It added substantially to its weight and limited the potency of the gun. At the start of the century, German engineers had discovered that it was possible to mount a substantially more powerful howitzer on a chassis employed for a field gun firing a much less potent shell.

Mount the gun in the hull of a tracked vehicle, and the same sort of economy of scale applied, only more so. The turret of the Czech 38t tank, for example, was designed for a puny 37-millimeter gun, and the hull and engine and transmission designed only for that gun-and-turret combination. But if the turret was removed, a high-velocity 7.5-centimeter gun could be installed in what was basically the same hull with a few steel plates added. The resulting vehicle, known as the Marder 3, weighed little more than the 38t and yet was capable of disabling any Russian tank it met.[5] The Germans were not as lucky with adaptations of the basic chassis and hull of the two German tankettes (Mark 1 and 2). Although attempts were made to mount a heavy gun on the Mark 1, the design was so bad that few vehicles were modified and put into service. They had better luck with the Mark 2, which, armed with either a high-velocity 7.5-centimeter antitank gun (Marder 2) or a standard field gun (Wespe), proved to be an invaluable asset on the Eastern Front.

An enormous industry sprang up, devoted to the modification of the tank designs so as to carry heavy, hull-mounted weapons; the result was a bewildering proliferation of designs. However, the basic pattern was simple enough. A tank chassis would be converted to mount a high-velocity gun firing armor-piercing shells, in which case it was a tank destroyer (Jagdpanzer). It could be used as a mobile field gun or, with a suitably enclosed compartment for the crew, in support of infantry (Stürmgeschütz). In this latter category it supplanted the role of the tank.

The tank enthusiasts were apoplectic. But Germany had no choice. It had no decent tank designs on the near horizon, and was incapable of producing in quantity what it did have. When the Panther, certainly the best German tank of the war, entered mass production in 1943, only 1,768 were manufactured, and only another 3,700 during the last year of the war. Production of the Tiger 1, the tank designed to give the German armored forces decisive battlefield superiority, was ludicrous: 78 in 1942 and 647 in 1943.[6] So the nearly 5,000 self-propelled guns derived from tanks (about 3,600 of them were based on obsolete models) became the backbone of German mechanized forces, even though men like Guderian remained bitterly opposed to them throughout the war.[7]

Despite the opposition of the experts, the assault guns soon proved themselves on the battlefield. Lieutenant Wilhelm Wegener, for example, an assault-gun commander in the elite Grossdeutschland Division, personally destroyed twelve Russian tanks in one action (at Stanowje); previously he had annihilated twenty-two artillery pieces and four tanks during an engagement at Alexandrowka. Wegener's record compares favorably with that of Michael Wittmann, usually regarded as one of the best tank commanders in the Wehrmacht.[8] Assault guns were indeed potent weapons.

Few of these modifications had reached the men in the field by April 1942, but the plans for a spring and summer offensive were well under way on both sides. From the first, Hitler had aimed at a drive deep into the Caucases that would seize the all-important oil fields to the east. In April his initial directive became an operation, Fall Blau, and the forces of Army Group South were heavily reinforced by the Fourth Armored Army and roughly forty additional divisions.

Stalin was planning as well, and had fallen back on the same somewhat unsuccessful plan as in the winter. There was, potentially, the possibility of cutting off German-occupied Kharkov from both sides, and Stalin duly approved a plan to that effect on April 10, only a few days after Hitler had activated Fall Blau. The weather in Russia made the timing of offensive operations rather predictable. What was not easily foreseen was where Hitler intended his blow to fall. Once again, Stalin misguessed, deciding that the main German thrust would be toward Moscow. The Russians were also wildly optimistic about the weakness of the German army, and reckoned their forces would greatly outnumber the hapless Germans. The Germans, on the contrary, had a reasonable idea of what was afoot.

What followed, the little-known Second Battle of Kharkov, was an epic Soviet disaster. Breaking through south of that city, the advancing units thrust deep into the German line, creating a vast bulge. The offensive began on May 8. By May 13, when the Germans in turn attacked, the Soviet forces were in an enormous pocket from which they were unable to extricate themselves. Ultimately, four armies were trapped and destroyed.

This was not the only bad news. At the same time, von Manstein, who had been charged with Crimean operations, overran the Kerch peninsula, resulting in another Soviet disaster: two out of every three soldiers engaged there were either dead or missing by the time von Manstein had cleared the area. He then turned his attention to Sevastapol, the historic fortress city that was the key to the Crimea, battering it into submission by July 4.

By then Fall Blau had begun in earnest. The attack began on June 28, and within ten days, the two advancing German armies, having crushed their opposition, were at Voronezh, and since that city lay at the core of what had traditionally been called "Black Earth" Russia, they now controlled the country's agricultural base. Once again, the German advance seemed unstoppable. Rostov fell on July 28, and the only thing that brought the advance to a halt was logistics. Army Group South was out of fuel, it was out of working vehicles, and its men were exhausted.

The Russians feverishly organized a defensive position along those portions of the Don River that they still controlled. But the Germans staggered on, and by August 23, they were at the Volga, to the north of Stalingrad. At that point, German offensive operations basically came to a halt.

Blau was a worse defeat for the Red Army than the opening blows of Barbarossa. Although the Russians were still fighting hard and having some local successes, and willing to absorb tremendous casualties, they were unable to stop a determined German offensive. Nor was the ceding of territory part of some grand plan. To the contrary, on July 28, 1942, Stalin had an order issued specifying that retreat was impossible and that any officer who retreated would be disgraced and assigned to a penal unit. If October 1941 was the great moment of panic for the Communist cadres in Moscow and Leningrad, July 1942 was the nadir of Soviet fortunes.

By August 1942, the Red Army was still hanging on to the Caucasus and the Grozny oil fields—small consolation, given the loss of so much other territory. Although the German victory was incomplete, it was a serious check to Stalin's delusions of spring 1942, when he had believed that the Germans were on the ropes and could be easily finished off.

For Hitler, the bad news was not in the east; it was in the Far East. After the December 7, 1941, Japanese attack on the American naval base at Pearl Harbor, Hitler had declared war on the United States. There was a logic to his decision: despite its professions of neutrality, the administration of President Franklin D. Roosevelt was sympathetic to Britain, and by the fall of 1941, there was an undeclared naval war sputtering along in the North Atlantic.

From past experience, the Germans knew that it would take some time before American troops could enter the fight—probably a year or more—and this time they would be deprived of the advantage they had enjoyed earlier. Hitler controlled France so there would be no place on the Continent to land, train, and build up forces. Then, too, looked at from a geostrategic point of view, it was reasonable to assume that the Americans would have to deal with Japan first. After all, the Japanese navy had the capability to threaten the West Coast as well as U.S. possessions in the Pacific. Not only had the Japanese destroyed a considerable number of capital ships at Pearl Harbor, but in the naval engagements that followed, the Japanese navy wiped out the British, Australian, and Dutch naval opposition, while its armies quickly overran Malaysia and the Philippines, with Singapore, the main British base in the East, surrendering on February 15, 1942.

Locked in a gargantuan naval campaign spread out across the world's largest ocean, the United States could devote few resources to Germany, and the declaration of war would allow the German navy an all-out attack against Britain's supply lines. Hitler's decision was reasonable and logical; it was also a fatal mistake. President Roosevelt had despaired of getting the American electorate to countenance another European war. In 1940, public opinion was firmly opposed to foreign interventions, largely thanks to the postwar shambles of Versailles and the perceived Anglo-French ingratitude. Quite possibly, the United States might have stood by and let Japan wrest control of British, French, and Dutch territory in the Pacific, just as the League of Nations had done little to counter Japanese aggression in China. Although Americans were sympathetic to Britain in its struggle against Germany, there was no public sentiment to offer substantive support. Most of the help Roosevelt was providing was done on the sly.

The Japanese declaration of war resolved one of Roosevelt's problems, but there is no evidence to suggest that the Tokyo declaration was tied to Hitler in anyone's mind. The war most Americans now felt was necessary was with Japan, not Germany. So Hitler's decision choked off what would have been a torturous internal debate.

Like everyone else, Hitler underestimated the military power of the United States. The Battle of the Coral Sea (May 4–10, 1942) was not a one-sided affair; and a month later, American naval forces badly mauled the Japanese fleet at the Battle of Midway (June 4–7). Almost precisely two months later to the day, U.S. ground forces were on Guadalcanal (August 7). By the end of August, it was clear that the war in the Pacific was not going to become a protracted stalemate: Japan was going to lose the war it had started nine months earlier.

Moreover, Hitler had fatally underestimated the extent to which the British and the Americans were able to keep Stalin supplied. By the end of that fatal summer of 1942, as long as the Russians could keep themselves awash in oil, their industrial capacity, when coupled with enormous Allied aid, would keep them in the war. The losses in manpower were crippling, but not immediately so, and Stalin didn't care how many dead Russians (or dead Communists) piled up, so long as he won militarily.

In this sense both Hitler and the Wehrmacht, despite their collective willingness to engage in a ferocious war against civilian populations, were very much locked into the ideas of Erich von Falkenhayn, ideas that campaigns from Poland to Greece had seemingly validated. Back in December 1915, von Falkenhayn had observed that it was no longer necessary to annihilate your enemy either through attrition or great battle. The trick was to destroy his will to fight. In spring 1941 the Germans had done that repeatedly.

The flaw was that the idea worked only when your enemy had a government dedicated to sparing the lives of their fellow countrymen as much as possible. The Netherlands was a good example: staggered by wildly inflated accounts of the bombing of Rotterdam (which was largely accidental), the Dutch government capitulated and went into exile. From a strictly military point of view, both the Dutch and the French could have fought on. But they didn't. The Germans never destroyed the czarist armies in the First World War, but they still forced them to sue for peace. His ideas were lost in the bristling thicket of Allied propaganda and the bitchery of the German high command, but von Falkenhayn was right. But as the Soviet Union (and Japan) would make clear, confronted with a state that regarded the slaughter of its citizenry with callous indifference, the idea that you could make your enemy quit through shock and despair failed.

By the end of July 1941, the Soviet Union had well over four million dead and missing, a figure that was already slightly larger than the combined Allied figures in the same categories for the entire First World War. In 1942 the Red Army had almost exactly the same number of killed and missing as in 1941. This was in some respects a misleading comparison, since in 1941 the fighting had been only for six months, but in absolute numbers it makes the point fairly. If the Russians were able to continue to absorb losses at the rate of a quarter of a million dead each month—or even half that—how was it possible to beat them using any of the conventional strategies that formed the foundation of military wisdom?

The solution was as simple as it was brutal. The way to deal with an enemy unwilling to surrender despite the odds against him was to kill him. If the state that supported and directed the enemy was indifferent to the fate of its citizens, the same principle applied. By the end of the Pacific war, the casualty ratio had reached the level of ten dead Japanese for every dead American—not even a populous country like Japan could sustain a war with that imbalance.[9]

The problem was that the Germans couldn't apply this solution to the Soviet Union, because they lacked the overwhelming technological edge that the United States had over Japan. Innovation is only a part of that advantage. The Japanese military-industrial complex was probably as ingenious as any comparable entity in the world. But the country lacked the industrial base that would allow for the mass production of war matériel, and it lacked the corresponding social structure needed for the training of proficient specialists (like air crews) in the requisite numbers. Germany had the latter, but not the former.

Consequently, while the American advantage in the casualty-exchange rate steadily improved over the course of the Pacific war, the German exchange advantage over the Red Army declined, even though, in absolute numbers, Berlin retained its edge. By the spring of 1945, the Red Army consisted of teenagers and geriatrics; its officers were mediocrities whose advances were at the expense of their men. Even at the end of the war, casualties in infantry units continued at appalling levels. The road from Stalingrad to Berlin was paved with Russian dead. But given the inability of National Socialism to mass-produce quality equipment, and Stalin's indifference to the human cost of war, there was no way the Germans could win outright in the east. The best they could hope for was a draw, and as 1942 came to a bitter end, a combination of Soviet ineptitude and German tenacity made this outcome more and more likely.

There is no better illustration of the stark imbalance between the two forces than the Red Army's next moves, a series of offensives named after the outer planets—Mars, Jupiter, Saturn, and Uranus.[10] As Stalin and his henchmen looked at the front, they saw two bulges in the line, a large one west of Moscow and a much smaller one centering on Stalingrad.

By the autumn of 1942, it was in the latter area that the fighting had intensified, as the Germans attempted to pierce the southern half of the line at Stalingrad, complete their breakthrough into the fertile underbelly of the Soviet Union, and essentially cut the country into two: the brains and the administrative centers were to the north, industry and agriculture to the south.

Overly optimistic as usual, the Russian high command envisioned two massive pincer movements that would penetrate the sections of the front on each side of the bulge, cut off the German defenders from the rest of their forces, and annihilate them. The idea was theoretically tempting. As the massive German offensives of spring and summer 1942 had driven southeast, the threat to Moscow had receded, and the Germans had made no serious attempt to regain the ground lost during the Soviet midwinter offensive, instead switching their attentions to the south. As a result, there was a vulnerable bulge centered on Rzhev. This bulge was about 150 kilometers wide, and ran—very roughly—from Belyi to about 30 kilometers southeast of Viazma (where the Red Army had suffered a horrific defeat in October 1941). From Rzhev the front line made an enormous concave arc, almost a semicircle, with a diameter of about 200 kilometers, the other end anchored on the small town of Velikie Luki, historically one of the key defensive positions guarding Moscow. The Soviet idea was to attack the salient from both sides and pinch it off.

Before 1914, French officers had been taught that it was dangerous to attack into a salient. Such an assault demanded a division of the offensive forces. Without almost perfect coordination of the attack, the defenders could, in theory, defeat each side of the pincers individually, shuttling their forces from one side to the other. What made the idea even more problematic was that as the forces on each side of the salient moved to the offensive, their axis of advance would be parallel to the rest of the enemy front, exposing them to fire from two sides and raising the possibility of flank attacks. There were exceptions to the rule: Verdun was a salient jutting into the German lines, for instance. But at Verdun the terrain on either side of the bulge precluded any attack by forces attempting to relieve pressure on the defenders.

Apparently the Soviet high command's approach to military theory was like Lysenko's approach to biology: the rules were all constructs of capitalism designed to enslave the masses; in Socialism, therefore, the rules didn't apply. Consequently, two parallel operations were planned. In the north, an offensive striking into each side of the Rzhev salient was planned: Mars, on the north side (around Velikie Luki), and Jupiter, on the south (by Briansk). At the same time, two additional operations— Saturn and Uranus—would trap the Germans fighting around Stalingrad.

The German bridgehead there was a slender bulge, nothing like the one at Rzhev, although when the planning for Saturn and Uranus was going on, it looked as though there would be German breakthroughs and a real salient would be formed. But the Stalingrad operation was more in the form of an attack on the flanks of the German position than an attack into a salient. Theoretically, then, the chances for success in the south were much better than in the north.

The Rzhev salient was definitely not an exception to the theory. The Red Army devoted over 800,000 men to Operation Mars and Jupiter,. which began on November 24, 1942. By the time the operation had been scrubbed (Jupiter on December 16, 1942, and Mars a month later), Zhukov, the Soviet commander, had lost one-quarter of them and about 90 percent of the substantial armored force committed to the operation (roughly two thousand tanks).[11]

To say that the collapse of Mars and Jupiter was eclipsed by the success of Saturn and Uranus at Stalingrad is hardly to do the situation justice. The catastrophic failure of the Rzhev operation disappeared into the Stalinist memory hole, while Stalingrad quickly passed to a mythical level as the symbol of how the Red Army had destroyed the Hitlerites and their Fascist allies.

There is a grain of truth in this perspective. Saturn and Uranus, launched on November 19, 1942, succeeded in cutting off Paulus's Sixth Army. A relief attempt led by Erich von Manstein failed, as did the Luftwaffe's effort to keep the besieged forces supplied by air. Although Hitler wanted Paulus to fight to the bitter end, he surrendered in early February

1943. Given the fate of most of the men under him as prisoners of war, his surrender was basically a betrayal of his command. Of the perhaps 123,000 prisoners of war, fewer than 5,000 had been repatriated by 1958.[12] And it gave Stalin a marvelous propaganda victory that he would otherwise not have had.

That Stalingrad was a Soviet triumph and a serious German setback can't be denied. What is highly questionable, however, is the magnitude of the victory in the context of the time frame. One measure of the extent of the victory is the casualties. For a long time, the Soviet Union did not release figures, but internally, Red Army losses are officially 154,885 killed or missing, with equipment losses of 2,915 tanks, 3,591 artillery pieces, and 706 aircraft.[13] In light of the consensus about German losses, this is frank admission, although it considerably understates the situation.

As is the case with any epic battle, the German casualty figures have been all over the landscape, but the most reliable data, taken from a variety of German sources, roughly agree that the totals for the dead and the missing (including prisoners of war) are roughly a quarter of a million men.[14] The interesting statistic in all this is that the estimates for the German dead all come in lower than the official Soviet figures for their killed. A victory, yes—but one achieved at a considerable cost.

But these figures give an impression of the fighting that is somewhat false. As the troops involved in Saturn and Uranus broke through the German lines on either side of Stalingrad and continued their advance, they encountered stiff opposition in the form of German counterattacks, directed mostly by von Manstein. On the German side these operations are rolled into one and named the Battle of Kharkov. On the Russian side they are broken down into separate offensive and defensive operations. But regardless of how they are identified, they have one thing in common: they are the culmination of the Saturn and Uranus operations after Soviet units penetrated the German defenses and thus, logically speaking, part of Stalingrad.

Red Army losses in these operations are hardly trivial: nearly one quarter of a million dead is the best estimate.[15] Seen that way, Stalingrad, far from being a great victory, was just another inconclusive slugging match. As the war was shaping up, given the size of the forces involved and the vast scale of the terrain, neither side would be able to annihilate the other.

Despite what by now should have been obvious even to the rankest amateur, the German and Soviet high commands continued on, apparently unshaken by the fact that their triumphs had produced nothing but piles of bodies. As the summer of 1943 arrived, both sides had far-reaching plans for decisive hammer blows, encircling battles of annihilation in the classic sense. The Red Army had gotten its blow in first. But by April 1943, the Germans had ambitious plans of their own.

Despite the loss at Stalingrad, the Wehrmacht was hardly a spent force. In many respects, it had more firepower than it had ever possessed. Although still badly outnumbered, German officers, two years into the war on the Eastern Front, had developed a certain confidence in their ability to prevail in combat, almost regardless of the odds against them. The retreats had already begun, and there was no longer much hope that Hitler's grand scheme for turning European Russia into a German province would succeed. But at the local level—on the ground—morale was good, and the soldiers were confident but wary.

Clearly, summer 1943 was the moment of decision. Despite an early victory against the Americans at Kasserine Pass, in Tunisia, in February 1943, Germany and Italy had lost the fight for North Africa by May. The next Allied move would be an amphibious invasion of some part of western Europe, probably Italy. But temporarily, Germany had the luxury of a one-front war. If it could smash the Red Army in a battle of annihilation, the military situation would dramatically reverse itself. Nor was this wishful thinking: the problems the Allies had encountered in North Africa did not bode well for their ground operations.

So Erich von Manstein, who had emerged as the strategic genius of the Eastern Front after his conquest of the Crimea and his victory at Kursk at the start of the year, proposed an ambitious plan. He had noticed not only that the Red Army was addicted to large-scale offensive operations but that once the operations began, they seemed unable to bring them to a halt. It was an uncanny repetition of the British and French disasters of the First World War, when operations would continue long past the point where it was obvious they couldn't possibly succeed, and were simply piling up bodies. But in that war, the Germans had never had the luxury of fighting only one enemy on one front, so they had lacked the resources to take the next step, luring the attacking forces further into the void and then smashing them with a massive flank attack.

Von Manstein was correct in his appreciation of Soviet tactics, and correct in his assessment of the chances of success. But the high command had never forgiven him for his audacity in going to Hitler in 1939–40 and proposing his own offensive plans; their resistance was almost automatic. So instead of an audacious stroke delivered against an off-balance enemy, the Germans decided on a repeat of Zhukov's Mars and Jupiter operations. There was a great bulge in the line between Orel and Kharkov: the Germans would attack from both sides, pinch it off, and destroy the trapped Russians.

Although the Germans were now beginning to equip themselves with serious armor, and their expertise in combat greatly excelled the Red Army's, all the same objections applied to Citadel (as the offensive operation was called) as had applied to Mars. So the German plan was yet another attack into a salient that, even if successful, would represent one more in a series of Soviet catastrophes and be of only tactical significance.[16] Given the size of the Soviet forces engaged, Citadel would hardly bring Stalin's war machine to a halt. Von Manstein's idea, on the other hand, held out that promise: his plan, if successful, would have split Russia in two and driven the armies to the south of the offensive back onto the Sea of Azov, east of the Crimea, where they would have been bottled up and unable to continue any serious fight.

Curiously, Hitler let the high command plan Citadel as they wished (although von Manstein was put in charge of carrying it out). If there was an instance in the war when he should have intervened, this was it. Citadel was the last chance to deliver a crippling blow against Stalin and inflict a defeat that would give Berlin the freedom to fight off the Allies in the west.

And again, the Germans had serious timing problems. Citadel should have been launched in May. Instead, operations didn't begin until July. True, the delay enabled more of the new and (in theory) vastly superior Panther tanks to be used, but it also gave the Red Army the opportunity to recover from the twin bloodbaths of Kharkov and Stalingrad. Von Manstein had wanted to take advantage of the obvious weakness of the Soviets: their field commanders were not capable of directing offensive operations in any coordinated way. Citadel played to what was, by contrast, a relative strength: the Red Army had plenty of people who would hold their ground and fight until they were killed. This was hardly surprising, since Soviet soldiers who retreated were regarded as traitors and their families were treated accordingly.

Not surprisingly, therefore, Citadel was a failure. All that the Germans managed to do in those two weeks in July was to inflict the usual horrific losses on the Red Army: the kill ratio was three to one, the losses in tanks and airplanes about five to one. The Red Army had about as many men killed as in Operation Mars, and the front line remained more or less where it had stabilized in May. In fact, Kursk was another inconclusive slugging match among the many. Its strategic importance was basically nil. Tactically, it should be remembered only as the greatest tank battle fought up to that time, and it is likely to hold that distinction well into the future.

In writing about the First World War, Winston Churchill opined that the French had won the battle of the communiqués. On the Eastern Front this statement—substituting the Red Army for the French—came true with a vengeance, as Stalin's propagandists created the fictional history of the Great Patriotic War: treacherously surprised by the Hitlerite attack of June 22, 1941, the heroic Red Army recovered, went on the offensive, and drove the invaders back to Berlin. It was the Red Army that won the war, and the twin victories of Stalingrad and Kursk were the proof. In other words, had Kursk not existed, it would have been necessary to invent it, although Stalingrad took pride of place—as scores of studies would demonstrate.[17]

Citadel certainly marked Germany's last chance to prevail in the east, and was thus roughly parallel to General Alexei Brusilov's famous offensive of June 1916. In both cases, when the offensive was contained, the ability of the attacking forces to mount future operations of the sort necessary to win the war had been exhausted. The result was the same, but the causes were different. Brusilov's offensive demolished the last of czarist Russia's troops. From then on, essentially, Russian forces could no longer mount a successful defense. After Kursk the Germans had plenty of men and an increasing flow of equipment. But they also faced a massive Allied invasion of Italy. The Russian front would continue to absorb resources and men, but the center of action now shifted to the west.

That this is only grudgingly recognized is hardly surprising. The one real triumph of Lenin's heirs had been to convince the world that Communism was a success. A regime that could persuade thousands of journalists, professors, and government leaders that seven million Ukrainians had not actually starved to death—that there was never any food shortage in the Soviet Union and certainly no famine—could easily rewrite military history. The task was made all the easier because, unlike other claims routinely made (and routinely accepted) in the West, this one contained several grains of truth. None of the defendants in the Moscow trials of 1937 had been guilty of treason, espionage, or any of the other fantastic charges leveled against them, but Paulus was forced to surrender his encircled forces at Stalingrad, von Manstein was unable to destroy the Kursk salient, and by mid-1943 the Wehrmacht was slowly but steadily retreating to the west. The myth was easy to create, and like its equivalent legend from the Great War—that the British army won it in the fall of 1918, and without much help from the United States—will doubtless prove to have a remarkable persistence. Truth has nothing to do with it.

There's no question that the Wehrmacht was ultimately defeated in the east, just as it was in Africa and in western Europe. What is arguable, however, is the dogmatic insistence that it was because of those encounters that Germany lost the war. At the risk of being accused of deconstructing the Eastern Front to make a controversial point, it seems to me that the Soviet case is wildly overstated and that it depends mostly on the suppression of key parts of the historical record.

Much of the claim, it seems to me—and particularly its moral force—rests on the appalling death toll the Soviet Union incurred. The problem, alas, is that a significant percentage of it was owing to the stubbornness and cruelty of one individual, Stalin. It was his decision, ultimately, that led to the disasters of the days and weeks following June 22, 1941—a period when the nation lost half its resources, three-quarters of its equipment, and nearly four-fifths of its active army. It was at his insistence that the Red Army massacred itself for four years in an ongoing series of offensives. It was because of his fanaticism that millions of Russians were murdered—not by the Germans but by the Bolsheviks themselves. It was Stalin who was responsible for the failure of the Soviet Union to sign the Geneva Conventions; doing so would have forced the Germans to treat Russian prisoners of war as they did the Allied prisoners, or at least to pay lip service to the concept. The Russian people may lay a claim to the sympathy of the world for their suffering; their failed government deserves neither sympathy nor credit.

When we turn to the military side of the ledger, the issue is considered far too narrowly. The war on the Eastern Front was a conflict of competing supply systems: the victory went to the side better able to move men and matériel by rail and road, because logistical success determined victory on the battlefield. British and American aid was not simply supplementary; it was the root cause of the Red Army's success. The figures make the point: Britain shipped 4,020 trucks and 5,218 tanks; the United States shipped 375,883 trucks, 51,503 jeeps, 8,701 tractors, and 7,537 tanks. By 1945, two out of every three trucks in the Red Army were American, while Allied armored vehicles constituted about one tank out of every two in service.[18]

The Red Army's march to the west was totally dependent on the nearly half a million British and American vehicles and the four million tires supplied. The Russian railroad system could not have functioned without the 11,155 railroad cars and 1,981 locomotives the United States provided.

That the contrary is not only believed but routinely accepted as fact should not surprise anyone familiar with the history of how the Soviet Union was perceived in the West, but in application it is still disturbing.

One reason the Great Patriotic War has become such an important part of Russian history, I think, is not that it marks a great victory but that it marks the beginning of the collapse both of Communism and of Russia as a great power. Without the war, the Soviet Union might have staggered on and become more or less like contemporary China. But the conflict simply left too deep a mark—too many tens of millions of dead, too wide a swath of destruction. To revert to a practical example: in 1941, the Russian T-34 tank was clearly the best tank in the world. But it was a prewar design, and Russian designers were never able to do much better, even though they kept on producing new tanks. Half a century later, the Western powers were building better tanks, and as a series of minor wars made clear, the initial Soviet advantage had been utterly lost.

FAILURE AND PHILOSOPHY:
THE END OF THE WAR

Let not axioms or "ideas" be the rules of your Being. The Führer himself and alone is the present and future German reality and its law.

Martin Heidegger[1]

Summer 1943 was the high-water mark for both Hitler and the Wehrmacht. The following year would bring about a remarkable transformation: the Germans, besieged on every side, had lost their initial advantages, together with much of their conquered territory. More important, they had lost faith in their leader. For every officer who aided the July 1944 plotters, there were dozens more who, at the least, understood their reasoning and sympathized with it—including senior SS generals such as Sepp Dietrich.

Strategically and tactically, the final period of the war is remarkably devoid of interest. Although the Wehrmacht was grossly outnumbered on all three fronts and had lost the ability to contest mastery of the air almost totally, it possessed one great advantage. Its officers and men had been in combat continuously for four years. Despite losses at Stalingrad and in Tunisia, in the main the army had been remarkably successful in the field, and this gave it a high level of self-confidence.

Although it was no longer capable of mounting the kinds of offensive operations it had executed in the first part of the war, the traditional excellence of the army in defense ensured that the Germans would be tough opponents, and this advantage was increased by two factors. On the one hand, the Allies kept dispersing their forces, mounting offensives in areas where their technical superiority in airpower and mechanization counted for little. As a corollary, the Allies had to keep throwing fresh, and therefore inexperienced, troops into battle. The result was to pit raw recruits against seasoned veterans defending a terrain that was perfect for defensive operations and a nightmare for the attackers.

Although the Americans were quick to catch on, in 1943 they were still learning, and rivalries among the Allied commanders prevented the sort of mentoring that had been used in the First World War, when seasoned French troops trained the newly arrived Americans and continued to provide them with technical support. The Allied decision to launch a sequence of attacks aimed at widely scattered objectives (Sicily, Italy, Normandy, southern France) exacerbated this problem.[2]

It meant that far too many American soldiers were being used in assaults without having had any serious combat experience beforehand. It also meant that manpower resources were being frittered away. The most experienced combat troops were simply being ground down to debris. Montgomery's best British troops in North Africa, the legendary Desert Rats (technically, the Seventh Armored Division), had been in almost continuous combat from June 1940 until the end of the North African campaign, in May 1943. They were then sent to Italy, withdrawn at the end of the year, given six months' respite, and landed at Normandy. Not surprisingly, the division was exhausted, as were a good many of the Commonwealth forces engaged in France. They had simply been used up.

Of course, so had many of the German units that were deployed to Italy and France, but as they were now on the defensive, the problem was not as acute. In terms of morale, it is less taxing to secure a position than to try to take it—particularly when the terrain assigned is so perfectly suited for defensive warfare. In North Africa, the vast Allied superiority in mechanization and airpower had put the German and Italian forces at an enormous disadvantage. But Sicily and Italy seemed almost expressly designed to nullify those advantages. The terrain was mountainous, road links were few and poor, and rail lines virtually nonexistent. As with many parts of the Mediterranean coast, the areas had been settled early and the population was relatively dense; the roads had an almost unbroken sequence of villages and hamlets, and each one was an ideal defensive position.

So the Allies planned operations that tended to nullify their tactical superiority and play to German strengths. As a result, after conducting a spirited defense of Sicily, the Germans managed to evacuate almost their entire force across the Strait of Messina, where they proceeded to wage a bitter fight for the peninsula itself. The Italian campaign, intended to divert German troops from France, dragged on until after the Normandy landings. The Allied involvement in Italy in the First World War had had a similar aim, and a similar result: in both wars more Allied troops were tied down than German. Seen from that point of view, the campaign was a waste of precious Allied resources. The Allies needed the troops in Normandy far more than in Italy.

The other reason for the Italian campaign was to provide better bases for the strategic bombing campaign; in this sense, the Allied offensive paralleled Hitler's strategically unsuccessful Balkan operations in the spring of 1941. In both cases the rationale was dubious, and in each case the failure stemmed from not considering the alternative uses of the forces available.

Strategically, the one exception to the intellectually uninspiring history of the final part of the war was caused by Hitler himself. From August 1944 on, he had decided that Germany's best hope was to force a decision in the west, and ordered his surly, recalcitrant generals to launch a series of ambitious offensive operations. The most famous was the Ardennes assault of December 1944; the most important was the Avranches offensive, which Hitler had demanded in August. The idea was to split the American and Commonwealth forces that were beginning to break through the western end of the Normandy bridgehead. Like Stalin's offensive ventures of 1942, this one was such a disaster that it hardly warrants mention.

But the consequences were profound. To mount the operation, the

Germans had to strip their resources from the front. Therefore, when the offensive quickly stalled, there was nothing left to hold their position. The line broke and the German army left France as fast as it could withdraw.[3] Undeterred, Hitler demanded another such operation, in the Ardennes, with much the same aims. When that, too, quickly foundered in the face of determined U.S. resistance, Germany was basically left without any reserves, and since Soviet troops had already occupied Romania, Germany's fuel supply was shut off as well. From then on, the end was obvious, but Hitler called for still more offensives, particularly in Alsace and in Hungary.

From a narrow military viewpoint, it is easy to say that this series of offensive operations, like Citadel before them, broke the Wehrmacht and brought a relatively speedy end to the war. But from a broader perspective, the situation suggests that Hitler was correct to gamble. By July 1944, it was clear that Germany could not hope to win the conflict that it had begun. The failure of Citadel condemned the country to the multiple-front war that German military thinkers had always opposed.

The problem confronting Hitler was not, however, purely military. Regardless of how many of his generals were aware of the facts, Hitler himself certainly knew that, at his direct order, at least fourteen million people had been murdered; in addition, smaller but more visible crimes had been committed against prisoners of war. As we shall see in the next chapter, these events alone would have ensured a bloody judgment exacted against the German leaders when they lost the war.

Hitler had always made it clear that Germany would either emerge triumphant or be destroyed. But there was a third alternative. If he could break the back of the Allied offensive in France, subjecting the Allies to a horrific loss, they might then be willing to negotiate an armistice. Both Britain and the Soviet Union were on the ropes. Like a good many people both then and later, Hitler believed that the United States would lose heart after a major setback.

Probably he was wrong: all along, his enemies had shown much more determination to fight to the bitter end than the Germans had thought possible. And in any event, the last offensives failed miserably, so the possibility of a draw was never considered. The point is that, like the decision to attack the Soviet Union, Hitler's idea of a series of desperate offensives was, all things considered, rational. It was the only hope Germany had for settling the war on any sort of terms. Clearly, in hindsight, the chance was slim, but then so was the prospect of a Japanese victory— or even a draw—in the Pacific.

Nor was the thought of snatching victory out of the impending battlefield defeat Hitler's only idea. As the war on the Eastern Front raged unchecked, the dictator more and more put his faith in a somewhat contradictory pairing of great men and new gadgets.[4] Revolutionary new weapons would win the war for Germany. In the meantime, a succession of great men would stave off defeat. Both ideas were consistent with Hitler's view of the world: National Socialism was, on the one hand, a philosophy of seizing the present—something that only great men could do—and, on the other, a revolutionary movement, radical and technologically sophisticated.

From early on, Hitler had been looking for a few great men who would work to carry out his vision and, by his definition, he had found them: Göring and then Goebbels, Reinhard Heydrich and Sepp Dietrich, and finally, Albert Speer—to name a few of the most well known. When he turned to the military, however, he hardly saw more than technical competence—enthusiastic toadies like von Blomberg, Keitel, and Jodl; apathetic technocrats like von Rundstedt. Consequently, he was unusually attuned to relatively junior officers who had the requisite qualities Hitler sought.

So he gave Kurt Student his way with the airborne assaults, and Erich von Manstein his head with the changes to the offensive in the west. He gave Rommel, who had been commanding his army bodyguard, command of an armored division. When Fritz Todt was killed in a plane crash on February 8, 1942, Hitler turned to Speer to direct the German armaments industry. Speer was an architect who knew nothing about armaments, but the choice turned out to be a good one: under Speer, German military production began to approach, for the first time, the levels required by the Wehrmacht. But the choice was also typical of Hitler, who tended to put his trust almost blindly in those who had the requisite qualities he sought.

The best proof that Hitler put a premium on the intangible quality of greatness is to be found in his handling of disputes. He regarded most of the leadership, military and civilian, as *die Herde*; he bullied and intimidated them—or simply ignored them. But for the select few, the treatment was different. He listened to what they had to say, and occasionally even agreed with it. He certainly tolerated dissent: there were screaming matches with Admiral Räder and Heinz Guderian, frosty disagreements with von Rundstedt, open sniping from Sepp Dietrich—but all of them survived the war intact.

Unlike Stalin, Hitler brought truly competent people to the front and gave them real authority. He also held them to account. Student pushed the aerial offensive against Crete over the objections of everyone on the senior staff. Hitler backed him, but then judged him harshly for the heavy casualties incurred. Student fell out of favor, but he was still on the scene. In the fall of 1944, his First Parachute Army, a hastily assembled force tasked to hold the Dutch front, was instrumental in stopping Montgomery's ambitious airborne offensive to seize the bridges leading to the Rhine (Operation Market Garden). The following spring, Student was given the command of Army Group Vistula, with the hope he could do the same thing in the east. There is nothing like this in Stalin's record, and much evidence to the contrary—one reason why the Soviet Union did so poorly at every level during the war.

There was, however, one major problem with Hitler's idea. It didn't work. Part of this was inevitable. In the First World War, the Germans had managed to fight the Allies on three separate fronts. In the Second World War, the Germans were less successful—first, because they did not enter the war with the substantial advantages they had in 1914, and, second, because the United States became an active participant at a much earlier point in the conflict. Besides, the Germans found themselves having to fight on two additional fronts: North Africa and the skies over Germany itself.

The air war was entirely predictable. Although the Wehrmacht had rejected the notion of a strategic bomber force and had, instead, opted for a tactical one, it was hardly a surprise that both the British and the Americans were pursuing the idea, almost obsessively. Anyone in Berlin who looked at *Life* magazine could learn all about the main U.S. strategic bomber being developed in the late 1930s—the difference between the American reports about U.S. planes and German reports about German planes was, chiefly, that the former represented hard news while the latter was simply propaganda.[5]

Unlike the airpower enthusiasts, who believed that ground-to-air defenses were useless and that the bombers would always get through, Göring was skeptical, and rightly so. The strategic bombing campaigns of the previous war had not been particularly successful, and in the intervening decades, antiaircraft systems had developed remarkably. True, there had been some infamous successes: Guernica, Barcelona, Warsaw, Rotterdam. But in none of them had German pilots been faced with antiaircraft defenses of any serious nature. And indeed, at the end of the first year of the war, all the data regarding strategic bombing supported the idea that the theorists were wrong. RAF losses in the fall of 1939 had been heavy, the gains trivial. The brief German aerial offensive against Britain had been more effective, but the costs in aircrews had been much higher, severely weakening the Luftwaffe's ability to provide the support for ground operations in the Soviet Union that the army desperately needed.

What Göring had failed to consider was, at bottom, the same thing that Hitler had failed to factor into his calculations about the war on the Eastern Front: the willingness of Germany's enemies to fight on, regardless of the human cost. Although I am extremely dubious about the success of the strategic bombing campaign, there is no denying the determination of the U.S. and British commanders to continue the air war to the bitter end, despite the loss of tens of thousands of trained aviators and thousands of aircraft. As the air war went on, the Allies developed techniques that reduced their losses: the bombers themselves were more heavily armed, their range and altitude dramatically increased. The realities of the air war scrapped the traditional theory that bombers could operate with impunity over enemy airspace, and increasingly (by the end of 1943) the enormous aerial fleets were accompanied by long-range fighter escorts capable of protecting the bomber force from German interceptors.

The costs remained high, the results feeble, but the conflict helped to reveal the structural weakness of the National Socialist state—its inability to match the two democracies at the technical level. German aircraft designers were never able to produce successful next-generation fighters to replace the aging Me-109, and the Luftwaffe could not train enough aircrews sufficiently well to make up for the loss rate.

The toll in human life was horrific by summer 1943. In late May the Allies had launched the first thousand-bomber raid (on Cologne), followed by a massive raid on Dortmund, and then, at the end of July, a series of raids on Hamburg, which created a firestorm of such intensity that it incinerated the target. So the German failure in one theater (the Eastern Front) occurred at about the same time as failure in another (the war in the air).

The Luftwaffe was much more successful in protecting industrial sites. In the August attacks against the Ploesti refineries and the frictionless-bearings plants at Schweinfurt, the Allies incurred heavy losses. But Göring and his commanders had clearly failed to stop the bombing raids, or to limit their damage. Although the level of injury to the German war industry was problematic, the increasing civilian death toll—by February 1945, it was about 350,000—brought home to the Germans in a peculiarly horrific way the failures of National Socialism.[6] It also marked the end of Göring's ascendancy in Berlin. Although he remained, technically, the head of the air force and the designated successor, Hitler increasingly directed the air war himself, putting his faith in a new generation of technology—guided missiles and jet aircraft, whose development and deployment were supervised by Speer and his rival, Heinrich Himmler.

Göring's moral and administrative failures are well known. He is hardly a sympathetic character. In that regard, Erwin Rommel, briefly Hitler's favorite general, is his polar opposite, except in one respect: both men had distinguished themselves in the First World War. Unlike Göring, Rommel had remained in the military and had no observable sympathies for either Hitler or National Socialism. He came to Hitler's attention as commander of his army security detachment, and saw no action in Poland. But when he asked Hitler for the command of an armored division, Hitler obliged, and his propagandists shaped the Swabian career officer into one of the great men of the Third Reich.

In the popular mythology, Rommel led the crossing of the Meuse at Sedan, attacked the Maginot Line, and routed the slow-moving French, who had failed to understand the realities of the new warfare. In reality, not much of this had actually happened. The man responsible for the crossing of the Meuse at Sedan was Balck, commander of the First Motorized Infantry Regiment, whose troops crossed the river in rubber boats and on foot after seizing the numerous bridges. Rommel's handling of armor had little to do with the maneuver.

So, too, with the much-trumpeted idea that Rommel had engaged the Maginot Line forts and defeated them. Rommel was an energetic and resourceful commander, but he had started to believe his own press releases. More important, Hitler did too, so when the moment came to bail out the hapless Italians, Rommel was given a few troops and sent to North Africa. No better illustration can be found of Hitler's belief that a great man can solve, almost single-handedly, whatever problem confronted him.

The course of the war in the North African desert, a conflict that raged simultaneously with the battles on the Eastern Front, is well known. In the two theaters, success was intimately bound up with logistics, and in both, the National Socialist state signally failed. The Germans could not produce enough equipment to keep Rommel competitive on the ground, and the Italians were unable to keep the supply routes to North Africa open. Meanwhile, the Allies poured resources into the theater. That Rommel managed to fight on for as long as he did, scoring notable successes, is testimony to his skills as a combat commander.

But his achievements came at a price, mainly in Italian blood. Rommel, who had fought the Italians in the First World War, had the sort of contempt for them that often characterizes insular and provincial Germans and Englishmen (in this he was curiously like his great adversary Montgomery). As a result, he treated his allies more or less the way the French high command had treated their African troops in 1917—using them as cannon fodder, without much concern for their fate, all the while denigrating their performance. The survivors of the Italian units in North Africa came to spit when his name was mentioned (and not just figuratively, either). Nor was Rommel's reputation with his own, German, officers much better.[7]

Fighting a determined and well-equipped enemy on a shoestring affected Rommel as well. By January 1943, he was, as he confessed to his wife, so depressed he could hardly attend to his duties; it was obvious, and by February he needed to be sent home.[8] In a predictable pattern, Hitler was furious: he had sent Rommel to North Africa to win, not to have a nervous breakdown. The facts of the case hardly mattered. Rommel should have prevailed, just as Student should have applied the lessons of the airborne attack against the Netherlands to Crete. In both cases there were clearly extenuating circumstances, but, at bottom, Hitler's judgment was no more unfair than Churchill's in deciding that the man who lost Crete, Freyberg, would never again hold an independent command, or in sacking Claude Auchinleck in North Africa.

Perhaps more judicious than Churchill, Hitler let Rommel stew for a while, then sent him to France to organize the defenses there. This is an interesting insight: Hitler apparently realized that Rommel's real competence lay in organizing defensive positions, particularly in the face of a determined, qualitatively superior enemy. Although this characterization is hardly recognized even today, it is not a bad appreciation of Rommel's expertise: his victory in the desert against the British stemmed, in fact, from the defensive, rather than the offensive, measures he employed.

In France, Rommel immediately became embroiled in a serious conflict over the disposition of forces along the coast. In North Africa, Rommel's attempts to conduct a modern war without air superiority had left an impression on him. It also made him unique in the ranks of the senior German commanders in northern Europe (particularly France), who had never had to operate with that handicap. In some cases they probably discounted tactical airpower altogether. Although, generally speaking, the consensus has been that Rommel was correct in his belief that if the defenders weren't already in position on the coast, they would never reach it, this is, as I've argued before, a distortion of events.

Two problems confronted the German defenders. They weren't sure where the Allies would land, or exactly when. What made this matter serious was that France had no decent rail and road infrastructure running parallel to the English Channel. If an armored division was deployed at one end of the coast, and the invasion was at the other end, the division would have to be shipped inland toward Paris and then back to the coast, because all the main rail lines spread out from the capital. The situation was made more acute by the German deduction that the best landing site was at the Pas de Calais region on the French coast. Forces positioned there would never be able to reach a landing site farther south. The best solution was to hold them back closer to the hub, so that they could move up to where they were needed.

In other words, both sides had a point. Rommel had certainly been right: German units moving up toward Normandy were, as it turned out, mauled by Allied airpower. But that would have happened in any event: no one supposed that the only invasion site was Normandy, and even after the landings began, there was no reason to assume that they would be concentrated there. From the German perspective, the Allies had an overwhelming advantage at every level and could easily afford multiple landing positions—indeed, they had used them earlier.

The real failure was neither Rommel's nor von Runstedt's (nor Hitler's, contrary to postwar rationalizations); it was that National Socialism had failed to produce quality weapons in quantities sufficient to allow the Wehrmacht to fight a modern war. The Germans had never had much in the way of technical superiority, and by 1944, they were the least mechanized of all the major combatants. Lacking sufficient vehicles (and armor with the necessary cruising range and reliability), they were forced to fall back on trains, horses, and feet, all of which made them highly vulnerable from the air.

Although, like Student, Rommel had fallen dramatically from Hitler's favor, he might have redeemed himself in the defense of the Normandy bridgehead.[9] But fate intervened. Seriously injured in an automobile accident, Rommel had to sit out the fatal summer of 1944. Implicated—without any real justification—in the July plot, he was forced to kill himself. Whether Rommel would have made the German defense even tougher than it was is an open question, but his forced suicide is certainly a sad end for a gallant officer of great ability who had served his country well in two world wars. In my view no higher praise can be given, nor should it be demanded. Contrary to his British hagiographers, though, a great captain Rommel was not. Great captains don't develop psychosomatic illnesses and abandon the battlefield.[10] Although an admirable human being, Rommel, like Göring, never lived up to Hitler's expectations, however unrealistic those might have been.

Regardless of how aggressive Hitler's aims were once he came to power, there was, as I noted before, a curious disconnect with the actual level of armaments production. Krupp had been given the contract to manufacture the original Mark 4 tank, which was supposed to equip one out of every four tank battalions, but it produced only 45 vehicles in 1939 and 280 in 1940.[11] Even though by the summer of 1941 it was obvious that the low-velocity L24 version of the 7.5-centimeter main gun in the Mark 4 was woefully inadequate for combat, Krupp kept on turning them out, and managed to build 480 in 1941. It wasn't until the following year that an upgraded Mark 4, armed with a more potent version of the 7.5-centimeter gun, appeared, and even then, the numbers were ridiculous: 837 vehicles for the entire year.

Figures for the Mark 3, intended as the main battle tank in prewar German thinking, were not much better: 157 of the pathetic 3.7-centimeter vehicle in 1939, and 392 in 1940. An upgunned Mark 3, equipped with a high-velocity 5.0-centimeter weapon, went into production in 1940, but even though the contract was spread out among several additional firms, only 470 were turned out. So the Wehrmacht entered the second phase of the war, in 1941, with far too few tanks, all of them far too feeble.

Initially, the shortfall was partially made up for by relying on Czech production of the standard prewar Czech tank, known in the German service as the 38t. During 1940–41, it was, after the Mark 3, the vehicle manufactured in the largest quantities. But the 38t was highly unsuited for the Eastern Front, and the Czech plant could produce them only in limited quantities: the 698 vehicles manufactured during 1941 hardly met the need for replacements.

The other alternative was to press captured foreign vehicles into service. By July 1940 the Germans had thousands of French tanks as well as tracked personnel carriers, and all saw service one way or another. But French equipment had been designed for purely defensive use, because the mission of the French army after 1918 had been fixed on defense of the country. Consequently the French equipment was unsuited for the Eastern Front, where speed (and cross-country mobility) were all-important. Then, too, the deployment of these vehicles so far away from their original point of service created severe logistical problems.

As the first phase of the war wound down, in the summer of 1940, what the Wehrmacht clearly needed was a modern tank produced in quantity. The 1,460 vehicles built that year barely replaced destroyed or worn-out machine, and three-quarters of the tanks built were obsolete. Once the Russian offensive began, the Germans discovered that there was a steep price to pay for their apathetic production schedules and the sublime indifference of experts like Guderian to what their opponents were doing in tank design.

Consequently, production was increased. In 1940, 1,460 tanks had been built; in 1941, the figure more than doubled—to 3,256. In 1942, after Speer took over as armaments director, it increased yet again, to 4,198 tanks, the vast majority of which were upgraded Mark 3 and 4 vehicles with high-velocity guns. Despite the strenuous objections of the tankers, Speer also supervised the most significant development in armor during the war—the production of self-propelled guns.

It was this weapon that enabled the Germans to maintain a rough parity with the Soviet T-34, as these vehicles all mounted guns with equivalent hitting power (and no wonder, since most of them were equipped with modified versions of the Soviet 76.2-millimeter gun). In 1942, 975 vehicles were produced, and, in the following year, production nearly trebled: 2,657 self-propelled guns were built, and 5,996 tanks. By this time—1943—the manufacture of modern tanks had finally begun, but the modified Mark 4 was still far and away the tank produced in the greatest quantities: of those 5,996 vehicles, 3,073 were Mark 4 tanks. In 1944, production went up yet again, to 8,224 tanks, but with a substantial decline in the figures for self-propelled guns—that number fell to 1,246.

Although the percentage increases were impressive, the numbers themselves reveal the staggering imbalance in production. Britain and the United States shipped 12,755 tanks to the Soviet Union, nearly the same number as Germany produced in 1943–44.[12] The United States turned out more than 40,000 Sherman tanks during the Second World War, and while Soviet statistics have to be treated skeptically, the Soviet claim to have manufactured more than 60,000 T-34 tanks during the war is not improbable. At any rate, even a cursory glance at the data makes clear the German shortfall in armored vehicles. German tankers could win every engagement, inflicting massive losses on the opponents, and still not prevail.

If Germany's tank production was appallingly insufficient, its truck production was even worse. At the start of 1940, the Wehrmacht was (by its rather penurious standards) reasonably well off. Its truck inventory was almost sufficient to equip itself—about 120,000 vehicles.[13] There were serious problems, however, none of which were ever solved, so January 1940 saw the army's truck pool at its peak. Many of the trucks were aging vehicles unsuitable for use in the field; they were simply civilian models pressed into military service. Vehicles with any sort of cross-country or rough-terrain performance were only a small fraction of the total inventory. To make matters worse, the allocation of truck production for the military that had been decided on was insufficient to replace normal losses even in peacetime.

One year later, the situation was, if anything, worse. In June 1941, three of the ten mechanized divisions had to make do with captured trucks (mostly French), and hardly any of the infantry organic to the armored divisions were fitted out with half-tracks. The vehicular situation was so bad that the force that invaded Russia was largely dependent on captured trucks and horses—625,000 of the latter were pressed into service. In fact, the Wehrmacht entered the Eastern Front with slightly more horses than motorized vehicles. Although 600,000 vehicles sounds like an enormous number, the figure has to be put into perspective. During the Second World War, the Canadians alone produced 350,000 trucks, or slightly fewer than the total shipped by the United States to the Soviet Union.

But enough has been said to make the point: when it came to industrial production, German industry failed spectacularly. The interesting question is why this was so. Part of the answer lies in the restrictions of Versailles, whose terms forced German industries to relocate their armaments development and production abroad, where, when successful, they were supplying matériel in small quantities. Countries like Spain, Turkey, the Netherlands, and Finland wanted quality weaponry but had no need for it in great quantity. Germany itself was deprived of a military big enough to require any serious mass-production efforts.

Then, too, a curious split had developed in war industries. Smaller items—rifles and machine guns, for example—had long been produced on assembly lines; with interchangeable parts, they were typical industrial products. But everything else was still being turned out in artisanal fashion, one or two at a time. Thus trucks and artillery pieces—and, later on, tanks—were manufactured the same way railroad locomotives and other large industrial items were. In the United States, tanks were increasingly constructed in plants set up by the automobile industry, which was accustomed to mass production on an assembly line. In Germany the firms responsible, like Krupp, were organized around batch production, and the contracts issued by the army typically called for just that: a small batch of, say, twenty-five vehicles, to be followed by another batch, and so forth.

We sometimes forget that fairly large quantities of industrial products can be turned out in this system—that a manufacturer can make complicated devices in the low thousands without mastering the principle of the assembly line. But the briefest reflection suggests this is certainly true: there were reasonably large numbers of cars and trucks on the world's roads long before Henry Ford built his first successful car. And the Model T of 1908 was built like every other complicated industrial device: a handful of workers built one car at a time, turning out a couple of vehicles a day.

To Ford, it was a slow and inefficient process. By 1913 he had hit on the idea of putting the vehicles on a huge conveyor belt: as the item being built moved across the factory floor, the workers, who remained in place, added parts, so the Model T was gradually assembled. Not only did workers specialize; they didn't waste time lugging parts. By 1918, half the cars in the United States were Fords; within three years, Ford had the largest automobile assembly plant in the world.

The Ford assembly line was as much a concept as a process. Ironically, the notion of mass production had an impact on manufacturing techniques just as Germany was being restricted by Versailles. Despite the reputation of German firms like Mercedes-Benz, Opel, and Auto Union, the German automotive industry was the least affected by Ford's methods—largely because of the limited market in the lean years following the war.

The German lands after 1918 were characterized by small farms and a dense rail network. Consequently, there was not the need for heavy equipment (trucks and tractors) on the scale that was required in Australia, Canada, and the United States, whose citizens, not coincidentally, had the wealth to purchase such items. American firms such as Holt (which then became Caterpillar) were already well established by 1914: Holt running gear was the basis for early British and French tank development. One reason Germany lagged in this area was that there was no German equivalent to Holt.

Early tank designers soon discovered that agricultural and industrial tracked vehicles made lousy tanks, as the requirements were totally different. But the size of the market that was developing led the civilian companies to emulate key aspects of Ford's manufacturing techniques. This was important because the assembly of heavy equipment presented a host of problems to be solved, simply because of the weight and size of the finished product. German firms never really dealt with any of this until well into the war. By contrast, even though the British spent the interwar years fiddling with dozens of designs, they were able to turn out many more tanks than the Germans were. For the same reason, the Czechs and the Russians, who as newcomers to the scene were more disposed to copy American methods, were much more efficient at turning out equipment in mass quantities.

As the war intensified, the Germans learned, but the impressive progress they made conceals their structural weakness. They became much more efficient at producing tanks and trucks, for instance, but they were never able to supply the army with enough tires, or the air force with enough engines. Indeed, in key areas the German approach remained firmly artisanal: craftsmen and engineers producing complex pieces of equipment that were technically fascinating—and often revolutionary—but were totally unsuited for mass production.

The enormous technological shifts in the interwar period disguised some of the problems. Thus the German manufacturers did pretty well with batch production in the first generation of aircraft (those produced before 1935 or so). But they were unable to make the break to the next generation, which required mass production of substantially more complex mechanisms. Basically, the aircraft industry was never able to move beyond planes like the Me-109 fighter, the Ju-52 transport, and the Ju-87 dive-bomber. They were all excellent planes for their day, but by 1941 that day had come and gone. The replacement aircraft were largely inferior to what was being produced elsewhere, and were not produced in sufficient numbers to overcome the qualitative edge.

This last point is often misunderstood or ignored. The best examples are to be found in tank design. When in late 1941, the Germans encountered Soviet tanks liked the T-34 and its larger relatives, the tankers realized, belatedly, that the Russians were a whole generation ahead of them. The T-34 had sloped armor, which vastly increased its resistance to armor-piercing shells. By contrast, the armor on German tanks consisted almost entirely of vertical plates. And the T-34 was superior in other ways: its high-velocity 76.2-millimeter gun, broader treads, and more powerful engine gave it substantially better all-terrain performance as well as speed.

From the point of view of the tankers, the solution was simple: build a German T-34. From an engineering standpoint, it was a sensible idea. As anyone who has poked around a T-34 can attest, the basic mechanism is simple to the point of primitive. There was only one problem confronting those doing this reverse engineering. Although the T-34 weighed about the same as the later versions of both the Mark 3 and the Mark 4, it had a much more powerful engine, a compact V-12 diesel turning out 500 horsepower. Motive power had always been the weak point in tank design, and it was one the Germans had never solved: the standard Maybach engine used in both the Mark 3 and the Mark 4 produced a relatively feeble 300 horsepower and was also a finicky gas hog. To reverse-engineer a German T-34, the Germans would therefore have to develop (or copy) the Soviet diesel.

There's no reason why this couldn't have been done. The engine was already at hand. Daimler-Benz had developed a 550-horsepower engine by mid-1937. This engine, later known as the DB-600, existed in both gasoline and diesel versions and, like the engine that powered the T-34, was adapted from an aircraft unit. The other unusual feature of the Russian tank, its modified Christie suspension and track system, was hardly novel: the American engineer Walter Christie had developed it in the 1920s, and the Russians had basically reverse engineered and then modified it for their own tanks. The Soviet Union had some brilliant engineers, but the idea that what they had done their German counterparts couldn't manage is preposterous.

The main reason it wasn't done was a typically insular attitude on the part of the tank designers, coupled with a certain stubbornness on the part of the army. The designers and engineers all knew better. If it wasn't invented by them, it was beneath contempt. The army would have to wait, and in due time a suitable superior tank would emerge. Besides,

German tank designers had been working on not one but two designs from early 1937 on. But the army didn't feel there was much need for a more powerful tank, and so development had puttered along.

It's tempting to blame this inertia on the problem. That is to say, had the army's tank experts wanted a decent tank, one would have been built, but the specifications for both vehicles make clear that, once again, the army had missed the mark. The first prototype, known as the VK-3001, weighed a staggering thirty-two metric tons, was powered by an anemic 116-horsepower engine, and mounted the fearsome 7.5-centimeter low-velocity gun that had proven itself worthless in combat from September 1939 on.[14] The only thing the VK-3001 had more of was its crew: it took five men to operate this monstrosity. Eventually, the VK-3001, suitably modified, ended up as the Mark 5, known as the Panther.

While the engineers piddled with the VK-3001, in the spring of 1941, Hitler ordered another heavy tank to be developed, and this vehicle, which entered service as the Mark 6 (generally known as the Tiger 1) went into production in August 1942. So in the confused world of German tank design, the Mark 6 (Tiger) was actually designed and in service before the Mark 5 (Panther), since the first Panthers didn't see service until July 1943.

Although the short design cycle of the Tiger 1 suggests what the industry could do if a gun was held to its head, both versions of this tank (one done by Porsche, the other by Henschel) were simply big fat versions of the Mark 4. The Tiger 1 had the same vertical armor, although its excessive weight (fifty-five tons) required a different steering and suspension system. Part of the weight was owing to the high-velocity 8.8-centimeter gun the Tiger mounted. This weapon, basically the same as the standard Luftwaffe antiaircraft weapon, enabled the Tiger to destroy with one shot any target it hit.

But the whole project—like all the other German designs—was a waste on a grand scale. The Russians had already figured out how to upgrade the T-34 to take an 85-millimeter gun almost as powerful as the

German weapon, and this in a package that weighed only 60 percent of the Tiger's fifty-five tons and had a substantially lower profile (302 centimeters high as opposed to the German tank's 373).

In a nutshell, the Tiger epitomized German tank design: too heavy and too high. When the Panthers rolled out on the battlefield, they continued the tradition. The Panther, although armed with a formidable high-velocity 75-millimeter gun, weighed 44 percent more than the T-34/85 and had a 26 percent higher profile. By contrast, the current American main battle tank, the Abrams, has a profile that is only 76 percent of the Panther's, and is actually lower than the T-34 in any of its variants. On the battlefield, a profile makes for a target, and the heavy sloped armor of the Panther did not compensate nearly enough for this failing. Just as the Mark 2 had been an overweight and overengineered machine-gun carrier, so with the Panthers and the Tigers. True, the firepower was formidable, but it was possible to get the same potency with a lot less.[15]

The consensus among tank experts has always been that the Panther was the best-designed German tank and could have been, potentially, the best tank of the war. This is doubtful. By early 1945, the British had already started producing the first versions of the Centurion tank. Centurion 1 tanks arrived in Europe too late to see action, but only by a few weeks. The Centurion was roughly the same size and weight as the Panther, and in no way inferior in hitting power or armor. Postwar, successive models of the Centurion were widely used, particularly by the Israeli Defense Force, where modified Centurions, called the Sh'ot, were the mainstay of the tank force for many years.

Despite a poor start in tank production, a decent American tank, popularly known as the Pershing, was in combat in March 1945. Armed with a 90-millimeter gun, the Pershing was more than a match for its German adversaries, and successive modifications resulted in a series of remarkable postwar designs. Because the war was over before the new Allied tanks could play a decisive role does not mean that they would not have been involved had the war continued past May 1945. By contrast, there was nothing in the German pipeline that would have resulted in anything better than the Panther.

There is another point to be considered. The initial batch of Panthers had severe problems. Hitler and his generals had pinned their hopes for the success of Citadel on the use of the Panther. Guderian had insisted that the tanks could not be used until July 1943. Despite Guderian's idea, when the battle began—in July 1943—the tanks were totally unfit for combat. Some—probably most—of the initial contingent never even made it to the battlefield, owing to engine fires and transmission failures, and the tank quickly established itself as a total lemon.

In the automotive industry, it is widely accepted that quality-control problems are, to a great extent, caused by design problems. They are not, in other words, simply a function of shoddy workmanship but often represent overly complex, highly fragile, or poorly thought out mechanisms. The same principle holds true in other areas. The serious defects in the Panther tank did not result from poor workmanship but were inherent in the design.[16] This bespeaks a serious problem, because one of the Panther's claims to fame was that it could be assembled in half the time it took to build a Tiger 1. That is to say, the Panther had the potential for mass production, while the Tiger would remain a batch-produced vehicle.

Unfortunately, the Panther's problems were typical of German designs, which, whether for planes or vehicles, tended to be mechanically unreliable, overly delicate, and underpowered, rarely if ever performed up to specification. The problem was not, in other words, simply the failure of National Socialism to organize industry properly. There was a general systemic failure to produce workable new deigns, a failure to get them into production in a timely fashion, and a well-nigh universal failure to produce them in sufficient quantity.

These German failures have long been recognized, albeit often grudgingly and only partially. What has not been recognized nearly enough is the extent to which the failure was not the result of ineptitude or even meddling from on high. Nor was it inevitable. In the First World War, German production had remained at a remarkable level until the end of the war.

At bottom, the German failure is a direct consequence of the philosophical roots of National Socialism. Since for decades it has been a tenet of faith that National Socialism was nothing but a jumble, and certainly not fit to be thought of as a philosophy, its impact on German affairs under Hitler has been resolutely ignored, and everything that happened reduced to personalities.

And in studying the Third Reich, it is quite clear that personalities were of great importance. But, as the quotation from Martin Heidegger that begins this chapter should make clear, personalities were important because a dependence on personality was at the base of National Socialist ideology. As I've suggested in the opening sections of this chapter, this principle was applied in reciprocal fashion. Just as all power and authority flowed from Hitler, the great man and national leader, so did Hitler put extraordinary faith in those he judged also to be great men.

But the emphasis on the *Führerprinzip* should not blind us to the fact that National Socialism had a fairly clear set of ideological positions, of which racism was only one. In fact, arguably the most important related to economics. Hitler, like Lenin, felt that industrialization "made the individual completely unfree . . . in bondage to capital and the machine . . . a work mill in which any originality or individuality is crushed." Freedom could be achieved only by "radically abolishing all the specious results of industrialization and restoring this development to the service of mankind and individualism."[17]

Both Hitler and Lenin argued that their peculiar forms of Socialism would solve the problem that they both felt existed. Where Hitler differed from Lenin was that for Lenin, the only way to solve the problem was for the proletariat to control everything. For Lenin and the Bolsheviks, the only key factor in social relations was class, and in practice, this led to class hatred and violence. For Hitler, rather more shrewdly, nationality, or ethnicity, trumped class distinctions. So long as the nation was controlled by the right leader, it made no difference who had ownership of what.

One key to Hitler's success in building his party was that the National Socialists espoused many of the same ends as the Socialists and the Bolsheviks—but they promised to deliver on those goals without resorting to class warfare. For most Germans, it was the social and economic foundations of National Socialism that were the most significant. Racial ideology was certainly there, but it was, for most people, a relatively minor issue, largely because the percentage of recognizable foreigners (Jews) living in Germany was such a small fraction of the total population, less than 1 percent. Then, too, when Hitler spoke of the need to reduce the influence of the Jews, he confined himself exclusively to that: it's not as though he came out and told everyone what he intended to do, i.e., to have them all murdered.

The link between economic and social concerns reflects their actual linkage in National Socialism. By the mid-1920s, one of the things about Communism that frightened people was the extent to which it loudly proclaimed its intentions to do away with the existing social order, as exemplified by such institutions as the family, motherhood, and community. Explicitly, National Socialism stood for a renewed emphasis on all three, and it was consistent in this belief. When Albert Speer pointed out that if the Germans made women work in factories (as the British and the Americans were doing), production would dramatically improve, he was quickly rebuffed. A series of decrees were passed, for the purpose of maintaining family relations in wartime, such as marriage by proxy and the automatic legitimacy of children borne out of wedlock to German women in cases where the father was a soldier.

In other words, mass industrialization—the all-important principle necessary to equip the Wehrmacht adequately for total war—was totally antithetical to National Socialism. As Speer attempted to import these principles into German industry, he therefore met with resistance, notably from Otto Ohlendorf, aided and abetted by Franz Hayler. Both men were seasoned party members, and highly educated. Hayler had a doctorate in political science, and Ohlendorf was a lawyer and no mean economist. Himmler had put both men in key positions in the government and in the SS.[18]

Whatever their politics, German industrialists were no more enthusiastic about having their systems tampered with than were their counterparts in the Wehrmacht, and indeed much of Speer's success stemmed from his realism about what he called "American" methods, i.e., mass-production techniques. Although it was clearly a case of too little, too late, there were substantial increases after Speer replaced Todt. Ohlendorf saw quite clearly that this was not a direction consistent with the goals of National Socialism. As he observed in a speech he delivered on July 15, 1944:

> We must view and test every economic structure in terms of whether it allows the full development of the basis characteristics of the German. . . . The goods we produce after the war are not so essential; what is essential is that we preserve and develop the substance of our biological values. . . . If we can carry out our *weltanschauung* even in the area of economic management, then we will finally achieve that order which, deep down, allows the development of human strength to be identical with man's mission towards his God.[19]

Just as Hitler was willing to tolerate exceptions, at least temporarily, to the principle of a military free of men of Jewish descent, so was he willing to see some exceptions to his economic principles. But his followers were not so pragmatic, and in the area of economics and industrial production, they were able to tap into a long-standing German fear of the soulless modern that had been raised to a fever pitch by the Bolsheviks.

In other words, true mass production was impossible in the Third Reich, because it violated one of the basic principles of National Socialism. In this one area, the Stalinist state had an advantage. Under the fiction that the workers owned the means of production and were free to enjoy the fruits thereof, Communists had no objection to the assembly line and the factory. Indeed, they celebrated it extensively. Alienation, it was argued, was a capitalist ailment. Psychologically and socially, the National Socialists were probably correct in their assessments of the corrosive effects of industrialization, although they failed to understand its benefits. Like Shakespeare's Richard III, Hitler went down with the National Socialist flag nailed to the mast, and refused to compromise his beliefs, even though in practice they doomed the Third Reich on almost every level.[20]

THE CRIMINALS

In the description of the Brianvillers trail [1772] this sentence:
"The greatest crimes, far from being suspected, cannot even be
imagined." That is quite true and derives from the fact that as
the magnitude of the crime increases, the more it rises above
the instinctive. The more intelligent it becomes, the more the
evidence disappears.

Ernst Jünger, October 16, 1943[1]

The military achievements of the Wehrmacht are perhaps not as impressive as they are sometimes made out to be, but the Germans proved
extremely tough opponents. Although from 1943 on, the Wehrmacht was
fighting on multiple fronts—and greatly outnumbered—it fought stubbornly on, mounting substantial offensive operations until the bitter end.
The Americans, and to a lesser extent the British, came away from their
victory with a respect for the Wehrmacht that grew almost obsessive as
the decades passed. Its virtues were magnified, its faults minimized.

The greatest fault, however, was not operational; it was moral, and it
is almost completely unremarked. In light of the Holocaust, this remark
may seem peculiar. But in the minds of a great many historians, the
wholesale murders by the Hitler regime were almost totally the work of
the SS. The regular army was simply a helpless bystander to a crime it
could do nothing to prevent. Alternatively, when the issue of war crimes
is raised at all, it is in connection with the Eastern Front, where whatever

sins the Wehrmacht committed can, with a certain truth, be blamed on the Bolsheviks and Stalin.

The matter is complex, and because of the amount of time that has passed, it may not be resolvable. But there is a clearer and simpler moral issue that we know a great deal about. From the first moment of combat, in September 1939, German officers violated the basic principle that had governed warfare among European nations for centuries. It was the expectation that uniformed soldiers—and particularly officers—had of experiencing good treatment at the hands of their adversaries once the killing stopped. These principles, codified by international treaties known collectively as the Geneva Conventions, had been accepted by professional armies since the middle of the eighteenth century.[2]

The code was schizophrenic. Uniformed soldiers essentially had one code of conduct for themselves and another for civilians, and the colonial wars of the nineteenth century exacerbated the dualism. Outside of Europe, the major powers slaughtered native populations mercilessly, with little concern about whether or not such conduct was allowable, legal, or moral.

Communism under Lenin brought the problem back to Europe with a vengeance. In the abortive Russo-Polish War of 1920, he exhorted the Red Army to crush the representatives of feudal or bourgeois Poland, using terms of the utmost savagery and violence. Lenin's followers had previously initiated a reign of terror in the Baltic states and Hungary, and the adversaries of Bolshevism responded in kind.

But those conflicts, although violent and on a large scale, had the look and feel of civil wars. The officers of the Wehrmacht, like their British and French colleagues, explicitly adhered to the same rules of war governing the treatment of their uniformed opponents that they had observed in the First World War. After 1945, they insisted that, although there were fanatical National Socialists who may have broken those rules on occasion, the regular army had, by and large, adhered to them, and whatever exceptions occurred had been caused by the atrocities committed by fanatical Communists on the Eastern Front.[3]

But this account of the Wehrmacht's behavior is not true. From the start of the war, the army simply pitched the tradition governing the treatment of uniformed prisoners of war that had been observed for centuries. On September 9, 1939, for example, the colonel commanding the third battalion of the Fifteenth Motorized Infantry Regiment had the three hundred Polish soldiers his men had captured in the fighting around Ciepelów lined up and summarily shot.[4]

No clearer violation of the conventions of warfare is to be found than the Ciepelów massacre. There were too many victims for this event to be classified as an isolated instance of indiscipline by a panicked soldiery. A direct order came from a senior officer who clearly understood the rules, since he attempted to create a scene that suggested the dead soldiers were actually civilians who had taken up arms against his men—illegal combatants, if you will. Photographs were taken. On that day in September, what the German officer corps had prized for centuries—its honor—was fatally wounded, and by the end of the month, it had, like Shakespeare's Julius Caesar, been systematically stabbed to death, by dozens of similar incidents. After the war, Polish researchers identified well over fifty similar incidents (most of them involving smaller numbers), far too many for the usual excuses to have any validity whatsoever.[5]

Most of the 700,000 Polish soldiers who became German prisoners of war fared better, in that they weren't murdered immediately, and many of them survived the war. That they did so was no testimony to the German army's observation of the rules governing prisoners of war. Polish soldiers who surrendered were beaten and starved. They were made to work at forced labor under primitive conditions, and were entirely at the mercy of their captors—who were, it should quickly be said, ordinary soldiers and not members of the SS. At the war's end, American photographers found their dead bodies stacked like firewood, as emaciated and gaunt in death as the civilian dead whose remains littered the Third Reich.[6]

Although the Polish case can be taken as an example of the corrosive effects of National Socialism on morals, I don't think this explanation comes anywhere near the mark. Given his rank, Colonel Wessel, who ordered the Ciepelów massacre, was far too old to have been brainwashed by National Socialism, and this seems true of many German soldiers in 1939.[7] For the next generations of recruits, and for the junior officers newly promoted, we might expect this to be the case, but the character and personality of the senior field-grade officers of 1939 were formed before Hitler came to power.

Moreover, the officer corps was that section of German society most resistant to the racism of National Socialism. There were dedicated party members, but the percentage of Hitlerite fanatics was rather small. That regular army officers would stand by and do nothing while someone else committed crimes is another matter, of course, and quite consistent with the passive side of the passive-aggressive behavior exhibited by the army's leaders after Hitler began interfering with their traditional prerogatives. But Wessel's behavior was active, it was clearly criminal, it was deliberate, it was obeyed — and it was not an isolated event. At the higher levels of the military, National Socialism was certainly a motivating factor, as was the force of Hitler's personality. But out in the field, in 1939, it doesn't provide us with an answer, any more than it explains why such war crimes became so widespread so quickly.

Nor can the matter be explained by some quasi-mystical reference to the barbarism of the Germans.[8] When the Russians seized their share of Poland, Stalin's creatures did exactly the same thing as their German counterparts; such behavior suggests that the idea of hatred bred into the German soul hardly stands up.[9] In general, the most brutal and enthusiastic of Hitler's murderers were not German at all, but Baltic, Ukrainian, Croatian, or even (and especially) Romanian.[10]

Although some army officers expressed reservations about the wholesale massacres of Polish civilians they witnessed in September 1939, the army itself did nothing to deal with criminal acts initiated by its officers against uniformed opponents. The usual excuse is to blame the SS for all this. But at bottom, this approach represents a fundamental misunderstanding. The vast majority of the field-grade officers of the SS had a traditional military background either as senior noncoms or junior officers. Reinhard Heydrich, the head of the most sinister branch of the

SS, the SD (Sicherheitdienst), was directly responsible for control of the Einsatzgruppen, the death squads that ranged across Poland right behind the army. He had been an officer in the Kriegsmarine, under Räder, and was thrown out of the navy for reasons that had little to do with his performance as an officer. Heydrich certainly knew the rules, and naval officers as a group were the cleanest section of the military.

Paul Hausser, the man who designed the training program for officers and noncoms in the SS (and then became inspector general of the schools), was one of the SS's most important senior officers. Hausser had an impeccable military background. The son of an officer, he had gone through the prestigious Lichterfelde cadet school and, as a captain, was retained postwar and retired from the Reichsheer as a major general. Hausser illustrates both the close relationship between SS and Luftwaffe officers and the obvious point that here was a man who clearly knew the rules of war.[11]

What began in Poland contravened those rules unambiguously. From the first, senior officers cooperated with the SS units charged with ethnic cleansing (murder on the wholesale level), while the Waffen-SS units simply did as they pleased. All of this was taking place under the noses of the soldiers of the army, often with regular units engaging in their own murders, as the example of Ciepelów makes clear.

What made the situation worse was that the traditional check on such behavior—the fear that if you mistreated your opponent, he would respond in kind—was absent, owing to the short duration of the fighting. Predictably, the army emerged from Poland with a taste for killing that the army commanders ignored (or denied), since they knew very well that it was precisely what Hitler demanded.

The dishonor of the Wehrmacht did not begin in June 1941. Nor did it start when the army sat by and watched the Jews being systematically murdered. In September 1939, that tragic event was still in the future. It began, both literally and metaphorically, one Friday in September 1939, when Colonel Wessel ordered three hundred Polish soldiers shot and left in a ditch by the side of a road.

Once the crimes began—and went unchecked—there was no turning back. And, of course, the easiest thing to do was to take the path of least resistance, to look the other way. On May 13, 1940, as the Germans fought their way through the French city of Sedan, one of the main roads out of the city was blocked by a concrete pillbox known as Blockhouse 220, garrisoned by French soldiers from the 147th Infantry Regiment. Many of their colleagues to the north of the city had died at their posts trying to stop the German advance, but the ten men here, isolated, cut off, and outnumbered, surrendered. They were then lined up and shot, presumably by men from Hermann Balck's First Motorized Infantry Regiment, part of Rommel's armored division.[12]

Nor was this an isolated event. Two weeks later, men of the second battalion of the Royal Norfolk Regiment were trying to block the German advance on Dunkirk, holding on to the tiny hamlets of Le-Cornet Malo, Riez-du-Vinage, and Le Paradis. Overwhelmed by the superior force, they surrendered to the Germans. They were then marched off into a field and murdered. In the French case, there were no survivors to press charges, and even less interest on the part of the De Gaulle government in conducting investigations into May–June 1940. But two of the one hundred–odd British victims managed to survive, and one of them, Bert Pooley, managed to get his story told. The officer responsible for this crime, Captain Fritz Knochlein, was eventually identified, tried, and on January 28, 1949, executed.[13]

In the context of a war in which millions of civilians were butchered, it seems almost perverse to focus on the deaths of handfuls of combatants—which explains why these incidents, while acknowledged, are then promptly ignored. But they are clear-cut violations both of warfare and of military discipline as they had evolved and been accepted by what was arguably the most professional and best-educated officer corps in the world.

Nor were these incidents confined to one theater or one section of the military. In May 1941, German airborne troops on Crete used captured British soldiers as a "screen for the advance of German troops . . . resulting in at least six of the said British prisoners being killed," while others were murdered for refusing to do forced labor, and still others (from the Royal Welsh) were murdered after surrendering, according to the British indictment of Kurt Student.[14]

There is little doubt that the murders and abuses took place—as well as numerous crimes against the Greeks fighting on Crete alongside the Commonwealth troops—and so Student was charged, tried, and convicted on several of these counts. But the British had made a mistake in concentrating on him. As overall commander of the airborne force, he had not personally been in the field giving orders, nor had he issued any general orders that could have reasonably led his subordinates to the crimes for which he was charged. Moreover, at this point in the campaign, he had been sacked by Hitler, so technically he wasn't even the senior officer to be held responsible. Consequently, although he was convicted on three serious charges, a British military appeals court acquitted him. And since the British had, for some reason, failed to identify and charge the men who were on the scene and had given criminal orders (possibly because they were all dead), no one was actually made to pay for the atrocities on Crete committed by German airborne and mountain troops.[15]

On March 29, 1944, of the seventy-odd Allied airmen who had escaped from Stalag Luft 3 (located at Sagan, now Zagan in Poland, southwest of Berlin) and were recaptured, fifty were murdered. This incident, generally referred to as the "Great Escape," is notorious. Actually it gives a misleading picture of the status of captured Allied prisoners, because Stalag 3 was perhaps the most humane and well run of the prisoner of war camps—possibly the only one in which the Geneva Convention of 1929, governing the treatment of prisoners of war, was observed in spirit as well as in letter. Allied prisoners held at other camps were treated much worse: in general, German compliance with the conventions was minimal, and conditions at stalags 17b and 13d failed to meet the standards mandated by the conventions.[16]

There is a widespread belief that the camps housing Allied airmen were run by the Luftwaffe, but this was not the case. Nor were all airmen automatically put into special camps. As at the other camps—including the concentration camps—the garrisons represented a cross section of the armed forces. Basically, the atrocious conditions that held in the Polish prisoner of war camps were recapitulated for British, French, and American military personnel. Conditions were much better—but this is getting into an argument of almost painful abstruseness. The Wehrmacht had abandoned any serious attempt to treat prisoners of war according to traditional rules.[17]

When Private Pooley tried to seek justice for the killings of his British comrades, his account was supposedly greeted with a good deal of skepticism; he was not, at first, believed by British investigators—or by senior British commanders. But the atrocity that he survived was hardly an isolated case. There's little point in reciting the record at length, but the examples I've cited are hardly isolated instances. After the war, in addition to those mentioned, Karl Buck, Josef Kisch, Willi Tessmann, Johannes Waltzer, Karl Winkler, and Johannes Balzer were all tried and convicted of the outright murder or brutal mistreatment of uniformed prisoners of war by the various courts formed for this purpose—and these men represent only the most notorious cases.[18]

In the West, crimes precisely like those in Poland occurred after D-day. Nearly fifty Canadian prisoners of war were murdered on June 7–9, 1944. Unlike Student in Crete, Kurt Meyer, the German commander charged with these murders, definitely ordered them (or let the orders be given).[19] On December 17, 1944, a German force commanded by *Obersturmbannführer* Jochen Peiper captured American soldiers of Battery B of the 285th Field Artillery Observation Battalion, at the crossroads known by the Americans as Five Points, outside of Malmédy, Belgium. On January 13, 1945, American soldiers recovered seventy-two partially frozen bodies, and, based on the testimony of other soldiers, concluded they were prisoners of war executed by Peiper's men.[20]

But by this point, the execution of uniformed soldiers had been established as Wehrmacht policy, by a directive from Hitler himself. On October 18, 1942, he approved an order stipulating that men captured in special operations, the personnel of so-called commando units, were to be summarily executed, even if they were in uniform.[21] There is no doubt that this order was carried out: in January 1945, uniformed American soldiers sent to the Balkans who were captured were transported to the Mauthausen camp in Austria and shot.

As the war came slowly to an end, Allied soldiers were firmly convinced that German soldiers were systematically violating the rules of war, as indeed they were—my brief survey here contents itself with enumerating the low points of German criminality; it makes no attempt to be exhaustive.

Although the mistreatment of civilians by the Wehrmacht is the most infamous aspect of its institutional criminality, it is also the area in which, by definition, the cases are the most complicated and, as I noted above, in which the code was most often ignored. Historically, armies have responded to illegal combatants with what often seems to be an indiscriminant use of force, whether the French army in Spain in the Napoleonic wars or the German army in France in 1870 (or in Belgium in 1914). The Geneva Conventions in force in 1939 extended certain protections to civilians in a combat zone, but they contained important exceptions. One exception was that a country that had not agreed to observe the convention beforehand could not claim to be under its protection. The rules apply only to those who have agreed to follow them, in other words. Nor can one side break the rules and then demand that the other be held accountable for a similar crime.

As a result, the Soviet situation is legally shaky, since the Soviet Union did not sign the 1929 convention. It is also morally untenable, given the practice of the Bolsheviks to conflate terror with warfare. Not only had they not agreed to observe its terms, but the Red Army had a history of committing atrocities.

This hardly lets the Wehrmacht off the hook. Poland, Greece, Czechoslovakia, and Yugoslavia—along with France, Britain, and the United States—had all signed the 1929 convention long before the war broke out, so the Soviet exception does not apply to the treatment of prisoners of war or civilians from those countries. Without going into the ghastly details, we have very clear and unambiguous cases of criminal behavior in countries signatory to the 1929 Geneva Convention. On May 27, 1942, Reinhard Heydrich was assassinated by Czech partisans. In retaliation, Hitler ordered draconian measures. The most notorious was the massacre of the inhabitants of the Czech village of Lidice. About three hundred adults were killed outright; another three hundred women and children were incarcerated (the women were sent to the Ravensbrück camp), most of whom died.

The Lidice massacre was not unique. On June 10, 1944, German soldiers moving up to the Normandy front killed the 642 inhabitants of Oradour-sur-Glane, allegedly in reprisal for Resistance activities they had encountered en route. Unlike Lidice, which was ordered by the leadership of the Third Reich, Oradour was carried out entirely on the initiative of a junior officer (*Sturmbannführer* Adolph Diekman). Although the Oradour massacre was carried out by Waffen-SS troops, this is mostly because of the disproportionately high number of these combat units deployed in France.

It is all too easy to find instances of atrocities committed by regular units of the army and air force. On September 4, 1939, soldiers of the Forty-Sixth Infantry Division took an unknown number of males from the town of Czestochowa, Poland, and shot them; most of the victims were gunned down in the town square. Judging from the photographs taken by one of the soldiers, there were certainly a hundred or more victims, executed allegedly in reprisal for shots fired from a house in the town.[22]

Sadly, the list of similar massacres is extensive. Nor can this behavior be rationalized by a cursory reference to the racial policies of National Socialism. When the German airborne and mountain troops went into Crete, they executed civilians, just as they abused British soldiers taken prisoner. On May 13, 1941, General Ringel (who had taken over command from Student after the heavy casualties being suffered had thrown Student out of favor) ordered draconian reprisals against the civilian population. The claim was made that the locals had been engaging in combat with German troops. When the village of Castelli was taken, on May 24, the Germans shot two hundred Cretans. On June 3, the Germans captured the town of Kandanos and burned it to the ground, along with more than 150 inhabitants and their animals.[23] So much for the idea that war crimes were committed only by the SS or by the army under the stress of the savagery on the Eastern Front.[24]

Although these examples show that there was a pattern of criminal behavior in the Wehrmacht and that, as we've stressed, the incidents were not isolated examples of a few fanatics taking matters into their own hands, the numbers pale to insignificance when compared with the millions of murders organized and carried out by the Einsatzgruppen and the Sicherheitdienst, the two components of the SS specially charged with these tasks.[25] But here, too, the Wehrmacht was more complicit than innocent. From the start of the war, military police units that were an integral part of the Wehrmacht, the Geheime Feld Polizei (GFP), operated in the occupied territories and were closely involved in the arrest, transport, and murder of civilians.

The role of both the military and the civilian police in controlling the population—a process that began immediately in Poland—smoothed over any embarrassing questions about legal jurisdictions. Frequently the GFP was directed by SS personnel, often from one of the branches of the police, since by September 1939, all of what might be called the ordinary police were administratively part of Himmler's expanding empire.

Like Colonel Wessel's orders that the Polish soldiers take off their tunics so that it could later be claimed that they were illegal combatants, these organizational twists seem designed to give the Wehrmacht deniability in case it was called to account. But the participation of the military police probably facilitated cooperation with local commanders in such logistical matters as the use of army trucks to transport civilians to places where they could be murdered.[26]

Who knew precisely what is unknowable. But even the most cursory research reveals an obvious truth: the systematic murders were hardly a secret to far too many ordinary soldiers, and emphatically not to their officers.[27] If much of the alleged resistance to Hitler was, in reality, nothing more than passive-aggressive behavior, much of the behavior of Wehrmacht personnel at lower levels can be termed its opposite: a passive acceptance of behavior that was wicked and in most cases illegal. Although often unable to judge the meaning of what they observed, many soldiers were aware of what was happening. It is difficult to believe that every eye-witness remained silent—that at some level the knowledge of these murders didn't spread.

That the pattern was widespread does not mean that there were no protests on the army side. However, most centered on jurisdictional problems. For instance, Himmler had ordered that all of the prisoners taken should be murdered as soon as possible—often right on the spot. But Himmler lacked the authority to give such an order, because he was not part of the army command structure for the campaign. Despite the intermingling of personnel, there was little love lost between the SS and the army. Much of the reported resistance on the part of the army has to be chalked up not to morality but to bureaucratic turf wars.[28]

The repetition of crimes from Poland in 1939 to Crete in 1941 (leaving aside the massacre at Le Paradis in 1940) suggests that, whatever the root causes, the tendency to commit murders that contravened the rules had spread quickly throughout the rest of the army. Rather than see the Waffen-SS units as islands of miscreants in an ocean of well-behaved soldiery, we would be more correct to view them as precedent setters in what seems to be a grisly competition with the regular army units.

The pattern established in Poland continued throughout the war. On the Russian front, it grew to monstrous proportions, and we have no shortage of eyewitnesses to the mass killings, often of the most horrifying sort, that became inextricably associated with the advances of the Wehrmacht into Russia and the Baltic. In some cases, the executions were justified, morally or legally, or both. But the overwhelming majority were not. And in some cases, officers protested; mostly they did not.

As individuals, the majority of these witnesses were innocent. At the lower levels—and this included most of the officer corps as well—there was little that observers could do about what they saw, not because of any fear for their lives, necessarily, but simply because the individual often feels helpless to do anything about wrongdoing when it is clearly sanctioned by the institution itself. The military mostly comprised people who went about their lawful duties and did nothing wrong whatsoever. My esti-

mate is that the percentage of criminals in the military was basically a constant throughout the war and strictly speaking was confined to a minority.

At the same time, it is easy to misunderstand—or to willfully
misinterpret—this conclusion, which Albert Speer understood perfectly.
In *Spandau: The Secret Diaries*, Speer, while insisting that he was not
guilty of the crimes attributed to him, nevertheless observed that he felt
himself guilty in another, more profound, way. His presence, his abili-
ties, enabled and empowered Hitler: "and yet—I drove with Hitler under
those streamers and did not feel the baseness of the slogans being publicly displayed and sanctioned by the government. Once again: I suppose
I did not even see the streamers . . . it even seems to me that my own 'purity,' my indolence, makes me guiltier."[29] There is such a thing as institutional guilt, and it applies here.

In the Second World War, the behavior of the Wehrmacht presented
the Allies with a moral and legal problem unprecedented in modern
times. Although there have been sporadic attempts to demonstrate that
the German army (and sometimes the Germans in general) historically
operated like a gang of criminals, at bottom such claims rest on wild generalizations and bizarre assumptions. In August 1914, Allied propagandists
made wild claims about atrocities in Belgium (and elsewhere). However,
there really never has been any evidence produced on this topic that can
withstand even the most cursory investigation. Telford Taylor, one of the
lead prosecutors at the Nuremberg trials, was right when he wrote that "in
nearly every case, there were serious evidentiary or legal questions
whether these acts could rightly be labeled 'war crimes.'"[30]

But at end of the Second World War, there was a pressing need to
find the men who had committed war crimes and bring them to judgment. In the minds of most people, that process meant a trial, and most
people are under the impression that, at Nuremberg, the Allies established a set of legal principles that would, it was hoped, ensure that the
behavior I've been describing would never be repeated. After 1947 the
very name—Nuremberg—passed into history as a symbol of the determination of civilized people to bring to judgment those who committed
horrifying atrocities against their fellow human beings.

This idea is difficult to sustain after any serious examination of what took place. Out of the many sorry examples to the contrary, here is what I think is the most disturbing. If there was any group of uniformed men with weapons clearly and unambiguously guilty of horrific crimes, it was the members of the Einsatzgruppen. They spent the war committing atrocity after atrocity. Indeed, their whole purpose was nothing but that, so, it seems to me, they represent the guiltiest of the guilty, the wickedest of the wicked.

Benjamin Ferencz, one of the members of the American legal team assembled for the Nuremberg trials, clearly thought so. In late 1946, he had discovered the Einsatzgruppen reports. Horrified, he went to Telford Taylor, who was then the chief prosecutor at Nuremberg, where, having tried the men the Allies believed to be the leadership of the Third Reich, they were now trying the lesser figures.

But Taylor could hardly be bothered. He was, in the succinct phraseology of Richard Rhodes, preparing for a series of trials that would demonstrate "the criminal participation of a representative cross section of German institutions, including medicine, the law, industry, and government ministries."[31] None of these people had murdered anyone, but their trials had already been scheduled. Ferencz, a youthful lawyer who had never prosecuted a criminal case, was on his own. And had he not been enterprising and industrious—and had he not had the luck of finding the reports—none of the Einsatzgruppen commanders would have been prosecuted at all.

The worst of the worst, in other words, were tried and found guilty only through a providential accident, and this is to overstate the extent to which justice was done. Ferencz was able to bring to trial only twenty-four of them, and over the next half a century, the West German government tried fewer than five hundred people for the murders committed both in the east and in the camps; the impression remains that a good many of the guilty escaped. The flight and consequent survival of men like Adolf Eichmann and Joseph Mengele suggests that this impression is not false. The Mengele case is particularly distressing. The man lived in Germany until a warrant was finally issued for his arrest—in 1959. He then fled to Argentina, where he lived for the rest of his life. It would be comforting to say that he did so in fear, but this hardly seems the case: he died while bathing in the ocean at age sixty-eight.[32]

How did these men—and a good many others—manage to escape? How did the Allies, who controlled all German territory and ruled it for some time, miss the most egregious criminals? Unfortunately, the answer is simple. They missed them because—as the Taylor example demonstrates—they weren't looking for them, could hardly be bothered.

Most people are under the impression that at Nuremberg the leaders of Hitlerite Germany were tried for mass murder, and that such terms as "war crimes" and "crimes against humanity" are simply complex legal terms describing different categories of mass homicide. As one theologian put it, war crimes are murders committed by soldiers at the front, while crimes against humanity are committed by soldiers and police officers behind the front.

This is a simple and elegant distinction. However, nothing could be further from the truth, as anyone who takes the trouble to read the actual indictment handed up at the start of the proceedings will quickly discover. In fact, one has only to look at the title of the published document to find an entirely new world of jurisprudence opening up. There it is, right there on the title page: *Nazi Conspiracy and Aggression*. The thrust of the prosecutors was to prove that the leadership engaged in a conspiracy to engage in an aggressive war against their fellow Europeans. The murders of military personnel and civilians only comes up on page 56, in connection with the treatment of prisoners of war. It is a scant five pages, most of which is concerned with the treatment of Soviet soldiers. The second section concerns "Murder and Ill Treatment of Civilian Population." It is barely six pages and mostly concerned with the murder of Communists.

In actual practice, the prosecutors spent most of their energies trying to prove that the men on trial were all part of a criminal conspiracy to wage war on the rest of the world. In other words, they spent most of their energies attempting to prove something that was clearly not true, interrogating men who, while certainly guilty of all sorts of lesser crimes, were hardly guilty of this one. No biographer of Hitler would subscribe to the notion that he spent much time consulting with Rosenberg and Streicher about his foreign-policy aims. If there's one thing we know about him it is that he didn't consult with anyone, repeatedly boasting that no one would ever know what he was thinking.

But at Nuremberg the prosecution pursued the ludicrous notion that Rosenberg was intimately involved with planning the Norwegian campaign. In fact, it was argued that most of the leaders participated in what was vaguely termed the "common plan" to wage an aggressive war. Since they weren't, and indeed in some cases had no idea what the prosecutors were talking about, the result was a monumental misdirection of effort, like trying to convict a serial killer of planning to steal coins from parking meters.

Not surprisingly, then, the basic and fundamental crime—the murders of millions of civilians, although dealt with, was not dealt with in any systematic way. Moreover, as the example of Ferencz and Taylor makes pretty clear, after the first round of the trials, in which Speer and Rosenberg and the other senior leaders were tried and convicted, the Allies launched an even more abstract legal action. Forget about trying to find Joseph Mengele and go after Martin Heidegger. It's no surprise, then, that for the rest of the century the myth that the Wehrmacht fought a clean war—and its corollary, that if there were any crimes they were in reaction to Communist barbarities—has flourished.

CONCLUSION: MYTHS,
REALITIES, AND ACHIEVEMENTS

A good man ought to love his friends and country, and should
share their hatreds and their loyalties. But once a man takes up
the role of historian he must discard all considerations of this
kind. He will often have to speak well of his enemies and even
award them the highest praise should their actions demand this,
and on the other hand criticize and find fault with his friends,
however close they may be, if their errors of conduct show that
this is his duty. For just as a living creature, if deprived of its
eyesight, is rendered completely helpless, so if history is
deprived of the truth, we are left with nothing but an idle,
unprofitable tale. . . . We must therefore detach ourselves from
the actors in the story, and apply to them only such statements
and judgments as their conduct deserves.

Polybius[1]

The main point of this book may, I think, be summed up easily enough.
In purely military terms, the superiority of the Wehrmacht lay in its institutional memory. The Germans had mastered many of the problems of
modern warfare, and they preserved the essentials of what they had
learned as they integrated the technologies that emerged in the next decades. Their advantage in combat thus was not a function of equipment
or even training: it was conceptual, and the two key concepts were speed
and integration.

The German army was never mechanized to the extent that its major opponents were. But its commanders were generally quicker to move than their adversaries, whether on offense or on defense. Their speed, immensely aided by the decentralization of command, meant that the Germans generally moved inside the decision cycle of their opponents.[2]

In the latter part of the war, for example, the Allies planned a daring airborne and armor seizure of a series of bridges through the Netherlands and across the Rhine (Market Garden). When they began planning, German forces in the west were in disarray. But by the time the operation was launched, the fleeing troops were organized into effective combat units in position along the Dutch frontier. The main road over which the Allies had to advance was now heavily defended. Despite every imaginable advantage, despite the deployment of some of the best troops in the world, Market Garden was not a success. Speed counted. It trumped mechanization.

So, too, with what we now call combined-arms tactics. By 1939, everyone paid lip service to the concept. Such curious concepts as the Royal Machine Gun Corps had long since bit the dust. The integration of combat engineers, heavy-weapons companies, and machine-gunners into line units, which had given the Germans such an advantage in 1914, was now widely practiced. But in the most important areas, airpower and ground-to-air defenses, the Germans were far ahead. The British and French air forces were left to wage their own wars; their ground troops lacked antiaircraft support on the German scale. And only in the Wehrmacht was airpower so clearly subordinated to the objectives of the troops on the ground. Instead of relying on heavy artillery, local commanders could call in air strikes at need, while their men were protected from enemy air strikes by the antiaircraft guns assigned to them.

These concepts could be learned. Over the course of the First World War, the Allied armies had grasped the importance of both speed and integration, just as they had begun to realize that troops armed with machine guns, mortars, and howitzers were substantially more lethal on the battlefield than units equipped only with rifles. Although in that war the

Germans generally had more and better weapons than their opponents, their superiority was not simply a function of better weaponry. It was conceptual. Howitzers under the direct control of battalion commanders were much more effective than the same weapons controlled by an army corps or group. As the war progressed, the Allies, particularly the French, adjusted, but once the war was over, they forgot what they had learned.

The Germans did not. The brutal conflicts of 1919–21, in which small groups of heavily armed and mobile soldiery annihilated their numerically superior opponents, ensured that, in the Wehrmacht, speed and integration would be permanently imprinted. In the west the military importance of this fighting was ignored or willfully misinterpreted. But nearly all the senior German commanders in 1939 had been involved in the fighting; it conditioned their view of warfare.

There was a third sense in which the Germans were superior. Although the successive German military movements into Austria and Bohemia met with no armed resistance, they gave German commanders the experience of coping with the logistical problems faced by modern armies. Nowadays, armies train as realistically as possible and work out the all-important details through intensive maneuvers. In the 1930s no one really did this, and certainly not on the grand scale afforded by the march into two neighboring countries. Transporting a mechanized division seven hundred kilometers (the distance the German Second Armored Division traveled to Vienna from its base in Würzburg) was a major accomplishment in its own right. So in September 1939, when the fighting started, the armies on both sides consisted of recent recruits, but only the Germans had dealt with the logistical problems of modern warfare. They were logistical veterans if nothing else.

Poland is a large country. In September 1939, not only were the Germans faced with a war of large-scale movement; they had to fight as well. So in May 1940, the German experience in logistics and combat gave them a decisive advantage. After the fall of France, the impact of their experience increased enormously, one reason why the Germans tore through the Balkans in April and May 1941, and through the Soviet Union in July and August. It is probably the chief reason that the Americans and their allies, despite their advantages, found the going tough as they began their great offensives in 1943. By then the German army had experienced four years of almost continuous combat, which gave it an invariable edge.

Like training, experience is difficult to quantify. Equipment is not. To shift the focus to these intangibles, I have devoted a good deal of space to explaining the inadequacies of German armament, since there is a widespread tendency to equate their success on the battlefield with simple technological superiority. Although there were interesting innovations and inventions, by and large the margin of technical superiority was nonexistent, which gives the lie to the notion that the Germans managed to evade the restrictions of the Versailles Treaty with much success. That claim, like the now discounted assertion that the Germans deployed two to three times as many tanks (or planes) in France in 1940 as the Allies, is simply another false idea.

From early on, the belief that the basis of German superiority was the blitzkrieg became a quasi-mystical concept used in explaining every German success. Insofar as the term characterized the concepts of speed and integration learned in the First World War, it conveys a grain of truth. As generally employed, however, the word *blitzkrieg* does not; yet as the war progressed, it began to have a great deal of influence, mostly on the way the stories of the conflict were told. At its simplest—suggesting that one could win by hurling masses of armor against the enemy—the term never worked. At its most sophisticated—and there has been no shortage of efforts to renovate the concept—it comes down to nothing more than speed and integrated tactics.

Up to a point, explaining the German advantage and the Allied deficiency is simple. The Allies had brave soldiers, competent commanders, and excellent equipment in great quantity. By any objective measure, the two sides were evenly matched. The Allies lost because they failed to learn from their experiences in the Great War and the Germans did not. But then again, how could they have learned anything? Their governments had lied systematically about the course of that war, claiming that while it had been a struggle between two evenly matched foes, they had ultimately prevailed on the field of battle.

As time passed, this delusion was regarded as an incontrovertible fact, as indeed it is today by the vast majority of British military historians. Although the months-long debacle of September 1939–June 1940 should have led to a fundamental reconsideration of the point, it did not. Instead, both the experts and their governments, unable to hide the extent of the defeat as they had done in the earlier war, invented three reasons to explain the devastating losses. The Germans had built up an enormous arsenal, largely by cheating on the Versailles Treaty, and simply overwhelmed us. We were the victims of a cunning conspiracy to wage an aggressive war. The Germans had invented a modern form of warfare, the blitzkrieg. There is, even today, no shortage of eloquent pleading on these three points. But as I have shown in this book (and elsewhere), they're simply not true.

As I studied both wars for more decades than I care to admit, I became convinced that tactics, training, and technology were only one part of the key to the achievements of the Wehrmacht. The German army of 1914 was substantially better than the British and French and Russian armies, and it was certainly better than the German army of 1939. Although the institutional memory that preserved the emphasis on speed and nurtured the evolution of integration of force gave it a serious advantage, it seems doubtful that this advantage, all by itself, could explain the victories of 1939–41.

To a great extent, those victories were a function of the leadership of the two sides. On the one side, the Allied, the record suggests what amounts to almost criminal incompetence. The only worse spectacle than French prime minister Paul Reynaud's hysterical phone call to Churchill on May 15, 1940, is Neville Chamberlain's desperate maneuvering to stay atop the floundering British government after September 1939.

Anyone who loves democracy and freedom must applaud Churchill's lonely fight from May 1940 to the end of the war. I would argue that as a result, he was his country's greatest prime minister, greater even than the Pitts, father and son, and Lloyd George. But most of his military decisions were simply wrong, beginning with his plans for stopping the shipments of iron ore from Scandinavia to Germany in the fall of 1939 to his insistence on invading Italy and his reluctance to back the cross-Channel invasion. Of course, these considerations pale in the face of Stalin's abysmal performance, but the case can be made that Hitler was extraordinarily lucky in the leaders who opposed him.

The mention of both names brings us face-to-face with a most unpleasant problem. The Allied leadership at the start of the war was wretched. But Hitler intuited that. Unlike everyone else in the German leadership, he was confident that they would cut and run at the first setback. The failure to come to terms with Hitler is a major stumbling block in understanding the Wehrmacht's success, perhaps the greatest stumbling block. As I have tried to explain, it is the missing element in the equation, and the single most important one.

It is Hitler who empowered the risky new strategies that resulted in May 1940 (and after), who gave Student and von Manstein the encouragement to develop their ideas and then insisted on their execution. The German high command was no more receptive to innovation in warfare than the high commands of its opponents. Similarly, it was Hitler who understood that at the first reverse his opponents would descend into hysterical impotency, lose the will to fight, and quit the war.

This last point, I think, is a perfect example of the collision between legend and reality, with historians almost united in a grim determination to show that Hitler's invasion of Poland was a grave error, because it united the Allies and forced them to fight. That overlooks a most inconvenient fact: by July 1941, the only one of Hitler's opponents still standing was Britain. True, Hitler would finally be beaten — but not by the French and the British.

Historically there have been two objections to the idea of Hitler as a shrewd strategist, the first being that the notion was hotly disputed by many of his generals. But their testimony is disingenuous and often flawed. Readers brought up on their testimony will probably find this judgment upsetting, but it is nonetheless true, or rather as true as anything can be, given the absence of any skeptical cross-examination. The examples cited in the text are simply the tip of the iceberg in that regard.

The second problem ties into the complex of false ideas that have come to dominate military history. Hitler was a supremely evil man. But wicked does not mean insane, incompetent, or stupid. On the contrary, the wicked are generally quite rational in carrying out their schemes — one reason why they are often so successful. True, they are frequently brought to justice, but not quickly. Until that final moment, they move from success to success. So it was with Hitler.

In fact, in terms of matters military, most of the prevailing wisdom about Hitler is not a bad description of Stalin. That too takes us into dangerous waters. That Stalin was not a bad military leader is as firmly entrenched in the received wisdom as the contrary image of Hitler. It may be even more firmly rooted, because the apologists and enthusiasts for the Soviet Union tend to take that country's claims about the Great Patriotic War at face value. It is, as I have tried to explain, a record of great disasters and unparalleled loss. I started out believing that the Soviet Union was the nation primarily responsible for Hitler's defeat, but I don't think the evidence supports the conclusion. Without massive Anglo-American aid, the war would have been lost in 1943, Stalingrad notwithstanding. Proponents of the idea that the Russians beat the Germans, who see Stalingrad as the turning point of the war, forget the catastrophic defeats of a bloody spring that turned into an even bloodier summer.

This view also neglects the fact that after mid-1943, Hitler was increasingly forced to divert resources to other theaters: North Africa, Italy, and then France. The numbers involved were hardly trivial. Albert Kesselring, the German commander in Italy, had somewhere close to half a million men. In the main, these troops were no great shakes, but they fought the Allies to what was almost a standstill, just as an even more wretched force held up Patton around Metz for months. Given the lethality of the German army in combat, regardless of the units deployed, such a force would have had an enormous impact on the Eastern Front. Stalin himself knew this; hence his bullying pleas for a second front in Europe.

For those devotees of the Soviet Union, such arguments won't carry much weight. But then the one lesson that military history teaches us is the imperviousness of its students to evidence. It is an article of faith among British analysts that the British army won the First World War in the fall of 1918 by destroying the opponent on the battlefield. No amount of contrary evidence will change that view. So the notion that the German army of 1914–18 was well on the way to understanding how to win in combat is nonsensical to them. In the Second World War, notions about the Red Army have the same provenance, enormously aided by the systematic misrepresentations about the Soviet Union, Stalin, and Communism in general.

As is often the case, the argument that the reasons for Germany's victories lay in the factors I've discussed appears to plunge us into yet another quandary. How was it that the Germans lost? There is another way of asking the question that leads to the same discussion: Since it seems hardly possible that the Germans could defeat the entire world, why did they keep on fighting as long as they did?

Basically Hitler lost because he never really understood the impact of the United States on the course of the war. This failure—the only serious mistake Hitler made on the grand strategic level—was more a function of his philosophical outlook than of his ignorance. For Hitler, the United States and the Soviet Union were more or less the same thing when it came to products. Both were systems that concentrated on soulless mass production, systems that prevented the heroic character from developing. The hero always trumped industry.

As Hitler and his lackeys received the news of the great Allied invasion force steaming toward North Africa, Hitler promptly flew into an extraordinary flight of the imagination. First he ventured the not entirely unreasonable suggestion that the target of the invasion was the beleaguered Afrika Korps. But then, in the words of Albert Speer, Hitler decided that

> the naval units were keeping together in this way . . . in order to advance through the narrow straits between Sicily and Africa under cover of darkness, safe from German air attacks. Or else, and this second version corresponded more to his feeling for perilous military operations: "The

enemy will land in central Italy tonight. There he would meet with no resistance at all. There are no German troops there, and the Italians will run away." It would never have occurred to him not to associate such a landing operation with a coup. To put the troops on land in safe positions from which they could methodically spread out, to take no unnecessary risks — that was a strategy alien to him.[3]

For Hitler, then, risk taking and audacity were always to be preferred to the methodical. It was not merely a preference when it came to strategy but also a preference for a means of organizing war and producing matériel. And as the war progressed, his insistence on this approach doomed the Wehrmacht, as in the first half of the conflict it had been the guarantor of victories.

Why, then, did the Germans fight on so desperately? There are, I believe, two answers to that question, closely related and involving the same emotion: fear. Part of that fear was innocent and entirely understandable. The Germans felt that there had been a systematic attempt to destroy them after 1918, that the terms of the peace treaty were constructed accordingly, and that the Allies tricked them into a surrender they could never have won on the battlefield.

Again, here is an area where false ideas have dominated our discourse. Rather than admit that this fear was legitimate, that it was what people felt and that there was a grain of truth in the idea, historians have devoted their energies to ridiculing the notion, suppressing the abundant evidence to the contrary. Hitler capitalized on those feelings, but he hardly invented them. He had no need to do so, as they were in the main justified. What he did do was to remind the Germans, once the Second World War began, that if they quit, they could expect treatment far worse than in 1919. Given the chaos of those early years — the determination of the French to destroy the country, the efforts of the Bolsheviks to transform it into a Soviet state — this prospect scared the daylights out of people.

The Allies then played into Hitler's strategy by making threats that were even more bloodthirsty than those of 1917–18. Unconditional surrender was hardly the right trump card to play. Put a rat in a corner, and he fights like a cornered rat. Nor did flying over civilians and incinerating them in large numbers dispose the population to feel much better about the alternatives they faced. Of course, this notion appalls the airpower enthusiasts, for whom it is an article of faith that strategic bombing hastened the end of the war, if it did not bring it about entirely. Another false idea, but one much beloved of air forces and airpower advocates — as were the notions of Hitler as a madman, the superiority of the British in every conceivable area, and the triumphs of the Red Army. For believers of these concepts no amount of evidence to the contrary will ever be persuasive.

To any reasonably objective observer, however, the European strategic-bombing offensive was mostly a failure. If the campaign had succeeded, the Wehrmacht would have run out of equipment by the end of 1944, the little equipment produced would never have reached the combat troops, and the troops would have never been able to maneuver into new defensive positions. But not one of those conditions was actually met. Mostly, as was the case with the German armored units stalled outside Dinant in December 1944, they simply ran out of gas. Although the airpower apostles invariably claim responsibility for the empty fuel tanks, the real reason was that by August 1944, the Red Army had overrun the Romanian oil fields.

Speculatively, a true holocaust from the air, such as the one visited on Japan, might have worked, provided, of course, that the United States and Britain had been willing to pursue that action. But they were not. By February 1945, about 350,000 Germans had been killed in the bombings. For anyone who values human life, that is a horrifying figure. But in this ghastly calculus, comparisons must be made. Over the course of the war, close to six million Polish civilians were murdered. But the Poles fought on, which suggests the ultimate futility of the murderous enterprise.[4]

Basically, the Allied bombings did for the Germans what the earlier German bombings had done for the British: far from demoralizing them, the losses made them more determined to fight on. In the German case, the bombings simply reinforced their fears that the Allies aimed at nothing less than their total destruction, hardly the best way to convince people to quit a war.[5]

The extent to which such fears motivated the Germans to keep on fighting is, like any intangible, not something we can quantify and throw onto the balance scale. But it seems a obvious factor to include. The Germans, remembering what had befallen them the last time they had stopped fighting, kept on at least partly because they deeply feared what would happen to them if they lost. It was a rational fear, compounded to a great extent by history, by the bombings, and by Allied declarations.

For a great many Germans in positions of authority, it was also rein-forced by a less benign set of fears, equally rational but more sinister. Criminals fear getting caught. By the end of the war, there were a great many criminals in Germany, and the rather bland denials about not knowing what was really going on hardly stand up to any serious exami-nation. In many cases the military leaders leading the charge of igno-rance were in fact beneficiaries of Hitler's largesse.

The idea that they had no idea what was happening is preposterous. In this sense, as I have tried to suggest, the focus on the murders of mil-lions of innocent civilians, although understandable, is misleading. Al-though everyone hoots down Göring's defense—that the numbers were so vast the whole thing was unimaginable—there's nothing outrageous about it. The military leadership may in some instance have actually not realized the enormity of these killings.

But Göring could hardly have claimed ignorance of the wholesale vi-olations of the Geneva Conventions, nor could anyone else in the Wehrmacht. I bring this up because it suggests two issues. First, that a contributing factor to the prolonged resistance was the rational fear of what would happen to individuals directing the war if the Allies won on their terms. Second, that this awareness makes Hitler's increasingly des-perate gambles seem sensible. Regardless of who else knew what and how much, Hitler certainly realized that his minions had murdered twelve to fourteen million innocent civilians, that at some point this in-formation would percolate into the Allied camp, and that there would be an accounting. The Allies might not destroy the entire country, level it to the ground, and turn it into a giant cow pasture, but they would exact justice from those who had been guilty of collaborating in this crime.

My point—to which, I hope, this chapter has given substance—is that from any reasonable perspective, there were an enormous number of men who had done something wrong, who were criminals. Given the way the investigations at the end of the war were botched, we will never know who was specifically guilty of what. But even the most cursory assembly of incidents suggests that war crimes were widespread, that they occurred right from the start of the war, and that regular army units took part. My judgment is that the percentage of men involved was essentially a constant and had relatively little to do with the horrors of the Eastern Front. But still, too many soldiers knew that crimes had been committed, or that their actions could be misinterpreted by hostile judges. That gave them a deep incentive to fight on. Considered in this light, the only real mystery is why so many of them surrendered.

This last, of course, brings up one of the more curious legends of the war. The army, so the story goes, fought a clean war. It was the SS that committed all the crimes. Perhaps there were draconian acts, but they were entirely in response to Bolshevik barbarities. That was true enough. From the beginning, Lenin had exhorted his followers to commit atrocities. In the Baltic they began in 1917, and gave the resulting mix of revolutions, counterrevolutions, and civil wars their peculiar horror. However, the situation hardly justified what, in the case of the Wehrmacht, rapidly became a de facto policy of crimes committed against uniformed prisoners of war.

The point is not that these were the worst of the crimes; the point is that they were the most unambiguous. Ordinary soldiers might well believe that a group of civilians are illegal combatants and deserve the death penalty. But there is no way that could be believed about uniformed soldiers who have just surrendered. The cases are unambiguous and all too frequent. That the contrary idea has been allowed to flourish—that half a century after the war, I find myself having to explain the situation case by case—seems to me an all-too-apt statement about the histories of this war. Bad history has a remarkable persistence, particularly when it is promoted by historians.

In the eighteenth century, it was well understood that armies were repositories not only of military prowess and valor but also of national virtue. The Marquis de Vauvenargues articulated the idea perfectly: "Vice" he observed, "starts wars. Virtue fights them."[6] War is a dirty business, a series of slaughters in which there is much that is bad as well as horrific. But that does not make the men who wage it wicked. On the contrary; as Frederick the Great told his assembled officers in 1778: "Before all things, I prescribe as your most sacred duty that in every situation you exercise humanity on our unarmed enemies."[7]

No matter how brilliant or amiable they appear, the officers of the Wehrmacht allowed one of the oldest and greatest armies in the world to descend to the level of thugs in uniform. As von der Marwitz's epitaph makes clear, when honor is gone, nothing remains. At some point in September 1939, that legacy was massacred and thrown into the ditch along with three hundred Polish soldiers. The army lost more than the war; it lost its honor.

NOTES

Introduction: Truth and Error

1. *Conversations with Eckermann*, translated John Oxenford [1850] (San Francisco: North Point Press, 1984), December 16, 1828: 282–283.

2. See Winston Churchill, *The World Crisis, 1916–1918* (New York: Scribner's 1927), 2:89; David Lloyd George, *War Memoirs* (London: Odhams, 1938), 2:1313.

3. Abel Ferry did the computations and reported them to the cabinet in October 1916. See his account in *La Guerre vue d'en bas et d'en haut* (Paris: Grasset, 1920), 129–132. André Maginot came to the same conclusion independently. When he revealed his and Ferry's finding to the Chamber of Deputies, there was pandemonium. See the account in Paul Allard, *Les dessous de la guerre révélés par les comités secrets* (Paris: Éditions de France, 1932), 14–15. For Churchill, see *The World Crisis, 1916–1918*, 1:38–39, 1:301–302. He was promptly smeared by apologists for the British army and defenders of the commander, Sir Douglas Haig. See Robin Prior, *Churchill's World Crisis as History* (London: Croom Helm, 1983), especially 212–213.

4. The drastic imbalance between Allied and German casualties is still hotly disputed by British historians, even though, as I explained in *The Myth of the Great War* (New York: HarperCollins, 2001), the basic data allowing such conclusions originated in the British War Office and was published as early as 1921. Nor am I alone in reaching this conclusion. See also Trevor Dupuy, *A Genius for War* (New York: Prentice Hall, 1977), 4. Niall Ferguson, in *The Pity of War* (New York: Basic Books, 1999), using the official British data from the War Office, computes Allied deaths at 5,421,000 and Central Powers deaths at 4,092,000. Thus he comes up with a casualty-exchange ratio in favor of Germany of 1.3:1, if we use what Ferguson calls

the "Revised Death Figures" (295). The problem is that the German totals in this column apparently include all the German prisoners of war at the end of 1918, and that they include 804,000 Turkish war dead. If we subtract out those questionable figures, the ratio is slightly better than 2:1. In *The Myth of the Great War* (9–12), I established the death figures for both sides on the Western Front alone; these numbers yield a ratio of about 3:1.

5. The author of the only work on the German army before this book is flatly dismissive. Speaking of the Polish campaign, Matthew Cooper observes that "the German Army gave no demonstration of *Blitzkrieg*." See *The German Army* (New York: Stein and Day, 1978), 169. See, as well, the technical study by Major Rick S. Richardson, *Fall Gelb and the German Blitzkrieg of 1940: Operational Art?* (Fort Leavenworth, KS: School of Advanced Military Studies, 1999). Although I certainly don't claim that my debunking of the concept in *The Blitzkrieg Myth* (New York: HarperCollins, 2003) has met with universal acceptance, the main criticism is that I went too far and may have oversimplified the issues, not that I was simply wrong. See the discussion of my work by Victor Davis Hanson (and others) in the summer 2005 issue of *Historically Speaking*, at http://www.bu.edu/historic/hs/.

6. The idea of Hitler's maniacal, meddling incompetence runs throughout Cooper, *German Army* (see, in particular, the opening paragraph of Chapter 32, page 528) and is the basic principle articulated in Ronald Lewin's *Hitler's Mistakes* (London: Seecker and Warburg, 1984). Ian Kershaw, the most recent serious biographer of Hitler, goes even further. See *Hitler, 1936–45: Nemesis* (New York: Norton, 2000), 332–334. (And this is to omit any consideration of the numerous fantastical accounts of Hitler.) Although deconstructed impressively by John Lukacs, *The Hitler of History* (New York: Random House, 1997), and, in more readable fashion, by Ron Rosenbaum, *Explaining Hitler* (New York: Random House, 1998), these false ideas soldier on, and will doubtless continue to do so for decades.

7. For a view contrary to the one cited in note 6, see the scathing remarks about the leading German commanders in Gerhard Weinberg's introduction to *Hitler and His Generals: Military Conferences, 1942–1945*, edited Helmut Heiber and David Glantz, translated Roland Winter, Krista Smith, and Mary Beth Friedrich (New York: Enigma Books, 2003), vi–viii. In Germany the idea of Hitler as militarily incompetent and his commanders as brilliant has been largely discarded, although it still lingers on in Anglo-American histories.

Chapter 1: *The German Army in 1918: Secrets of Success*

1. This passage is one of the many profound observations in Konrad Heiden's early biography of Adolf Hitler, easily the best extended essay ever done on the German leader; the work is all the more remarkable for having been written mostly before 1937. The sentence is taken from Heiden's comments on Ernst Rohm. See *The Führer*, translated Ralph Manheim (New York: Carrol and Graf, 1999), 30.

2. William Harbutt Dawson, *German Life in Town and Country* (New York: Putnam's, 1901), 90. An interesting book could be written comparing the thought-

ful, perceptive British analyses of Germany before 1914 with the accounts penned once the war began.

3. Although much has been written describing the German staff system, few writers explain its importance in comparison with other systems. The basic text is Bronsart von Schellendorf [general, German Great General Staff], *The Duties of the General Staff*, translated H. A. Bethell, J. H. V. Crowed, and F. B. Maurice (London: Harrison and Sons, 1905). A more recent appreciation is found in Rod Paschall, *The Defeat of Imperial Germany* (Chapel Hill, NC: Algonquin Books, 1989); see, especially, 24.

4. This revealing document is buried in the official German army history of the First World War. See "Anlage 1," in volume 12: Reichsarchiv, *Schlachten des Weltkrieges* (Berlin: G. Stalling, 1924).

5. See Martin Samuels, *Doctrine and Dogma: German and British Infantry Tactics in the First World War* (New York: Greenwood, 1992), especially 17–19, where Samuels discusses the fact that important innovations were introduced at relatively low levels—and that historians have consistently missed this point.

6. As reported by Jean Feller in *Histoire de l'armée française* (Paris: Flammarion, 1961), 49. See also the discussion in Samuels, *Doctrine and Dogma*, 102, notes 20–21.

7. These data are taken from William Serman, *Les officiers français dans la nation, 1848–1914* (Paris: Aubier Montaigne, 1982), 90.

8. The only military historian to take note of these numbers is Samuels (*Doctrine and Dogma*, 105); he does not comment on the implications. The scarcity of comment is particularly true concerning the number of reserve officers in Germany and Austria. One looks in vain in Martin Kitchen's *The German Officer Corps, 1890–1914* (Oxford: Clarendon, 1968) for a discussion of the topic. To grasp the magnitude of the reserve officer phenomenon, one must leave the field of military history and turn to social history. Thus, for example, the best source of data on the reserve officer situation is Kevin McAleer, *Dueling: The Cult of Honor in Fin-de-Siècle Germany* (Princeton: Princeton University Press, 1994), from which the 3-to-1 figure is taken (103; the figure agrees with the Samuels estimate of 120,000 men). McAleer's study, like the earlier analyses done in Germany, establishes the significant impact of the reserve officer population on German society. See, in addition, Ute Frevert, *Ehrenmänner: Das Duell in der bürgerlichen Gesellschaft* (Munich: Beck, 1991).

9. This description is taken from the anonymous *The German Army from Within, by a British Officer Who Has Served in It* (New York: George H. Doran, 1914), 36–38. The book was written and published in October or November 1914, since it refers to the opening battles of the war. Because the purpose of these propaganda exercises was to instill contempt and hatred in the Anglo-American reader, the positive evidence must be taken seriously.

10. Heinz Guderian, *Panzer Leader*, translated Constantine Fitzgibbon (New York: Da Capo Press, 1952), 16.

11. Emile Fayolle, *Carnets secrets de la grande guerre*, edited Henry Contamine (Paris: Plon, 1964), entry of April 13, 1918 (271). See also 78, 160. The British quotation

is taken from F. S. Oliver's *The Anvil of War* (New York: Macmillan, 1936), 113, as quoted by John Terraine, in *The Smoke and the Fire* (London: Sidgwick and Jackson, 1980), 105. The remarks parallel one made by Edward Louis Spears, who was the British liaison with the French in 1914. See his *Liaison 1914: A Narrative of the Great Retreat*, 1st ed. (London: Heinemann, 1930), 108–110.

12. See the photographs and description of this remarkable weapon in Ludwig Jedlicka, *Unser Heer: 300 Jahre Österreiches Soldatentum in Krieg und Frieden* (Vienna: Fürlinger, 1963), 288, 320. Although little noted by British writers, batteries of this Austrian weapon were deployed in 1914 with devastating impact. See the summaries in General J[ean-Joseph] Rouquerol, *Les hauts de Meuse et Saint-Mihiel* (Paris: Payot, 1939), 48–50.

13. After I had written this chapter, I had the good fortune to attend a lecture given by Professor Bradley J. Meyer at the U.S. Marine Corps University (September 20, 2003), in which he outlined exactly the same approach, even using some of the same terms. Where I think we differ is in our account of the *how* of these tactics. I believe Meyer sees them from the point of view of the analyst studying written doctrines, while in *Myth of the Great War*, I emphasized the idea of responsive innovation in the field. We also differ in our evaluation of the success of the tactics, since my accounts derive chiefly from the point of view of the French survivors, who saw all too well how the tactics worked. Both of us owe much to the pioneering research of Bruce I. Gudmundsson, *Stormtroop Tactics: Innovation in the German Army, 1914–1918* (New York: Praeger, 1989), as well as to Martin Samuels, *Doctrine and Dogma*. One key quote from Gudmundsson sums up the situation in World War II perfectly: "It was their ignorance about how the Germans had fought World War I that prevented the majority of French, British, Dutch, and Belgian leaders from adequately preparing for the German attack. . . . Seeing tactics as an exercise in engineering, these writers were looking for the formula for German tactics—how many guns per yard of front and how many waves of infantry per battalion. They thus missed the intangibles. . . . Like all members of their generation, military writers were affected by wartime propaganda, which depicted Germans as heartless automatons who were as incapable of independent action on the battlefield as they were of human feeling" (xii–xiii). Writings in German are extensive, beginning with Generalleutnant Max Schwarte's *Die militarischen Lehren des Grossen Krieges* (Berlin: Mittler und Sohn, 1923) and Generalleutnant Hermann Balack's *Development of Tactics*, which was translated by Harry Bell and issued by the U.S. Army (Fort Leavenworth, KS: General Service Schools Press, 1922).

14. Little has been written about this important branch of the German army. The standard German source is Paul Heinrici's *Das Ehrenbuch der Deutschen Pioniere* (Berlin: Wilhelm Rolf, [1931]), which gives the following strengths: in peacetime, 21,000 men organized into 35 battalions; in wartime, nearly 80,000 men in 70 battalions, or 379 companies (47).

15. Technically there were eleven Jäger battalions in the Prussian army, two Saxon, two Bavarian, and one Mecklenburg Jäger battalions, plus two guards units, the Garde-Jäger and the Garde-Schützen. Captain Rohr, who directed the special

unit in 1915, was from the last named—a good indication of the priority attached to it by the army high command.

16. John Terraine sees the Sturmbataillone as some type of commando force, and he echoes British field marshal Slim, who observed that such "private armies" "lower the quality of the rest of the army, especially of the infantry." This quotation is taken from Terraine, *The Smoke and the Fire*, 206. See the elaborate discussion of this in Samuels, *Doctrine and Dogma*, 20–23.

17. The phrase "inside the decision cycle" refers to a concept developed by John T. Boyd as part of what is called the "OODA Loop" (observation, orientation, decision, action). Although Boyd's work (which mostly took the form of briefings to military personnel) has had a noticeable impact on American military performance in recent years, the concepts don't seem to have penetrated into the world of military history. For a brief discussion of Boyd, see Colin S. Gray, *Modern Strategy* (Oxford: Oxford University Press, 1999), 90–93. There is a detailed exposition of Boyd's life and impact on the military in Grant T. Hammond, *The Mind of War: John Boyd and American Security* (Washington: Smithsonian Institution Press, 2001).

18. Fayolle had figured this out by summer 1915; the passage summarized in the text was written in his diary on June 1, 1915. See Fayolle, *Carnets secrets*, 109.

19. Jean Norton Cru, who was both a historian and a combat veteran, puts it perfectly: "If orders had always been obeyed to the letter, the whole French army would have been massacred before August 1915"; see *Témoins* (Paris: Etincelles, 1929 [reprinted Nancy: Presses Universitaries, 1993]), 20.

20. Erich von Falkenhayn, *Die Oberste Heeresleitung, 1914–1916* (Berlin: Mittler, 1920), 181–182. The standard English translation muddles the point. See von Falkenhayn, *The German General Staff and Its Decisions, 1914–1916* [no translator given] (New York: Dodd, Mead, 1920), 243. I've chopped von Falkenhayn's convoluted sentences into smaller pieces to make them easier to read, but the discussion pretty well preserves the sense of what he was saying.

21. Confirmation of the importance of this idea comes from an unlikely source: speaking of the reasons for the Nationalist victory in the Spanish civil war, Hugh Thomas says, "German technical training, particularly in signals, played a considerable part there. But equally important was the availability of so many middle-class young men as *alféreces provisionales*, provisional lieutenants, whose education made them more effective than the junior Republican officers"; see Thomas, *The Spanish Civil War*, 3rd ed. (New York: Harper and Row, 1986), 938.

Chapter 2: The Army Before Hitler: Hollow Victories, Shattered Illusions

1. Sebastian Haffner, *Geschichte eines Deutschen: Die Erinnerungen, 1914–1933* (Munich: Deutscher Taschenbuch, 2002), 271. Born in 1907, Haffner emigrated, three decades later, to Britain, where he worked as a journalist. He returned to Germany in 1954, and became a best-selling author and respected contributor to *Die Welt* and *Sterne*. His memoirs of 1914–32 lay undiscovered until after his death in 1999.

2. Emile Fayolle, *Carnets secrets de la grande guerre*, edited Henry Contamine (Paris: Plon, 1964), 322. For the failure of the blockade to starve Germany, see Herbert Bayard Swope, *Inside the German Empire* (New York: Century, 1917), especially xx.

3. In Ernst Hanfstaengl, *Hitler: The Missing Years* (New York: Arcade, 1957), 40–41.

4. No one would print George Seldes's account of his German expedition; it appeared in *You Can't Print That! The Truth Behind the News, 1918–1928* (Garden City, NY: Garden City Publishing Co., 1929), 24–40. To my knowledge no historian has made use of this interview.

5. "Ideas about what happened in 1914 must not be influenced by knowledge of what happened afterwards" is how the best of Wilhelm's biographers puts it; he goes on to say, "Nor do I consider that the Kaiser really did run the country." See Michael Balfour, *The Kaiser and His Times* (New York: Norton, 1972). These remarks are taken from the afterword added to the American edition, 527–529. The idea that Wilhelm II had any real impact on military affairs has been thoroughly demolished by Lamar Cecil, citing half a dozen documentary sources on this point. See *Wilhelm II: Emperor and Exile* (Chapel Hill: University of North Carolina Press, 1996), 209–211.

6. The military aspect of the Friekorps has long been denied: "The Freikorps were an extremist right-wing influence in German politics during the Weimar era. Not an organized political party, they were rather demobilized German soldiers who kept their weapons from the war. Without any regular jobs available, these ex-grunts organized themselves into gangs, hiring themselves out to the highest bidder." This quotation represents the conventional wisdom (found at http://www.dingwall.bc.ca/history/main.php3?cat=personalities&listing=Freikorps), which follows the lead of Robert G. L. Waite, who views the phenomenon in such political terms as to demilitarize it entirely. See *Vanguard of Nazism: The Free Corps Movement in Postwar Germany, 1918–1923* (Cambridge: Harvard University Press, 1952).

7. The only serious account of the situation in Central Europe is Henry Bogdan, *De Varsovie a Sofia* (Paris: Editions de l'Université et de l'Ensiegnement Moderne, 1982). For the Baltic, the key work is George von Rauch, *The Baltic States: The Years of Independence*, translated Gerald Onn (Los Angeles: University of California Press, 1974).

8. There was no secret about what Guderian was doing. When he wrote his famous memoir, he put all this information right there, in the first appendix. See Heinz Guderian, *Panzer Leader*, translated Constantine Fitzgibbon (New York: Da Capo Press, 1952), 468.

9. Divisional organizational tables of the units operating in the Baltic in 1919 were first published in Josef Bischoff, *Die Letzte Front: Geschichte der Eisernen Division im Baltikum 1919* (Berlin: Schützen Verlag, 1935), 263–264. A more comprehensive display of the organizational charts is to be found in Reichsministerium, *Der Feldzug im Baltikum bis zur Zweiten Einnahme von Riga* (Berlin: Mittler und Sohn, 1937), 143–159.

10. Analysts who have discussed Germany's attempts at clandestine rearmament have oversimplified the situation by ignoring the conflicts that wracked Central Europe (and the Baltic) in 1919–21. See, for example, Barton Whaley's *Covert German Rearmament, 1919–1939: Deception and Misperception* (Frederick, MD: University Press of America, 1984). This work rules out of bounds, at the outset, any concept of Germany as requiring a legitimate national defense. Such a view ties neatly in with the belief that Germany and Austria were wicked powers that started the war and deserved to be punished—Versailles being the just punishment mechanism.

11. By 1939, eighteen countries had taken delivery of this gun, and eight more had bought the license and were producing it themselves, with suitable modifications. In 1941 the United States, reluctantly deciding that the weapon was far superior to the 37-millimeter M1A2 gun, bought the license; production problems delayed its introduction until 1943. Suitably modified, it was produced until 1974. See the excellent brief summary in Peter Chamberlain and Terry Gander, *Anti-Aircraft Guns* (New York: Arco, 1975), 40–41.

12. To avoid confusion, I've used the English translations for terms designating the German army (and navy) whenever possible. But in certain places the German phrases are important. The official title of the army before 1935 was Reichsheer, and the navy was called the Reichsmarine. As there was no separate air force, those two branches comprised the entire military, technically known as the Reichswehr, and the cabinet minister in charge was the *Reichswehrminister* (in American English we would say "secretary of defense," but this translation, I think, strips the connotations from the title). There is a tendency, though, to use this latter term to refer to the army, even though technically the term includes the navy as well. To add to the confusion, in the initial months of the republic, until March 1919, the army was called the Provisional Reichsheer. The main distinction, however, is between the Reichswehr—that is, the armed forces (or army) of the Weimar Republic—and the Wehrmacht, the army of National Socialist Germany.

13. There is no biography of von Seeckt in English (the German ones are less than illuminating); see the brief summary in James S. Corum, *The Roots of the Blitzkrieg* (Lawrence: University Press of Kansas, 1992), 25–29. The most useful biographical reference work on the Germans is Samuel Mitcham's *Hitler's Field Marshals* (New York: Cooper Square Press, 1990) and *Hitler's Commanders* (New York: Cooper Square Press, 2000); however, as the titles suggest, Mitcham restricts himself to senior officers who actually served after 1933, so he doesn't include men like von Seeckt, and there are curious omissions—Guderian, for instance.

14. Here are the actual German titles. For the northern command, von Seeckt was *Stabschef des Armeeoberkommandos Grenzschutz Nord*. In July he was appointed *Chef der Generalstabes der deutschen Armee*; in October this title changed, as the general staff was now called the *Truppenamts im Reichswehrministerium*, to conform to the Versailles diktat.

15. The exact number is in Corum, *Roots of the Blitzkrieg*, 46. By comparison: before 1914 the German army had 42,000 noncommissioned officers, for a premobilization army of well under a million men. Data are taken from the discussion in

Jean Feller, *Le dossier de l'armée française: La guerre de cinquante ans, 1914–1962* (Paris: Perrin, 1966), 49.

16. Bismarck's successors had complacently assumed that no alliance was possible between an aggressively Republican, anti-Monarchist France and a Russia widely viewed as the epitome of despotism. They were wrong. The Franco-Russian alliance is thus a cautionary tale, with much relevance to contemporary history. Despite the pact in August 1939 between Hitler and Stalin, however, the conventional wisdom persists that adversaries do not make alliances.

17. See, for example, the controversy in the British navy before 1914, when Sir John Fisher attempted to "break down the traditional barriers of social class that afflicted the navy," as Massie puts it, as he describes one of the most feudalistic, anti-intellectual structures imaginable. And this was the navy, which by contrast with the army was a bastion of intellectual egalitarianism. Quote from Robert K. Massie, *Dreadnought: Britain, Germany, and the Coming of the Great War* (New York: Ballantine Books, 1992), 449.

18. In 1926, at the annual maneuvers, von Seeckt invited the crown prince (the kaiser's eldest son) to attend. Since the crown prince had spent most of the First World War as the commander of the Fifth Army, the invitation seems harmless, but von Seeckt had been far too neutral during the abortive Munich coup staged by Hitler and Ludendorff. So the distinguished jurist Otto Gessler, who had been defense minister since the fall of Noske after the Kapp–von Luttwitz putsch in March 1920, used the invitation to drive von Seeckt out of office. Von Seeckt's behavior during the Hitler putsch attempt was perilously close to treason, but sacking him represents the perfect example of how classical liberals contributed to the demise of German democracy (Gessler was a member of the DDP, or German Democratic Party). There were plenty of important men in Germany who, one way or another, aided and abetted the future dictator in the 1920s, but von Seeckt can hardly be counted in their number. See the brief mentions in Ian Kershaw, *Hitler, 1889–1936: Hubris* (New York: Norton, 1999), 194–195. Left unexplored is the extent to which Gessler, who managed to hang on to the job of *Reichswehrminister* for eight tumultuous years, was actually the driving force behind the formation of the new army. There are extensive analyses of the day-to-day politicking involved in John W. Wheeler-Bennett, *The Nemesis of Power* (London: Macmillan, 1961), 83–288.

19. This figure was derived by collating the entries in Mitcham (*Hitler's Field Marshals and Hitler's Commanders*) and F. W. von Mellenthin, *German Generals of World War II as I Saw Them* (Norman: University of Oklahoma Press, 1977). In *Covert German Rearmament*, Whaley cites figures showing that the proportion of aristocratic officers was over 20 percent (19).

20. Thus Baron Kurt von Hammerstein-Equord is mostly remembered for his attempt to prevent Hitler from becoming chancellor and Wilhelm Adam isn't remembered for anything much at all. Von Hammerstein-Equord is to be praised for being the first—and, practically speaking, the only—high-ranking officer in the Reichsheer to try to stop Hitler. See the explanation in Mitcham, *Hitler's Field Marshals*, 17–19, the only competent account in English. Far too much is made of the hostility of von Seeckt (and the officer corps in general) toward Weimar. But the of-

ficers corps was hardly more hostile than the *Ordinarien*—the professorial elite who ran the universities—or their students: when Hitler came to power, the universities proved themselves the first and in many ways the most enthusiastic supporters of National Socialism. We often forget that the books being burned were ignited by the students.

21. This bizarre incident is reported by Manfred Rommel, and recorded in David Fraser, *Knight's Cross* (London: HarperCollins, 1993), 132.

22. One way to look at the development of warfare in the twentieth century is to see it as a period in which there was an increasing gap between the two, a gap filled by what some recent military theorists have called the "operational art," an "intermediate field of military knowledge situated between strategy and tactics." These quotations are from Shimon Naveh, *In Pursuit of Military Excellence* (London: Frank Cass, 1997), xiii. Interestingly, one of Naveh's examples of this gap is Fall Gelb, the German offensive of May 1940. See the discussion in Major Rick S. Richardson, *Fall Gelb and the German Blitzkrieg of 1940: Operational Art?* (Fort Leavenworth, KS: School of Advanced Military Studies, 1999), especially 15–17.

23. For decades a more or less contrary view has prevailed in Anglo-American military history. It has long since been discarded by German researchers: "For the most part, we have been able to see Hitler the military leader only through the eyes of these generals. Especially during the years of self-justification this often led to grotesque situations. . . . It is not true that—in simple black and white terms—the reasonable and promising ideas of Hitler's General Staff were regularly overridden by the stupid ignorance of a nonsense-planning and nonsense-demanding amateur," Helmut Heiber, *Hitler and His Generals: Military Conferences, 1942–1945*, translated Roland Winter, Krista Smith, and Mary Beth Friedrich (New York: Enigma Books, 2003), xxx. In his introduction to this text, Gerhard Weinberg is even more forthright: Hitler "had a clear view of his aims, or broader strategic issues and their economic and political implications; in these matters he saw reality more clearly than the narrowly focused military professionals" (vi–vii). Weinberg's concluding sentence can hardly be bettered: "It might well be suggested that Hitler and his generals deserved each other" (viii). Although the English edition of this text appeared in 2003, the German text, *Hitlers Lagebesprechungen*, dates from 1962; the evidence in the stenographic records has been around for some time.

Chapter 3: Breaking Out of the Cave: Hitler and the Wehrmacht's Jewish Problem

1. As quoted by Ron Rosenbaum, *Explaining Hitler* (New York: Random House, 1998), 345.

2. François Furet, *The Passing of an Illusion: The Idea of Communism in the Twentieth Century*, translated Deborah Furet (Chicago: University of Chicago Press, 1999), 162, note 13.

3. This point cannot be overstressed. Right up until the collapse of the Soviet Union, the conventional wisdom among Sovietologists was to minimize the scale of

the Bolshevik terror, to rationalize it, and then basically to ignore it. Those researchers who revealed what we now know is the truth were frequently reviled as cold warriors or anti-Communists. As Walter Laqueur notes, "Some Western sovietologists claimed that the importance of the purges and forced labor had been grossly overstated, both quantitatively and qualitatively." In fact, this was the academic consensus. See *The Dream That Failed: Reflections on the Soviet Union* (New York: Oxford, 1994), 134; for discussion of the losses and post-1990 data, see 136–146. See also Alan Bullock, *Hitler and Stalin: Parallel Lives* (New York: Knopf, 1992), 277, 507, 1003; Dmitrii Antonovich Volkogonov, *Stalin: Triumph and Tragedy*, translated and edited Harold Shukman (New York: Grove Weidenfeld, 1988), 167, 307, 562. The traditional source of much of these data in the West was Robert Conquest. See *The Great Terror: A Reassessment* (New York: Oxford, 1990). But it would be a mistake to suppose that the figures have not been produced independently elsewhere. Olga Shatunovskaya, a member of the control committee under Khrushchev, claimed that "between 1935 and 1941[,] 19,800,000 people had been arrested," as recorded by David Remnick in *Lenin's Tomb* (New York: Random House, 1993), 115.

4. Two of Germany's nineteen elite Jäger battalions used the word *Schütze* (the Garde-Schützen, one of the elite units of the Prussian army, and its Saxon equivalent, the Schützen Regiment Prinz Georg). The former had been one of the first test-bed units in the development of what was later called storm-troop tactics, back in 1915. The Freikorps units carried both terms into the post–World War I era, as well as the designation of *Sturm*, and Hitler's use of both terms was a shrewd propaganda decision.

5. These figures have always distressed most chroniclers of Hitler's rise to power, and one often sees comments such as the following: "In the last free elections of November 6, 1932, the National Socialists gained 33.4 percent of the votes. In the March 5, 1933, elections, after the Reichstag fire, after the elimination of the Communist Party and the massive intimidations of the rest of the opposition, the Nazis still did not have the majority of the people behind them." These are the words of Rüdiger Safranski in the excellent biography *Martin Heidegger: Between Good and Evil*, translated Ewald Osers (Cambridge: Harvard University Press, 1998), 291. But the perspective is simply one of wishful thinking. In *Hitler, 1889–1936* (New York: Norton, 1999), Ian Kershaw puts the case fairly: "Still . . . 43.9 per cent of the vote was not easy to obtain under the Weimar electoral system" (461). But anyone in the West who was reading the papers would have been told the same thing: "Where Hitler's Majority Comes From" was the subhead in the *Manchester Guardian Weekly*, March 10, 1933, 190. There wasn't much doubt, at the time, about the majority and how it was obtained.

6. I believe that this is a fair summary of the basic conclusions reached in John Lukacs's exhaustive analysis in *The Hitler of History* (New York: Random House, 1997). The idea that Hitler was not a revolutionary is another example of the way Marxists have distorted the historical fabric: a revolutionary must be a fellow traveler. But as Hugh Thomas points out in his discussion of the leaders of the two sides in Spain, it was the Nationalist leaders who were young and had radically new

ideas. See *The Spanish Civil War*, 3rd ed. (New York: Harper and Row, 1986), especially 186, 193, 328.

7. See the discussion in Hugo Ott, *Martin Heidegger: A Political Life*, translated Allan Blunden (New York: HarperCollins, 1993), 140–171; the quotation is on 165. Ott's evidence about Heidegger's complicity is convincing (the relationship was torturous and complex) and, by and large, accepted by Safranski, the best of Heidegger's biographers (see note 5 above). A good example of the orientation of most Hitler analysts is the fact that they simply ignored the parallelism with Heidegger, together with the philosopher's clear statements of the principles Hitler embodied.

8. And as well: "For every two children born in Germany in 1932, three were born four years later. In 1938 and 1939, the highest marriage rates in *all* of Europe were registered in Germany. . . . From 1932 to 1939 the number of suicides committed by Germans under twenty dropped 80 *percent* during the first six years." See Lukacs, *Hitler of History*, 97–98 (emphasis in original).

9. John Lukacs lists the German biographers—all of them serious and responsible men—who would have more or less agreed with this remark and whose views, in several cases, preceded it (*Hitler of History*, 97). I am indebted to Lukacs for this illuminating quotation.

10. The data here and below are taken from the invaluable Bryan Mark Rigg, *Hitler's Jewish Soldiers: The Untold Story of Nazi Racial Laws and Men of Jewish Descent in the German Military* (Lawrence: University of Kansas Press, 2002), 67–70. A typical case is to be found in Martin Kitchen, *The German Officer Corps, 1890–1914* (Oxford: Clarendon, 1968), 40. Kitchen cites French and Austrian data, is wrong on the German, and ignores the British figures entirely, thus setting up a misleading comparison, rigged against the Germans.

11. Another point of confusion: prior to 1914 there was a Prussian, a Bavarian, and a Saxon army, each with a distinct identity, command structure, and cultural attitude. Even in those historic states that no longer maintained a national army per se, individual units retained the historic traditions. Thus, for example, the Fourteenth Jäger, recruited from Mecklenburg, was known as the *Großherzoglich Mecklenburgisches*. In 1914, Allied propagandists deliberately blurred the distinctions, smearing all Germans with the sobriquet *Prussian*. Although there is no solid data on the subject, it appears that in Roman Catholic Bavaria, for instance, there was much greater tolerance of Jewish officers than in Protestant Prussia; some of the confusion on the subject may stem from the erroneous assumption that the terms *Prussian* and *German* were interchangeable.

12. One could construct a torturous case based on the fact that the ratios of Jewish officers to non-Jewish officers as a percentage of the population were much smaller than they should have been, and similar calculations have been made about suffrage in attempts to prove that Wilhelmine Germany was neither tolerant nor democratic. Although fashionable among political scientists, such analyses are basically rubbish.

13. Only more so: Milch may have had two Jewish parents, while the majority of the officers classified as Jewish by the National Socialists had only one or two

Jewish grandparents. However, Rigg was able to find almost one hundred Jews (as opposed to men with one or two Jewish grandparents) who served in the Wehrmacht (see *Hitler's Jewish Soldiers*, 64).

14. The Milch story was known long before Rigg published his book. Samuel Mitcham summarizes it in *Hitler's Commanders* (New York: Cooper Square Press, 2000), 174.

15. A quotation from a little jewel of a story, entitled "Veronica," and found in Theodor Storm, *Gesammelte Werke* (Stuttgart: Cotta, 1965) 1:498–502.

16. Indeed, much the same thing holds true today, with, say, Americans who consider themselves observant Roman Catholics dissenting from the Church's position on key subjects. The pre-1914 Jewish and Protestant migrations roughly parallel the confused state of affairs with regard to ethnicity in Central Europe. For example, the inhabitants of historic Bohemia were forced to choose between being (or were forcibly divided into) Germans and Czechs (and Jews). But as Jeremy King has observed, the process was tangled, which is why he titles his book *Budweisers into Czechs and Germans* (Princeton, NJ: Princeton University Press, 2002). The inhabitants of Budweis/Budějovice tended not to think of themselves along ethnic or national lines until fairly late in the nineteenth century; rather, they considered themselves to be inhabitants of the town, as subjects of the Hapsburg emperor, or as Bohemians. One could make the same claim—with reservations—about certain sectors of the Jewish and German communities. Curiously, the synagogue in Budweis "was the most obviously church-like structure created for Jewish worship" in Europe (King, 77).

17. In this regard, Hitler betrayed the religious orientation and traditions of his childhood, giving the most cynical interpretation possible of Jewish assimilation or migration: the Jews, he claimed, converted in order to empower themselves socially. I think it's relevant here to note that Hitler was born in the part of Austria from which the Protestants had been expelled and that this prototype of ethnic cleansing had taken place long after the supposed Enlightenment had begun. In fact, it was the last such occurrence in Europe proper. In the Protestant lands of the north and northwest, the idea of a shared ethical base enabling individuals to shift from one confession or sect to another was much more widely accepted, a fact that doubtless aided the migration of Jews from their traditional faith to what is now called Reform Judaism.

18. Passive-aggressive behavior was first diagnosed and named by psychologists working with American army personnel in the Second World War. Although today it is a frequently observed behavior pattern, the concept is "more widely accepted among practicing clinicians than among research psychologists," as the authors of one textbook put it. Basic features are "indirectly expressed resistance and hostility in the face of common environmental demands for adequate performance and behavior. There is hostility toward others, though the passive-aggressive denies this hostility and may even act insulted when confronted with it. . . . This resistance is expressed through such indirect behaviors as stubbornness, intentional inefficiency, deliberate forgetfulness, and procrastination." Quotations are from Robert G. Meyer and Yvonne V. Hardaway Osborne, *Case*

Studies in Abnormal Behavior (Boston: Allyn and Bacon, 1982), 261; for discussion of the typology, see 261–268.

19. It is on this basis that I have so much skepticism about much of the testimony of surviving German senior officers. Passive-aggressive behavior is highly persuasive, simply because, over time, the individual comes to believe that he is not at fault, that the failure is the responsibility of other people.

20. In other words, although Hitler was supremely evil, most of his observed behaviors can be viewed as ordinary responses to the situation at hand. Conversely, the Allied interrogators, who for justifiable reasons tended to see him in negative terms, played into the hands of many of the senior officers they interviewed, whose combination of blame, transference, and excuse is pretty much the range of behaviors that passive-aggressives display.

21. The figure of 200,000 French children born of liaisons between French woman and German military personnel is taken from Jean-Paul Picaper and Ludwig Norz, *Les enfants maudits: Ils sont 100.000 on les appelait les "enfants de Boches"* (Paris: Editions des Syrtes, 2004). The title makes the point clear enough, but see the estimate on 13.

22. Or for other reasons as well. These declarations began to be issued at least as early as October 1937, as Rigg reprints one (*Hitler's Jewish Soldiers*, following page 71), and the criteria of the individual in question were that he had several nephews in the military. The key phrase: *"als arisch in Sinne der Vorschriften der NSDAP."*

23. In his suicide note, Ernst Udet, who killed himself on November 15, 1941, specifically named Milch and von Gablenz as Jews and accused Göring of having let them destroy the air force. The note represents a good example of passive aggression to the last, since, in any objective accounting, Udet would bear a heavy responsibility. Von Gablenz, who became head of the air force planning office, was killed in a plane crash on August 21, 1942.

24. The data are a mess, as Rigg patiently explains, but I think this is a fair reading of his summaries (*Hitler's Jewish Soldiers*, 191–194). In the discussion of the German army in 1914, I pointed out that there were only 42,000 officers holding active-duty commissions for the entire army, and that Versailles limited the officer corps to 4,000 men; the 16,000 officers of Jewish descent is thus a significant number. And even small numbers force us to reconsider the situation. Moreover, the most conservative data we have demonstrate that hundreds of individuals were, in fact, granted exemptions personally by Hitler. For example, during the period from January 1940 to September 1943, Hitler approved 295 applications for *Genehmigung* and decided to grant 33 applicants the status of *Deutschblütig*.

25. As quoted by Ott, *Martin Heidegger*, 176. Ott does not identify the source.

26. *The Speeches of Adolf Hitler*, edited Norman H. Baynes (London: Oxford University Press, 1942), 1:7. It is easy to find examples from these early speeches that are explicitly and unambiguously racist (see pages 8–10). But the later, more public speeches of the 1930s take a much different tack. See note 28 below.

27. The Czech distaste for the Jews of the region continued through Communist times, when it was exploited deliberately. Franz Kafka (1883–1924) was treated

as a nonperson. The standard government printed guides to Prague never mentioned his name. And in the purges of the Communist Party occurring in Czechoslovakia after 1947, those singled out were mostly Jews, as the Czech Communists slavishly followed Stalin's moves to eliminate Jews from the party.

28. See, for example, the repeated linkages in Hitler's speeches on Bolshevism, *Speeches of Adolf Hitler*, 1:674, 676, 682, 686, 695, 700, 710, 713. "Though the speeches of Hitler are filled with attacks on the Jewish-Bolshevik opposition and upon the Jews as an international force which everywhere supported world revolution, who as emigrants were always inciting the other powers to oppose the National Socialists and the Germany of the Third Reich, is it surprising to observe how little the Führer has said on the treatment of the Jews by the National Socialist state" (editorial note to *The Speeches of Adolf Hitler*, 1:721). For those who remain skeptical—these arguments are, I know, difficult to accept—here is a contemporary example: the insistence that one's opposition to Zionism in no way can be taken as an indication of hatred of the Jews. It just so happens that all Zionists are Jewish. The distinction is an intellectual sleight of hand—and transparently so. But in my experience it is stoutly maintained, and nowhere more fervently than in the professorate, where it is often accepted by those who themselves are of Jewish descent.

Chapter 4: Planes, Personalities, and Conflict in the Luftwaffe

1. A quote that appears in many texts. The one used here is taken from Ray Wagner and Heinz Nowarra, *German Combat Planes* (New York: Doubleday, 1971), 303.

2. Data are taken from Jules Poirier, *Les bombardements de Paris (1914–1918): Avions, Gothas, Zeppelins, Berthas* (Paris: Payot, 1930), 18–19. Casualties from the bombing and shelling of Paris: 527 dead and 1,261 wounded.

3. According to an unpublished study by the American naval officer John F. O'Connell, the Germans abandoned their daylight bombing attacks against Britain after three months of missions because their loss rate approached 30 percent. They eventually resumed bombing missions at night but found that the loss rate was still too high (about 14 percent).

4. Quotation is from the War Department's Technical Manual 30–450, *Handbook on German Military Forces* (Washington, DC: War Department, 1941), 328–329. The quotation is allegedly from a German document, unidentified. The manual goes on to say: "The manner in which the German Luftwaffe has been employed since the commencement of hostilities shows that the war in the air is being waged for the purpose of expediting and increasing the effectiveness of the general operations" (329). The poorly written statement is entirely correct.

5. As Robin Higham observes: "At the very time when the counter-strike deterrent force policy was accepted, when the Cabinet adopted the idea that a weaker democracy could protect itself by threatening to devastate the cities of any potential aggressor, the RAF ceased to issue specifications for long-range heavy bombers. In-

stead, the cadre force maintained was equipped with medium bombers with a striking range inadequate for any target beyond Paris." See *Air Power: A Concise History* (New York: St. Martin's, 1972), 71.

6. See the discussion in Herbert Molloy Mason, *The Rise of the Luftwaffe* (New York: Dial, 1973), 254. For obvious reasons, the concept of accuracy in bombing is usually passed over in silence by airpower analysts, as indeed it was by the bomber commanders themselves. When, at Churchill's insistence, an analysis of bombing results was done (the Butt Report), the findings showed that "the aiming error was something like about five miles; under those conditions there was little hope that Bomber Command could hit anything smaller than a city." See the discussion in Higham, *Air Power*, 132 (the source of the quotation).

7. In the frantic Allied attempts to stop the Germans from crossing the Meuse on May 14, 1940, the RAF lost 40 bombers out of the 70 it deployed: in proportion to the number of planes involved, it was the worst single day in the history of the RAF. For a brief account, see Mason, *Rise of the Luftwaffe*, 363. There is some minor confusion about the exact numbers. In the British official history, L. F. Ellis comes up with a loss rate of approximately 50 percent; see *War in France and Flanders* (London: Her Majesty's Stationery Office, 1953), 55–56. In *Comme des Lions, Mai–Juin 1940* (Paris: Calmann-Levy, 2005), Dominque Lormier calls this disaster *"l'episode du Pont Saint-Menges,"* after the name of the bridge the Allies were trying to destroy, and lists combined French and British aircraft losses at 150 planes — without the bridge even being hit (page 33).

8. See the brief description by R. S. Hirsch, "The Junkers Ju-87 'Stuka,'" in Heinz Nowarra and Edward Maloney, *Junker Ju-87* (Fallbrook, CA: Aero Publishers, 1966), no pages given. The 20-millimeter-cannon-equipped Ju-87 was the D-7 version; the 37-millimeter version was the G-1, which entered service in 1942.

9. See the detailed discussion in Hanfried Schliepahke, *The Birth of the Luftwaffe* (Chicago: Regnery, 1971), 37–40.

10. It was not widely known that the Ju-88 had been designed by Americans working for Junkers until William Green revealed the fact in the late 1950s. See *Famous Bombers of the Second World War* (Garden City, NY: Hanover House, 1959), 71–72.

11. For these problems and others, see R. S. Hirsch and Uwe Feist, *Heinkel 100*, 112. (Fallbrook, CA: Aero Publishers, 1967), 7 [pages of monograph are not numbered].

12. "Losses mounted alarmingly, and in August [1940] it was decided to withdraw the Defiant from daylight operations and use it as a night-fighter" is how Owen Thetford puts it in *Aircraft of the Royal Air Force Since 1918* (New York: Funk and Wagnalls, 1968), 102. See also the comments of William Green in *War Planes of the Second World War: Fighters* (New York: Doubleday, 1960), 1:54–55.

13. This was the only area in which the Allies were remarkably deficient in equipment. Data are taken from Dominique Lormier, who shares my conclusion. See *Comme des Lions*, 30–31.

14. The Republican commander of the Army of the North, Colonel Prada, in a communication to Azaña, then president of the republic, and quoted by him in the

fourth volume of his memoirs, page 848. As recorded by Hugh Thomas, *The Spanish Civil War*, 3rd ed. (New York: Harper and Row, 1986), 787.

15. The one major exception was the Ju-87 dive-bomber, still under development. Only one or two were sent to Spain; consequently, the Allies were unprepared for it later on.

16. As late as summer 1937, the Republicans had more planes—and their Spanish pilots, trained in the Soviet Union, were competent enough. See the remarks by Thomas, *Spanish Civil War*, 787.

17. The bombing of Durango followed a pronouncement by the Nationalist general Mola: "If submission is not immediate, I will raze Vizcaya to the ground, beginning with industries of war." Thomas is of the opinion that the bombing was the practical application of the threat. See the discussion in Thomas, *Spanish Civil War*, 616–617 (whence the quotation).

18. The issue of April 11, 1938: 25. Although Guernica became the symbol of terror from the air, contemporary observers were more struck by the Nationalist attacks on Barcelona. So was Italian foreign minister Ciano, who, according to what he wrote in his diary, was horrified. By the standards established later, of course, Barcelona was hardly touched.

19. That Allied bombers were ultimately decisive factors in the German defeat is a deeply cherished belief that seems impervious to skeptical inquiry. In addition to my analysis in *Blitzkrieg Myth* (190–209), see Gian P. Gentile, *How Effective Is Strategic Bombing?* (New York: New York University Press, 2001). By examining the internal correspondence and reports of the surveyors, it casts doubt on their (highly positive) conclusions about the efficacy of strategic bombing. Part of Gentile's conclusion: "Second, as in previous conflicts involving the application of air power—World War II, Korea, Vietnam, and the Gulf War—efforts to assess the effectiveness of strategic bombing remain clouded with ambiguity" (191).

Chapter 5: Paper Tigers: Hitler's Tanks

1. As reported by Heinz Guderian, *Panzer Leader*, translated Constantine Fitzgibbon (New York: Da Capo Press, 1952), 29. "I was amazed at the clarity with which the old man pointed out the mistakes that had been made," Guderian says (29). As well he might be.

2. See the discussion in Michael Scheibert, *The Secret Beginnings of Germany's Panzer Troops*, translated Ed Force (Altglen, PA: Schiffer Military/Aviation History, 1999), 3–4. As to the state of German armor in 1939–40, see the comments by F. M. von Senger und Etterlin in *German Tanks of World War II*, translated J. Lucas, edited Peter Chamberlain and Chris Ellis (New York: Galahad, 1967), 22.

3. Guderian, *Panzer Leader*, 27. The Soviet base did provide one valuable service: it trained hundreds of Soviet tankers. Based on their performance in Spain, the training was first-class.

4. The major producers were Czechoslovakia, France, the Soviet Union, and the United States. Although there were dozens of tanks of various sorts designed in

Britain, the army had not settled on a standard tank (or tanks) and put it into quantity production at this time: "The number of fighting vehicles to be shared between the fifty-nine RAC regiments at the start of the war was some 2000 tanks, of which 300 were completely obsolete, while most of the rest were light tanks of very little combat value." See David Fletcher, *The Great Tank Scandal* (London: Her Majesty's Stationery Office, 1989), 1:3.

5. Specifications and design data here and below are taken from von Senger und Etterlin, *German Tanks:* Mark 1, 21–23; Mark 2, 24–28; Czech tanks, 29–33; Mark 3, 34–42; Mark 4, 43–48. This text is vastly preferable to the original German one. The tons specified in the text are all metric tons of 1,000 kilograms.

6. See the definition in Werner Regenburg, *Captured Tanks in German Service: Small Tanks and Armored Tractors* (Altglen, PA: Schiffer Military/Aviation History, 1998), 3.

7. The German system of tank nomenclature, like the American, is cumbersome in the extreme. Technically the first tank in service would be called the *Panzerkampfwagen I*, abbreviated *Pz Kw I*, the next model would be the *Pz Kw II*, and so on. Within each series there were numerous modifications and upgrades, identified by the legend *Ausfuhrung* A, B, and so forth. Given the hastily applied patches and upgrades, the Germans went through the alphabet at a good clip. There was, for example, a *Panzerkampfwagen III Ausfuhrung* N. Around 1943 the Germans pretty much gave up and started using animal names. Thus the *Pz Kw V* was called the *Panther*, and the VI the *Tiger*, which existed in two entirely different versions, *Tiger* 1 and *Tiger* 2. In this book I'm reducing the terminology drastically and using Mark 1, Mark 2, Mark 3 (or Mark 3-N), and Mark 4 for the initial designs, and the animal names for everything else (confusingly, there was another system of names as well, using a three-digit number, but fortunately few analysts refer to it). The American system, if possible, was even worse. Probably in desperation the British gave the American tanks that formed the basis of their armored force after 1940 names, and even though designations are in some cases technically inaccurate, the system makes for a much easier read: *Sherman* instead of *Medium Tank M4A1*.

8. There's a certain confusion about the numbers of tanks deployed; one reason was that the Germans began, early on, removing the turret from their tanks and mounting a heavier gun (or something else) on the hull—what we would call self-propelled guns of various types. In May 1940, the most authoritative count gives a total of 3,695 tracked vehicles derived from Marks 1–4, of which 3,238 were tanks—that is, they had turrets—and 1,133 armored cars and weapons carrying half-tracks. These data are from the table in appendix 2 of von Senger und Etterlin, *German Tanks* (193). Clearly not all these vehicles were assigned to the May 1940 offensive. The French colonel Georges Ferré, working from German documents, gives a figure of 2,683 tanks, broken down by division. See *Le défaut de l'armure* (Paris: Charles-Lavauzelle, 1948), 108. A report to Hitler from the inspector general of armored troops in 1944 lists 2,574 tanks, broken down by type (these totals don't agree with Ferré's figures), but the variance is under 5 percent. This report is reprinted in Guderian, *Panzer Leader*, appendix 3 (472–473).

9. Guderian, *Panzer Leader* (27). The claim is repeated in von Senger und Et-

terlin, *German Tanks* (35). But this didn't happen. The first armored division had only Mark 1 and 2 tanks. And in May 1940, as a result of the reclassification of the Mark 3 as a medium tank, the same armored division was now evenly divided between the tankettes and the Mark 3 (or one of the Czech tanks). See the organizational tables Guderian prints as appendixes 24 and 25.

10. Although the Americans had guns that were more powerful than the inadequate 75-millimeter gun on the main U.S. battle tank (the Sherman), the turret wasn't big enough to accommodate them, and the British problem was even worse. The British figured out how to mount the 17-pounder, a potent 76.2-millimeter gun, in the Sherman turret by making all sorts of ingenious patches. Vehicles thus equipped, which the British called the Sherman Firefly, were the only Allied tanks able to survive encounters with German machines such as the Mark 4-F and, later, the Panther and the Tiger. It's an interesting comment on the lack of technological expertise of many writers that one of the Sherman's chroniclers asserts that in the mounting of the British gun, the recoil mechanism was removed. Minus the recoil mechanism, of course, the gun, when fired, would have blown the turret (together with bits and pieces of the gun crew) into the blue.

11. After I made this point in *The Blitzkrieg Myth* (New York: HarperCollins, 2003), I was sent a paper a senior U.S. Army officer (who perhaps best remains anonymous) wrote for the National Security Council, neatly dissecting the army's historical position: "The Army's rationale for mass producing a smaller, undergunned tank (the Sherman), was less for reasons of shipping requirements (deployability), as it was for the vision of how mechanized forces would conduct operations"; his point was that the doctrine underlying the tank was a mistake. As indeed it was.

12. Guderian, *Panzer Leader*, 21. Von Senger und Etterlin puts it rather differently: "It was intended to fit these vehicles [Mark 4] with a larger calibre gun . . . to fulfill a support role for the light tanks during combat and engage targets which the smaller armor-piercing weapon . . . was not able to affect or penetrate" (*German Tanks*, 62).

13. Archival material as quoted by Dominique Lormier, *Comme des Lions, Mai–Juin 1940* (Paris: Calmann-Levy, 2005), 27–28. This detailed accounting lists some definite areas of German superiority. I've abbreviated Kühne's remarks drastically.

14. Data on production are taken from Walter Spielberger and Uwe Feist, *Halbkettenfahrzeuge* (Fallbrook, CA: Areo Publishers, 1968). Unfortunately the data are not given in any systematic way—apparently no figures were available until 1942, but as our summary makes clear these vehicles were intended as prime movers of one sort or another, and even after two years of war, the army lacked the requisite numbers. The "tons" referred to in the ratings are all metric tons, or 1,000 kilograms.

15. See the comments in this regard by Wilhelm von Thoma, justly regarded as one of Hitler's better armored commanders, as interviewed in Basil H. Liddell Hart, *The German Generals Talk* (New York: Quill, [1948] 1979), 98.

16. Over the course of the Spanish civil war, about 17,000 German military and

civilian personnel served; there were about 5,000 men just in the Condor Legion, and Germany sent a total of about 200 tanks, together with a thousand guns. Since von Thoma was also in command of the thirty antitank companies Germany sent (180 antitank guns and their crews), his estimate is way off. This interview is to be found in Liddell Hart, *German Generals Talk*, 92–97. The figures for antitank guns in this paragraph are from the interview (page 92); other data are from Hugh Thomas, *The Spanish Civil War*, 3rd ed. (New York: Harper and Row, 1986), appendix 7, 985.

17. The actual quotation is "For it was seen that Spain would serve as 'the European Aldershot'" (Liddell Hart, *German Generals Talk*, 92). A curious phrase for a German to use, and the passive voice ("it was seen") makes it even curiouser. The best summary of the conventional wisdom on this is, as one might suspect, in Thomas, *Spanish Civil War*, 944–945.

18. This sentence, buried in volume 9 of the testimony, was ferreted out by Thomas, who quotes the relevant passage (*Spanish Civil War*, 355). The problem is that in the first part of the paragraph, Göring says that Franco "asked for support, particularly in the air. . . . He could not get his troops across, as the fleet was in the hands of the communists." But the actual letter Franco had delivered to Hitler asked only for fighter planes and antiaircraft guns—there was no mention of an airlift. It is difficult to escape the conclusion that (1) it was Hitler alone who decided to send the transport planes and (2) the idea of Spain as a testing ground came up only retrospectively. One thing is for sure: if Hitler had said, "We're going to test out our new toys in Spain," there would have been no shortage of fingers pointing to his statement as yet another sign of whatever sin the speaker was crediting to his account.

19. Note the recurrent use of the first person pronoun, particularly striking in light of the fact that the lessons never seem to have penetrated into the rest of the army. Quotation is from Liddell Hart, *German Generals Talk*, 92.

20. For this incident, see Thomas, *Spanish Civil War*, 468. Some other examples: in January 1937, a handful of Russian armored cars, armed with the less potent 37-millimeter gun, destroyed twenty-five Mark 1 tanks (493). Ironically, the armored cars were equipped with the Soviet version of the original 3.7-centimeter gun designed by the German firm of Rheinmetall and manufactured in the Soviet Union under license. It was the same pathetic weapon that was the basic German antitank and tank gun. The Soviet version was much better, mainly because of the ammunition it used. Thomas charitably says that this ammunition was "soon" adopted by the Germans, but the shell didn't make it into service until the end of 1940; "soon" in this context was actually three years. These details account for the discrepancies in evaluating the gun, such as the one found in Lormier, *Comme des Lions*, 35.

21. Guderian, *Panzer Leader*, 143. This is a good example and prototype when it comes to the disingenuous remarks of Hitler's commanders. It was Guderian's business to know what his potential opponents were up to and what kind of equipment they had. It's hard to escape the conclusion that as the result of their unbroken string of victories, the senior commanders were just as complacent as Hitler was.

Chapter 6: Bloodless Victories, or Nearly So: Toward a Greater Germany,
1935–39

1. Hugh Thomas, *The Spanish Civil War*, 3rd ed. (New York: Harper and Row, 1986), 194. To make this quotation read better, I have eliminated a connective: as written, the sentence begins "Yet . . ."

2. The Chaco War, between Paraguay and Bolivia, began with sporadic fighting as early as 1928, but the actual conflict started in 1932 and continued through 1935. The United States, together with the major South American powers, finally managed to broker a peace, which was formally signed in 1938. The fact that the settlement was made independently of the League of Nations was one of the straws breaking that organization's back, ignored mainly because the war involved two obscure (for Europeans anyway) countries.

3. As reported—without comment—by Denis Richards in the first volume of the official RAF history, *The Fight at Odds* (London: Her Majesty's Stationery Office, 1953), 2–3. By 1940, Baldwin was blamed for failing to build up armaments during his term as prime minister. A. J. P. Taylor's take on the issue is similar to that of the epigraph at the head of this chapter; albeit from another perspective: "People turned against Baldwin and blamed him, very often, for their own faults and failings. Baldwin had been perhaps only the representative man at the time and he had shared, indeed, its faults and failings. He had also shared in its good qualities." See *British Prime Ministers and Other Essays*, edited Chris Wrigley (London: Allen Lane, 1999), 57.

4. See the figures and analysis in Thomas, *Spanish Civil War*, 156–157. The Popular Front (the parties of the left) received 4,654,116 votes, or 34.3 percent; the National Front (parties of the right) got 4,503,505, or 33.2 percent; and the center parties garnered 526,515, or 5.4 percent. As Thomas explains, the outcome translated into a win for the Popular Front because of the way the seats were selected (it got 263 deputies, the National Front 133, and the center 77). In terms of the population, however, the country was evenly divided—probably why so few historians have mentioned the figures, or disputed them, even though they may not be entirely accurate. In the mythology of the Spanish civil war, the "people" were all on the Republican side—a nice myth but hardly true in any sense of the word.

5. See the conclusion by Thomas: "Azana and his ministers behaved as if they were dealing primarily with constitutional or cultural problems. Even the socialist ministers (between 1931 and 1933, Prieto and Largo Caballero) did not seem to recognize the need, in a world financial crisis, of the importance of the direction of the economy" (*Spanish Civil War*, 186).

6. Recent information strongly suggests that Pierre Cot was a Communist agent, although it is not clear whether he was working for the Soviet Union in 1936. But judging from his actions, he pursued a policy in line with the one Stalin was developing: aid would be funneled through the various Communist-front organizations; for the time being, the Soviet government would appear to be neutral. Cot was identified as a Soviet agent in the Venona decryptions, as reported by Nigel West, *Venona: The Greatest Secret of the Cold War* (London: HarperCollins, 1999), 90–92.

7. In *Panzer Leader*, translated Constantine Fitzgibbon (New York: Da Capo Press, 1952), Heinz Guderian bitterly disputes Churchill's description (in volume 1 of *The Second World War*) of the whole affair as a shambles (54–56) but grudgingly admits that breakdowns were not insignificant. He claims that they were certainly less than 30 percent, a figure suggesting that probably at least one out of every four vehicles broke down (if the figure had been below 25 percent, he might well have used that number).

8. As quoted in an extensive essay on Central Europe in *Life*, November 8, 1937, 96–100. The essay then gives two well-chosen examples: "The Carpathian Russians [Ruthenians] have not been given self-government and the Slovak Popular Party leader, Dr. Tuka, who most noisily demanded Slovak autonomy, is in jail."

9. The Poles believed that Ukrainians agitating for an independent Ukraine were operating with relative impunity out of the Czech-controlled portion of Ukraine (Ruthenia). Probably so, given the republic's comparative tolerance of such things. In the discussions of the collapse of the Czech Republic, one often reads that Stalin was ready to come to its aid and that the Allies should have convinced Poland to allow him to do so. This reading of history turns foreign affairs into a board game: the Poles were about as likely to permit the Red Army passage through Poland as pigs were to fly—not least because from Warsaw's point of view, Czechoslovakia was a threat and a nuisance, not an ally.

10. The idea that the Germans would have been so obliging as to attack the one area of the border that was fortified is interesting, given the historical preference of the German army for flanking movements. More likely, in light of the incredible ignorance (which still prevails) about the nature and extent of the much better known Maginot Line, the analysts making these comments didn't know exactly where the Czech fortifications were. Even the Czech publications detailing these fortification are all recent, dating from after the collapse of the Communist state.

11. Technically, the Trianon was the name given to the treaty involved, but the decisions were all made at Versailles. In the chronology here, I am closely following the pioneering study by Stanislav J. Kirschbaum, *A History of Slovakia* (New York: St. Martin's Press, 1995), especially 179–186; the work is a useful corrective to the traditional accounts, in which the legitimate concerns of the Slovaks and the Ruthenians are ignored.

12. See Wolodymyr Kosyk, *The Third Reich and Ukraine*, translated Irene Rudnytzky (New York: Peter Lang, 1993), 53, together with reprinted documents cited. Kosyk is, I believe, one of the first scholars to call attention to the ambassador's statement.

13. The text of the treaty, together with one of the best explanations of what it really meant, may be found in Bronis J. Kaslas, *The USSR-German Aggression Against Lithuania* (New York: Robert Speller and Sons, 1973), 109–112. This book, a collection of documents and memoranda indispensable to any student of the period, is ignored in most of the conventional accounts of the beginnings of the war. See, for example, Donald Cameron Watt's *How War Came: The Immediate Origins of the Second World War* (New York: Pantheon, 1989). The conventional wisdom

was that Stalin was trapped into this agreement by the dilatory way the French and British pursued their own negotiations about a possible alliance; this view was espoused or at least tolerated by many historians in the West. See the account in Leonard Mosely, *On Borrowed Time* (New York: Random House, 1969), 267–310, for a good illustration of this point of view. Most analysts, while recording the pact's existence, wrote their accounts as though it didn't exist. As the existence of the pact became harder to controvert, fellow travelers like A. J. P. Taylor quickly developed benign interpretations consistent with the initial Communist Party formulations: the provisions of the treaty, defensive and tactical, bought time for Stalin and were forced on him by the unreasonable anti-Communism of the British and French governments. See Geoffrey Roberts, *The Soviet Union and the Origins of the Second World War* (New York: St. Martin's Press, 1995), 1–2, and *The Origins of the Second World War Reconsidered: The A. J. P. Taylor Debate After Twenty-five Years*, edited Gordon Martel (Boston: Allen and Unwin, 1986), especially 162–187. When François Furet wrote his account of the rise and fall of Communism, he pointed out that Stalin had attempted a rapprochement in 1934, and again in February 1939. See *The Passing of an Illusion: The Idea of Communism in the Twentieth Century*, translated Deborah Furet (Chicago: University of Chicago Press, 1999), 258.

Chapter 7: The Fall of the West, September 1939–June 1940

1. As quoted in S. Fischer Fabian, *Prussia's Glory: The Rise of a Military State*, translated Lore Segal and Paul Stein (New York: Macmillan, 1981), 232.

2. Besides the discussion in John Mosier, *The Blitzkrieg Myth* (New York: HarperCollins, 2003), 36–40, the only treatment in English is found in J. E. Kaufmann and H. W. Kaufmann's *Maginot Line Imitations* (New York: Praeger, 1998), 9–50. For Hitler's involvement, see Dieter Bettinger and Martin Büren, *Der Westwall* (Osnabrück: Biblio Verlag, 1990), 1:92–95. Albert Speer, in *Inside the Third Reich*, translated Richard and Clara Winston (New York: Macmillan, 1970), says that the only plans Hitler personally drafted were for his house on the Obersalzberg, but as this example shows, Speer's observation is not correct.

3. On German planning maps, each division was given roughly the objective of the same linear advance. These dispositions are clearly marked on the OKW maps reprinted in the U.S. Army study of the Polish campaign, written by Robert F. Kennedy, *The German Campaign in Poland (1939)* (Washington, DC: Department of the Army, 1956), as maps 6 and 9. See also map 2, "The German Concept of Ground Operations."

4. The (mostly silent) treatment accorded the Saar offensive is a good example of how accounts of the war were quickly rewritten to suit political ends and then passed into the historical record. Here is Gerhard Weinberg's conventional account, in *A World at Arms: A Global History of World War II* (Cambridge: Cambridge University Press, 1994): "All available evidence shows that there was never any intention of implementing the central portion of these promises—a major offensive starting on the fifteenth day of mobilization" (68). Actually, the forces in-

volved were substantial: two mechanized divisions and the equivalent of an armored division (5 independent tank battalions, or 180 tanks), as well as ten regular infantry divisions, including two of the North African divisions—some of the best infantry France had. Considering that war between France and Germany officially began only that weekend, this was a creditable effort.

5. In addition to my discussion in *Blitzkrieg Myth* (62–77), there are several excellent accounts of the Polish campaign: Kennedy, *The German Campaign in Poland* (1939); Matthew Cooper, *The German Army* (New York: Stein and Day, 1978), 169–177; J. E. Kaufmann and H. W. Kaufmann, *Hitler's Blitzkrieg Campaigns* (Conschocken, PA: Combined Books, 1993), 68–92; and Andrzej Suchcitz's unpublished monograph distributed to the Polish Ex-Combatants Association, in Britain in 1995, to commemorate the fiftieth anniversary of the end of the war. Cooper understands that the campaign had little to do with new tactics and technology—a startling judgment, in light of the year the book was written, but he is dismissive of the Polish armed forces: "an enemy as deficient in the military art as the Poles then were" is how he puts it (169).

6. Personnel losses were light: 8,028 killed, 5,029 missing, and 27,278 wounded, according to the U.S. Army's study (Kennedy, *The German Campaign in Poland [1939]*, 120). Suchcitz has a slightly higher figure: 16,000 killed (he lumps the killed and the missing together) and 32,000 wounded (3). The difference arises from the fact that the army figures include only German army personnel and exclude air force losses. Equipment losses were more substantial. During the course of the fighting, the Poles put 674 tanks out of commission, along with 319 armored cars, 6,046 trucks, and 5,538 motorcycles. Data from Kennedy (120), Suchcitz (cited in note 5, page 3), and the Kaufmanns (*Hitler's Blitzkrieg Campaigns*, 92) are all in broad agreement. In *The German Air Force* (London: Jane's, 1981), Matthew Cooper gives losses of about 500 aircraft out of 1,939 engaged (100), while in Robin Higham, *Air Power: A Concise History* (New York: St. Martin's Press, 1972), the figures come to 1,581 aircraft engaged, 285 lost, and another 279 damaged (100).

7. The best instance is Donald Cameron Watt's *How War Came: The Immediate Origins of the Second World War* (New York: Pantheon, 1989), particularly 479–529. As to the dismissal of the Polish military as incompetent, see Cooper, *German Army*, 169, and Nicholas Bethell, *The War Hitler Won* (New York: Holt, Rinehart, and Winston, 1972), 30–31.

8. Information from Basil Henry Liddell Hart, *The German Generals Talk* (New York: William Morrow, 1953), whose account (108–109) is still the best, far superior to more recent ones—e.g., Ian Kershaw's convoluted discussion in *Hitler, 1936–1945* (New York: Norton, 2000), which begins on 266, only to be interrupted by digressions concerning internal affairs.

9. The quotation is from Liddell Hart's interview with Siewert in *German Generals Talk*, 109. Liddell Hart links von Brauchitsch's actions to the alleged plots to depose Hitler, but this interpretation is highly questionable. Rather, the incident stands as proof of the passive-aggressive response on the part of the senior leaders. "Indirect resistance (e.g., forgetting, procrastinating, inefficiency, making irrelevant excuses) to demands or assumed demands of others even when a direct challenge

would be possible" is the first quality listed in the standard clinical texts: see Francis J. Turner (editor), *Adult Psychopathology: A Social Work Perspective* (New York: Free Press, 1984), 212. Note the wording of the quotation in Liddell Hart: he "began to think" of resigning. He avoided a direct challenge even though he could have resigned.

10. The extent to which the British were far from united on the issue of opposing Hitler has been ignored until recently. See the account in John Lukacs, *The Duel: 10 May–31 July 1940: The Eighty-day Struggle Between Churchill and Hitler* (New York: Ticknor & Fields, 1990), especially 60–61, 77–79, and 139–140. Hitler came closer to a peaceful accomplishment of his aims here than is generally realized. See the discussion in Bethell, *The War Hitler Won*, 17–35.

11. Data are taken from Cooper, *The German Air Force*, 111.

12. The best account of the Norway campaign is François Kersaudy's *Norway 1940* (Paris: Editions Tallandier, 1987). Translated by the author, the text was published in Britain (London: William Collins Sons, 1990), in the United States (New York: St. Martin's Press, 1991), and in paperback (Lincoln: University of Nebraska Press, 1998). For the listing of units taken from Kersaudy, see the index under *France* and *Great Britain*. During spring 1940, the British systematically moved equipment from France to Norway, particularly antiaircraft systems, much to the distress of the commanders of British forces on the Continent. See also my discussion in *Blitzkrieg Myth* (92–101).

13. As Brian Bond explains in *Britain, France, and Belgium* (London: Brassey's, 1990): "In the knowledge of the outcome of the German onslaught on the Low Countries and France in May 1940 it now seems almost incredible that in the period from January to April inclusive the Allies were more concerned, one might fairly say obsessed, with extending the war to Scandinavia" (48).

14. See my analysis of these dispositions in *Blitzkrieg Myth* (102–104). As with Poland, most accounts of May 1940 are driven by the desire to exculpate the British, in this case either at the expense of the French (or the Belgians) or by positing a radically new form of warfare that caught them by surprise. Hitler's propagandists were, of course, only too happy to oblige.

15. Heinz Guderian, *Panzer Leader*, translated Constantine Fitzgibbon (New York: Da Capo Press, 1952), 92. See also Major Rick S. Richardson's remarks that "there was no coherent operational design in the *Fall Gelb* plan. . . . Although the plan was flexible it lacked clearly defined objectives," in *Fall Gelb and the German Blitzkrieg of 1940: Operational Art?*, an essay written for the School of Advanced Military Studies, U.S. Army Command and General Staff College, Fort Leavenworth, Kansas (document identification: 19991109 062), 30.

16. Figures for losses are taken from Frans S. A. Beekman and Franz Kurowski, *Der Kampf um die Festung Holland* (Herford: Mittler und Sohn, 1981), 212–213. The authors tally German airborne casualties of all kinds as coming to 38 percent. The men taken prisoner were recovered after the Dutch surrender, a fact that disguised the casualty rate. The heavy losses during this operation were not recognized by the Germans, the Allies, or historians.

17. Among the many accounts, the best and most accurate chronicle is in Jean

Paul Pallud's *Blitzkrieg in the West* (London: Battle of Britain Prints, 1991), 146–149. That the bombing was basically an error seems to be the current consensus. See Robin Neillands (who is not shy in apportioning blame on the Germans whenever possible), *The Bomber War* (New York: Overlook, 2001), 41–42.

18. Even today the exact details of these operations are confused, with many authors still speaking of parachute drops. There is an excellent account by Colonel James E. Mrazek, *The Fall of Eben Emael* (Washington, DC: Luce, 1971). The key German eyewitness account is by Gerard Schacht, who commanded one of the assault teams. According to Mrazek (203), Schacht's account was originally published in the *Wehrwissenschaftliche Rundschau* (May 1954), 217–233. I am indebted to the U.S. Army Military History Institute for the typescript of its translation of this article. There is a good explanation of the hollow charge in Mrazek (55–57).

19. These forts were actually underground (or in the case of Eben Emael, tunneled into the sides of the great rock), so that all that was visible was a set of partially concealed turrets emerging from the ground. Their location made them basically invulnerable to bombs and shells, and indeed the Germans tried both without doing any damage, particularly at Schoenenbourg, the most easterly of the Maginot fortification complexes. Fortifications like these would become vulnerable only with the advent of precision-guided missiles, in the 1990s. Even the older structures—those built before 1914—were difficult to destroy, as Patton's soldiers found out in the fall of 1944, when they had to take Metz.

20. These major clashes of armor have long been denied by historians. When I wrote *The Blitzkrieg Myth*, I was the first analyst to call attention to the size and scope of these armored engagements, and to the fact that they were hardly French routs. The point is important because of the long-standing myth that the French did not know how to use armor, only the Germans did. A more detailed and authoritative account of the fighting has now appeared in France, which makes clear the scope and intensity of the armored combats. See Dominique Lormier, *Comme des Lions, Mai–Juin 1940* (Paris: Calmann-Levy, 2005), 41–55, 79–126.

21. The significance of this move can hardly be overestimated. Hitler clearly thought the war in the west would go on for some time, or he would hardly have planned on relocating his headquarters and then relocated, which quashes the idea that Hitler had gauged the Allies correctly and knew they would quickly fold. On the contrary, he was preparing for a long war. His staff began looking for the site as early as May 19. The work was done speedily, and Hitler arrived on June 6, remaining there for the duration. Typically, the relocation is either ignored or passed over in bland silence by Anglo-American historians. See the extensive study by René Mathot, *Au ravin du loup: Hitler en Belgique et en France* (Brussels: Editions Racine, 2000).

22. The British—including Churchill—began trying to blame the Belgians for the collapse almost immediately. Only the prompt response of Admiral Sir Roger Keyes, a distinguished veteran of the Great War who happened to be a member of Parliament in 1940, aborted the government's campaign. See the account by his son, Roger Keyes, *Outrageous Fortune: The Tragedy of Leopold III of the Belgians*

(London: Seecker and Warburg, 1984). Although the initial attempt to smear the Belgians was a failure, the idea has had a long life.

23. See the precise accounting of casualties in Pallud, *Blitzkrieg in the West*, 607–609; the figures used in the following paragraphs come from that work. There is a growing consensus in France that French casualties were closer to the 100,000 mark than to the traditional figure of 92,000 dead. The ratio suggests that the fighting was much more intensive than is usually claimed.

24. These battles, when mentioned at all, are simply dismissed. In addition to Lormier, *Comme des Lions*, 44–49, consult the following: for the Glembloux Gap, see Michel de Lombarès, *Histoire de l'artillerie française* (Paris: Charles-Lavauzelle, 1957), 308; Pallud, *Blitzkrieg in the West*, 158, 165; Mosier, *Blitzkrieg Myth*, 131–141; Ernest R. May, *Strange Victory* (New York: Hill and Wang, 2001), 402–403. The Battle of Stonne has been virtually ignored in English accounts; there is a brief mention in May, *Strange Victory* (433), who seems not to understand exactly where the fighting took place. There is an excellent, detailed account of the fighting in the French Ardennes in Gérald Dardart, *Ardennes 1940* (Charleville-Mézières: Editions Ardennes 1940, 2000).

25. The reality of Dunkirk exemplifies the fact that a great deal of the scholarship on this phase of the war collapses under scrutiny. The defense of the port was directed by the French, whose sacrifices made the evacuation work. Royal Navy losses were heavy: 226 out of the 693 ships involved, including 32 out of the 41 destroyers. RAF performance was competent but nothing more. The Germans were justifiably reluctant to engage in the intensive ground fighting that would have been required, so the famous halt order, given by General von Rundstedt (and approved more or less automatically by Hitler) was hardly miraculous. At that point, the Germans realized that all their energies would be required to fight the French. For further details, see Robert Jackson, *Dunkirk* (New York: St. Martin's Press, 1976) and Arthur Durham Divine, *The Nine Days of Dunkirk* (New York: Norton, 1959). Data are taken from Jackson (172).

26. See the citation in Gordon Williamson, *Infantry Aces of the Third Reich* (London: Arms and Armour, 1991), 36–37. The Knight's Cross of the Iron Cross was instituted in 1939 as an equivalent to the traditional award for outstanding valor established by Frederick the Great—the Pour le Mérite. Holders of the Knight's Cross who received successive awards for bravery under fire were given Oak Leaves—a metallic sprig that was tacked on to the cross. Only 758 of these were awarded to the roughly seven thousand holders of the Knight's Cross: Pössinger received his in February 1945.

Chapter 8: A Few Distractions on the Road to Armageddon

1. Walter Goerlitz, *History of the German General Staff, 1937–1945*, translated Brian Battershaw (New York: Barnes and Noble, 1995), 388. This remark was made in conjunction with the period this chapter covers.

2. The total was derived by counting the individual losses enumerated in the

first volume (1939–40) of W. R. Chorley, *Royal Air Force Bomber Command Losses of the Second World War* (Earl Chilton, UK: Midland Publishing, 1992).

3. By October 1916, Allied losses, which were averaging over 20 percent, forced the French (and later the British) to switch to night raids. The Germans went through the same learning cycle, only at a later date: the bombing of London began on May 25, 1917, and by August the Germans, too, had switched to the cover of darkness after suffering even more serious losses than the French had. These data are courtesy of an unpublished manuscript on airpower by Captain James T. O'Connell (USN), who sent me portions of it to read as a supplement to what I had written—somewhat erroneously—in *The Blitzkrieg Myth* (New York: Harper-Collins, 2003), 52–54.

4. The data are taken from Alfred Price's succinct and accurate *Pictorial History of the Luftwaffe, 1933–1945* (New York: Arco, 1969), 24. Although the literature on the air war over Britain is voluminous, Price gives most of the needed information in fewer than five pages (24–29). There are a few additional details relating to the effectiveness of the air-defense system that I discuss in *The Blitzkrieg Myth* (54–60).

5. See the data reproduced in Richard Overy, *The Battle of Britain: The Myth and the Reality* (New York: Norton, 2000), 162. The figures are for single-engine fighters only, but since we're talking about bombing missions here, the data for crews can hardly be any better. See also Overy's analysis of combat experience (125). Curiously, he then concludes that "the Battle of Britain did not seriously weaken Germany and her allies" (113), although the evidence cited suggests quite the contrary.

6. Thus in *Hitler, 1936–1945: Nemesis* (New York: Norton, 2000), Ian Kershaw characterizes Hitler's assessment as a "crass underestimation of Soviet forces" (335 and following). But then Kershaw is always at pains to paint the Soviet Union in the most flattering light.

7. It's a telling commentary on Hitler's penchant for keeping his ideas to himself that Mussolini apparently thought that Operation Sea Lion, which was probably never contemplated with any seriousness, was actually going to take place in September 1940.

8. Understandably, ascribing human virtues to Hitler upsets a good many people. But as we shall see, loyalty is certainly a component of his personality. He stuck by Göring long past the point at which self-interest—and national needs—dictated his replacement. Nor is this the only example. For a conventional account of the Balkan campaigns explicitly from the German point of view, see the U.S. Army monograph *The German Campaigns in the Balkans (Spring 1941)* (Washington, DC: Center of Military History, 1953). This document makes the best case for the grand strategic thinking allegedly underlying what was going on.

9. Franco did cooperate with Hitler in various ways; one of the most important was that he sent an expeditionary force to Russia. This force, the Blue Division, gave a good account of itself on the battlefield; had the Germans supplied them with decent equipment, they would have done even better. But Franco was also very clever: packing volunteers off to fight the Communists was not a bad way of making sure he'd have no opposition from the right as he remade Spain.

10. An exact count of which units were originally intended for which operation is difficult, because of the Yugoslavian operation, so I've added them together: seven armored, three motorized, three mountain, and thirteen infantry divisions were committed for Greece and Yugoslavia. This does not count two units nominally tagged as regiments but that in reality were at divisional strength (the Herman Göring armored regiment and Gross Deutschland, the premier army unit, by now motorized) and the airborne division deployed by the air force. Since two of the motorized units were Waffen-SS, it is clear that a substantial proportion of Germany's best (or, anyway, best-equipped) troops were to be involved.

11. Figures on losses are taken from Churchill's correspondence, as reproduced by Callum MacDonald, *The Lost Battle: Crete, 1941* (New York: Free Press, 1993), 126, 134.

12. The distances here and elsewhere are calculated according to Great Circle routes, i.e., the shortest distance between two points on a sphere, which is not the same as a straight line drawn on a flat map. For obvious reasons, combat aircraft can rarely fly an exact match to the Great Circle distance, so the distances given here should be considered as the bare minimum.

13. A point generally lost in the shuffle, but see the discussion, in MacDonald (*Lost Battle*, 71–72), of Bernard Cyril Freyberg, commander of British forces in Crete. The British ability to read the German codes impacted commanders in the field negatively. A lot of military intelligence is flat-out wrong; and since the high command couldn't tell Freyberg why this intelligence was absolutely correct, it only added to his dilemma: Should he be preparing to mount an all-out fight for the airfields, or should he be worried about stopping a naval assault? In retrospect, most analysts act as though the first option was the only one, but, lacking a time machine and a crystal ball, Freyberg hardly knew this.

14. Crete may well be the most extensively researched and recorded campaign in the twentieth century. In addition to the texts cited in this chapter, see, among the many: Ivor Stewart, *The Struggle for Crete: A Story of Lost Opportunity* (London: Oxford University Press, 1966); David Thomas, *Nazi Victory: Crete, 1941* (New York: Stein and Day, 1972); Christopher Buckley, *Greece and Crete, 1941* (London: Her Majesty's Stationery Office, 1977); Tony Simpson, *Operation Mercury: The Battle for Crete, 1941* (London: Hodder and Stoughton, 1981).

15. In the German airborne system, the men jumped without packs or weapons, which were dropped separately. Regardless of the theory justifying the procedure, this technique has to be one of the most idiotic ideas in military history. Crete made this clear: many of the weapons containers fell in places the British troops controlled.

16. Data are taken from S. W. C. Pack, *Battle for Crete* (Annapolis, MD: Naval Institute Press, 1973), appendixes F and H (124, 126). Listing the evacuees ship by ship, Pack concludes that 16,511 men were transported to safety in Egypt, but that figure omits those who died en route; thus about 17,000 were actually taken off the island.

17. Seven months later—December 1941—a powerful British surface force, consisting of the *Prince of Wales* and the *Repulse*, was caught by Japanese aviators

and promptly sunk. The army was not the only branch of the service that was slow to learn lessons.

18. There's been confusion over the exact figures on the German side. The latest and best—used here—come from MacDonald, *Lost Battle*, 301.

19. This quotation is from MacDonald, *Lost Battle*, 298–299. This had certainly always been Churchill's instinct—my point is that Crete brought it out into the open, perhaps unfairly to Freyberg, but Crete was a major disaster for the British.

20. In the conclusion to *Blitzkrieg Myth*, I discuss the reasoning behind this analysis, and cite the relevant earlier works, mainly Trevor N. Dupuy, *A Genius for War: The German Army and the General Staff, 1807–1945* (Englewood Cliffs, NJ: Prentice-Hall, 1977). Dupuy appended an updated summary of his work on this subject in Trevor N. Dupuy, David L. Bongard, and Richard C. Anderson Jr., *Hitler's Last Gamble* (New York: HarperCollins, 1994), appendix H (498–501).

Chapter 9: The Soviet Collapse

1. D. H. Lawrence, *Lady Chatterley's Lover* (London: Penguin, 1928), 35.

2. The extent to which Soviet information consisted largely of distortions and prevarications, initially a controversial subject, is increasingly accepted today, albeit often grudgingly. For the best summary of the case, see Walter Laqueur, *The Dream That Failed: Reflections on the Soviet Union* (New York: Oxford, 1994), especially 110–119. For a direct application to military history, consider the remark made by one of the best historians working in the field: "While many detailed Soviet works on the war display sound scholarship and are accurate, unfortunately the most general and most accessible to Western readers tended to be the most biased, the most highly politicized, and the least accurate. Even the soundest works have been vetted ideologically, and the authors have been forced to write their accounts with the narrowest of focuses." See David Glantz, "The Failures of Historiography: Forgotten Battles of the German-Soviet War (1941–1945)," Fort Leavenworth, Kansas, Foreign Military Studies Office (1997) 1; available at http://rhino.shef.ac.uk:3001 /mr-home/rzhev/rzhev2.html.

3. Norman Stone argues that the Battle of Lake Narocz, launched three days after the German assault on Verdun in February 1916, was "one of the decisive battles of the First World War. It condemned most of Russia's army to passivity." See *The Eastern Front, 1914–1917* (New York: Scribner's, 1975), 231. The one exception was Brusilov's offensive in June 1916, which marked the end of the Russian army as an effective combat force. It seems likely that the Russo-German war of 1914–17 would be the departure point for any serious analysis of the 1941 war, since the Wehrmacht tended to be dominated by senior officers who had fought there. That conflict, however, is generally dismissed with a few sentences.

4. The size of this alliance is usually dismissed, but the contributions were hardly minimal. The Hungarian army deployed twenty-five infantry divisions, one cavalry division, two armored divisions, and two brigades of Jäger. Data are from

Franz von Adonyi-Naredy, *Ungarns Armee im Zweiten Weltkrieg: Deutschlands letzter Verbundeter* (Neckargemund: Klaus Vowinckel, 1971), 29. The Romanian contribution was even more substantial. Although the Finnish army confined itself to operations inside what Helsinki regarded as national territory, its participation was significant. The divisional-strength Italian, Spanish, and Slovakian forces all gave good accounts of themselves. In 1941 the real military alliance was on Hitler's side—the only country contributing anything significant to the Allied effort was Poland.

5. Right up until 1989, when the Soviet Union collapsed. Nor was the inaccessibility of accurate information a function entirely of Soviet secrecy or propaganda. Laqueur's comment regarding the situation in East Germany (the DDR) can be taken as the definition of the overall problem of knowledge about the Soviet state after 1918: "If Western experts were misled, it was only to a small degree owing to the cunning of DDR propaganda. Far more important was the fact that some of their basic assumptions and attitudes had been wrong for more than twenty years" (*Dream That Failed*, 179). If we say "almost all" instead of "some," and "seventy years" instead of "twenty," we have a fair assessment of the difficulty stretching over many decades and involving scores of government officials and academic experts. German intelligence in 1941 was no better, and no worse, than what came afterward. A practical example: most analysts list effective strength by citing the number of divisions, but Soviet divisions were substantially smaller (and less powerful) than their German counterparts. In 1940–41, numerous Soviet divisions were being maintained at a skeletal strength of 6,000 men, and few active divisions had anything like their full complement of men or equipment.

6. Nikita Khrushchev's comment, in *Khrushchev Speaks*, edited Thomas P. Whitney (Ann Arbor: University of Michigan Press, 1963), that the Red Army had fewer rifles in 1941 than in the days of the czar is probably a fair assessment (235). Or, to quote Norman Stone: "The problem with the Russians in 1914 wasn't that they were unprepared, but that they, like everyone else, were woefully unprepared for the war that followed. But by prevailing standards, they were certainly prepared" (*Eastern Front*, 48).

7. "Red Army commanders continued to make costly mistakes as late as the Battle of Berlin" is how David Glantz understates the issue. See *When Titans Clashed* (Lawrence: University Press of Kansas, 1995), 288. Glantz himself narrates the story of one of the worst of those disasters, Operation Mars (fall 1942). The title of another of his works indicates Glantz's attitude toward this engagement: *Zhukov's Greatest Defeat* (Lawrence: University Press of Kansas, 1993).

8. These figures—together with the course of the fighting—are summarized in John Mosier, *The Blitzkrieg Myth* (New York: HarperCollins, 2003), 77–83. Casualty data are taken from William R. Trotter's excellent and detailed *A Frozen Hell* (Chapel Hill, NC: Algonquin Books, 1991); the Soviet leader's comments are from *Khrushchev Remembers*, translated Strobe Talbott (Boston: Little, Brown, 1970), 155.

9. The best summary of these reforms is in Glantz (*When Titans Clashed*, 23–25); he provides an admirable recent account of the conflict. As Glantz himself

notes, however, despite the lack of access to much valuable information, the best chronicle is one of the earliest: John Erickson's *The Road to Stalingrad* (London: Weidenfeld and Nicolson, 1975).

10. The relatively few historians who mention these factors promptly dismiss them. See, for example, Bryan Fugate's *Operation Barbarossa: Strategy and Tactics on the Eastern Front, 1941* (Novoto, CA: Presidio Press, 1984), 74–75. Fugate sandwiches these concerns between discussions of Russia's enormous population and then begins talking about Napoléon.

11. There is a succinct description of the final constructions (those between 1938 and 1941) in Gabriel Gorodetsky, *The Grand Delusion: Stalin and the German Invasion of Russia* (New Haven: Yale University Press, 1999), 242–244.

12. It is an integral part of the mind-set of many analysts that the Soviet Union — even under Stalin — was, in general, a peaceful nation and that any threatening moves it made were in response to Western provocation. In the words of Laqueur: "While Soviet policy was essentially peaceful, or at least not aggressive, Stalin's crudity and mistakes played into the hands of American hawks, who were out to have their confrontation" (*Dream That Failed*, 124). Again, although Laqueur is speaking specifically about the Cold War era, his remark is a fair characterization of how the situation before 1941 was viewed. See, for example, Ian Kershaw's bland assessments of Stalin's foreign adventures in *Hitler, 1936–1945: Nemesis* (New York: Norton, 2000), 332–334.

13. To an older generation of military historians, the von Schlieffen plan was a given in any discussions of 1914. More recent analysts, myself included, have deconstructed this particular myth. In addition to my discussion in *The Myth of the Great War* (New York: HarperCollins, 2001), 32–37, see the useful abstract of research in David Fromkin, *Europe's Last Summer* (New York: Knopf, 2004), 31–36.

14. For the failures of Soviet farming, see Zhores A. Medvedev, *Soviet Agriculture* (New York: Norton, 1987), tables 5 and 6 (119). "In 1909–1913 Russia was the world's largest exporter of grain, exporting 12 to 14 million tons a year. It has now [1987] become the largest grain importer, importing 30 to 50 million tons . . . the highest reported yields in 1976–80 . . . are lower than the yields reported in all other East European countries for the same period" (237).

15. "There was moreover a gradual deterioration in the quality of the orders issued on the German side" is how Warlimont puts it — immediately quoting Eisenhower's February 1944 directive for the invasion of Europe as the counterexample. See Walter Warlimont, *Inside Hitler's Headquarters, 1939–45*, translated R. H. Barry (London: Weidenfeld and Nicolson, 1964), 30.

16. General Franz Halder's comments, widely cited, were a good example. At the end of June, he thought the war was won; on August 11 he began to complain how the Russian strength had been underestimated. See the full complaint in Glantz (*When Titans Clashed*, 74). Glantz cites it approvingly, noting that "not all German leaders saw the situation so clearly and pessimistically" (75), but it seems more like the response of the classic passive-aggressive, who blames others for failures: apparently Halder was simply a bystander when the planning was being done and the situation was being estimated.

17. Gorodetsky, *Grand Delusion*, 281. Gorodetsky makes a convincing case that Stalin was not tricked, nor was he naive. His other argument, that Stalin was not planning a future war against Germany, is less convincing.

18. Gorodetsky argues vigorously to the contrary, that Stalin was well informed about the deficiencies in the military and was working frantically to correct them (see, in particular, his summary remarks in *Grand Delusion*, 318–319). Based on his research, however, it seems more accurate to infer that Stalin approved key changes only reluctantly (see, for example, the discussion of tanks, on 243—it hardly sounds like a man who feels under pressure). The flaw in the argument is that the existence of a document in the file (assuming the document was actually written at the time and not inserted afterward by people trying to save their necks) does not mean it was read or that anyone paid attention to it.

19. The defector was one V. Rezun, who, under the nom de plume Victor Suvarov, wrote a fascinating, wildly exaggerated book arguing that Stalin planned to attack Hitler but that the Germans simply beat him to the punch: *Icebreaker: Who Started the Second World War*, translated Thomas Beattie (London: Hamish Hamilton, 1990). As was usual with Soviet defectors, Rezun was smeared by all and sundry for a host of reasons unrelated to his argument. Gorodetsky subsequently called the claim "preposterous and unsubstantiated" (*Grand Delusion*, 18). Glantz (*When Titans Clashed*, 326, note 29) discusses why the argument became controversial.

First, Glantz's characterization of Rezun as an "émigré" is disingenuous. He was in the GRU, or Soviet military intelligence, and thus had both military training and access to information denied outsiders. There's a historical pattern relating to the information passed on by Soviet defectors: each defector has been smeared and vilified, the intelligence treated skeptically by the experts—and then, later on, we find out it's surprisingly accurate. One could expand the category to include not only actual defectors but anyone questioning the moral superiority of the Soviet Union. The fact that Suvarov's argument is smeared so viciously suggests he may have had a point. According to Suvarov, Stalin intended a strike directly through Romania to get the oil Hitler needed. The notion is logical, and it resonates with Hitler's otherwise curious interest in the Balkans. It also explains why the Germans initially had so much trouble in the Ukraine: there was a sizable concentration of forces there.

20. Traditionally, analyses of the problems in the Soviet military referred exclusively to the obvious bad effects of Stalin's decimation of the officer corps; little attention was paid to the state of the combat units themselves—a flaw in Erickson's otherwise astute analysis of the situation (*Road to Stalingrad*, 26–36). Glantz is the first analyst to lay bare how woefully underequipped and undermanned the units were (among the many examples, see *When Titans Clashed*, 35).

21. See the summary of the scale of losses in the military purges, in Dmitrii Antonovich Volkogonov, *Autopsy for an Empire*, translated Harold Shukman (New York: Free Press, 1998), 209. Erickson gives a chilling account of those events (*Road to Stalingrad*, 5–7). The more recent information—referred to by Volkogonov— suggests that, if anything, the death toll was worse than we had originally thought.

22. Erickson's figures are 287,704 prisoners and 2,585 tanks: "On 9 July, German 'mopping-up' operations came to an end" (*Road to Stalingrad*, 159).

23. Ukrainian estimates of the death toll in 1932–33 are four million to seven million people. See Stanislav Kuchitsky, deputy director of the Ukrainian History Institute, as quoted by the AP wire service, May 12, 1993, 21:27 (EDY V0037). No one knows the exact figures. See the summary by Alan Bullock, *Hitler and Stalin: Parallel Lives* (New York: Knopf, 1992), 277.

24. Kursk fell on November 3, 1941. There is some discrepancy between German and Russian accounts of the collapse of Kursk, with October 24 and 30 being given. Most historians give the impression that this vital area was not taken until much later, when the Soviet winter offensives had reclaimed some of the territory lost in the fall. Not so, as the dates for these cities make clear. See the misleading maps in Glantz, *When Titans Clashed*, 84, 85.

25. "On that day, most of the factories and shops, as well as public transport, had suddenly ceased to function. Almost all the ministers and hundreds of thousands of private citizens left the city," Walter Laqueur, *Stalin: The Glasnost Revelations* (New York: Scribner's, 1990), 221.

26. Data are taken from Glantz, apparently from archival materials (*When Titans Clashed*, 360). I find these figures dubious: Did the 17,900 aircraft lost constitute only 34 percent of the Soviet air force? If 20,500 tanks had been lost (three quarters of the total tank park), then Soviet production must have averaged about 3,000 tanks a year all through the 1930s, since we know that the first Soviet tanks were not built much earlier than 1932. The conventional estimate of the Soviet air force pegged it at 4,000 aircraft (in 1936). It's difficult to reconcile the enormous tank losses with the woefully understrength armored units the Germans encountered. Nor are the figures internally consistent: Gorodetsky says Stalin was told (in May 1941) that Soviet industry could possibly produce 2,800 T-34 tanks by the end of 1941 (*Grand Delusion*, 243); Glantz says that 1,861 T-34 and KV-1 tanks had already been produced by June, "with over half going to 4th Mechanized Corps in the Kiev Special Military District" (*When Titans Clashed*, 36). This last point suggests that Suvarov's analysis of force distributions is not entirely fanciful. It does not necessarily support his claim that Stalin aimed to attack Germany, but it certainly doesn't contradict it. As Malcolm Muggeridge, who covered the Soviet Union in the 1930s for the *Manchester Guardian*, remarked, "Soviet statistics have always been almost entirely fanciful, although not the less seriously regarded for all that." See his comments in *Chronicles of Wasted Time I: The Green Stick* (New York: Morrow, 1973), 217–218. In Communist societies lying is a reflexive art, one that starts at the most basic levels. It's not as though the wildly misleading Soviet statistics were massaged in some central office in the basement of the Kremlin by the Office of Statistical Fudge. Rather, the data were spun, from the start, by men whose lives depended, quite literally, on substantiating the party line.

27. U.S. Army, *The German Campaigns in the Balkans (Spring 1941)* (Washington, DC: Center for Military History, 1953), 20. The exact figures: 11,840 out of 53,051. Many of these were either wounded or prisoners, so the precise exchange ratio is unknown; however, no totals of dead and missing Greeks and Yugoslavians

have been published. We do know that the Germans had 90,000 Yugoslavian and 270,000 Greek prisoners of war.

28. Soviet figures lump the dead and the missing together. In conventional military operations, of course, the missing are not presumed to be dead until a final accounting is made. But in this theater of operations, the missing can fairly—and tragically—be considered to be dead men walking. They would either die of abuse in German camps or, if they escaped to their own side, be slowly murdered there as well. Not that either Hitler or Stalin cared one way or the other.

Chapter 10: The Death Ride: Russia,
December 1941–December 1944

1. Gabriel Gorodetsky, *The Grand Delusion: Stalin and the German Invasion of Russia* (New Haven: Yale University Press, 1999), x.

2. Total wartime production of the Ju-52 amounted to only 2,804 aircraft, and only 5,415 were produced over the roughly thirteen-year life of the plane. By contrast, the Soviet GAZ factory built nearly 3,000 copies of the American C-47 transport during the war (the Li-2), and about 6,000 were made in the United States during the war. Although it was a much faster plane with a much greater cruising range, the C-47 actually had less transport capacity than the Ju-52, so sheer numbers produced were important. Key data are taken from Alfred Price, *Pictorial History of the Luftwaffe, 1933–1945* (New York: Arco, 1969), 63. The title does the author a disservice: Price's short essay on the Luftwaffe is one of the best that has been written.

3. See the summary of reorganizations in David Glantz, *When Titans Clashed* (Lawrence: University Press of Kansas, 1993), 65–68. He argues that much of the reorganization was part of an attempt to create smaller units that Soviet commanders could manage. Most of the cavalry divisions were annihilated in 1941. Although recent analysts are unwilling to go the next step, they cite abundant evidence supporting the contention that the Red Army's commanders were, at best, minimally competent.

4. Glantz, in *When Titans Clashed*, has the most reliable Soviet and German data (295–298).

5. The Germans made similar modifications to a host of other vehicles, including French Hotchkiss and Renault tanks. The final development of the 38T, known as the Hetzer, was the best tank destroyer of the war.

6. Tank production figures are from F. M. von Senger und Etterlin, *German Tanks of World War II*, translated J. Lucas (New York: Galahad Books, 1968), 211–212.

7. Figures for the various forms of self-propelled guns are taken from von Senger und Etterlin, *German Tanks*, 211. In an interesting indication of internal turf wars, assault-gun crews were not allowed to wear the distinctive black uniforms of the tank crews and were in every way possible treated as orphans. Guderian was more successful in these areas than on the battlefield.

8. Wittmann got his start as an assault-gun commander on the Russian front, before rocketing to fame as a Tiger tank commander (in this capacity he was credited with destroying 128 tanks). See the discussion of Wittmann in Samuel Mitcham, *Hitler's Commanders* (New York: Cooper Square Press, 2000), 298–300. For Wegener, see the citation in Gordon Williamson, *Infantry Aces of the Third Reich* (London: Arms and Armour, 1991), 79–82.

9. Ratio is from the Okinawa campaign (April–June 1945). But the loss figures there also suggest why the strategic bombing effort was necessary. Losses on Okinawa were "the highest experienced in any campaign against the Japanese. Total American battle casualties were 49,151 of which 12,520 were killed or missing and 36,631 wounded. . . . Nonbattle casualties during the campaign amounted to 15,613 for the Army and 10,598 for the Marines. The losses in ships were 36 sunk and 368 damaged, most of them as a result of air action. Losses in the air were 763 planes from 1 April to 1 July." See Roy E. Appleman, James M. Burns, Russell A. Gugeler, and John Stevens, *Okinawa: The Last Battle* (Washington, DC: Center of Military History, U.S. Army, 1948), 473. The data seem proof that an assault on Japan would have been a bloodbath. Since over 110,000 Japanese were killed on Okinawa, the argument that there would have been a saving of Japanese lives by resorting to an invasion of Japan seems weak.

10. Until David Glantz wrote his account of Mars and Jupiter in *Zhukov's Greatest Defeat* (Lawrence: University Press of Kansas, 1993), these disastrous operations—and the extent to which our understanding of the war had to change accordingly—were virtually unknown in the West.

11. This is a good time to mention the (probably deliberate) confusion about Soviet losses caused by the way operations were categorized. Glantz, in *When Titans Clashed*, reprints the latest official figures for two maneuvers identified simply as "Rzhev" and "Velikie Luki" (296). The dates make clear these are the Mars and Jupiter operations. Losses are as follows: 291,674 men killed and missing, 1,847 tanks, 1,100 artillery pieces, and 120 aircraft destroyed. In his more detailed study of the Rzhev operations, though, Glantz uses much lower figures for the casualty rates, without attempting any reconciliation of the differences. See Glantz, *Zhukov's Greatest Defeat*, xxx. The main point, however, is that to piece together Soviet losses, we have to combine separate listings—an issue that becomes important in discussing successive operations in 1943.

12. Data are taken from Heinz Schröter, *Stalingrad*, translated Constantine Fitzgibbon (New York: Ballantine, 1958), vii–viii. Schröter was a war correspondent with the Sixth Army.

13. These are the official data reprinted in Glantz, *When Titans Clashed*, 295. When Earl F. Ziemke wrote his U.S. Army study, *Stalingrad to Berlin: The German Defeat in the East* (Washington, DC: Military History Office: 1968), he noted that "the Soviet Union has not made public its own losses" (79).

14. The German (and Soviet) estimates are discussed in Walter Kerr, *The Secret of Stalingrad* (New York: Doubleday, 1978), 240. To summarize: German sources for killed in action come to 166,000, while the Russian sources report 197,000. German sources for prisoners are 123,000, while the Russian estimates are much

lower—93,000. Kerr quotes Manfred Kehrig's *Stalingrad* (Stuttgart: Deutsche Verlag–Anstalt, 1974) to the effect that German dead came to 72,885, with prisoners at 201,191. He also refers to an essay in *Die Welt*, by Walter Goerlitz (February 26, 1977), which gives figures of 110,500 and 107,500. Although there are variations in the categories, the totals seem to be roughly the same. Despite some of the enormous figures cited, it appears that the Sixth Army never had more than 220,000 men during the Stalingrad operation.

15. A number derived from adding the figures for the separate January–March operations listed under designations such as "Voronezh–Kharkov." The total is 216,135 men killed in action, with equipment losses of 3,209 tanks, 2,106 artillery pieces, and 307 aircraft (Glantz, *When Titans Clashed*, 296–297).

16. There are numerous studies of Citadel, the most recent being David Glantz and Jonathan House, *The Battle of Kursk* (Lawrence: University Press of Kansas, 1999). Although my reading of the battle differs from theirs, this study is preferable to earlier works such as Martin Caidin, *The Tigers Are Burning* (New York: Hawthorn Books, 1974).

17. One way or another, most accounts of Stalingrad derive from the 1943 Soviet general staff study, translated as *The Battle for Stalingrad*, edited Louis C. Rotundo (New York: Pergamon-Brassey's, 1989).

18. The source for most Lend-Lease data is Joan Beaumont, *Comrades in Arms: British Aid to Russia, 1941–1945* (London: Davis-Poynter, 1980). These figures are taken from the tables on 205–206. Glantz (*When Titans Clashed*) cites some of these data early on (150) but then, in his conclusion, argues the contrary point of view, which suggests the difficulty the "easterners" have in these matters. Glantz, in fact, asserts that "left to their own devices, Stalin and his commanders might have taken 12 to 18 months longer to finish off the *Wehrmacht*; the ultimate result would probably have been the same" (285). Given the scale of aid— and the deficiencies of the Soviet system—it seems considerably more likely that it would have been the other way around: left to their own resources, Stalin and his commanders would have lost the war in the summer of 1943 or the spring of 1944.

Chapter 11: Failure and Philosophy: The End of the War

1. As quoted by Rüdiger Safranski, *Martin Heidegger: Between Good and Evil*, translated Ewald Osers (Cambridge: Harvard University Press, 1998), 232–233.

2. For an exposition of the purely military issues involved, see John Mosier, *The Blitzkrieg Myth* (New York: HarperCollins, 2003), 154–189.

3. There is an extensive analysis of this little-known offensive and its consequences in *Blitzkrieg Myth*, 211–243.

4. The term *great men* is used in the sense that the British jurist and novelist Henry Fielding use it in his novel *Jonathan Wild*; or, for a German example, Robert Musil's complex and ironic application of the term *a man without qualities*, in his novel of the same name. A great man, Fielding opined, is by definition not a good

one but not necessarily evil, either. As Musil put it: "The outstanding personalities of history are criminals." See *The Man Without Qualities*, translated Sophie Wilkins and Burton Pike (New York: Knopf, 1995), 2:1755.

5. The history of and the specifications for the B-17 were published at the time. The December 21, 1936, issue of *Life* had pictures of the plane, gave key details ("one ton of bombs 3,000 miles at 250 mph"), and revealed that the first model crashed on takeoff, in October 1935, at Wright Field, in Dayton, Ohio, and that the second plane crash-landed when the brakes locked, on December 7, 1936 (page 15). Less than a year later, there was a photo essay showing six of the new bombers flying over Manhattan; the army now had thirteen. Directly below is a picture of the XB-15, identified as the "big brother" of the B-17 (*Life*, October 11, 1937), 87.

6. The argument against the results of the Strategic Bombing Survey has been made extensively—and, to my mind, unconvincingly—by Richard Overy, in *War and Economy in the Third Reich* (Oxford: Clarendon Press, 1994), especially 259–314. Overy's points are well taken, so long as we discount entirely the work of the Strategic Bombing Survey, the production statistics for German industry, the alternative uses to which the forces employed could have been put, and the casualty rate in aircrews. Conceptually, the airpower apostles postwar, in discussing the third item (alternative uses), confuse cost-benefit analysis with opportunity-cost analysis, and thus fail to understand that the basic issue is not whether the Allied losses were fewer than the German but, rather, what the Allies could have achieved had they committed those resources elsewhere.

7. Rommel's reputation derives, essentially, from admiring accounts by his (mostly British) adversaries. There was no shortage of Rommel criticism on the German side, from Paulus and Julius Streicher to von Rundstedt, who openly mocked Rommel's competence. See the brief summaries in Matthew Cooper, *The German Army* (New York: Stein and Day, 1978), 357. Much of this criticism stems from the events at Tobruk in 1941, which, as one sympathetic biographer admits, "undoubtedly show Rommel at his worst—leading troops into battle hastily and without preparation or coordination, sacrificing method to speed in a way which the situation condemned." See David Fraser, *Knight's Cross* (London: Harper-Collins, 1993), 146.

8. Although generally glossed over by his admirers, Rommel's illness was psychosomatic. See the comments made by Captain Alfred Berndt in a letter to Rommel's wife: "At the beginning of February [1943] the physical and mental condition of your husband had reached such a state that Professor Hörster considered an immediate course of at least eight weeks' treatment to be indispensable. . . . An aggravating factor contributing to your husband's condition was the unresolved command situation"; quoted in Erwin Rommel, *The Rommel Papers*, edited B. H. Liddell Hart, translated Paul Findlay (New York: Harcourt, Brace, 1953), 410. To say that Rommel had problems is not an inference. He admitted them. See his letter to his wife, January 21, 1943: "I'm so depressed I can hardly do my work" (391). Nigel Hamilton, in *Master of the Battlefield* (New York: McGraw-Hill, 1983), refers to this correspondence as well (136). Hamilton is still the best account of the North African fighting, preferable to other leading works on the subject: Barrie Pitt, *The*

Crucible of War: Western Desert 1941 (London: Jonathan Cape, 1980) and Samuel W. Mitcham Jr., *Rommel's Desert War* (New York: Stein and Day, 1982).

9. Whether his attempts to fortify the coast were worthwhile is an open question. Von Rundstedt (hardly an unbiased source) called the whole thing a "humbug," observing that the bunkers and fortifications were largely useless, because they could not defend themselves from land-based attacks. Despite the old man's dislike of Rommel, his judgment seems reasonable enough. Cooper reprints the extended comments in *The German Army*, 494.

10. When I expressed this judgment more delicately in *The Blitzkrieg Myth* (New York: HarperCollins, 2003), 161–162, some outraged readers threw back at me Liddell Hart's judgment that Rommel was one of history's "great captains," which I think fairly expresses the standard British point of view. This seems entirely based on the fact that he gave them a very tough time in North Africa and is entirely consistent with a deep-seated national belief that only a military leader of great genius could ever beat the British in the field. If this were actually true we should have to expand the list of "great captains" considerably, including, for example, Andrew Jackson. At the Battle of New Orleans, on January 8, 1815, Jackson's mixed force confronted roughly 10,000 British soldiers. After three successive assaults, about 4,000 of them were either dead, wounded, or prisoners. Total American casualties came to 71. Although there is some debate about the actual total for among Sir Edward Pakenham's hapless soldiery, New Orleans may well be the worst defeat, in terms of the casualty rate, the British army ever suffered.

11. Production statistics are taken from F. M. von Senger und Etterlin, *German Tanks of World War II*, translated J. Lucas (New York: Galahad Books, 1968), appendix 4, 211–212.

12. Data on tanks shipped to the Soviet Union are taken from Joan Beaumont, *Comrades in Arms: British Aid to Russia, 1941–1945* (London: Davis-Poynter, 1980), 205–206. American tank data in the sentence following are taken from Peter Chamberlain and Chris Ellis, *British and American Tanks of World War II* (New York: Arco, 1969), 114–115. Soviet figures are from Horst Scheibert, *Russian T-34 Battle Tank* (Altglen, PA: Schiffer Military History, 1992), 3. After the collapse of the USSR, an enormous amount of technical material has been released into the Internet by enthusiasts. Although all Soviet-era data must be viewed with skepticism, these figures are as good as any. See, for example, the data at http://en.wikipedia.org/wiki/Soviet_tank_production _during _World_War_II, as well as http://www.battlefield.ru/specific.html.

13. See the discussion in Cooper, *The German Army*, 211. The figures in the following two paragraphs are taken from there.

14. See the extensive discussions of both tanks in von Senger und Etterlin, *German Tanks*, 59–67 (Mark 5 Panther), 70–74 (Mark 6 Tiger).

15. In addition to the T-34/85, there was the British-engineered Sherman modification, known as the Firefly, which mounted a 17-pounder (76.2-millimeter) high-velocity gun in a modified turret. For a brief description, see Chamberlain and Ellis, *British and American Tanks*, 203–204. There is a good deal of confusion about this modification among Sherman tank enthusiasts, but its combat records were

good. The 17-pounder had an explosive force of slightly over 3 million kilograms per meter, more than three times that of the standard Sherman 75-millimeter gun and almost the same as the German 88-millimeter weapon. Since this specification translated into the ability to penetrate 120 millimeters of 30-degree sloped armor plate at 500 meters, and since even the massive Tiger 2 had only 100 millimeters of 40-degree sloped armor, the Firefly could hold its own on the battlefield—neither tank could survive a direct hit from its adversary.

16. Buried discreetly in the text is a similar conclusion in von Senger und Etterlin, *German Tanks*: "There were not only the usual teething troubles of a new design, but deep-rooted problems which could only be eradicated after thorough tests and fundamental alterations, and the armored units had little confidence in the vehicle" (62).

17. From a 1932 conversation with Otto Wegener, his economic adviser, as quoted by Albert Speer, in *Infiltration*, translated Joachim Neugroschel (New York: Macmillan, 1981), 76.

18. There is a good summary of their backgrounds in Speer, *Infiltration*, 71–72. Men like Hayler give the lie to the claim that the National Socialist leadership consisted, in the main, of uneducated dolts. At every level the party had a complement of intelligent and well-educated men. Speer, Hayler, and Ohlendorf were as typical as Sepp Dietrich. Unfortunately, education and intelligence hardly inoculate a person against evil. In 1941–42, Ohlendorf, a *Gruppenführer* (lieutenant general), had commanded Einsatzgruppe D, responsible for the murder of nearly 100,000 people, mostly in Ukraine. After the war he was tried and executed, as well he should have been.

19. As quoted by Speer, *Infiltration*, 77. Essentially Speer and Ohlendorf were dueling over the matter through the last year of the war, as Ohlendorf belatedly realized the threat to what the National Socialists saw as core German values posed by Speer's wartime production strategies.

20. Germany would have been more successful in the Second World War had it not embarked on its murder campaigns against the Jews. As we saw in an earlier chapter, Jews were enthusiastic supporters of the army (and of all things German), out of all proportion to their numbers (not even counting the high percentage of talented, educated men and women in other fields of great relevance to the war effort). But to say this is to miss the point: Hitler was perfectly willing to lose the war in the narrow military sense if that meant he could rid Europe of Jews. In that ghastly calculus, he emerged as the clear victor.

Chapter 12: The Criminals

1. From his diary. A portion of this work has been translated and appears in *German Writings Before and After 1945*, edited Jürgen Peters (New York: Continuum, 2002). This quotation is on page 26. The title of this chapter is borrowed from the third part of Robert Musil's *Man Without Qualities*, which bears the subtitle *Ins Tausenjährige Reich (Die Verbrecher)* [*In the Thousand Year Reich (The Criminal)*].

2. I use the plural, since technically there were three Geneva conventions before 1939. However, the form suggests a misleading diversity in the rules. These
agreements go back to 1864, when the first one was established. It was amended by
a second convention, in 1906. The Hague Conventions of 1899 and 1907 basically
extended the Geneva Conventions to the war at sea, and the 1929 agreement specified how prisoners of war are to be treated. The core issues were thus expanded but
never fundamentally altered until recently, by parties pushing political agendas.

3. This is the argument in Omer Bartov's *The Eastern Front, 1941–45: German
Troops and the Barbarisation of Warfare* (New York: St. Martin's Press, 1986). The title makes the point clear enough.

4. In *Hitler Strikes Poland: Blitzkrieg, Ideology, and Atrocity* (Lawrence: University of Kansas Press, 2003), Alexander B. Rossino summarizes this atrocity and includes photographs taken on the scene by German witnesses (182–184).

5. See the brief discussion in Rossino, *Hitler Strikes Poland* (185). The main
Polish text is Szymon Datner, *Crimes Committed by the Wehrmacht During the
September Campaign and the Period of Military Government* (Poznán: Institute for
Military Affairs, 1962). Documents produced under the auspices of the various
Communist governments are highly suspect, as the grossly inflated death toll displayed at Auschwitz-Birkenau makes clear. The Polish government insisted that a
figure of four million dead be used; after the collapse the more accurate figure of 1.3
million was cited. See James Young, *Texture of Memory* (New Haven: Yale University Press, 1993), 152–154. But about some things, people were allowed to tell the
truth, and particularly in Poland in the early 1960s.

6. Although subject to interpretation, photographic evidence is more convincing than second- and thirdhand accounts by distraught witnesses. In the case of Polish prisoners of war, the photographic evidence is compelling. See the photographs
in SC-111 (WW2), Box 61A in the National Archives Still Photograph Section, particularly photographs 203357S, 203356D, and 203360, all taken at the Ohrdruf
camp. Eloquent testimony to the Wehrmacht's treatment of prisoners of war is a
motion picture directed by the great Polish filmmaker Andrzej Wajda. In the opening scenes of *Landscape After Battle*, we see the liberation of a concentration camp.
It takes some time for the viewer to realize that the inmates are actually Polish prisoners of war—that it is a camp for captured soldiers, not civilians. There wasn't
much difference between the two.

7. The colonel should not to be confused with *Oberst* (or Colonel) Wessel
Freiherr von Freytag-Loringhoven, who was briefly head of the Abwehr's Section 2,
and one of the conspirators in the 1944 plot to assassinate Hitler. Ironically, Wessel
is also a reasonably well-known Polish name, e.g., the painter Jakub Wessel.

8. The thesis has been around a long time, often expressed in coded language
by references to Prussian militarism. Although the idea is unsustainable, it keeps
popping up in new guises, a recent one being Daniel Jonah Goldhagen's *Hitler's
Willing Executioners: Ordinary Germans and the Holocaust* (New York: Random
House, 1996). For a good overview of the reaction to this thesis—which makes clear
why Goldhagen is flat-out wrong—see the discussion in Ron Rosenbaum, *Explaining Hitler* (New York: Random House, 1998), 337–368.

9. In April and May 1940, those officers in Russian Poland were promptly murdered by Stalin—who then blamed the slaughter on the Germans and instructed his minions to insert the charge into the Nuremberg trials. But everyone knew that the 14,000 Polish bodies found in the Katyn Woods outside Smolensk in 1943 had all been executed by the Russians. Mikhail Gorbachev admitted (on April 13, 1990) that the Soviet security services had committed these crimes. The point was long denied, even though at Nuremberg the Allies knew the claim that the Germans were responsible was entirely bogus. See the discussion in Allen Paul, *Katyn: The Untold Story of Stalin's Massacre* (New York: Scribners's, 1991). Paul makes the point that "from that moment [April–May 1940] prospects for an independent postwar Poland were set on the road to oblivion" (ix). The exact number of men murdered is not known, and many of the victims have still not been identified. The most recent Polish publication is able to list only 4,406 names, even though the remains of over 14,000 bodies have been recovered.

For the list of those identified, see the anonymous *Ksiega Cmentarza Polskiego Cmentarza Wojennego* (Warszawa: Rada Ochrony Pamieci Walk i Meczenstwa, 2000). The Katyn Woods massacre is not the only instance of the murder of uniformed members of Poland's military by Stalin's minions. The primary documents detailing these crimes have not been translated, but see the English-language summary (prepared by Barbara Bulat of the Jagellonian Library of Kraków) at www .library.uiuc.edu/spx/class/Biography/Polishbio/polvictims.htm. By my count, over 18,000 prisoners of war were murdered by the Soviets—in addition to the roughly 14,000 shot in the Katyn Woods. A brief English summary of the documents is available at www.library.uiuc.edu/spx/class/Biography/Polishbio/polcems.htm.

10. The situation in Romania is of particular relevance to any judgment of Germany. There is a long, grotesque history of anti-Semitism in that country, which came to a head in the late 1930s. By 1945 the Romanians, on their own, had murdered at least a quarter of a million Jews. Although there have been intensive efforts to suppress this information (both during the Nicolae Ceausescu regime and afterward), there is no doubt that it happened and that the Holocaust in Romania was entirely independent of Hitler and National Socialism. See the account by Radu Ionid, *The Holocaust in Romania* (Chicago: Ivan R. Dees, 2000), from which the figure of a quarter of a million is taken (xxii).

11. There were certainly senior SS commanders who came up from the ranks; Theodor Eicke and Sepp Dietrich are the most obvious examples. But as decorated combat veterans of four years of warfare (1914–18), they emerged as senior enlisted men—precisely the sort of soldier who would be familiar with the rules governing the treatment of enemy soldiers. At the same time, "over the past four decades historical opinion has moved from a position in which the *Wehrmacht* was regarded as essentially distinct from the SS/SD, both in terms of attitudes and behavior, to a stance where little differentiation is made between these two 'institutions of the Third Reich,'" says Theo Schulte, in *The German Army and Nazi Policies in Occupied Russia* (Oxford: Berg, 1989), 211.

12. The blockhouse, located at the intersection of D6 and D6E, the road going from Bazeilles into Sedan, still stands. It is almost directly on the autoroute, and a

plaque marks the crime, listing the names of the ten soldiers the Germans murdered. I know of no French source detailing this war crime, but as I make clear in chapter 6, serious research into May–June 1940 is just beginning in France. See Dominique Lormier's *Comme des Lions, Mai–Juin 1940* (Paris: Calmann-Levy, 2005).

13. Photocopies of the relevant documents taken from German eyewitnesses are at the Liddell Hart Center for Military Archives, King's College London, reference GB 0099 KCLMA MISC 6. In this case the murderers were men from the SS Totenkopf Division, a technicality that has enabled defenders of the regular army to claim that all the dirty deeds were done by others and that the Wehrmacht had no way to stop the evildoers. The men who carried out the Royal Norfolk massacre — and the man who ordered it — were part of the Twenty-Seventh Army Group and, as such, at least technically subject to regular-army control. At this stage of the war, Hitler certainly had no animus against the British. On the contrary, his feelings were both well known and unexceptional. Anyone in the Twenty-Seventh Army Group or in Army Group A who had cared to could have brought the massacre to his attention. Why did no one do so? Because by then no one cared is one answer. Another: by May 1940, the army was too implicated in similar actions in Poland. No one complained because of what would then have been brought up against him (or his command or his unit). See John Keegan's different — but equally damning — take on this incident, in *Waffen SS: The Asphalt Soldiers* (New York: Ballantine Books, 1970), 65.

14. Excerpted from the passage cited by Callum MacDonald, *The Lost Battle: Crete, 1941* (New York: Free Press, 1993), 304–305.

15. MacDonald (*The Lost Battle*, 305–306) reprints the key passages, accepting it as a fair decision: "I do not imagine [Lord Russell wrote] that this proposition would find much favor with those who have to plan and execute difficult and dangerous operations in which it is essential that the fighting qualities of the troops engaged should not be hampered by the constant thought that every action must be measured up and considered as if a policeman or umpire was at hand." Oh really? Soldiers need umpires on the scene to keep them from killing enemy soldiers when they surrender? This exemplifies a British postwar failure: everything possible was done to give the accused the benefit of the doubt. The same line of reasoning led to the numerous commutations of the sentences of those senior German commanders who had the good fortune to fall into the British jurisdiction. This was venue shopping with a vengeance.

16. The best information on the camps comes from U.S. Army Air Forces reports prepared during the war. The relevant parts of these accounts, together with eyewitness testimony, may be found at http://www.b24.net/pow, an invaluable source for inside reports on a strangely neglected aspect of the war. The treatment of Soviet prisoners of war is well known, but Bartov has a good summary of the situation, in *Eastern Front*, 106–107. Again, it is worth pointing out that the perpetrators were members of regular-army units — although I am dubious as to Bartov's argument that this is largely (or even partly) the result of ideology, as described in his section "Indoctrination and the Need for a Cause," 68–100.

17. I use the word *rules* here as opposed to the technical citation of the Geneva Conventions, to emphasize the point that the proper treatment of prisoners of war had been accepted by European armies long before 1929. The German treatment of prisoners in that conflict was at least as humane as the treatment afforded by the French, a situation leading one former French officer and historian to raise a question: Given what prisoners of war could expect in the way of treatment, why didn't more soldiers surrender? A profound question, and one to which there's no easy answer. For what it's worth, the consensus among those unfortunates who were incarcerated in both systems was that Stalin's was worse.

18. For a comprehensive list, see UN War Crimes Commission, *History of the United Nations War Crimes Commission and the Development of the Laws of War* (London: Her Majesty's Stationery Office, 1948), 536.

19. Although convicted, Meyer had the good fortune to have killed Canadians rather than Americans and thus fell under British military justice jurisdiction. Consequently, although he was convicted and sentenced to death, his sentence was commuted. Released as a result of poor health in 1954, he died in 1961. Meyer was a brilliant tactical commander, but that hardly means he should have been pardoned for the deaths of the Canadians.

20. What actually happened is still controversial. The account of Malmédy put together by Trevor N. Dupuy, David L. Bongard, and Richard C. Anderson Jr., in *Hitler's Last Gamble* (New York: HarperCollins, 1994), concludes that "somewhere between fifty and eighty-six American prisoners of war were murdered in cold—or at least cool—blood by their German captors . . . a clear and unjustifiable violation of the laws of war" (491). The real problem came up at the trial, which was a mockery of any pretense at justice (493–495). "We do not know for certain who the guilty German soldiers were, because some Americans—by acts of omission and commission—prevented us from knowing. . . . Germans should be ashamed of the Malmédy massacre. Americans should be ashamed of the Malmédy trial" (497).

21. Both the order and the example given are specifically cited in the Nuremberg indictment. See Office of the United States Chief of Counsel for Prosecution of Axis Criminality, *Nazi Conspiracy and Aggression: Opinion and Judgment* (Washington, DC: Government Printing Office, 1947), 58.

22. The chief photographs are reprinted in Rossini, *Hitler Strikes Poland*, 144–152. Again, I have deliberately chosen a Polish example to show that these behaviors started with the war itself, and were committed against the civilian population of a country that had signed the 1929 Geneva Convention. Nor, during the first month of the war, did the Polish government try to use its civilian population deliberately as a shield for irregular warfare, as was the case with the Soviet Union. Unfortunately, there is no shortage of Wehrmacht eyewitnesses to such murders. See the depressing collections of testimonies in Hannes Heer, *Tote Zonen: Die deutsche Wehrmacht an der Ostfront* (Hamburg: Hamburger Editions, 1999), 257–286. In this text, most of the attention to these murders centers on the Eastern Front; the work unintentionally gives the impression that the Wehrmacht fought a war *ganze normale* elsewhere.

23. See the summary in MacDonald, *Lost Battle: Crete, 1941*, 256–257. In all

these instances, the Germans claimed they were retaliating for atrocities committed against their troops. This may well be true, and in such instances revenge is tempting. But getting revenge by killing octagenarian ladies is not just illegal and immoral; it is an act of wickedness. Nor were these isolated events. British prisoners of war waiting evacuation witnessed firing squads killing Cretan civilians on what MacDonald calls "a daily basis" (295). Some of this may have well been justified, but given the early precedents, one is hardly inclined to give the airborne and mountain troops the benefit of the doubt. Interestingly enough, at least some of the mountain troops had seen action in Galicia, where they apparently had witnessed atrocities committed by the Poles against ethnic Germans. See the sampling of reactions by mountain troops, in Rossino, *Hitler Strikes*, especially 103.

24. The statement should not be taken to imply that the Wehrmacht did not commit serious crimes in the Soviet Union, only that the case is a strong one without examining such crimes. This is an important consideration, since much of the evidence is tainted: although this hardly excuses the Germans, it was, in Stalinist logic, no bad thing to foment resistance activities that would result in massive German reprisals against the local population. For a brief review of the more serious crimes committed by the regular army in the Soviet Union, see Schulte, *German Army*, 130–131.

25. Again, an oversimplification that telescopes the various reorganizations. The overall authority was vested in the *Reichssicherheitshauptamt* (RSHA), which directed both the *Sicherheitdienst*, the criminal police, and the state police (the infamous Gestapo). After its creation in 1939, Heydrich directed its activities; he died in July 1942, and the position was not filled until early 1943, when Ernst Kaltenbrunner replaced him. Heydrich had not been in charge of the camp system: that man reported directly to Himmler.

26. Their participation also contributed to the impressions of the survivors that these activities embraced the entire German military establishment. For a practical example of the use of army trucks, see Eugen Kogen, Hermann Langbein, and Adalbert Rückerl, *Nazi Mass Murder: A Documentary History of the Use of Poison Gas*, translated Mary Scott and Caroline Lloyd-Morris (New Haven: Yale University Press, 1993), 39. The original text was published in 1983.

27. To cull examples from a recent study, in Richard Rhodes, *Masters of Death* (New York: Knopf, 2002), we have the eyewitness testimony of a young officer about the killing of Ukrainian children (and the subsequent protests by enlisted men and their chaplains, 130–131), a letter to a senior Wehrmacht general from a police officer detailing his murderous activities (160), and Hitler's response to a report relayed to him by Admiral Canaris relative to the Rumbala massacre ("I have to do it, because after me no one else will," 212). It would be easy to compose an enormous list of similar cases. Deniability through bureaucratization may be thought of as a deliberate strategy on the part of senior army officers. How many of the criminal orders emanating from Hitler (such as the orders for reprisals against the Czechs after Heydrich's death or the order to shoot the airmen of the Great Escape) were in reality urged on him by members of the high command anxious to clear themselves by being able to point to a directive from the führer? In *Inside the Third Reich*, trans-

lated Richard and Clara Winston (New York: Macmillan, 1970), for example, Albert Speer recounts instances of both Goebbels and Bormann manipulating Hitler in similar ways (122, 124–125). See also Speer's comments about attempts to keep Hitler from the "unconsidered signing of decrees" (252). Do these incidents in any way imply that Hitler was not directly responsible for ordering the mass murders of millions of people? No; they only suggest that his military subordinates may be much guiltier of war crimes than we realize.

28. For a practical example, see Rossino, *Hitler Strikes Poland*, 82–84. As the circle of murders expanded and became more public, there were certainly complaints made by officers on moral grounds, although here again motivation is hard to determine. Elementary logic suggests that killing large numbers of innocent people is not the best way to proceed during an occupation—and many German officers doubtless remembered how the Red terror after 1917 had backfired against Lenin's disciples, depleting whatever goodwill the Bolsheviks may have possessed and hardening the resolve of the population against them. Of course, those men of good quality who were appalled may have attempted to couch their objections in pragmatic and tactical terms, so the attitudes are, at bottom, unknowable.

29. The passage is taken from *Spandau: The Secret Diaries*, translated Richard and Clara Winston (New York: Macmillan, 1976), 24. This passage apparently looks back (or, rather, forward) to scenes described in Speer's *Inside the Third Reich*. I am well aware of the subsequent controversies relating to the more literal question of Speer's guilt, although they strike me as excellent examples of the contemporary "deconstruction" that is both contentious and problematic. They are irrelevant to the point being made regarding the moral culpability of senior officers in the German military.

30. See Telford Taylor, *The Anatomy of the Nuremburg Trials* (New York: Knopf, 1992), 13. It's no surprise that Taylor's judgment isn't mentioned in John N. Horne and Alan Kramer, *German Atrocities, 1914: A History of Denial* (New Haven: Yale University Press, 2001). But then neither are the relatively objective accounts by journalists on the scene in 1914. See, among many, an Associated Press dispatch published in the *New York Times* (September 17, 1914), "Finds German Army Polite and Kindly." The subheads are relevant: "American Correspondent, Who Was a Prisoner, Cannot Verify Reports of Atrocities"; "Says Sniping Is Prevalent." Unfortunately, this sleight of hand, in which all contrary evidence is ignored, has become typical. The charge is based on unsubstantiated second- and thirdhand reports, themselves based on documents that have disappeared. In American legal terms, the book is a lengthy indictment—but we know how frequently such cases collapse when brought to trial and subjected to counterfactuals and cross-examinations. Historians may not be lawyers, but they should at least convey an awareness of legal principles.

The same flaw bedevils many of the accounts of Wehrmacht atrocities on the Eastern Front: on the one hand, not all dead civilians are innocent; on the other, few if any standards seem to be used in evaluating the veracity or accuracy of the testimony of the witnesses. The result is often a kind of unintentional descent into the pornography of violence, an endless litany of ghastly brutalities, which is not to downplay what actually happened. See, for instance, the judicious account of a major Italian atrocity in Michael Geyer, "Civitella della Chiana on 29 June 1944," in *War of Extermination: The German Military in World War II*, edited Hannes Heer and Klaus Naumann (Oxford: Berghahn, 2000), 175–207.

31. As recounted by Rhodes, *Masters of Death*, 275. That these trials were managed by a young, inexperienced lawyer suggests the priorities of the Nuremberg prosecutors.

32. Mengele drowned in 1979, so he had been avoiding arrest for over three decades. His fate is not so uncommon in Brazil, given the coldness of the water and the high daytime temperatures. Foreigners are routinely warned to be careful. There is a certain grim irony that Mengele, who was in fact a medical doctor, died because he ignored a common safety warning. But thus do the wicked perish.

Chapter 13: Conclusion: Myths, Realities, and Achievements

1. Polybius, *The Rise of the Roman Empire*, translated Ian Scott-Kilvert (London: Penguin, 1979), book 1, paragraph 14, page 55.

2. As I noted in Chapter 1, "moving inside the decision cycle" is the concept enunciated by John T. Boyd as part of the "OODA Loop" (observation, orientation, decision, action). Although Boyd's briefings of military personnel has had a noticeable impact on the American military, the concepts don't seem to have penetrated into the world of military history. For a brief discussion of Boyd, see Colin S. Gray, *Modern Strategy* (Oxford: Oxford University Press, 1999), 90–93. There is a detailed exposition of Boyd's life and influence on the military in Grant T. Hammond, *The Mind of War: John Boyd and American Security* (Washington, DC: Smithsonian Institution Press, 2001).

3. Albert Speer, *Inside the Third Reich*, translated Richard and Clara Winston (New York: Macmillan, 1970), 246.

4. German bombing losses are taken from U.S. Strategic Bombing Survey, *Over-all Report (European War)* (Washington, DC: Overall Economics Effects Division, September 1945). Polish data are from Witold J. Lukaszewski, citing various Polish and British studies, in *The Sarmatian Review* 18.2 (www.ruf.rice.edu/~sarmatia/498/losses.html).

5. One of the disquieting findings of the strategic bombing surveyors was the relatively small shift in civilian attitudes caused by the bombing. "Allied bombing widely and seriously depressed German civilian morale, but depressed and discouraged workers were not necessarily unproductive workers" is the initial conclusion in Strategic Bombing Survey, *Over-all Report*, 37. But the supporting evidence is problematic. In heavily bombed cities, 64 percent of those surveyed were tabulated as "willing to surrender," while in unbombed cities, the percentage was 57 percent, a difference that seems negligible, given the errors inherent in such measurements. Moreover, the survey found no difference between those bombed once and those bombed repeatedly (95–98).

6. From *Réflexions et maximes* (1746). Collections of Vauvenargues's axioms are numerous. See *Dictionnaire des citations françaises* (Paris: Larousse, 1997), 566, for the French.

7. As quoted by David Fraser in *Frederick the Great* (New York: Fromm, 2001), 627. The original speech is to be found in Benjamin H. Latrobe, *Characteristics, Anecdotes, and Miscellaneous Papers Tending to Illustrate the Character of Frederick the Great, Late King of Prussia* (London: n.p., 1788), 222–223.

ACKNOWLEDGMENTS

I am indebted to the following institutions for their help: the National Archives (Washington, D.C.), and particularly the Still Photographs Section; the Austrian Army Museum (Vienna); the Imperial War Museum (London); the Bavarian Army Museum (Ingolstadt); the Aberdeen Proving Ground; and numerous small museums and collections in Belgium, France, and Luxembourg. The support offered by Patricia Doran of the J. Edgar and Louise S. Monroe Library of Loyola University in New Orleans has been exemplary.

Over the past years numerous people have enriched my knowledge of this topic by sending me photographs, essays, detailed comments, and even documents. Thanks to Jeff Coufal ("Dutch") for materials on the Freikorps; Balbino Katz (France) for materials on Jewish officers in the Wehrmacht; Skelly McCay for Heidegger; Doug Hanson and John O'Connell for unpublished manuscripts of great value; Thomas Wictor, Gerard Potel, Rabbi Robert H. Loewy, and Bob Lembke for their thoughtful comments; numerous veterans and serving officers (who wish to remain anonymous) for their invaluable help; and Albert and Annick Casciero for long-suffering logistical support.

I also want to thank my agent, Jim Hornfischer, no mean military historian himself; Mary McCay, always enthusiastic and supportive in a way that few departmental chairs manage; and, of course, my best critic and editor, my wife, Sarah. Last but by no means least, my editor at Holt, Jack Macrae, whose persistence has made this book several orders of magnitude better than it was when I first wrote it.

INDEX

Abrams tank, 223
Adriatic Sea, 150
Aegean, 160
agricultural resources, 170, 179, 180, 190
airborne troops
    Belgium and, 139
    Crete and, 156–161, 164, 183, 209
    Netherlands and, 136, 137, 183
    Norway and, 134
aircraft, 17, 70–83, 85–86, 147, 169, 210–11, 220
    German vs. American, 210
    production increases, 187
    See also bombers; fighter planes; and specific makes
air defense system, 128, 145–46
air power, 8, 129–30, 245. See also bombing
    integration of, with ground operations, 183, 184
    strategic vs. tactical, 69–76, 87–88
air transport, 183
Albania, 148, 149
Alexandrowka, battle of, 189
Algeria, 148
Allies. See also specific countries
    antiaircraft defenses, 84
    bombing and, 71–72, 83, 253
    checkmating of, in 1939, 5

Czechoslovakia and, 118
    Hitler's push into Central Europe of 1936–38 and, 112
    invasion of Italy and, 201, 205–6, 250
    invasion of Normandy and war France and, 206–8, 214–15, 250
    invasion of North Africa and, 198
    invasion of Norway and, 134
    invasion of Poland and, 31, 123, 124, 127, 129–33
    Market Garden and, 245
    offensive of 1940 and, 2, 72, 135–38, 140–43, 248–50
    POWs, 202, 234–36
    rearmament and, 32
    strategic bombers and, 76, 77, 78, 209–11
    strategy of, 132–33
    strategy of, vs. Hitler's, 42, 249–53
    tanks and, 223–24
    Versailles treaty and, 31–32
    war crimes and, 240–43, 254–55
    WW I and, 1–3, 16–17, 20–23, 25, 27, 245–48
Alsace, 76, 108, 110, 207
André, General, 60
Anglo-German naval agreement (1935), 110

Anschluss. See Austria
antiaircraft defenses, 32, 71, 73–74, 83–84, 86–87, 210, 245
anti-Semitism, 66. *See also* Jews
antitank weapons, 85, 96, 98, 99, 103, 187, 188
Antonescu, Ion, 169
appeasement, 115
Arado, 79
   Arado 80 plane, 81
Ardennes Forest, 136, 206, 207
Argonne, 26–27
armaments production, 32–33, 132, 187, 208, 214–27. *See also specific types*
armored divisions, 90–91, 93, 102–6, 113–14, 130, 152, 154, 163–64, 169, 174, 178. *See also* tanks
armor-piercing ammunition, 96
artillery, 16–21, 32, 102–3, 218
Auchinleck, Claude, 213
Australia, 160, 162, 219
   navy, 191
Austria, 91
   Anschluss of 1938, 25, 112–14, 148, 151, 246
   war of 1866 with, 12
Austria-Hungary, 13–15, 27, 51, 53
Austrian Army, 33, 34, 39, 114
Austrian Jews, 51, 65
Avranches offensive (1944), 206
Azov, Sea of, 199

B-17 bomber, 70, 76, 77, 83
Balck, Hermann, 37–38, 212, 233
Baldwin, Stanley, 111
Balkans, 33, 127, 148
   invasion of, 149–51, 153–55, 157, 180–81, 183, 206, 246
   murder of POWs and, 236
Baltic sea, 181
Baltic states, 43, 231. *See also specific states*
   civil war of 1919, 29–31, 34, 44, 46, 65, 229, 255
   invasion of 1941, 175, 176
   Red Army invades, in 1940, 168
   Soviets cede in 1918, 165
Balzer, Johannes, 235
Barbarossa operation, 153, 154, 190. *See also* Soviet Union, invasion of
   Crete and, 157–59, 164, 172–73
   Greece and, 163–164
   lessons from opening of, 180–81

Barcelona, 210
Basques, 87
battle of annihilation, 24, 42, 43, 198, 193
Bavaria, 29, 46, 51
Beck, Ludwig, 41
Belarus, 168
Belgian air force, 140
Belgian army, 95, 99, 104
Belgium, 18, 19, 33, 76
   WW I and, 33, 240
   WW II and, 123, 132, 134–36, 138–43, 159
Belgorod, 179, 185
Belorussia, 31, 175–77
Belyi, 195
Beneš, Eduard, 115, 116
Bialystock, 175
Bilbao, battle of, 106
Bismarck, Otto von, 34
Bitterfeld uprising, 30
Black sea, 181
blitzkrieg, 3–4, 247–48
Blomberg, Frau von, 40–41, 208
Blomberg, Werner von, 15, 40, 59
Blum, Léon, 111, 112
BMW, 78
Bock, General von, 186
Bofors manufacturer, 32–33
Bolivia, 110
Bolsheviks, 28–29, 36, 40, 45–47, 165, 167, 225, 229, 255
   Jews and, 65–67
bombers, 69–80
   dive-bombers, 72–75, 79, 83
   fighter planes vs., 82
   design failure, 74–75
   level-flight, 88, 73, 140
   strategic, 69–71, 75–80, 83, 89, 127–29, 145, 163
   tactical vs. strategic, 69–73
   tactical, 71, 145–46
bombing (air war), 8, 77, 127
   of Britain, 69, 145–46
   of Germany, 206, 209–11, 253–54
   of Rotterdam, 138
   Spanish civil war and, 86–87
Brauchitsch, Walther von, 131, 186
breakthrough tactic, 18, 21–24, 95, 96
Brest-Litovsk treaty (1918), 36, 165
Brialmont, Henri-Alexis, 138
Briansk, 196

Britain, Battle of, 146–48, 157, 164, 210. *See also* Great Britain
British aircraft, 8
    Lancaster bomber, 70
    Hurricane, 70
    Spitfire, 70, 81
    Wellington bomber, 77
British army, 162, 205
    officers and, 13, 15
    training of soldiers and, 16
British Royal Air Force (RAF), 8, 69–71, 76, 82, 83, 140, 145–46, 129, 156, 163, 183, 210, 245
    Bomber Command, 70, 145
British Royal Navy, 33, 133–35, 145, 158, 160, 163, 191
    Mediterranean fleet, 160
British Royal Norfolk Regiment, 233
British Seventh Armored Division (Desert Rats), 205
Broch, Hermann, 39
Brusilov, Alexei, 33, 42, 201
Buck, Karl, 235
Budapest, 169
Bulgaria, 151, 154, 164, 169

Cambrai, battle of, 96–97
Canada, 3, 218, 219
Canadian POWs, 235
Castelli massacre, 237
casualties. *See also* civilian deaths
    Crete and, 161, 162
    Greece and, 155
    Japanese, 194
    offensive of 1940 and, 142
    Soviet, 176–78, 180–81, 186, 190, 193–94, 197–98, 200, 202, 203
    WW I and, 3, 16–17, 22–23
Caucusus, 165, 167, 180, 189, 191
Centurion tank, 223
Chamberlain, Neville, 115–18, 133, 248
China, 192
Christian Protestants, 55–56
Christie, Walter, 221
Churchill, Winston, 1, 3, 9, 113, 114, 137, 140, 161–62, 169, 200, 213, 248–49
Ciepelów massacre, 230–31, 232
Citadel offensive, 199–201, 207, 224
civilian deaths, 211, 236–39, 242–43, 253–55
coal, 179, 180
Cologne, bombing of, 211

combat engineer units, 19–20
Communism, 28–29, 37, 132, 201, 203, 229
    National socialism vs., 226, 227
Communist parties, Hitler-Stalin pact of 1939 and
Coral Sea, battle of the, 192
Cot, Pierre, 112
Crenaica, 150
Crete, 156–63, 172, 183, 209, 213
    war crimes in, 233–34, 237–39
Crimea, 178, 190, 198
Croatians, 155, 231
Czechoslovakia, 25, 114–20, 123, 124, 126, 127, 148, 246
    tanks, 91, 94, 95, 99, 188, 216
    war crimes and, 236
Czestochowa massacre, 237

Daimler-Benz, 78, 221
Daladier, Edouard, 117, 118
Danzig, 124
Dawson, William Harbutt, 11
declaration of racial purity, 54, 62
defensive warfare, 13, 18–21
De Gaulle, 233
Denmark, 12, 123
Dessau uprising, 30
Diekman, Adolph, 237
Dietrich, Sepp, 204, 208, 209
doctrine, 4–5, 20, 36, 42–43, 69, 75, 83–84, 176, 185
Dornier bombers (Do-19), 76–77, 78–80
Dortmund, bombing of, 211
Douhet, Giulio, 41, 69, 76, 88, 89, 96
Drang nach Osten (expansion to east), 43–44
Dunkirk evacuation, 141, 155, 233
Durango, bombing of, 87

easterners, 34–36, 76, 43–44, 165
Eastern Front. *See also* Soviet Union, invasion of
    WW I and, 23, 36, 37, 38
    WW II and, 6, 7, 74, 184, 201–3, 208, 211, 216, 228–29, 238, 250
Eben Emael fortress, 138–40
Ebert, Friedrich, 28, 29
Egypt, 149, 150, 156
Eichmann, Adolf, 241
Eisenhower, Dwight, 43
Eiserne Division, 30

enemy's will to fight, 42–43, 193
Estonia, 29, 168, 175
Ethiopia, 110, 148, 149, 151

Falkenhayn, Erich von, 23–24, 34, 36, 42, 193
Fall Blau (Caucasus operation), 189–91
Fall Gelb, 171
Fall Weiss, 171
Fayolle, Emile, 16, 21–22, 25–26
Ferencz, Benjamin, 241, 243
Ferguson, Niall, 3
Ferry, Abel, 3
Fiat Ansaldo CV3 tank, 91
field fortifications, 20–21
fighter planes, 81–83
    long-range, 146, 211
Finland, 131, 132, 167, 169, 165, 218
Five Points massacre, 235
flamethrowers, 19, 20
Focke-Wulf, 82
    Fw-159 plane, 81
    Fw-189 plane, 82
Ford, Henry, 219
Formidable (British aircraft carrier), 160
Förster, Colonel, 125–26
France
    Allied invasion and war in, 6, 205–7, 213–15, 237, 249, 250
    antiaircraft defenses, 84
    checkmated before WW II starts, 108
    Czechoslovakia and, 117, 120, 121
    Hitler and, 76
    iron ore, 163
    Italy and, 148, 151
    Jews in, 55
    occupation of, 191
    offensive of 1940 and, 93, 123, 130–33, 135–37, 140–43, 172, 193, 249
    Pacific and, 192
    Poland and, 31, 123, 125, 128, 129
    Popular Front in, 84, 112
    Resistance, 237
    resources of, for defense, 80
    Russo-Polish war of 1920, 31
    Saarland, Rhineland and, 109–11
    Spanish civil war and, 84–85, 112
    tanks, 91, 93, 95, 96, 99, 100, 142, 216
    war crimes and, 233, 236
    WW I and, 1, 16–19, 22–24, 27, 35–36
Franco, Francisco, 84, 105

Franco-Prussian war of 1870, 12, 236
Frederick the Great, of Prussia, 12, 123, 143, 256
Freiburg University, 47–48, 59, 63
French air force, 69, 70, 71, 83, 140, 245
French army, 13–15, 22–23, 60, 101–4, 141–42
French Communist party, 132
French Corps de Cavalerie, 142
French Fifth Motorized Infantry Division, 142
French 147th Regiment massacre of, at Sedan, 233
French Revolution, 66, 67
French Third Armored Division, 142
Freyberg, Bernard, 159–62, 213
Fritsch, Werner von, 30
fuel supplies, 113, 190, 207, 253
Führer, The (Heiden), 11
Führerprinzip, 59, 75, 225
Fuller, John F. C., 41, 95, 96, 101
Furet, François, 45

Gablenz, Kar-August von, 61
Galician offensive, 33
Gamelin, Maurice, 128, 129, 132
Gdynia, 124
Geheime Feld Polizei (GFP), 238
Gembloux Gap, battle of, 142
Geneva Conventions, 202, 229, 234, 236, 254
Gercke, Achim, 52
German Afrika Korps, 152, 251
German army (Wehrmacht). *See also* German officer corps; *and specific battles, campaigns, equipment, and units*
    Allied bombing and, 253
    all-volunteer army idea, 42
    armament production problems and, 216
    armored divisions, 14, 102–3
    casualties of, in WW I, 1–2, 22
    Central European takeover of 1938 and, 120=21
    combat engineer units or Pioniere, 19
    combined arms tactics, 245
    communications, 21, 22
    education and training of, 4, 11–16, 20, 44, 146
    elite infantry and, 19
    engineering and, 19
    equipment of, 3, 17–18

experience of, 25
fight desperately at end WW II, 7, 252–53
final period of war and, 204–10, 228–29
Hitler's strategic thinking and, 249–53
infantry, 19, 101–6, 162–63
institutional memory of, 4, 108, 244–48
Jews in, 7–8, 51–54, 57–63
mountain troops, 159
near-paralysis of, on June 6, 1944, 44
POWs and, 235–36, 197
Soviet invasion and, 164, 171, 176, 180–83, 198, 201–2
success and prestige of, in 1914, 12
success of 1939–41 and, 3–4, 108–9, 140–43, 248=50
success of spring 1918, 22
summer 1943 as high water mark of, 204
Versailles limits on, 32–34
von Blomberg and, 40–41
von Seeckt and, 36–37, 42
war crimes and, 7, 8, 67, 228–31, 232–33, 235–40, 243, 254–56
WW I and, 1–3, 11–24, 26–27, 248, 251
German Army Group A, 13, 141
German Army Group Center, 185, 186
German Army Group North, 128
German Army Group South, 129, 186, 189, 190
German Army Group Vistula, 209
German Baltische Landwehr Division, 30
German codes, broken by British, 162, 171
German Condor Legion, 85
German Eighth Air Corps, 159
German Eighth Army, 129
German Einsatzgruppen, 8, 232, 238, 241
German Eleventh Air Corps, 157, 158
German Eleventh Army, 33
German empire of 1871, 51
German Fifteenth Motorized Infantry Regiment, 230
German Fifth Cavalry, 38
German Fifth Mountain Division, 158
German First Armored Group, 178
German First Army, chief of staff, 13
German First Guards Reserve Division, 30
German First Motorized Infantry Regiment, 38, 212, 233
German First Parachute Army, 209
German Forty-Sixth Infantry Division, 237
German Fourteenth Army, 129
German Fourth Air Force, 157, 158

German Fourth Armored Army, 189
German Fourth Army, 54, 128
German Freikorps, 29, 30, 41
German Grossdeutschland Division, 189
German intelligence, 100, 159, 178
German Luftwaffe (air force), 8, 54
  airborne units and, 84
  aircraft design and, 72–80, 90
  antiaircraft defenses and, 84
  Battle of Britain and, 145–47, 210
  Belgian invasion and, 140
  bomb production and, 80–81
  Crete invasion and, 157, 159, 161
  decline in, 83, 146–47, 164
  as tactical not strategic force, 68–71, 75–78
  final period of war and, 211
  Jews in, 54, 61
  Norway invasion and, 133, 134
  Polish invasion and, 130
  Soviet invasion and, 183–84, 196, 210
  Spanish civil war and, 83–89
  SS and, 232
German navy, 8–9, 192, 133–34
German Northern Defense Command (Bartenstein), 30
German Northern Frontier Command, 34
German officer corps, 4, 44
  authority of, in WW I, 21
  background of, in Freikorps, 30
  Central European successes of 1938 and, 121
  chain of command and, 21, 171
  code of honor and, 39, 256
  conflict of, with Hitler, 4, 5, 8, 40–41, 43, 44, 50, 57–61, 100–101, 170–71, 177–78, 186, 204
  east vs. western front debate and, 34–36, 43–44
  education of, 11–16
  field commanders, 171, 174
  filled with captains, not generals, 43, 44
  general staff, 12–13, 34–36, 157, 169, 170–71
  high command, 8, 34, 95, 100–101, 136, 158, 171, 174, 177–78, 184, 186, 199–200, 249
  Jews and, 50–55, 57, 61
  July 1944 assassination plot and, 204
  junior officers, 12–13, 39, 208

German officer corps (*cont'd*)
  literary treatments of, 39
  National Socialism and, 50
  noncommissioned officers, 13–14, 34
  passive-aggressive behavior of, 58–59, 68,
    81, 101, 171
  reserve commissions in, 14, 51
  social background, conservatism, and
    naïveté of, 36–44, 100
  Soviet invasion and, 170–171, 186, 198
  war crimes and, 229–32, 233–34, 256
German Reichsheer, 34, 38–40, 52, 59, 72,
  90, 112–13, 125
German Reichstag, 46, 47
German Schützstaffel (SS), 46, 62, 204, 226,
  228, 230–32, 238, 239, 255
German Second Armored Army, 186, 246
German Second Armored Division, 113,
  246
German Second Armored Group, 178
German Second Reich (1872–1918), 36
German Seventh Airborne Division, 158
German Seventeenth Army Corps, 142
German Sicherheitdienst (SD), 8, 232,
  238
German Sixth Army, 196
German Sixth Mountain Division, 158
German Socialist Party, 27, 28
German Southern Frontier Defense
  Command, 30
German *Strurmabteilungen* (SA or storm
  troops), 19–20, 46
German Tenth Army, 129
German Tenth Jäger battalion, 30, 38
German Tenth Reichswehr Brigade, 30
German Third Army, 128
German Third Army Corps, 33
German Truppernamt (training
  organization staff), 34
German Waffen-SS, 165, 232, 237, 239
German War College, 15
Germany. *See also* German Army
  (Wehrmacht); German Luftwaffe (air
  force); German officer corps; Hitler,
  Adolf; *and specific military campaigns,
  units, and special forces*
  Allied bombing of, 89, 206, 209–11,
    253–54
  civil war of 1919–1920, 28–29, 46
  Communist revolts, post-WW I, 28–29,
    37

conflicts of 1919–1921, 246
creation of, by army in 1871, 12
elections of 1932–33, 46–47
feels tricked into loss of WW I, 27
reasons for success and losses of in WW
  II, 3–6, 9, 25–26, 201–2, 209, 227, 251
Spanish civil war and, 85–88
state of, at end of WW I, 28–29
tanks and, 94
uprisings of 1918–19, 37
victory vs. Russia in 1917–18, 165
Weimar Republic, 28, 30, 38, 40, 46–49,
  59
WW I and, 25–26
Gessler, Otto, 59
Geyer, Captain, 13
Gibraltar, 147
Gleichschaltung, 48, 49, 60
Goebbels, Josef, 208
Goerlitz, Walter, 144
Goethe, 1
Goltz, Rüdiger von der, 29–30
Göring, Hermann, 49, 54, 61, 68–69, 73, 74,
  77, 78, 81, 84, 98, 105, 145, 146, 157, 158,
  164, 208, 210–12, 215, 254
Gorlice, battle of, 33
Gorodetsky, Gabriel, 182
Grant, Ulysses S., 15
Graziani, Rodolfo, 149, 153
Great Britain
  aids Soviet Union, 187, 192–93, 202, 217,
    250
  air war and, 84, 145–47, 149, 210
  Austrian takeover and, 114
  casualties and, 181
  checkmated before WW II starts, 108
  colonial empire of, 152
  Crete and, 156, 156–63
  Czechoslovakia and, 120–21
  final period of WW II and, 207, 210–11
  offensive of 1939–40 and, 130–32, 141,
    143
  Greece and, 152–56, 163
  House of Commons, 111
  invasion of, planned, 144–45, 147
  naval blockade by, 127–28
  naval competition with, 76
  North Africa and, 149, 150, 152, 153, 155,
    205, 213
  Pacific and, 192
  Poland and, 31, 123, 125, 127–28, 249

resources of, for defense, 80
Saarland and Rhineland and, 109–111
Soviet invasion and, 171, 172
tanks, 91, 92, 95, 96, 99, 223
U.S. and, 6, 192
vehicles to move infantry, 103–4
war crimes and, 236
weapons and, 32–33
WW I and, 1, 2, 17, 21, 22, 27
Greece, invasion of, 147, 149–56, 158, 163, 172
war crimes and, 236
Gross-Lichterfelde cadet school, 15
ground-to-air defenses, 86, 210, 245
Grozny oil fields, 191
Guadalcanal, 192
Guderian, Heinz, 3, 14–15, 30, 38, 90–93, 95, 97, 98, 100–102, 105, 112–13, 136, 186, 187, 189, 209, 216, 224
Guernica, 86–89, 210
guns, development of, 16, 17, 19–21, 32, 41, 86, 91, 98–99, 102–4, 106, 187–89, 215, 217, 221–23

Haffner, Sebastian, 25
Halder, Franz, 178
half-tracks, 103, 218
Hamburg, bombing of, 211
hand grenades, 18–20
Hanfstängel, Ernst, 26
Hannut, battle of, 142
Hapsburg empire, 66, 112, 115, 165
Hausser, Paul, 232
Hayler, Franz, 226
Heidegger, Martin, 47–49, 59, 75, 136, 204, 225, 243
Heiden, Konrad, 11
Heinkel, Ernst, 81, 82
Heinkel planes, 78–79, 82
    He-50, 72, 78
    He-51, 81, 85–86
    He-100, 82
    He-111, 79, 80, 86
    He-112, 81
    He-177, 79
Henschel planes, 222
    dive-bomber (Hs-123), 72
Herzl, Theodor, 66
Heydrich, Reinhard, 208, 231–32, 236–37
Hildesheim uprising, 30
Himmler, Heinrich, 211, 226, 238, 239

Hindenburg, Paul von, 23, 26–27, 40, 42–43, 76, 90, 165
Hitler, Adolf
air war and, 76, 211
assassination attempt vs., 50, 204, 215
assumes control of army, 186
Austrian invasion and, 112–14
Central European takeover by, 112–13, 121
conflict with officers and, 4, 5, 8, 40–41, 43, 44, 50, 57–61, 100–101, 170–71, 177–78, 186, 204
Crete invasion and, 157–59, 163
Czechoslovakia and, 115–20
decision-making and management style, 49, 59, 73, 75, 78
decisions of, and German war machine, 3
decisions of, during last months, 7
declares war on US, 6, 191–93, 251
Germany's detractors and, 2
Göring and, 68
great man philosophy of, 6, 208–9, 211–13, 225–27, 251
Greek invasion and, 152, 154, 161
guns and butter provided by, 49–50
high-water mark of, in 1943, 204
invasion of Britain planned by, 144–45, 147
Jews and, 6–8, 50, 57, 62–65, 67
Luftwaffe and, 68, 71–74, 80, 82
Mussolini and, 148–52, 163
National Socialism and, 225–27
nonaggression pact with Stalin and, 121–22
North African invasion and, 152
offensives of 1939–40 and, 108, 131, 132, 136–37, 139, 141, 143
offensives of 1944 and, 206–8
Pacific and, 191
Pearl Harbor and, 191
Polish invasion and, 123–28, 130–31
remilitarization and, 110
Rhineland and, 110
rise of, 38, 45–49, 52
Rommel and, 41, 210–13, 215
Saarland plebiscite and, 109–10
Soviet invasion and, 144, 147–48, 164–73, 177–180, 183, 185–86, 189–90, 193–94, 196–97, 199–200
Spanish civil war and, 85, 105, 112
strategic thinking of, 5–6, 44, 249–53

Hitler, Adolf (*cont'd*)
  surface fleet and, 80
  tanks and, 90, 98, 102, 107, 222, 224
  war crimes and, 7–9, 207, 231, 235–37,
    240, 243, 254–55
  WW I and, 26–28
  Yugoslavian invasion and, 154–55
Hoffman, Max, 36–37, 39
Holocaust, 228
Holt company (Caterpillar), 219
howitzers, 17, 103
Hungary, 65, 114, 127, 154, 165, 229
  Czechoslovakia and, 117, 119, 120
  offensive of 1944, 207
Husserl, Adolf Abraham, 54
Husserl, Edmund, 49, 54, 56–57, 63
Husserl, Gerhard Adolf, 54
Husserl, Julie Selinger, 54
Husserl, Malvine Steinschneider, 54
Husserl, Wolfgang, 54

Incident at the Kretchetovka Station
    (Solzhenitsyn), 179
India, 148
iron ore, 132, 163, 169, 248
Israeli Defense Force, 223
Italian air force, 149–50
Italian army, 22
  mechanized divisions, in North Africa, 153
  tanks, 91, 106
Italian *Fascisti* party, 151
Italian navy, 127, 150, 158, 159, 160
Italian Tenth Army, 149
Italy, 114, 127
  Allied invasion of, WW II, 6, 201, 205–6,
    249, 250
  Czechoslovakia and, 119
  Greece invaded by, 149–52, 155
  North Africa and, 149–51, 182, 198, 205,
    212–13
  offensive of 1940 and, 147–48
  Soviet invasion and, 165
  Spanish civil war and, 85, 86, 106, 151
  WW I and, 21, 42

Jagdpanzer (tank destroyer), 188
Jäger battalions, 19, 30, 38
Japan, 83, 110, 191–92, 194, 208
Jews, 7–8, 41, 48–67, 226, 232
  Aryanization of, 54–55, 62
  army and purge of, 7–8, 51, 54–55, 58–62

Jodl, 208
Joffre, General, 21, 142, 176
Joseph, Archduke, 33
Jünger, Ernst, 228
Junkers planes
  Ju-52 transport, 85–86, 87, 137, 183, 220
  Ju-87 (Stuka) dive-bomber, 72, 74, 220
  Ju-88 bomber, 74–75
  Ju-89 bomber, 77
  strategic bombers, 77–80
Jupiter offensive, 194, 196, 199

Kaiserreich, 42
Kalinin, battles of, 179, 185
Kama training facility, 90
Kandanos massacre, 237
Kapp putsch, 34
Kaslow, Major, 13
Kasserine Pass, battle of, 198
Kaunas, 168
Keitel, 208
Kerch peninsula, 190
Kerensky, Aleksandr, 28
Kesselring, Albert, 78, 79, 92, 97, 250
Kharkov, battles at, 179, 189–90, 197,
    199–201. *See also* Citadel offensive
Khrushchev, Nikita, 167, 171–72
Kiev, 168, 170, 177
Kisch, Josef, 235
Kitchener, H. H., 142
Knochlein, Fritz, 233
Königsberg, 168
Kriegsmarine, 8–9
Krupp company, 32, 215, 218
Kuhn, Bela, 65
Kühne, General, 99, 100
Kursk, 179
  battle of, 198–201

L'Adultera (Storm), 39
Latvia, 29, 168, 175
Lawrence, D. H., 165
League of Nations, 109, 110, 115, 124, 192
Le-Cornet Malo, 233
Lenin, 28, 31, 45, 225, 255
Leningrad, 167, 168, 170, 175, 177, 179–81,
    184–85
Le Paradis massacre, 233, 239
Libya, 148–50, 152, 153
Lidell Hart, Basil, 105–6
Lidice massacre, 237

Liège fortifications, 12, 138, 139
Life magazine, 88, 116–17, 210
Lithuania, 29, 124, 168, 175
Lloyd George, David, 1, 248
Loehr, Commander, 158
logistics, 25, 246–47
    Austrian invasion and, 113
    North Africa and, 212–13
    Soviet invasion and, 175, 178, 182, 184,
        190, 202–3
London bombings of WW I, 69
Losberg, Colonel, 13
LTM tank, 91, 92
    LTM-35 tanks (or German 35t), 94
Ludendorff, Erich, 12, 21, 23, 34, 35–37, 39,
    42–43, 76, 132, 134, 165
Lufthansa, 78
Luxembourg, 136, 140

Mackensen, August von, 33, 76
Maginot, André, 3
Maginot Line, 109, 126, 148, 212
Malaysia, 191
Malta, 158
Manchuria, 110
Manstein, Erich von, 133, 135, 136, 190,
    196–201, 208, 249
Marder 2 tank, 188
Marder 3 tank, 188
Marita operation, 147, 153–55, 164
Mark 1 tank, 91–93, 95, 97, 130, 188
Mark 2 tank, 92, 93, 95, 97, 130, 188, 223
Mark 3 tank, 93–95, 97–99, 215–16, 221
Mark 4 tank, 93–95, 97–99, 187, 215, 217, 221
Mark 5 tank. *See* Panther tank
Mark 6 tank. *See also* Tiger 1 tank
Market Garden, Operation, 209, 245
Mars offensive, 194, 196, 199
Marwitz, von der, 256
Marxism-Leninism, 48
Masaryk, Tomá_ Garrigue, 115–18
massed infantry assaults, 19
massive battle tactic, 21–22
Mauthausen camp, 236
mechanized divisions, 37–38, 102, 113–14,
    189
    Greece and, 154, 163–64
    lack of adequate vehicles, 217–18
    Soviet invasion and, 169, 178, 179
Mediterranean, 127, 147, 148, 158, 160
Mein Kampf (Hitler), 75–76, 77, 144

Memel, sacrifice of, 44
Mengele, Joseph, 241–42, 243
Mercedes-Benz, 219
Mercury operation, 157
Messerschmitt, Willy, 81, 82
Messerschmitt planes
    long-range fighter-bombers, 82
    Me-109 fighter, 70, 81–83, 86, 146–47, 211,
        220
    Me-110 fighter, 146
Meyer, Kurt, 235
Midway, battle of, 192
Milch, Erhard, 54–55, 61, 77, 78
mineral resources, 170, 180
Minsk, 168, 175–77
Moltke, Helmuth von, the Elder, 35, 143
Moltke, Helmuth von, the Younger, 12, 34,
    35, 132, 134, 139, 169
Montgomery, Bernard, 205, 209, 213
mortars, 18–20
Moscow, advance on, 167–69, 175, 177–81,
    184, 185, 187, 190, 194 195
Moscow trials, 201
Mosse, George, 45
Mossner, Walther, 51
motorcycle battalions, 102, 104–5
motorized artillery regiments, 102
motorized infantry brigades, 102–4
motor vehicles, 103–5, 113, 184, 190, 214,
    217–18
Munich accord (1938), 65, 115, 117–19
Mussolini, Benito, 110, 112, 117, 148–53, 163
Myth of the Great War, The, 6

Napoléon, 113, 236
Narvik fjord, battle of, 135
National Socialism
    airborne troops and, 157
    ascends to power, 38, 45–50
    Guernica and, 88
    "Horst-Wessel Lied" (anthem), 48
    ideology of, and industry, 224–27
    ideology of, and racism, 6–7
    Jews and, 7–8, 52–54, 57–60, 63–64
    leadership and great men and, 75, 208,
        212–13
    Luftwaffe and, 71, 75–76, 81, 82
    military and, 38, 40–41
    secular messianism and, 65–66
    state police as branch of, 68
    war crimes and, 230–31, 237

naval blockade, 127, 132
Netherlands, 33, 192, 209, 218
    air force, 137
    army, 138
    invasion and occupation of, 88, 123, 132,
        134, 136–38, 159–61, 183, 193, 213
    Market Garden and, 245
    navy, 191, 192
New Zealand, 160, 162
Nicholas II, czar of Russia, 166
Nietzsche, 136
Normandy invasion, 6, 205, 206, 213–15, 237,
    249
North Africa, 148–53, 155, 156, 158, 182,
    212–13
    Allied invasion of, 6, 198, 205, 209, 250–52
North Atlantic, 191
Norway, invasion and occupation of, 8–9,
    123, 131, 133–35, 145, 157, 169, 172, 183,
    243
Nuremberg trials, 7, 240–43

Odessa, fall of, 177–79
offensive tactics, 19–21
Ohlendorf, Otto, 226, 227
oil, 163, 169, 177, 189, 191, 253
Opel, 219
Operation 25, 155
Oradour-sur-Glance massacre, 237
Otto, Case, 112–13, 169

Pacific, war in, 194, 208
Panther tank, 189, 200, 222–24
Panzer divisions, 102. *See also* armored
    divisions; tanks
Panzer IV tank, 107
Paraguay, 110
Patton, George S., 250
Paulus, Friedrich, 196–97, 201
Pearl Harbor attack, 6, 191
Peiper, Jochen, 235
Pershing, John J., 15, 43
Pershing tank, 223–24
Philippines, 43, 191
Pioniere combat engineer units, 19–20
Pittsburgh Agreement, 115
Plan Z, 80, 124
Plato, 47, 48
Ploesti oil fields, 156, 169, 211
Poland, 114. *See also* Russo-Polish War of
    1919–20

armaments, 33, 99
    invasion of 1939, 25, 43, 92, 117–19, 122–27,
        130, 246–47, 249
    Jews in, 63
    Soviet occupied, 168, 175
    Soviets cede in 1918, 165
    war crimes in, 230–32, 234–36, 238–39,
        253, 256
Polish Corridor, 124, 128
Polybius, 244
Pooley, Bert, 233, 235
Porsche, Ferdinand, 17, 82, 222
Pössinger, Michael, 142
Priapit Marshes, 167=68
prisoners of war, 207, 230–35, 239, 255–56
production problems and industry, 18, 80,
    170, 180, 182, 218–27, 251
Prussian army, 12, 51
Prussian State Police, 68
Pskov, fall of, 175
public opinion, 114–15, 120, 121, 192

racism, 226, 231, 237
Räder, Erich, 8–9, 80, 101, 133, 134, 135, 136,
    209, 232
Radetsky March, The (Roth), 39
Ravensbrück camp, 237
reconnaissance battalions, 104–5
reconnaissance planes, 71
Red Army, 6, 29. *See also* Soviet Union
    armored divisions, 185
    Finland invaded by, 167
    high command, 176, 184, 196
    historians on, 251
    infantry divisions, 174
    invasion of 1941 and, 166–69, 173–79,
        184–85
    casualties, 176–78, 180–81, 186, 190,
        193–94, 197–98, 200, 202–3
    offensives of 1942–44 and, 186, 190–91,
        193–200, 202–3, 253
    officers, 166
    in Poland and Baltics, 168–69, 173–74
    Russo-Polish war and, 31, 167
    Spanish civil war and, 112
    state of, in 1945, 194
    tank and infantry brigades, 185
    war crimes and, 236–37
Renault
    FT17 tank, 91, 93
    VE tank, 91

reparations, 32

resources. *See also specific raw materials*
    allocation vs. scarcity of, 79–81
    controlling strategic, 163, 169–71

Reynaud, Paul, 140–41, 248

Rhineland militarization, 110–11, 114

Rhodes, Richard, 241

Richthofen, Wolfram von, 73–74, 159

Riez-du-Vinage, 233

rifles, 16, 19–20

Riga
    fall of (1941), 166, 168, 175
    fall of (1919), 31

Riga, Treaty of (1921), 167

Ringel, General, 237

Rohr, Captain, 13, 19, 20

Romania
    oil fields, 156, 163, 169, 253
    WW I and, 22, 42, 165
    WW II and, 120, 124, 127, 129, 151, 154, 158,
        165, 169, 207

Romanian army, 22, 169, 231

Romanian Fourth Army, 178

Romantic, The (Broch), 39

Rommel, Erwin, 3, 41, 152–53, 208, 211–15,
    233

Roosevelt, Franklin D., 191, 192

Rosenberg, Alfred, 243

Rostov, advance on, 177, 179, 190

Roth, Joseph, 39

Rotterdam, bombing of, 88, 138, 193, 210

Ruhr uprising, 30

rules of war, 7, 229, 230–32, 236. *See also* war
    crimes

Runciman, Lord, 116

Rundstedt, Gerd von, 186, 208–9, 214

Russia, czarist, 13. *See also* Soviet Union
    Bismarck's policy toward, 34
    WW I and, 12, 33–36, 42–43, 165–66, 193

Russia, Jews in, 65

Russian army (czarist), 13, 22. *See also* Red
    Army

Russian Revolution of 1917, 67

Russo-Finnish War, 132

Russo-Polish War of 1920–21, 29, 31, 34, 167,
    229

Ruthenia, 115, 116, 117, 119, 120

Rzhev, 185, 195, 196

Saarland, 108–11, 129

salient, attack into, 195, 196, 199

Sarraut, Albert, 111

Saturn offensive, 194, 196–97

Scandinavia, 33, 127, 131–32

Schlieffen, Alfred von, 35, 169

Schweinfut bombing, 211

SD. *See* German Sicherheitdienst

Sea Lion operation, 147

Sedan, battle of, 38, 136, 140–41, 212
    massacre at, 233

Seeckt, Hans von, 33, 34, 36–44, 54, 59, 75

Serbia, 33, 154, 155

Sevastopol, 167

Sherman tank, 94, 96, 217

Sicily, Allied invasion of, 205–6

Sidi Barrani, battle of, 150

Siewert, General, 131

Silesia, 31, 44

Singapore, 191

Slovakia, 115–16, 119–20, 123, 154

Slovenes, 155

small-unit assault tactics, 19, 21, 22

Smolensk, 168
    fall of, 175–78

Solzhenitsyn, Aleksandr, 179

Somaliland, 149

Somme, battle of (1916), 13, 23

Soviet air force, 183

Soviet Fourteenth Mechanized Corps, 174

Soviet Union, 209. *See also* Red Army
    aircraft, 82, 86, 166
    Allied aid to, 192–93, 250
    arms, 187
    Bolshevik revolution in, 28
    defeat of Hitler and, 3, 5, 250–51
    final period of war and, 207
    Finland and, 132
    German retreat and, 201–3
    Hitler plans to invade, 5–6, 144, 147–48,
        151–54, 163–67
    invasion of, and logistics, 166, 182–84,
        187–89, 246–47
    invasion of, and loss by Germany, 201–3
    invasion of, and plan of attack, 167–72
    invasion of, and production problems,
        216–18
    invasion of, and tank design, 92, 94,
        187–89
    invasion of, begun and early victories,
        171–82
    invasion of, counter offensive of 1941–42,
        184–87, 189–91, 193–95

Soviet Union (*cont'd*)
  invasion of, offensives of 1942 and battle
    of Stalingrad, 194–98
  invasion of, offensives of 1943, 198–201
  nonaggression pact (1939), 121–22, 125, 132
  Poland and, 124, 125, 129
  POWs and, 202
  propaganda and, 200–201
  Spanish civil war and, 92, 105–6, 112, 166
  strategic airpower and, 76
  tanks, 74, 90, 92, 99, 105–6, 166, 174, 187,
    188, 189, 203, 216–17, 220–223
  terror in, 45
  war crimes and, 231, 236–37, 239
  WW II as beginning of collapse of, 203
Spain, 127, 165, 218
Spandau: The Secret Diaries (Speer), 240
Spanish Army of Africa, 84, 85
Spanish civil war, 70, 111–12, 122, 148, 151, 166
  air war and, 83–89
  Munich and, 117, 119
  tanks and, 92, 105–7
Speer, Albert, 187, 208–9, 211, 216, 226–27,
  240, 243, 251–52
SS. *See* German Schützstaffel
Stalag 17b and 13d, 234
Stalag Luft 3 war crimes, 234–35
Stalin, Josef, 86, 229, 249
  casualties and, 194, 202
  counteroffensive of 1942–44 and, 184–87,
    189–91, 193–97, 199, 200
  Finland invaded by, 131, 132
  invasion of 1941 and, 166, 169–75, 177,
    179, 180
  as military leader, 6, 166, 174, 209, 250,
    251
  nonaggression pact of 1939 and, 121–22,
    132
  Poland and, 125, 129
  Spanish civil war and, 106, 112
Stalingrad, 167, 170, 190
  battle of, 194–98, 200, 201, 204, 250
Stanowje, battle of, 189
Storm, Theodor, 39, 55–56
strategy, 5–6, 8, 16, 18–24, 41–44, 69, 76, 171,
  249–53
Streicher, Julius, 243
Student, Kurt, 136, 157–59, 161, 208, 209, 213,
  234, 235, 237, 249
Stuka dive-bomber. *See* Junkers Ju-87
submarine war, 8–9

Sudan, 149
Sudetenland, 116–19
Suez Canal, 147, 156
supplies. *See also* logistics; production
  German retreats and, 207
  North Africa and, 212
  Soviet invasion and, 178, 183–84, 196,
    202–3
surface fleet, 8, 80, 160
swastika, 40–41, 46
Sweden, 32, 163

T-26 tank (Soviet), 106
T-34 tank (soviet), 74, 107, 187, 203, 216–17,
  220–21, 222–23, 223
tactics, 16, 18–22, 41–42, 44
Tallinn, 168, 175
Tancik Vz33 tank, 91
tank destroyer, 188
tanks, 32, 41, 74, 130, 142, 153, 202, 247
  development of, 90–107
  production and design problems, 164,
    187–89, 215–24
  Spanish civil war and, 85, 105–7
Taylor, Telford, 240–43
technology, 3, 16–17, 41–42, 208
Teschen, Duchy of, 117, 119
Tessmann, Willi, 235
Thoma, General von, 105–6
Thomas, Hugh, 108
Tiger 1 tank, 189, 222–24
tire production, 220
Tobruk, fall of, 150
Todt, Fritz, 82, 187, 208, 227
Trianon treaty, 120
trucks, 101–4, 202, 217–20
Tukhachevsky, Mikhail, 174
Tula, battles of, 179, 185
Tunisia, 198, 204
Turkey, 218

Udet, Ernst, 73–75, 77, 78, 79
Ukraine, 43, 115, 201
  invasion of 1941, 167–70, 175, 177–78,
    180–81
  Soviets cede in 1918, 165
Ukrainian troops, 231
United States
  aids Soviet Union, 187, 192–93, 202, 217,
    218, 250
  air war and, 8, 76, 82, 83, 210

armored vehicles, 187
Czechoslovakia and, 115
enters WW I, 26–27
enters WW II, 6, 163, 191–94, 198, 205,
207, 209–11, 251=52
production in, 187, 218–19
resources of, 80
tanks, 95–96, 223–24
war crimes and, 236
U.S. Army, 13, 15, 102
U.S. 285th Field Artillery Observation
Battalion, 235
universal conscription, 53, 110–11
universities, 47–48, 50, 57
Uranus offensive, 194, 196–97

Vauvenargues, marquis de, 256
Velikie Luki, 175, 185–86, 195–96
Verdun, 23, 195
Versailles Treaty, 25, 31, 34, 167, 192, 218, 219,
247, 248
Czechoslovakia and, 115–17, 119, 120
German navy and, 8
rearmament despite, 31–34
Saarland and Rhineland and, 109–11
Viazma, 185, 195
Vilnius, 168
VK-3001 tank prototype, 222
Voronezh region, 170, 190
Vosges Mountains, 19–20

Waffen-SS. *See* German Waffen-SS
Waltzer, Johannes, 235
war crimes, 7–9, 32, 207, 228–43, 254–56
war of attrition, 22–23
Warsaw, bombing of, 137–38, 210
Wavell, Archibald, 153
weaponry, 11, 15–20, 208, 246
Wegener, Wilhelm, 189
Wellington, duke of, 43
Wessel, Colonel, 230–33, 238
westerners, 35–36

Western Front
in WW I, 1–2, 17, 165
May–June 1940 attack, 137–43
Wever, Walter, 75–78, 79, 144
Weygand, Gen. Maxime, 13
Wilberg, Helmuth, 54, 61, 85
Wilhelm II, Kaiser of Germany, 23, 27, 38,
51
Winkler, Karl, 235
Wittmann, Michael, 189
World War I, 152, 185, 199, 200, 212
aftermath of, 27
armored combat and, 96–97
British and, 251
casualtiesppppppin, 1, 3
doctrine and, 4–5
easterners vs. westerners and, 35–36
German production during, 224
Jewish officers and, 51, 54
June 1916 offensive, 42, 201
lessons of speed and integration and,
245–48
lessons on airpower and, 69, 72
myths of, 2–5
Russia defeated in, 165, 166, 168
success of German army in, 1–2, 11–28
as three-front war, 209
training and equipping of soldiers and,
16–18
U.S. and, 6, 205, 206
war crimes and, 236
Zionism and, 66
World War II. *See specific countries; armies,*
battles, military units, and campaigns

Yellow, Case, 157
Yugoslavia, 114, 151, 236
invasion of, 154–55, 172

Zhukov, General, 196, 199
Zionism, 66
Zog, King of Albania, 148

ABOUT THE AUTHOR

A former film critic and member of the Camera d'or Jury at the Cannes Film Festival, JOHN MOSIER is currently a professor of English at Loyola University. His background as a military historian dates from his role in developing an interdisciplinary curriculum for the study of the two world wars, a program funded by the National Endowment for the Humanities. He lives in Jefferson, Louisiana.